PAYING ATTENTION TO FOREIGN AFFAIRS

PAYING ATTENTION TO FOREIGN AFFAIRS

How Public Opinion Affects
Presidential Decision Making

THOMAS KNECHT

The Pennsylvania State University Press
University Park, Pennsylvania

Library of Congress Cataloging-in-Publication Data

Knecht, Thomas, 1971–
Paying attention to foreign affairs : how public opinion
affects presidential decision making / Thomas Knecht.
    p.   cm.
Includes bibliographical references and index.
Summary: "Examines the relationship between public
opinion and U.S. foreign policy. Argues that policy making under
intense public scrutiny differs from policy making when no
one is looking"—Provided by publisher.
ISBN 978-0-271-03753-0 (cloth : alk. paper)
1. United States—Foreign relations—Decision making.
2. Public opinion—United States.
I. Title.

JZ1480.K58 2010
327.73—dc22
2010020744

Copyright © 2010 The Pennsylvania State University
All rights reserved
Printed in the United States of America
Published by The Pennsylvania State University Press,
University Park, PA 16802-1003

The Pennsylvania State University Press is a member of
the Association of American University Presses.

It is the policy of The Pennsylvania State University Press
to use acid-free paper. Publications on uncoated stock
satisfy the minimum requirements of American National
Standard for Information Sciences—Permanence of Paper
for Printed Library Material, ANSI Z39.48–1992.

This book is printed on Natures Natural,
which contains 50% post-consumer waste.

Contents

List of Figures and Tables vii
Preface and Acknowledgments ix
A Note on the Surveys xiii

Introduction 1

1
Foreign Policy in the Shadows and the Spotlight 13

2
The Five Stages of Decision Making 37

3
Patterns of Public Attention 55

4
The Persian Gulf Crisis:
Problem Definition and Option Generation 81

5
Operation Desert Storm:
Decision, Implementation, and Review 113

6
The Ethiopian Famine:
Problem Definition and Option Generation 141

7
The Ethiopian Famine:
Decision, Implementation, and Review 177

Conclusion 203

Appendix A: Quantitative Methods 221
Appendix B: Case Study Methods 227
Bibliography 235
Index 255

Figures and Tables

FIGURES

1 Causal pathways explaining the public opinion–foreign policy correlation   4
2 Salience of foreign policy issues   61
3a Pattern-conforming noncrises, 1970s–1980s   62
3b Pattern-conforming noncrises, 1990s–2000s   63
4 Pattern-breaking noncrises, option generation   67
5 Pattern-breaking noncrises, implementation (Star Wars)   68
6 Pattern-breaking noncrises, policy review (Elián González)   69
7a Pattern-conforming crises, 1970s–1980s   73
7b Pattern-conforming crises, 1990s–2000s   73
8 Pattern-breaking crises, policy decision   77
9 Pattern-breaking crises, option generation   79
10 Pattern-breaking crises, policy review (Angola)   79
11 Television coverage of the 1990–91 Persian Gulf conflict   89
12 Public approval of President Bush's handling of the Persian Gulf crisis   107
13 Public opinion that the situation in the Persian Gulf is/was worth going to war over   117
14 Change from preceding period in real GDP (2005 dollars)   121
15 Reasons for initiating war with Iraq   128
16 Television coverage of the Ethiopian famine   147
17 *New York Times* coverage of the Ethiopian famine   148
18 Increases in U.S. food aid to Ethiopia   185
19 Ethiopians affected by famine, 1982–87   189
20 USAID economic assistance to Ethiopia   200
21 The congruence procedure   230

TABLES

1 The political contexts   23
2 Political context and presidential action at the problem definition stage   45
3 Political context and presidential action at the option generation stage   47
4 Political context and presidential action at the policy decision stage   49
5 Political context and presidential action at the implementation stage   52
6 Political context and presidential action at the policy review stage   54
7 Television news coverage of crisis and noncrisis foreign policy cases   60
8 Problem representations in the Ethiopian famine   152
9 U.S. food and nonfood aid to Ethiopia, 1984–86   197

Preface and Acknowledgments

In a democracy, it is generally assumed that citizen preferences inform public policy. But do American presidents really consider public opinion when making foreign policy decisions? For a variety of reasons, foreign policy has always posed a difficult challenge for democratic governance. Citizen oversight of public officials requires an active and informed electorate, yet the American public is only sporadically attentive to and knowledgeable about foreign affairs. Additionally, citizens' foreign policy preferences sometimes conflict with the policies that presidents believe to be in the national interest, forcing the White House into a difficult choice between political expediency and strategic effectiveness. Further complicating matters are national security concerns that prevent a full disclosure of information to the public. These and other challenges have been especially apparent in recent history. The U.S. intervention in Kosovo, the Kyoto Protocol, and the Iraq War have led some observers to question what role, if any, the public plays in the construction of American foreign policy.

This book examines whether presidents lead, follow, or simply ignore the American public when making foreign policy decisions. Our exploration into the public's role in U.S. foreign policy departs from a rather unusual place: a personal story that has nothing to do with international affairs. About a year ago, I was at home playing with my kids when the phone rang—it was a local survey organization wanting to hear my opinion of the new hospital being built in my community. Fortunately, ours is a relatively healthy family, and I only think of hospitals when one of our kids breaks a leg (or when a pollster asks me questions about hospitals). But being a college professor in the field of American public opinion, I believe it is important to respond to surveys, even those concerning topics I have little interest in or knowledge of. I agreed to be interviewed, so the pollster asked what kind of services I thought the local hospital should provide: Should it have an eye institute? Should the emergency room staff include a pediatric specialist? Should the hospital perform hip and knee replacements? Should it have a cosmetic surgery wing? I replied to all of these queries with an emphatic "yes!" After all, I wanted the best hospital money could buy just in case, God forbid, a member of my family should ever need it. I hung up the phone and did not think about hospitals again until my daughter had a high-grade fever seven months later.

This anecdote may seem a bit off topic, but it does offer several insights about the nature of public opinion in general that we will relate to the specific issue of public opinion and foreign policy. First, it is easy to offer an opinion to pollsters. I had given no thought to our new hospital before the survey call, so when answering the questions, I paid little mind to the problems that hospital administrators surely deal with, such as budgets, staff, and space. My responses, although genuine, were probably a bit poorly considered, but I offered them anyway. Second, just because a clear and definitive opinion is expressed in a survey does not mean that the issue is important to the respondent. Again, I rarely had thought of hospitals, so I was not going to base my vote in the upcoming election on a candidate's hospital platform, and I was not planning on marching in the streets to demand a cosmetic surgery wing. The issue was simply not that important to me at the time, but again, that lack of salience didn't stop me from staking a clear and definitive position when asked for my opinion. Third, the importance of an issue can change over time. While hospital services were not that salient to me at the time of the survey, they suddenly became very important when my daughter became ill. (Her illness turned out to be minor, but we did have to drive twenty miles to the next hospital because ours did not staff the appropriate pediatric specialist.)

The final and most important lesson is that the interaction of preferences and issue salience prompts both citizen action and government response. Even though my preferences for hospital services had not shifted one little bit in the seven months after the survey call, the salience of those very same opinions increased dramatically when my daughter became ill. The confluence of strong preferences and high issue salience eventually prompted me to become more active toward our local hospital (I consider "active" to be writing a letter of complaint about the lack of pediatric specialists on staff), something I would not have done if my child had stayed healthy or if I were ambivalent about which services were important for the hospital to have. On the other side of the ledger, I expect that a hospital administrator comes under the greatest pressure to respond to citizen demands when a significant majority of the public holds similar opinions *and* is highly attentive to local health care. On that score, my one little letter demanding that a pediatric infectious disease specialist be on the hospital's payroll was probably insufficient to produce any real change.

This book takes lessons about public opinion drawn from the hospital story and applies them to U.S. foreign policy; but instead of looking at opinion from the perspective of the respondent, we examine what the situation looks like from inside the Oval Office. While presidents may be able to ignore the public when Americans are divided on the issues or are inattentive to what is going on, it is politically dangerous to snub a large majority of people who care deeply about an issue. And if presidents are indeed most sensitive to public opinion when a large majority of Americans hold the same preference *and* the issue is highly salient, then the obvious question arises: can we forecast *when* that convergence will occur? The evidence provided in this book suggests that we can. The American people tend to be a predictable lot when it comes to foreign policy. The public is generally interested in some aspects of foreign policy while giving a collective yawn to others. Likewise, the public tends to unify around some foreign policy options, only to divide on others. This movement of public opinion and attention is not random but rather conforms to predictable patterns. By tracing these patterns, we can forecast when presidents are likely to lead, follow, or ignore the public.

This book is the culmination of work that began as a rather small idea in a graduate school paper, somehow blossomed into a dissertation, and has (hopefully) reached some level of maturity in this text. As one might imagine, numerous people have helped nurture this project, and me, along the way and deserve special mention. I especially would like to thank the wonderful members of my dissertation committee at the University of California, Santa Barbara. Kent Jennings has been an outstanding mentor and advisor. Kent is a fount of knowledge and insight; I consider it a great honor to have studied under him. As a graduate student, I probably spent as many hours in Stephen Weatherford's office as my own; I'm very grateful for both his wisdom and his patience. He also collaborated with me on an *International Studies Quarterly* article, which helped me to better conceptualize this current project and learn how to navigate the publishing process. I'm indebted to Aaron Belkin for teaching me the art of writing and the skill of developing an idea. Aaron's margin notes—especially the ones reading "what does this mean?" and "how do we know?"—pushed me to refine my thinking. These men have my profound gratitude and respect.

My project has also benefited from the insights of other scholars, friends, and students who have commented on conference papers, chapters, and/or the full manuscript. To this end, I wish to thank Ole Holsti, Richard Sobel, Lori Gronich, Richard Flickinger, Samuel Hoff, Helene Orr, Steve McCarl, Spencer Welhoffer, Susan Sterett, Lisa Conant, Rob Hinckley, Eric Patterson, and several anonymous reviewers. The Junior Faculty All-Stars at the University of Denver certainly lived up to their name, and I thank Seth Masket, Nancy Wadsworth, Jing Sun, and David Ciepley for all of their help and support. I'm very grateful for Susan Penksa, Jesse Covington, and all of my new colleagues at Westmont College. In addition, this work has benefited from the research assistance of Josh Bernstein, Nyssa Dickman-Frank, Jason Everitt,

Kelly Lack, Tyler Shaw, Jonathan Solorzano, Alicia Durst, Katie Mulligan, Jordan Cass-Boyle, and Chris Hinckhouse. Heartfelt thanks to Linda for her fantastic job editing an earlier draft. Finally, a special thanks for the outstanding work of my friend Jim Carr. Jim's absolute wizardry with Excel helped transform a mountain of jumbled and intimidating data into a thing of pure beauty (at least, I think it is beautiful). All of these people have been instrumental in helping me to complete this book; any mistakes that still exist are, of course, entirely my own fault.

I was fortunate to receive a Faculty Research Fund Grant from the University of Denver that allowed me to make several important research trips. I wish to thank the people at the George H. W. Bush Presidential Library in College Station, Texas, and the Ronald Reagan Presidential Library in Simi Valley, California, for their help in locating and copying documents. I also appreciate those individuals who gave of their time and agreed to be interviewed for this book: Steve Weissman, Julia Chang Bloch, Chester Crocker, Princeton Lyman, M. Peter McPherson, David Korn, and Kenneth Hackett.

I am very thankful to Penn State University Press and its former director, Sandy Thatcher, for publishing this book. Sandy has helped me navigate the publishing process, as has editorial assistant Kathryn Yahner. I am deeply indebted to manuscript editor Julie Schoelles for clarifying and sharpening my writing. Julie's suggestions were always spot-on and helped produce a much better book. Blackwell Publishers has granted permission to republish portions of chapters 3 and 6 that first appeared, respectively, in Thomas Knecht and M. Stephen Weatherford, "Public Opinion and Foreign Policy: The Stages of Presidential Decision Making," *International Studies Quarterly* 50, no. 3 (September 2006): 705–27, and Thomas Knecht, "A Pragmatic Response to an Unexpected Constraint: Problem Representation in a Complex Humanitarian Emergency," *Foreign Policy Analysis* 5, no. 2 (2009): 135–68.

Last, but certainly not least, I want to thank my family. I am blessed to have wonderful parents, Gary and Kathy, who have been faithful in their love, prayer, and support. The encouraging calls from Krista and Lance have meant so much to me. I am extremely grateful to Tom and Laurel for their heroic editing job and last-minute babysitting expedition to Santa Barbara. To Wanda, Craig, and Lynn, thanks for all of your love and support. Most of all, I want to thank my lovely wife, Nicole, and my children, Jake and Annie. Without your understanding, encouragement, and love, this book would not have been possible. I dedicate this book to you.

A Note on the Surveys

The majority of the surveys cited in this book were retrieved online from the Roper Center for Public Opinion Research at the University of Connecticut, via the LexisNexis database, at http://web.lexis-nexis.com/universe/form/academic/s/s_roper.html. LexisNexis no longer carries the center's data, but all of the surveys herein can now be accessed directly from the Roper Center's iPOLL Databank at http://www.ropercenter.uconn.edu/ipoll.html.

INTRODUCTION

Does public opinion influence U.S. foreign policy? The prevailing wisdom in the foreign policy literature is that public opinion can, at times, influence presidential decision making. Two examples in particular serve to illustrate the potential effect of the public on presidents' policy choices. In March 1999, NATO warplanes bombed Serbian targets in an effort to end the violence against ethnic Albanians in the Kosovo region. In the prelude to conflict, only a plurality (46 percent) of Americans approved of using U.S. military force to protect Kosovars from Serbian ethnic cleansing.[1] Despite such minimal public support for intervention, President Clinton believed that the situation in the Balkans justified U.S. military involvement. After committing U.S. forces to Kosovo without the backing of a majority of the American public, President Clinton opted for a low-risk military strategy specifically designed to minimize U.S. casualties in hopes of increasing domestic support for intervention. This strategy was largely a political success: no U.S. military personnel lost their lives in the Kosovo intervention, and public approval of Clinton's decision to use force jumped to 68 percent by the end of the conflict.[2]

While campaigning for office in 1988, George H. W. Bush promised, if elected, to address the issue of global warming during his presidency. Despite

---

1. Survey by the Harris Organization, March 19–23, 1999, from LexisNexis, Roper Center for Public Opinion Research, University of Connecticut (accessed April 1, 2004). "The Americans and some of our NATO (North Atlantic Treaty Organization) allies have said that they will launch air attacks against the Serbs in, or near, Kosovo if the Serbs refuse to accept the peace agreement including the use of 25,000 NATO troops. Do you favor or oppose launching air attacks against the Serbs if they refuse to accept NATO troops in Kosovo?"

2. Survey by Princeton, June 9–13, 1999, from LexisNexis, Roper Center for Public Opinion Research, University of Connecticut (accessed April 12, 2004). "All things considered, do you think that the U.S. and NATO made the right decision or the wrong decision to conduct airstrikes against Serbia to force them to agree to the terms of the peace agreement and end the fighting in Kosovo?"

this pledge, and despite the public's concern with climate change (63 percent), little effort was made to tackle global warming until late in Bush's presidency.[3] In June 1992, a framework to reduce greenhouse gas emissions was introduced at the Earth Summit Conference in Rio de Janeiro. Over 60 percent of the public believed that the United States should commit to the Rio Treaty, even at a potential cost of billions of dollars to the American taxpayer.[4] This high degree of public support influenced the Bush administration's decision to sign the treaty, even though the administration believed it to be fundamentally flawed and detrimental to U.S. interests. Two years after Rio, however, emission of greenhouse gases in the United States not only had failed to decline but had actually increased.

These two examples demonstrate that public opinion can affect foreign policy making, and also that the public sometimes exerts influence at different points in the decision-making process. In the case of Kosovo, the public appeared influential in shaping how the United States would carry out its military intervention, but not in the actual decision to intervene. Conversely, the public influenced the George H. W. Bush administration's decision to sign the Rio Treaty but seemed to play little role in subsequent enforcement of emission standards. Additionally, the point at which public opinion entered the decision-making process shaped policy outcomes in both cases. In Kosovo, a zero-casualty military strategy was effective in increasing public support for intervention, yet it proved strategically flawed when the United States made a number of military blunders, not the least of which was bombing the Chinese embassy in Belgrade. In the global warming case, the decision to sign the Rio Treaty enjoyed strong popular support, yet lax enforcement of the treaty later undermined the public's mandate to "do something" about global climate change.

The purpose of this book is to develop and test a theory on the relationship between American public opinion and presidential foreign policy making.

---

3. Survey by the Gallup Organization, May 4–7, 1989, from the iPOLL Databank, Roper Center for Public Opinion Research, University of Connecticut (accessed August 10, 2008). "(I'm going to read you a list of environmental problems. As I read each one, please tell me if you personally worry about this problem a great deal, a fair amount, only a little, or not at all. First, how much do you personally worry about) . . . the 'greenhouse effect' or global warming?" Percent reporting "a great deal" or "a fair amount."

4. Survey by Cambridge Reports/Research International, September 1992, from the iPOLL Databank, Roper Center for Public Opinion Research, University of Connecticut (accessed August 10, 2008). "Now, I am going to read you some things that might happen if the United States was the only country to take actions to substantially reduce the emissions that might be causing global warming. As I read each one, please tell me whether or not you think the United States should single-handedly take actions to substantially reduce emissions that might be causing global warming, even if that thing happens. . . . If it cost US businesses and taxpayers billions of dollars?"

The argument is one of *conditional responsiveness,* where presidents sometimes lead, sometimes follow, and sometimes ignore the American public. In a sense, then, the American public loosely holds the reins of U.S. foreign policy, periodically giving them a tug but all too often just going along for the ride. To better understand the role of public opinion in U.S. foreign policy, it is useful to first review the current literature. This will set the stage for a brief overview of the conditional theory of political responsiveness and the tenuous relationship between the American public and U.S. foreign policy.

The American Public–Foreign Policy Connection

We assume in a democracy that mass opinion is eventually translated into public policy, either by citizens electing leaders who closely match their own opinions and/or by rational politicians who are clever enough to discern and meet their constituents' preferences between elections.[5] Political representation is especially important when it comes to foreign policy. After all, a decision for war means that American soldiers might die; a free trade agreement can mean that your job will soon be outsourced; and international environmental agreements entail the difficult choice between a sustainable future and current economic growth. In short, the foreign policy choices made in Washington, D.C., affect us all, whether we recognize it or not. Unfortunately, the relationship between public opinion and American foreign policy is only poorly understood.[6] We do know that a strong correlation exists between the preferences of Americans and the foreign policy choices that leaders make.[7] However, *how* to explain this relationship has given rise to considerable debate about three possible causal pathways: political leadership, political representation, and political responsiveness (see figure 1).

The first explanation for the correlation between opinion and foreign policy is *political leadership,* which means that politicians lead the American public to hold certain views. The first wave of public opinion research in the 1950s and 1960s found most Americans to be ill informed and ambivalent about foreign affairs, and as a result, it was thought that leaders generally ignored

---

5. Stimson, Mackuen, and Erikson, "Dynamic Representation."
6. Aldrich et al., "Foreign Policy," 496; Powlick and Katz, "Public Opinion/Foreign Policy Nexus," 30; Holsti, *Public Opinion and American Foreign Policy,* 196; Sobel, *Impact of Public Opinion,* 9.
7. Burstein, "Estimates of the Impact of Public Opinion"; Monroe, "Public Opinion"; Page and Shapiro, *Rational Public.*

Political Leadership

[Politicians' foreign policy preference] ⟶ [The public's foreign policy preference]

Political Representation

[Politicians' foreign policy preference] = [The public's foreign policy preference]

Political Responsiveness

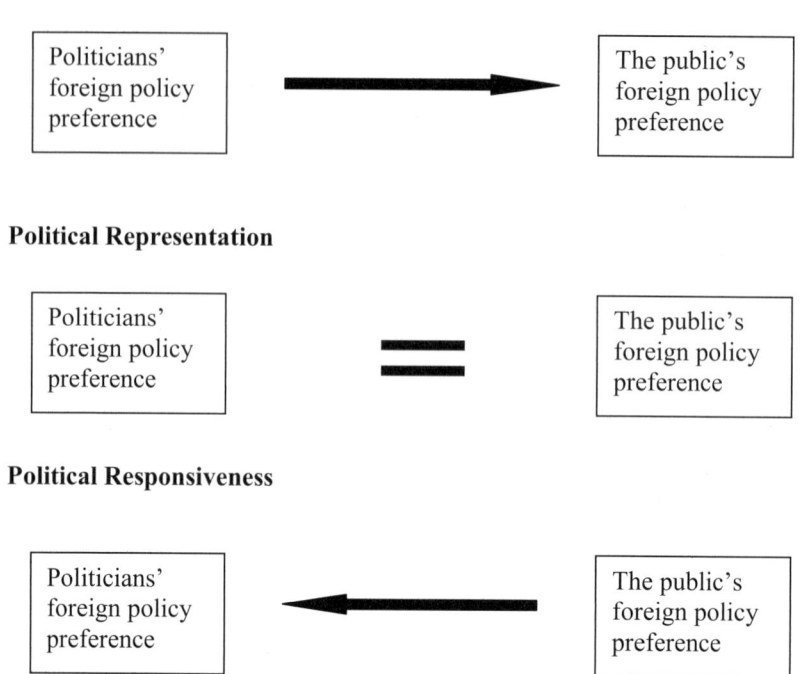

[Politicians' foreign policy preference] ⟵ [The public's foreign policy preference]

Fig. 1 Causal pathways explaining the public opinion–foreign policy correlation

mass preferences when making their foreign policy choices.[8] More recent studies also contend that public opinion plays little role in the actual formulation of policy, but with the caveat that policy makers work hard to convince the public to support the *decisions they have already made.* For instance, presidents can utilize the "bully pulpit" of the White House and extensive opinion polling to manipulate American opinion by framing an issue in a certain way and engaging in "crafted talk."[9] The ability of decision makers to lead public opinion is especially pronounced in foreign policy; most Americans hold weaker opinions and have less knowledge about international affairs than they do on bread-and-butter domestic issues.[10] The executive branch can also shape

---

8. Almond, *American People*; Lippmann, *Essays in the Public Philosophy*; P. Converse, "Nature of Belief Systems"; Kelman, "Social-Psychological Approaches"; Morgenthau, *Politics Among Nations*; B. Cohen, *Public's Impact on Foreign Policy*. For a review of this literature, see Holsti, *Public Opinion and American Foreign Policy*; Holsti, "Public Opinion and Foreign Policy"; Powlick and Katz, "Public Opinion/Foreign Policy Nexus"; Baum and Potter, "Mass Media, Public Opinion"; and Aldrich et al., "Foreign Policy."

9. Jacobs and Shapiro, *Politicians Don't Pander*; Ginsberg, *Captive Public*; B. Cohen, *Public's Impact on Foreign Policy*; Entman, *Projections of Power*.

10. Murray, "Private Polls"; Entman, *Projections of Power*; Canes-Wrone, *Who Leads Whom?*; Zaller, *Nature and Origins*; Zaller, "Converse-McGuire Model"; Western, *Selling Intervention and War*.

public opinion through its considerable control over and selective dissemination of information.[11] The mass media are often seen as complicit in this political arrangement by faithfully reporting, and rarely challenging, the White House position.[12] While decision makers may not be responsive to public opinion overall, this view contends that politicians are quite clearly sensitive to the needs of influential political interest groups,[13] international business leaders,[14] and/or partisan activists.[15]

The public opinion–foreign policy correlation might also be explained by *political representation*, in which decision makers and the American public, independent of any reciprocal influence, just so happen to hold the same view of an issue. This account seems plausible since citizens will presumably send to Washington the candidate who most closely mirrors their own policy preferences.[16] Additionally, both policy makers and the public react to the same foreign policy events.[17] For instance, there is little reason to expect that 9/11 affected Washington politicians any differently than it did the average American; after all, politicians are Americans too. When the American public and elected politicians hold similar opinions on foreign policy issues, there is no political leadership or political responsiveness. Instead, political representation occurs as elections work as they were arguably designed to work. However, the empirical evidence on the congruence of opinion between leaders and the masses is somewhat mixed. Although decision makers and the public do share a number of foreign policy preferences, there remain considerable gaps on certain important issues.[18] For instance, the public tends to be more concerned than its leaders about foreign economic competition and globalization, less concerned about security policy, and less willing to deploy U.S. troops abroad.

In the final explanation for the correlation between mass opinion and foreign policy, *political responsiveness*, rational politicians set aside their own beliefs and dutifully follow public opinion. In contrast to the first wave of opinion

---

11. Fisher, *Politics of Executive Privilege*; Fisher, *Presidential War Power*; Tiefer, *Semi-Sovereign Presidency*; Adler and George, *Constitution and the Conduct*.
12. Bennett, Lawrence, and Livingston, *When the Press Fails*; Entman, *Projections of Power*; Bennett, "Theory of Press-State Relations"; Herman and Chomsky, *Manufacturing Consent*; Hallin, *Uncensored War*.
13. Jacobs and Shapiro, *Politicians Don't Pander*; Mearsheimer and Walt, "Israel Lobby."
14. Jacobs and Page, "U.S. Foreign Policy"; Bauer, de Sola Pool, and Dexter, *American Business*.
15. Aldrich, *Why Parties?*; Jacobs and Shapiro, *Politicians Don't Pander*.
16. Stimson, Mackuen, and Erikson, "Dynamic Representation."
17. Hill, "Policy Agendas of the President."
18. Page and Bouton, *Foreign Policy Disconnect*; Page and Barabas, "Foreign Policy Gaps"; Kull and Ramsay, "Elite Misperceptions"; Kull and Destler, *Misreading the Public*; Holsti, *Public Opinion and American Foreign Policy*; Holsti, "Public Opinion and Foreign Policy."

research, recent studies have shown that the American public both cares about foreign affairs and holds foreign policy opinions that are "rational," "prudent," and "stable."[19] Indeed, Americans often base their voting decision on foreign policy issues, giving presidents an electoral incentive to do the public's bidding.[20] Additionally, the need for presidents to maintain or increase political capital can influence the foreign policy decisions of first- and second-term presidents alike.[21] Unpopular foreign policies can quickly erode approval ratings, damaging a president's prospects for a successful, and possibly more important, domestic agenda.[22] Public opinion may also influence lame-duck presidents as they attempt to set the electoral stage for their heir apparent.[23] Finally, while presidents may desire to lead the American public, they often find that their ability to do so is surprisingly limited.[24] Rather than attempt to lead a reluctant and sometimes inattentive electorate, therefore, it is often easier for the savvy politician to simply cave in to public demands.

We are thus left with three very different causal pathways, each of which seems plausible and is backed by a wealth of evidence. Before we discuss which perspective is "correct," it is important to make a simple clarification. Political leadership is fairly easy to understand, but representation and responsiveness are sometimes confused. Representation is distinguished from responsiveness in that the former tells us only that politicians and constituents hold the same opinion while the latter describes a more active relationship in which the public influences politicians.[25] This book is interested in finding evidence of political responsiveness and identifying the process that produces it. After all, political responsiveness is really what is explored in the question "Does public opinion influence U.S. foreign policy?" The word *influence* signifies a power relationship—making someone act in a way that he or she would not have otherwise acted. We can then rephrase the central question

---

19. Shapiro and Page, "Foreign Policy and the Rational Public"; Page and Bouton, *Foreign Policy Disconnect*; Aldrich et al., "Foreign Policy"; Page and Shapiro, *Rational Public*; Shapiro and Page, "Foreign Policy and Public Opinion"; Page and Shapiro, "Changes in Americans' Policy Preferences"; Jentleson, "Pretty Prudent Public"; Jentleson and Britton, "Still Pretty Prudent"; Oneal, Lian, and Joyner, "Are the American People 'Pretty Prudent'?"; Wittkopf, *Faces of Internationalism*.

20. Geer, *Tea Leaves to Opinion Polls*; Eichenberg, Stoll, and Lebo, "War President"; Karol and Miguel, "Electoral Cost of War"; Gelpi, Reifler, and Feaver, "Iraq the Vote"; Aldrich, Sullivan, and Borgida, "Foreign Affairs"; Aldrich et al., "Foreign Policy"; Bartels and Zaller, "Presidential Vote Models"; Hibbs, "Bread and Peace Voting"; Eichenberg, "Victory Has Many Friends."

21. Sullivan, "Bank Account Presidency"; Light, *President's Agenda*; Neustadt, *Presidential Power*.

22. Voeten and Brewer, "Public Opinion"; Eichenberg, Stoll, and Lebo, "War President"; Gelpi, Feaver, and Reifler, "Success Matters."

23. Rottinghaus, "Rethinking Presidential Responsiveness."

24. Brace and Hinckley, *Follow the Leader*; Edwards, *On Deaf Ears*.

25. Eulau and Karps, "Puzzle of Representation."

of this book to make it even clearer: "When are presidents likely to abandon their preferred foreign policy for one favored by the public?"

Uncovering evidence of political responsiveness is a difficult task. Two key observations are necessary to determine whether responsiveness has or has not occurred. First, there must be some evidence that a decision maker's choice differed from what he or she would have otherwise preferred. This means that the researcher must have considerable insights into the policy-making process and, more interestingly, into the mindset of the leaders who make these decisions. Second, if a policy choice is found to be different from the decision maker's true preference, there must be some evidence that public opinion caused that deviation and not some other factor. In other words, we must rule out all of the other pressures that can lead presidents to have a change of heart, such as demands from international allies, interests groups, bureaucrats, or Congress. Although finding evidence of responsiveness is a challenging task, uncovering what role, if any, the American public plays in U.S. foreign policy decisions is important enough to warrant the effort.

Why Focus on the White House?

This book focuses on presidential foreign policy making. Included in the analysis are the president, vice president, political advisors in the Executive Office of the President and the White House Office, and political appointees in the executive branch. There are several reasons to focus exclusively on the White House rather than broadening the analysis to include Congress or other political elites. First, presidents are uniquely positioned to play the most dominant role in U.S. foreign policy making.[26] It is, of course, inaccurate to say that presidents have an unchallenged authority in foreign policy,[27] but usually they have significantly more influence in international affairs than do other domestic political actors.

Second, presidents are more likely than other domestic political actors to feel the dual pressures of international and domestic politics. As the only nationally elected public official, the president has a strong incentive to represent the American public. At the same time, presidents are charged with advancing U.S. interests in world affairs. When these pressures conflict, as they often do, presidents are forced into a difficult political trade-off between

26. Wildavsky, "Two Presidencies"; Schlesinger, *Imperial Presidency*; Peterson, "President's Dominance."
27. Rose, *Postmodern President*.

domestic and international goals. By contrast, voters usually evaluate members of Congress on how well they respond to domestic policy and local issues.[28] That presidents must reconcile conflicting demands from the international and the domestic levels makes the Oval Office a more theoretically interesting unit of analysis than Congress.

A Conditional Theory of Political Responsiveness

From a conceptual or theoretical standpoint, it would be fairly easy to understand the role of the American public in U.S. foreign policy if presidents always led or always followed mass opinion. However, the truth of political life is far too complicated to be captured by such simple, absolute statements. Rather than adopting an all-or-nothing approach, the emerging consensus in the literature is that political responsiveness is *conditional.* As Paul Burstein writes, "No one believes that public opinion always determines public policy; few believe it never does."[29] The task, then, taken up by a number of foreign and domestic policy scholars, is to identify the factors that can increase or decrease politicians' sensitivity to public opinion.

The literature on conditional political responsiveness is vast and growing. For instance, Douglas Foyle, in *Counting the Public In,* examines how presidents' normative and practical beliefs about the role that public opinion *should* play in foreign policy affect the role that it *does* play. Motivators for responsiveness can come from political factors, such as temporal proximity to the next election,[30] or the level of presidential approval.[31] Responsiveness can also vary according to the quality of information that presidents possess about mass opinion,[32] or the degree to which citizens' views seriously constrain a president's freedom of action.[33] In a sense, then, a conditional approach to political responsiveness suggests that all three causal explanations of the correlation

---

28. Mayhew, *Congress*; Fiorina, *Congress.*
29. Burstein, "Impact of Public Opinion on Public Policy: A Review," 29. See also Manza and Cook, "A Democratic Polity?"; Canes-Wrone and Shotts, "Nature of Presidential Responsiveness"; and Foyle, *Counting the Public In.*
30. Nincic, "U.S. Soviet Policy"; Jacobs and Shapiro, "Politics and Policymaking"; Manza and Cook, "A Democratic Polity?"; Geer, *Tea Leaves to Opinion Polls*; Canes-Wrone, *Who Leads Whom?*; Canes-Wrone, Herron, and Shotts, "Leadership and Pandering."
31. Towle, *Out of Touch*; Brace and Hinckley, *Follow the Leader*; Hibbs, *American Political Economy*; Manza, Cook, and Page, *Impact of Public Opinion*; Canes-Wrone, *Who Leads Whom?*; Canes-Wrone, Herron, and Shotts, "Leadership and Pandering."
32. Geer, *Tea Leaves to Opinion Polls.*
33. J. Cohen, *Presidential Responsiveness.*

between opinion and policy can be correct. Presidents can lead, follow, or ignore public opinion depending on the details of the situation.

This book presents and tests a theory of conditional responsiveness, integrating three concepts found in the conditional responsiveness literature—decision stages, public preferences, and issue salience—into a single model of the public opinion–foreign policy link. The theoretical model rests on five simple propositions outlined in chapter 1, which allow us to precisely identify when the American public might have a greater or lesser influence on foreign policy. As a starting point, I conceptualize presidential foreign policy making as a five-stage sequence consisting of problem definition, option generation, policy decision, implementation, and policy review (also detailed in chapter 1). The relative importance of public opinion as a presidential decision premise will be assessed at each of these five decision stages.

The theory then explores two mechanisms that can influence presidential responsiveness to public opinion: issue salience and public preferences. Presidents are likely to feel increased pressure to respond to public opinion when a large percentage of Americans are attentive to an issue (i.e., high issue salience). Likewise, presidents will likely feel increased pressure to respond when a significant majority of Americans hold the same preference on an issue. Therefore, it stands to reason that presidential sensitivity to public opinion reaches its apex when an issue is highly salient *and* enjoys widespread support. When public attention is focused elsewhere, or when Americans are divided in their preferences, political responsiveness is likely to decrease accordingly.

The analytical task then becomes to predict which of the five decision stages will see a convergence of high issue salience with a large majority preference. To do this, I compare the nature of public preferences and issue salience in foreign policy crises and noncrises. Although foreign policy crises usually produce a highly attentive public throughout the stages of the decision-making process, interest tends to peak during the implementation of a policy decision. Americans typically agree about what should take place at this stage of crises, particularly if the implementation of crisis policy means military conflict, which it often does. This confluence of high issue salience and unified public preferences offers presidents a strong incentive to be responsive during implementation. Noncrises are a different story. While certain types of noncrises can stimulate a high degree of public interest, that interest generally focuses on the government's most visible policy decision and little else. Further, while the American public often demands that something be done about noncrisis problems, it usually offers little guidance on the precise solutions. Therefore, political responsiveness should be most evident at the policy decision stage of noncrises.

Implications of the Theory

This conditional theory of political responsiveness offers us several insights into the relationship between public opinion and U.S. foreign policy. First, by conceptualizing a single foreign policy case as a sequence of choices, we can examine the possibility that the causal direction between opinion and policy can change over the life of the event. Put differently, presidents can lead, follow, *and* ignore the American public, all within the same foreign policy case. As such, the model offers an improvement over theories that attribute unidirectional causality to the public opinion–foreign policy relationship.

Second, the book demonstrates that public opinion can indeed influence U.S. foreign policy—just not at the stages where we might expect, or hope, that it naturally would. For instance, one of the central conclusions of the analysis is that while mass opinion may have little influence on a president's decision to go to war, the American public plays a surprisingly large role in shaping what the subsequent battle will look like. Perhaps the greatest revolution in military and strategic affairs since Vietnam has not been advances in weaponry or the end of the cold war, but rather the pervasive belief among political leaders that the American public is casualty phobic. This belief has impacted the ways that wars are fought and the steps that presidents now take to initiate military conflict. From a normative perspective, however, we might wish that the situation were reversed—that citizens would enjoy greater say in the crucial decision for war or peace, and that wars, if they must be fought, be conducted in a manner that is strategically effective and militarily efficient (within reason, of course). Yet it seems that presidents usually lead reluctant Americans into battle, only to turn around and follow the public once the decision for war has been made.

Third, our analysis shows that what the public does or does not pay attention to matters in foreign policy. Consider, for instance, the public's interest in noncrisis foreign policies. A large percentage of Americans are attentive when a president signs an arms control treaty, agrees to limit global warming, or pledges U.S. aid to foreign nations ravaged by natural disasters. But how many people pay attention to whether the weapons are actually dismantled, whether corporations are taking advantage of undue loopholes in the implementation of a global warming accord, or whether U.S. aid actually reaches those in dire need? The answer: not too many. Instead, the public usually assumes that the policy decided on will be the policy implemented. We also assume that *someone* must be paying attention to ensure that everything is going according to plan. And we assume that *someone* will notify us if and when the plans go awry.

These assumptions, while often justified, are sometimes misplaced. When the public turns its attention away from what is going on in Washington, D.C., U.S. foreign policy can veer dramatically off its original course, no matter what Americans prefer. After all, there are no political costs for the president who deviates from popular opinion when no one is looking.

Plan of the Book

The remainder of the book is organized as follows. Chapter 1 puts forth a theory of the policy-opinion link. The key aspect of the model is an examination of the interplay of public preferences and issue salience throughout the foreign policy process. Chapter 2 offers expectations of presidential sensitivity to public opinion at each decision-making stage—problem definition, option generation, policy decision, implementation, and policy review—for crises and noncrises. Chapter 3 empirically tests the expectation that issue salience moves in predictable ways. These data include some of the most important events in American foreign policy over the past forty years and bring breadth to the analysis. Having examined the fluctuation of issue salience in a large number of cases, the analysis then turns to two in-depth case studies—one crisis and one noncrisis—to assess the actual role of public opinion in presidential decision making. Chapters 4 and 5 examine presidential decision making in the 1990-91 Persian Gulf crisis. The Persian Gulf case is indicative of most crises in that the public remained highly attentive for the duration of the conflict, with interest being most intense during the actual conduct of the war. Although President George H. W. Bush attempted to lead the American public throughout most of the case, the influence of mass opinion became stronger during the implementation of policy. Chapters 6 and 7 assess a noncrisis case—the U.S. response to famine in Ethiopia during the mid-1980s. Although the Ethiopian famine lasted more than four years, the American public was only attentive for a period of roughly three months. Given a selectively attentive public, a close congruence between mass preference and U.S. food aid policy existed for only one brief decision-making stage. The book concludes with a discussion of the major findings of the analysis and their implications for American foreign policy, democratic theory, and political representation.

1

FOREIGN POLICY IN THE SHADOWS AND THE SPOTLIGHT

At what point, if at all, does the American public matter in the construction of U.S. foreign policy? To help us think about this question, consider three foreign policy problems that occurred during President Jimmy Carter's term in office. First, Carter faced the question of whether or not to turn over control of the Panama Canal to the Panamanians. Under the leadership of General Omar Torrijos, the Panamanians had long demanded the abrogation of the Hay-Bunau-Varilla Treaty, which gave the United States control of the canal in 1903. President Carter was eager to comply with this demand since he believed that U.S. ownership of the canal had become a flash point of anti-American sentiment in Latin America. The American public, however, was opposed to Carter's position. In May 1977, 78 percent of the public felt that the United States should continue its ownership and control of the Panama Canal.[1] But despite this widespread sentiment, the issue did not seem particularly important to the American public. The very same month that 78 percent of Americans expressed their support for continued U.S. control of the canal, there were exactly *zero* minutes of television coverage on the issue. Moreover, 62 percent of Americans admitted that they knew very little or nothing at all about the Panama Canal controversy.[2]

---

1. Survey by the Opinion Research Corporation, May 4–7, 1977, from LexisNexis, Roper Center for Public Opinion Research, University of Connecticut (accessed April 2, 2004). "Do you favor the United States continuing its ownership and control of the Panama Canal, or do you favor turning ownership and control of the Panama Canal over to the Republic of Panama?"

2. Survey by the Opinion Research Corporation, May 4–7, 1977, from LexisNexis, Roper Center for Public Opinion Research, University of Connecticut (accessed April 9, 2004). "As you may know, the Panama Canal is the waterway in Central America that connects the Atlantic and Pacific Oceans. The United States secured full ownership and control of the Canal Zone by way of a treaty signed with the Republic of Panama in 1903. How much, if anything, have you heard or read about the possibility of negotiations on a new Panama Canal Treaty—a great deal, a fair amount, very little, or nothing at all?"

President Carter faced a second, more serious problem when radical Islamic students stormed the U.S. embassy in Tehran, Iran, on November 4, 1979, and held sixty-six Americans hostage. In response, the Carter administration engaged in vigorous international diplomacy, froze Iranian assets in the United States, and refused to purchase Iranian oil. These steps, however, were not enough to free the hostages. The question then turned to whether the United States would attempt to rescue the hostages in a manner similar to that of the 1976 Israeli raid on Entebbe. By December 1979, the American public was split on the question of a rescue: 46 percent of the public believed it should be attempted while 49 percent felt it should not be an option.[3] Although Americans were divided on a rescue attempt, they were united in their attention to and concern about the hostage crisis: 99 percent[4] of Americans said they had heard about the crisis; 92 percent[5] remarked that they were following the situation closely; and 80 percent[6] felt that the taking of American hostages in Iran was the most serious crisis the United States had faced since the end of the Vietnam War.

Already dealing with the Iranian hostage crisis, President Carter encountered a third foreign policy problem when Soviet troops invaded Afghanistan in late December 1979. The United States was concerned that the Soviets would continue their offensive into Iran and would eventually gain control of the Middle East and its oil. The Soviet invasion was highly salient: 90 percent of Americans said they were attentive to the situation.[7] Moreover, the

---

3. Survey by the Roper Organization, December 1–8, 1979, from LexisNexis, Roper Center for Public Opinion Research, University of Connecticut (accessed April 12, 2004). "If Iran won't release the hostages, another approach that has been suggested is to have a U.S. military strike force invade Teheran to try to rescue them. Some say we should do this. Others say we shouldn't because the hostages would be killed before we could get to them. Still others say we should do it, even if we don't succeed in rescuing the hostages in order to retaliate for Iran's actions and show we won't be pushed around. Do you think we should or should not make a military attempt to rescue the American hostages in Teheran?"

4. Survey by the Gallup Organization, December 7–10, 1979, from LexisNexis, Roper Center for Public Opinion Research, University of Connecticut (accessed April 12, 2004). "Have you heard or read about the situation in which students are holding the occupants of the U.S. (United States) Embassy in Iran hostage demanding the return of the Shah?"

5. Survey by the *Los Angeles Times*, December 16–18, 1979, from LexisNexis, Roper Center for Public Opinion Research, University of Connecticut (accessed April 12, 2004). "(Of course, everyone is more interested in some things in the news than in others.) Is the situation in Iran something that you have been following closely, or just following casually, or not paying much attention to?"

6. Survey by ABC News/Louis Harris and Associates, November 26–29, 1979, from LexisNexis, Roper Center for Public Opinion Research, University of Connecticut (accessed April 14, 2004). "How serious do you feel the crisis has been of Iran seizing our Embassy there and holding 49 Americans as hostages—one of the most serious crises since the Vietnam War started, only somewhat serious, or hardly serious at all?"

7. Survey by ABC News, January 16, 1980, from LexisNexis, Roper Center for Public Opinion Research, University of Connecticut (accessed April 16, 2004). "Have you heard or read anything about the Soviet Union's invasion of Afghanistan?"

public was unified in many of its preferences, including a widespread preference (73 percent) that the United States boycott the upcoming 1980 Moscow Olympic Games.[8]

If we put ourselves in President Carter's shoes, in which of these three foreign policy problems would we be most sensitive to public opinion? This is a rather difficult call in two of the cases but a fairly easy choice in the third. In the Panama Canal case, the widespread public preference for retaining the canal might convince us that advocating a policy that called for relinquishing control of the canal could harm our political future. On the other hand, the fact that very few Americans seemed interested in the situation suggested that the political costs of defying public opinion might not be all that great. The high issue salience of the Iranian hostage crisis certainly increased the political pressure for a successful resolution. However, the division in public preferences over a rescue attempt offered little guidance on that particular option. In both the Panama Canal and Iranian hostage cases, low issue salience or a division in public preferences raises doubts about whether we, in President Carter's position, would have responded to public opinion. By contrast, the third case, the Soviet invasion of Afghanistan, presents a stronger and more clear-cut motivation for political responsiveness to public opinion. Here, the American public expressed a strong majority preference (i.e., boycott the Moscow Olympic Games) on a highly salient issue. In this case, defiance of public opinion would be bound to carry some political costs.

As it turns out, Carter defied public opinion by signing the Carter-Torrijos Treaty, relinquishing U.S. control of the Panama Canal. Unfortunately for the president, the return of the canal to Panama eventually became salient to the American public, and only 29 percent of Americans gave Carter a positive rating on his handling of the issue.[9] Carter also authorized a high-risk rescue operation of American hostages in Iran, dubbed Operation Eagle Claw, on April 7, 1980.[10] The mission was an unqualified disaster: a sandstorm forced the United States to scrub the rescue attempt, and in the retreat, eight U.S.

---

8. Survey by NBC News/Associated Press, January 29–30, 1980, from LexisNexis, Roper Center for Public Opinion Research, University of Connecticut (accessed April 12, 2004). "If the 1980 Summer Olympics are not moved out of Moscow, do you think that the U.S. should withdraw from them (because of the Soviet military intervention in Afghanistan), or don't you think so?"

9. Survey by Louis Harris and Associates, September 18–26, 1977, from LexisNexis, Roper Center for Public Opinion Research, University of Connecticut (accessed March 3, 2004). "(Now let me ask you about some specific things President Carter has done.) How would you rate him on . . . his new treaty to give control of the Panama Canal to the Panamanian government by the year 2000—excellent, pretty good, only fair or poor?"

10. Paterson et al., *American Foreign Relations*; Houghton, *U.S. Foreign Policy*; McDermott, "Prospect Theory."

soldiers were killed when their helicopter collided with a C-130 transport plane.[11] Finally, in a manner consistent with public preferences, Carter announced that the United States would boycott the Moscow Olympic Games on March 21, 1980.

Uncovering how much public opinion actually influenced President Carter in each of these cases requires significantly more insights than what is presented here. Nevertheless, the point is that presidents face different political contexts that can make them more or less responsive to the opinions of the American public. This chapter offers a theory of conditional political responsiveness in which presidents sometime lead, sometimes follow, and sometimes just ignore the American public. We begin by distinguishing between crisis and noncrisis foreign policies, before examining the five simple propositions that comprise the theoretical model and proposing hypotheses about the nature of public attention and preferences. After addressing two caveats, the chapter will conclude with a discussion of some of the assumptions that undergird the theoretical model.

Crises and Noncrises

In this book, a critical distinction is made between foreign policy crises and noncrises. A crisis is defined as "a situation in which three conditions, deriving from a change in a state's external or internal environment, are perceived by the highest-level decision makers of the state: (a) a threat to basic values, (b) an awareness of finite time for response to the external threat to basic values, and (c) a high probability of involvement in military hostilities."[12] Examples of crises include the 1991 Gulf War, the Cuban Missile Crisis, and the recent wars in Afghanistan and Iraq. Noncrises are situations in which the option of using military force is extremely unlikely and the time horizon for making and implementing a policy decision is comparatively long. Relevant noncrises include international economic agreements, arms control treaties, global environmental issues, and foreign aid.

It is rare to find studies that directly compare foreign policy crises with noncrises, for the simple reason that the two seem so totally incomparable. Crises are high-stakes events that attract massive public interest. Additionally, crises are often equated with "high politics," in which presidents are relatively

---

11. Paterson et al., *American Foreign Relations.*
12. Brecher and Wilkenfeld, *International Crisis Behavior Project.*

insulated from the normal political constraints that come with the job. As a result, many scholars contend that the state behaves as a unitary actor during crises (i.e., acts with one voice).[13] By contrast, noncrises often seem less important and less pressing, and garner significantly less public interest. Moreover, while presidents enjoy considerable deference and autonomy in crisis situations, a number of strong political actors compete with the president for power in noncrisis policy making, including Congress, interest groups, bureaucrats, and political parties.[14] When the two types of foreign policies are compared, it is usually to illustrate that Americans are highly attentive to crises but pay little mind to routine noncrisis issues.[15]

Although this traditional view of crisis and noncrisis foreign policy contains elements of truth, it is also somewhat misleading. American presidents are not completely insulated from domestic pressures during foreign policy crises, nor are they completely constrained during noncrises. And while crises are typically more salient to the public, we will see that the public does, at times, pay close attention to noncrisis problems. For our purposes, the important distinction between crises and noncrises is that the American public tends to take an interest in different aspects of each. In crises, especially those involving the use of military force, the public is inclined to be most interested in how policy is implemented. By contrast, in noncrises, public interest typically focuses on the policy decision and little else (i.e., not the decision stages before or after the president announces his policy).

Five Propositions of Conditional Political Responsiveness

The theoretical model of conditional presidential responsiveness in American foreign policy is composed of five simple propositions. First, presidents make a number of choices during the various decision stages of a foreign policy event, any one of which can potentially be influenced by public opinion. Second, presidential sensitivity to public opinion partially increases as the size of majority opinion increases. Third, presidential sensitivity to public opinion partially increases when an issue is highly salient to the public. Fourth, presidents are under the greatest pressure to respond to public opinion when the public holds a clear preference on a highly salient issue. And finally, both

---

13. Waltz, *Theory of International Politics*; Morgenthau, *Politics Among Nations*.
14. Peake, "Presidential Agenda Setting"; Lindsay, *Politics of U.S. Foreign Policy*; Destler, *American Trade Politics*.
15. Baum and Potter, "Mass Media, Public Opinion"; Graber, *Mass Media and American Politics*.

the public's attention to and preferences on foreign policy issues move in predictable ways across the decision stages. The following sections discuss each of these propositions in greater depth.

Proposition 1: Presidents Make a Number of Decisions in a Foreign Policy Case (the Decision Stages)

With important exceptions, the relationship between public opinion and U.S. foreign policy is usually assessed by looking at one juncture of the decision-making process (e.g., the decision to use military force or the decision to sign a treaty). Although a narrow analytical focus is understandable given the practical challenges that research across the policy spectrum entails, the drawback to such a "snapshot" approach is that it may overlook other choices made within the same case where public opinion was more or less influential. Put more bluntly, looking at only one aspect of a policy case can be like a blindfolded man describing an elephant: the picture is certainly incomplete, segmented, and often misleading.

An alternative approach in assessing political responsiveness is to conceptualize presidential foreign policy making as a series of interrelated decisions and examine the role of public opinion at each stage of that process.[16] This sequential decision-making, or "moving-picture," approach offers three advantages over the snapshot method. First, it recognizes that presidents make not one but several important choices in any foreign policy event. This understanding opens up the possibility that the influence of opinion on policy can vary over the life of the event. It also avoids the tendency inherent in the snapshot method to over- or underestimate the role of public opinion by focusing exclusively on a single policy choice. Second, the sequential approach understands that a president's current decision is conditioned by past ones and will likewise shape future choices. As such, the approach accounts for the process by which policy is made. Finally, the decision-stages approach allows for the possibility that presidents may lead the public at some stages, only to follow the public at others. In this way, the method improves upon existing theories that attribute unidirectional causality in each foreign policy case.

A number of scholars have employed a decision-stages approach in assessing the role of public opinion in U.S. foreign policy. For example, Douglas

16. For literature on sequential decision making in foreign policy, see Hermann, "Changing Course"; Billings and Hermann, "Problem Identification"; Beasley et al., "People and Processes"; Beasley, "Collective Interpretations"; Ozkececi-Taner, "Reviewing the Literature"; Kuperman, "Dynamic Framework"; and deLeon, "Stages Approach."

Foyle conceptualizes decision making as a four-stage process—problem representation, option generation, option selection, and policy implementation—and finds that public opinion has the greatest influence while presidents are generating options. Thomas Graham also describes a four-stage policy process, but with a slightly different characterization of the stages: getting on the agenda, negotiation, ratification, and implementation. In his examination of nuclear arms control from 1945 to 1980, Graham discovered that public opinion was influential in getting an issue on the political agenda and during the ratification stage. Jeffrey Cohen specifies another four-stage process—problem identification in agenda setting, position taking in agenda setting, policy formulation, and position taking on roll call votes before Congress—and finds the influence of the public to be greatest during problem identification. Finally, Richard Sobel examines the influence of public opinion at different "benchmarks," or key junctures, of policy making in his case studies of U.S. policy toward Vietnam, Nicaragua, Bosnia, and the Persian Gulf.[17]

Drawing on these works, our model begins by conceptualizing presidential foreign policy making as a five-stage process. Following the work of Foyle in *Counting the Public In,* the first stage, *problem definition,* incorporates two types of observations: agenda setting and problem representation. Agenda setting refers to constructing the "list of subjects to which government officials and those around them are paying serious attention";[18] problem representation examines how decision makers interpret constraints and specify policy goals in response to a perceived problem.[19] At stage two, *option generation,* the president and his advisors compile a menu of options for dealing with the defined problem. *Policy decision,* stage three, is the key decision made in a foreign policy case. Stage four, *implementation,* refers to the strategy and tactics involved in carrying out a policy decision. And the fifth stage, *policy review,* presents the choice of continuing, modifying, or abandoning a particular policy course. This framework allows us to assess whether presidents lead, follow, or ignore the American public at different stages of the same foreign policy event.

Proposition 2: Public Preferences Are a Partial Motivation for Presidential Responsiveness

Preferences, the central focus in the responsiveness literature, refer to the public's views on specific policy issues. To assess these preferences, survey organizations

---

17. Foyle, *Counting the Public In*; Graham, "Foreign Policy Decision Making"; Graham, "Politics of Failure"; J. Cohen, *Presidential Responsiveness*; Sobel, *Impact of Public Opinion.*
18. Kingdon, *Agendas.*
19. Sylvan and Voss, *Problem Representation.*

ask questions like "Do you support President Bush's decision to go to war at this time, or not?"[20] or "In general, do you think that free trade agreements—like NAFTA, and the policies of the World Trade Organization—have been a good thing or a bad thing for the United States?"[21]

Since Franklin Roosevelt, presidents have employed their own pollsters to provide them with a wealth of information on the preferences of the American public.[22] Yet even in situations where decision makers may lack specific data, they can often infer what Americans want by looking at the media coverage,[23] assessing the overall liberal-conservative public mood in the nation,[24] or simply relying on their own intuition.[25] James Druckman and Lawrence Jacobs examine whether politicians are influenced by the public's specific policy preferences gathered from survey data (i.e., splitters) or by the public's overall liberal-conservative policy mood (i.e., lumpers). The authors find that decision makers act as splitters on high-salience issues and act as lumpers on low-salience issues.[26] We should therefore expect that, because crises are usually highly salient and noncrises are usually less salient, presidents are generally splitters in times of crisis and lumpers in noncrises.[27]

All things considered, presidents come under greater pressure to cater to the public's preferences when a large majority of Americans coalesce around a particular policy option. For example, Thomas Graham found that at the "unanimous level" of opinion (80 percent and higher), presidents almost always select policies favored by the public. Mass opinion at the "preponderant level" (70–79 percent) has a strong but not automatic effect on presidential decision making. In the "consensus range" (60–69 percent), presidents again

20. Survey by the *Los Angeles Times*, January 17–18, 1991, from LexisNexis, Roper Center for Public Opinion Research, University of Connecticut (accessed April 12, 2004).
21. Survey by Pew Research Center/Council on Foreign Relations/Abt SRBI, April 23–27, 2008, http://www.pollingreport.com/trade.htm (accessed June 7, 2008).
22. Eisinger, *Evolution of Presidential Polling*; Geer, *Tea Leaves to Opinion Polls*; Heith, *Polling to Govern*; Jacobs, "Recoil Effect"; Jacobs and Shapiro, "Issues, Candidate Image"; Jacobs and Shapiro, "Rise of Presidential Polling"; Murray and Howard, "White House Polling Operations."
23. B. Cohen, *Public's Impact on Foreign Policy*; Arterton, *Media Politics*; Mutz and Soss, "Reading Public Opinion"; Cook et al., "Media and Agenda Setting"; Powlick and Katz, "Public Opinion/Foreign Policy Nexus."
24. Kingdon, *Agendas*; Erikson, MacKuen, and Stimson, *Macro Polity*; Stimson, Mackuen, and Erikson, "Dynamic Representation."
25. Powlick, "Sources of Public Opinion"; Powlick and Katz, "Public Opinion/Foreign Policy Nexus"; B. Cohen, *Democracies and Foreign Policy*; Foyle, *Counting the Public In*; Powlick, "Attitudinal Bases for Responsiveness."
26. Druckman and Jacobs, "Lumpers and Splitters."
27. This situation is expected to hold unless the crisis moves too quickly for surveys to be taken, or the noncrisis problem achieves sufficient interest to warrant polling, in which case presidents would be lumpers in crises and splitters in noncrises.

feel the strong pull of public opinion, yet are able to exercise discretion in decision making. Finally, popular presidents can safely ignore public opinion in the "majority range" (50–59 percent).[28] Graham's framework suggests that we might be able to predict presidential responsiveness if we can also forecast the size of majority or plurality opinion.

Proposition 3: High Issue Salience Is a Partial Motivation for Presidential Responsiveness

There is a subtle, yet vitally important and often overlooked, distinction between public preferences and issue salience.[29] Whereas public preferences refer to mass opinions on policy issues, issue salience is the amount of public attention an issue receives.[30] Although preferences and salience are often conflated, the two concepts are analytically distinct and can vary independently. For example, knowing that 68 percent of the American public *prefers* that the federal government do more to curb global warming tells us nothing of the issue salience or the importance these same individuals attach to the issue of climate change.[31]

Compared with public preferences, issue salience has received considerably less attention in the foreign policy literature.[32] Several factors suggest that this oversight is a mistake. First, high issue salience can raise the political stakes,

---

28. Graham, "Foreign Policy Decision Making."
29. Burstein, "Public Opinion and Congressional Action"; Manza, Cook, and Page, *Impact of Public Opinion*; Soroka, "Media, Public Opinion"; Jones, *Reconceiving Decision-Making*; Geer, *Tea Leaves to Opinion Polls*; Knecht and Weatherford, "Public Opinion"; Kollman, *Outside Lobbying*; Zaller, *Nature and Origins*.
30. A number of scholars have pointed out the potential problems in conflating the terms "issue salience," "attention," and "importance." While the admonition is valuable, such fine-grained distinctions are probably more vital for individual-level studies than for research that examines governmental responsiveness. From the perspective of the White House, it is difficult to judge whether the public is casually attentive to an issue or whether the public really feels that the issue is of great importance. Because decision makers often judge public attention through the proxy of media coverage, they are likely to conflate the terms "attention" and "importance" just as we do here. Therefore, throughout the analysis, the terms "public attention," "issue salience," "importance," and "concern" are all used interchangeably. On the distinctions between these terms and related questions of measurement, see Wlezien, "Salience of Political Issues"; Wlezien, "Patterns of Representation"; Kiousis, "Explicating Media Salience"; Baum, "Use of Force"; and Mutz and Soss, "Reading Public Opinion."
31. Survey by ABC News/*Time*/Stanford University, March 9–14, 2006, http://www.pollingreport.com/enviro.htm (accessed July 11, 2008). "Do you think the federal government should do more than it's doing now to try to deal with global warming, should do less than it's doing now, or is it doing about the right amount?"
32. Edwards, Mitchell, and Welch, "Explaining Presidential Approval"; Everts, "After the Cold War"; Burstein, "Impact of Public Opinion on Public Policy: A Review."

increasing decision makers' sensitivity to public opinion.[33] Simply put, politicians incur political costs when deviating from majority opinion *only if* the public is aware that its views are being ignored. Second, issue salience can change rapidly while public preferences generally remain more stable.[34] The rapid fluctuation of issue salience is especially common in foreign policy, where unexpected events can quickly grab the public's attention. Finally, presidents may attempt to manipulate the level of issue salience in order to prime issues on which the public already agrees with the White House position.[35] Indeed, presidents generally have an easier time affecting the level of salience than they do changing people's opinions on an issue.

Recently, more scholars have begun to incorporate salience into their models of foreign policy responsiveness. For example, both Stuart Soroka and Brian Jones show how issue salience strongly influences levels of defense spending. Matthew Baum examines presidents' incentive to "go private," or minimize issue salience, when public opinion is contrary to their preferred policy. In his analysis of security policy in the Netherlands, Philip Everts finds that "for public opinion to have an impact on an issue, the issue must be salient to the public." Finally, Philip Powlick and Andrew Katz assume that public opinion becomes the "barking dog" only when events or elite disagreements raise issue salience.[36]

Proposition 4: The Interaction of Public Preferences and Issue Salience Influences Presidential Responsiveness

Public preferences and issue salience are both partial mechanisms in political responsiveness, but either alone is usually insufficient to convince presidents to abandon their favored policies and cater to mass opinion. Instead, it is the *interaction* of preferences and salience that typically affects policy makers. This interaction can produce different political contexts for presidents. Again, preference and salience can vary independently: the public's preference can be unified (i.e., a significant majority opinion has formed on an issue) or divided,

---

33. Burstein, *Discrimination, Jobs, and Politics*; Burstein, "Public Opinion and Congressional Action"; Burstein, "Impact of Public Opinion on Public Policy: A Review"; Burstein, "Estimates of the Impact of Public Opinion"; Everts, "After the Cold War"; Geer, *Tea Leaves to Opinion Polls*; Kollman, *Outside Lobbying*; Powlick and Katz, "Public Opinion/Foreign Policy Nexus"; Baum, "Going Private."

34. Page and Shapiro, *Rational Public*.

35. Druckman and Holmes, "Does Presidential Rhetoric Matter?"; Jacobs and Shapiro, "Issues, Candidate Image"; Murray, "Private Polls"; Druckman, Jacobs, and Ostermeier, "Candidate Strategies"; Krosnick and Brannon, "Impact of the Gulf War."

36. Soroka, "Media, Public Opinion"; Jones, *Reconceiving Decision-Making*; Baum, "Going Private"; Everts, "After the Cold War," 187; Powlick and Katz, "Public Opinion/Foreign Policy Nexus."

Table 1 The political contexts

	Salience High	Salience Low
Preference Unified	Constrained	Guarded
Preference Divided	Contested	Insulated

and the salience of the issue can be either high or low.[37] Preferences are assumed to be unified when over 60 percent of Americans hold the same opinion on an issue; salience, as measured by nightly television news coverage, is assumed high when the three major television networks devote a combined twenty minutes of coverage to a single issue per week (see appendix A for a justification of these measures). Table 1 illustrates how variation in preferences and salience can produce different political contexts.

Public opinion is expected to factor most heavily into decision making in the *constrained* category, since high issue salience raises the political stakes and the public expresses an unambiguous preference. In the *contested* category, preferences are divided (i.e., close to a 50-50 percent split), so there is no clear-cut opinion to which presidents might respond. The divided preferences and high issue salience at this stage often produce fierce political debates as presidents and their opponents try to shift public opinion to their respective sides. In the *guarded* category, presidents can usually ignore majority opinion but must be cautious about an inattentive public suddenly turning attentive sometime in the future. Finally, presidents enjoy the greatest autonomy in the *insulated* category because the public is divided in its opinion and is uninterested in policy making.

Although table 1 offers a typology of the political contexts that presidents face, it does not offer a predictive theory of presidential responsiveness. To predict when presidents will lead, follow, or ignore the American public, we need some means of forecasting whether the political context surrounding an issue will be constrained, contested, insulated, or guarded at each of the five decision stages.

Proposition 5: Issue Salience and Public Preferences Move in Predictable Ways

Is it possible, then, to predict which foreign policy issues Americans will attend to and what preferences they will hold? In large part, the theory presented here

---

37. Obviously, both preferences and salience are continuous variables, but for the purposes of elucidating our model I treat each as a dichotomy.

hinges on the answer. If issue salience and public preferences are completely erratic, then the framework offered above can be no more than a post hoc typology of the political contexts that presidents faced when they made their choices. In other words, the typology would be useful in analyzing presidential foreign policy making *after the fact* but could not tell us in advance when to expect political responsiveness. If, however, both salience and preferences move in ways we can anticipate, then the model will be able to predict the political context at all five stages of decision making for both crises and noncrises. Although prediction need not be considered the *sine qua non* of theoretical progress, it is useful to have a theory that can tell us when political responsiveness is likely to occur. The following paragraphs draw upon the extant literature to posit hypotheses concerning the nature of public attention and preferences for crisis and noncrisis foreign policy.

ISSUE SALIENCE

The ability to offer a predictive theory of the opinion-policy link relies on identifying systematic patterns of public attention to foreign policy across the five decision stages. If we are able to identify such patterns, then we have some means of forecasting when presidents are most likely to incorporate public opinion into their policy decisions. One particular aspect of issue salience that deserves more attention is the potential of a systematic "issue-attention" cycle in foreign policies. An issue-attention cycle describes the regular ebbs and flows of public attention to various policy issues. Anthony Downs first noted the existence of such a cycle in environmental policy, suggesting that an initial spike in public concern to "do something" about an ecological problem eventually eroded as the public became aware of the magnitude of the costs involved in solving the problem and grew bored with it.[38] The issue-attention cycle has subsequently been identified in the debates surrounding global warming,[39] humanitarian relief efforts,[40] and long-term political change.[41] To the extent that issue salience acts as a mechanism prompting political responsiveness, identifying fluctuations of mass attention offers a partial means of forecasting when presidential responsiveness is most likely to occur.

There are several reasons to expect high issue salience throughout the duration of most crises. The American public is usually aroused by the drama,

38. Downs, "Up and Down with Ecology." See also Hilgartner and Bosk, "Rise and Fall"; McCombs and Zhu, "Capacity, Diversity, and Volatility"; Neuman, "Threshold of Public Attention"; and Henry and Gordon, "Tracking Issue Attention."
39. Brossard, Shanahan, and McComas, "Issue-Cycles."
40. Bosso, "Setting the Agenda."
41. Vasquez and Mansbach, "Issue Cycle"; Vasquez, "Domestic Contention."

conflict, and potential violence inherent in crises.[42] Crises are also relatively short in duration and usually have a definitive conclusion, thus satisfying the public's limited attention span and cognitive need for problem resolution.[43] But even within these highly salient crisis events, the public tends to be most interested in the implementation of policy, especially if that implementation means the use of military force. War has become a public spectacle in an era of real-time television coverage and twenty-four-hour news channels. For example, Doris Graber demonstrated that nightly television news coverage of the start of the Iraq War in 2003 attracted more viewers than the two most popular shows of the time, *CSI* and *Friends*.[44] This leads to our first hypothesis:

H₁: Public attention to crises, while fairly high throughout the decision process, will peak during the implementation of policy.

For a number of reasons, noncrises typically garner less public attention than crises. Many noncrises, like poverty in the less developed world, seem remote to the average American.[45] Moreover, noncrises frequently involve subjects (e.g., international finance) with which the average American has little familiarity. Compared to crises, noncrises tend to be longer in duration and often have no definitive conclusion. As a result, the public eventually becomes bored with noncrisis issues. For instance, nuclear arms control, international trade and monetary policy, environmental protection, and foreign aid have been on the political agenda for decades and will likely remain there for the foreseeable future without ever reaching a definitive solution. And unlike crises, noncrises only periodically feature salient events that will garner extensive media coverage. As Powlick and Katz note, "The media need a 'peg,' or discrete event, on which to 'hang' a story."[46] Consider, for instance, the issue of global warming and the presence or absence of a peg. For decades, environmental activists have sounded the alarm about climate change to little avail; until recently, the American media really only covered the issue when an Earth Summit was being held, when Al Gore released a documentary, or when the summer was particularly hot. At other times, the concern about global warming was frozen during the winter months or drowned out by the crisis *du jour*.

42. Baum and Potter, "Mass Media, Public Opinion"; Graber, *Mass Media and American Politics*; Gans, *Deciding What's News*; Tuchman, *Making News*; Baum, *Soft News Goes to War*.
43. Neuman, "Threshold of Public Attention," 163.
44. Graber, *Mass Media and American Politics*, 130.
45. Almond, *American People*; Rielly, *U.S. Foreign Policy, 1999*.
46. Powlick and Katz, "Public Opinion/Foreign Policy Nexus"; Graham, "Foreign Policy Decision Making"; Graham, "Politics of Failure"; Bosso, "Setting the Agenda."

As global warming activists have learned, it is hard to get a noncrisis issue on the public's agenda and even more difficult to keep it there.

Although noncrises are typically less salient than crises, the public can at times be highly attentive to these issues. For instance, there was extensive American media coverage and public concern toward the 2008 Chinese earthquake and Myanmar cyclone disasters; the tsunami that struck Southeast Asia in 2004; arms control treaties such as SALT and START; the debate over NAFTA and the WTO; the 1980 Moscow Olympic boycott; the Camp David Accords; U.S. policy toward apartheid South Africa; and the Ethiopian famine of the mid-1980s.[47] However, the public's attention to these noncrisis issues was usually short-lived, focusing almost exclusively on the government's most visible policy decision. The details of most noncrisis policies—which tend to be hashed out during the option generation and policy implementation stages—are complicated, bureaucratic, and, quite frankly, normally about as exciting as watching paint dry. Still, the political devil is in those details, and the lack of public engagement with the nuances of policy affords presidents and bureaucrats alike considerable leeway to ignore public preferences and do what they want. This leads to our second hypothesis:

H_2: Public attention to noncrises, while fairly low throughout most of the decision process, will peak during the policy decision stage.

PUBLIC PREFERENCES

Compared to issue salience, there is a virtual mountain of research on the foreign policy preferences of the American public. This book draws upon this vast and rich reservoir of scholarship to offer predictions of what types of policies the public wants and when they want them.[48] The growing consensus in the literature is that public opinion is indeed rational, prudent, and stable. Although some preferences are undoubtedly shaped by the details of a particular case, the American public generally reacts in predictable ways to events and outcomes.[49] In crises, for instance, the public tends to initially rally around the president;[50] prefers that the use of force be authorized by both the UN and

---

47. For some of the seminal works on the American public's foreign policy preferences, see Holsti, *Public Opinion and American Foreign Policy*; Page and Shapiro, *Rational Public*; and Page and Bouton, *Foreign Policy Disconnect*.

48. Powlick and Katz, "Public Opinion/Foreign Policy Nexus," 40.

49. Jentleson, "Pretty Prudent Public"; Jentleson and Britton, "Still Pretty Prudent"; Page and Bouton, *Foreign Policy Disconnect*; Aldrich et al., "Foreign Policy"; Page and Shapiro, *Rational Public*.

50. Brody, *Assessing the President*; Mueller, *War, Presidents*.

the U.S. Congress;[51] strongly supports multilateral burden sharing in the conduct of military action;[52] and generally withdraws support for war as U.S. casualties increase,[53] but will tolerate casualties if a war looks like it will be a success or the cause for fighting is particularly just.[54] With few exceptions, these strong preferences emerge in most foreign policy crises.

The picture is more muddled for noncrisis foreign policies. The public holds several strong preferences on noncrisis issues, but it tends to have fewer opinions about the nuances of such policy. For instance, the public typically supports global environmental protection,[55] wants to protect U.S. jobs from foreign competition,[56] favors arms control agreements,[57] and supports the provision of emergency humanitarian aid to countries in need while opposing foreign aid to middle-income allies.[58] However, while the public may want the government to "do something" about a noncrisis, there is often little consensus on the actual solution. In the early 1990s, for instance, 77 percent of Americans viewed Japan as an economic threat to the United States.[59] The public, however, was roughly split on whether the problem would be best addressed by increasing tariffs (37 percent) or decreasing tariffs (41 percent) on Japanese imports.[60] Perhaps more illuminating is that a large percentage (22 percent) of

---

51. Eichenberg, "Victory Has Many Friends"; Holsti, *Public Opinion and American Foreign Policy*; Kull and Destler, *Misreading the Public*; Page and Bouton, *Foreign Policy Disconnect*.

52. Kull and Destler, *Misreading the Public*; Holsti, *Public Opinion and American Foreign Policy*; Sobel, "To Intervene or Not to Intervene"; Todorov and Mandisodza, "Public Opinion"; Page and Bouton, *Foreign Policy Disconnect*.

53. Mueller, *War, Presidents*; Gartner and Segura, "War, Casualties"; Gartner, "Multiple Effects of Casualties"; Feaver and Gelpi, *Choosing Your Battles*; Gelpi, Feaver, and Reifler, "Success Matters"; Larson and Savych, *American Public Support*; Voeten and Brewer, "Public Opinion."

54. Klarevas, "'Essential Domino'"; Eichenberg, "Victory Has Many Friends"; Eichenberg, Stoll, and Lebo, "War President"; Gelpi, Reifler, and Feaver, "Iraq the Vote"; Gelpi, Feaver, and Reifler, "Success Matters"; Feaver and Gelpi, *Choosing Your Battles*; Jentleson and Britton, "Still Pretty Prudent"; Oneal, Lian, and Joyner, "Are the American People 'Pretty Prudent'?"; Jentleson, "Pretty Prudent Public"; Kriner and Shen, *Casualty Gap*; Kriner and Shen, "Iraq Casualties."

55. Nisbet and Myers, "Polls Trends"; Page and Bouton, *Foreign Policy Disconnect*.

56. Page and Bouton, *Foreign Policy Disconnect*.

57. Ibid.; Graham, "Foreign Policy Decision Making"; Graham, "Politics of Failure."

58. Page and Bouton, *Foreign Policy Disconnect*; Kull and Destler, *Misreading the Public*; Otter, "Domestic Public Support."

59. Survey by the Gallup Organization, November 21–24, 1991, from LexisNexis, Roper Center for Public Opinion Research, University of Connecticut (accessed April 12, 2004). "Do you consider Japan to be an economic threat to the United States today, or not?"

60. Survey by the Gallup Organization, September 28–29, 1989, from LexisNexis, Roper Center for Public Opinion Research, University of Connecticut (accessed April 12, 2004). "Some people think the U.S. (United States) should impose stiffer tariffs and quotas on Japanese goods to reduce America's trade deficit with Japan. Others oppose such steps because they might lead to higher prices for popular imported products in the U.S. and Japan might make it more difficult for U.S. companies to sell their products in Japan. Still others oppose such steps because they might make Japan a less reliable military ally. Which comes closest to your view?"

Americans responded "don't know" when asked how tariffs might solve the U.S.-Japanese trade imbalance.[61] In short, the public usually demands that something be done about noncrisis problems but leaves it up to the political leadership in Washington to decide on the appropriate course of action.

Two Caveats About the Theoretical Model

In summary, the theory of conditional responsiveness ties together five simple propositions. However, while the propositions constitute the core of our theoretical model, two complicating factors must also be addressed. First, presidents may be more concerned about future decision-making contexts than they are with the current one. And second, presidents have an incentive to lead public opinion and manipulate issue salience. We address these caveats in turn and discuss their implications for our theory.

Caveat 1: Future Preferences and a Potentially Attentive Public

Although the theory has thus far focused on the current state of the public's preferences and attention, there is an implicit time dimension in modeling the political context. It is frequently the case that the preferences of the moment are less important to presidents than what Americans might think at the time of the next election.[62] Therefore, the appropriate question becomes, when do presidents rely on current opinion and when do they anticipate future preferences?

The tendency for public preferences to remain relatively stable over time, or at least to move in predictable ways in the course of policy making and events, means that politicians can draw on historical experience when anticipating the trajectory of public opinion. This is not to say that presidents are prescient and always anticipate future opinion correctly.[63] Although they may misread public opinion from time to time, presidents perhaps more commonly overestimate the effectiveness of their own policies. For instance, a president

---

61. In this book, "don't know" survey responses are treated as an indication of lack of knowledge or a lack of engagement with the issue. See Schuman and Presser, *Questions and Answers*. For a different take on "don't know" responses, see Berinsky, *Silent Voices*.

62. Zaller, "Elite Leadership"; Key, *Public Opinion*; Holsti, *Public Opinion and American Foreign Policy*; Arnold, *Logic of Congressional Action*; Foyle, *Counting the Public In*; Powlick and Katz, "Public Opinion/Foreign Policy Nexus"; Baum and Potter, "Mass Media, Public Opinion"; Sobel, *Impact of Public Opinion*; Page, "Toward General Theories"; Rosenau, *Public Opinion*.

63. Geer, *Tea Leaves to Opinion Polls*.

contemplating military involvement may believe that a short, successful war will produce a rally while a protracted, costly war will lead to an erosion of public support. In this case, there is little uncertainty about how the public will react to the two possible policy outcomes. There may be, however, considerable uncertainty as to the cost, length, and effectiveness of military action. Therefore, the key variable for presidents is not their ability to divine the opinions of the future, but rather the ability to predict actual policy success or failure.

Likewise, presidents must anticipate the trajectory of public attention. A number of factors—unexpected events, elite debate, investigative journalism, or policy failure—can quickly and unexpectedly change the salience of an issue. But while these abrupt shifts do sometimes occur, it is perhaps more common for public attention to follow the issue-attention cycles hypothesized earlier. When the president has good reason to suppose that issue salience will increase in the future, he will seek to anticipate and meet the public's preferences at that stage. Before that stage, the relative weight of current opinion on the president's decision will be less. Furthermore, unless attentiveness is expected to remain high, the importance of public opinion will decline as public attentiveness also declines. For crises, this typically means that presidents will anticipate the political context at the implementation stage; for noncrises, it means that presidents generally anticipate the political context at the policy decision stage.

Although the concepts of future preferences and a potentially attentive public are listed as a "caveat" here, they nevertheless fit nicely with our theory. It is precisely because issue salience and public preferences move in predictable ways across decision stages that we are able to hypothesize whether presidents will be more responsive to public opinion in the current political context or will anticipate public opinion at a future point in time. These hypotheses are discussed more fully in chapter 2.

Caveat 2: Are Presidents Leaders or Followers?

A second complicating factor in our theoretical model is that it does not quite address the problem of causal direction, telling us simply when a strong correlation between opinion and policy is likely to occur. Presidents have an interest in leading public opinion and manipulating issue salience in order to carry out their favored policies. However, they also confront situations where they are unable to convince the public to support their policies and/or where the level of issue salience works against them. As such, the political context may be endogenous to presidential leadership or it may be an exogenous constraint. Put differently, presidents may at times create the political context in which they operate or, at other times, find themselves prisoners of a political context they did not create.

To illustrate these two possibilities, consider how a specific political context might become constrained (i.e., high issue salience, unified preferences). First, a president may successfully convince the public of the virtues of his policy and, in the process, raise the salience of the issue. In such a case, the political context is constrained, but only because of presidential leadership and in a manner that benefits the White House and usually silences political opponents. In the second situation, the political context becomes constrained independent of presidential action and in a manner opposed to the president's policy. In this case, the political context works to the detriment of the White House and in favor of the political opposition. Therefore, the task for the researcher is to determine the extent to which presidential leadership produces the political context.

A closer theoretical look at foreign policy making is needed to assess whether the political context results from presidential leadership or serves as an exogenous constraint. By examining the nature of presidents' choices throughout the foreign-policy-making process, and then by assessing the likely interplay of public preferences and issue salience throughout that process, we can arrive at more specific hypotheses on whether presidents will lead, follow, or ignore public opinion. These expectations are presented in chapter 2.

Assumptions

Like all political science theories, the one presented here offers a stylized version of reality to explain a wide range of U.S. foreign policy cases. As such, it relies on a number of simplifying assumptions to make the theory less complex (i.e., more parsimonious) and more portable (i.e., generalizable to a number of different cases). To allow the reader the chance to fully evaluate the theory, it is important to be explicit about the seven main assumptions that undergird the model.

First, there are five interrelated, yet analytically distinct, decision stages for each foreign policy event. Although this decision-stages approach offers a powerful analytical tool to assess the role of opinion in policy making, a qualification is still in order. The problem faced by all scholars who model the foreign policy process is that decision making often proceeds in a nonlinear or haphazard fashion.[64] For example, a president may decide on a course of action, only to revisit his policy options at some later time. This makes it difficult to judge when one stage ends and another begins. The possibility that policy making is inherently messy has led some scholars to question the entire utility of the decision-stages framework.[65] While this concern does deserve serious attention, no scholar has argued, nor do I, that decision makers sequentially progress through each stage of the process in a deterministic fashion. Instead, the decision-stages approach is useful as a parsimonious framework from which to examine more precisely the diversity of choices that are made in a single foreign policy case.

Presidents are sensitive to aggregate public preferences. The theory assumes that the president, as the only nationally elected politician, is interested in the preferences of all Americans. But an equally strong argument can be made that presidents are not responsive to opinion in the aggregate, but rather are responsive only to a subset of the electorate. This subset may include partisan supporters, a reelection constituency, or big-money donors. Although it is likely true that presidents are more responsive to some constituents than to others, using aggregate preferences is a convenient and fairly reliable shortcut. Consider, for instance, a situation in which the public is united (i.e., preferences above the 60 percent level) *against* a president's policy. Given a relatively close partisan split in America since the 1990s, a supermajority opinion means that a number of erstwhile supporters have defected from the president's side.[66] Therefore, presidents encountering a supermajority realize that their policy is disliked by partisans and nonpartisans alike.

Presidents are sensitive to aggregate levels of issue salience. The theory assumes that presidents feel the political heat only when a large percentage of Americans are attentive to policy making. Yet for virtually any issue, there is a small subset of the population—often called "issue publics" or "attentive publics"—that is highly attentive.[67] Although issue publics are often influential,

    64. Hermann, "Changing Course," 14; Jann and Wegrich, "Theories of the Policy Cycle," 44; J. Cohen, *Presidential Responsiveness*.
    65. Sabatier, "Need for Better Theories"; Sabatier and Jenkins-Smith, *Policy Change and Learning*; Jenkins-Smith and Sabatier, "Public Policy Processes."
    66. According to the American National Election Studies, in 2004 the partisan breakdown stood at 49 percent Democrat, 10 percent Independent, and 41 percent Republican. This means that even if the Independents broke entirely Democratic or entirely Republican, and the parties managed to hold 100 percent of their voters, the maximum support a president could enjoy would be 59 percent (Democrats) or 51 percent (Republicans). In short, a strong majority in the range of 70 percent means broad bipartisan support. American National Election Studies, *ANES Guide to Public Opinion*.
    67. Rosenau, *National Leadership*; Key, *Public Opinion*; Sobel, *Impact of Public Opinion*; Hutchings, *Democratic Accountability*; P. Converse, "Nature of Belief Systems"; Arnold, *Logic of Congressional Action*.

it is reasonable to assume that there is also strength in numbers. For presidents, ignoring ten average people is usually pretty easy; ignoring 135 million angry voters is considerably more difficult. This is one reason celebrities can be so important in raising public awareness of otherwise neglected international problems, such as poverty in the less developed world (Bono), genocide in Darfur (Mia Farrow, Brad Pitt, George Clooney, Matt Damon, Don Cheadle), the global AIDS epidemic (Alicia Keys), Tibetan freedom (Richard Gere, Sharon Stone), and global warming (Sheryl Crow, John Travolta). For each of these causes, the prospects for political success hinge on raising public awareness and convincing a large number of voters to pressure their elected representatives.

It is possible to gauge the public's preference. The analysis assumes that public opinion surveys from organizations like Gallup and Roper provide a fairly accurate picture of American preferences. However, a number of critics contend that biases inherent in mass surveys make a determination of "the public opinion" meaningless, at best.[68] There are a myriad of potential biases in surveys (e.g., nonresponse, question ordering effects, social desirability effects, etc.), but consider one specific problem of question wording and how it might affect our analysis. Pollsters have long recognized that different phrasing of a question, however subtle, can produce dramatic changes in the results. During the 1991 Gulf War, for instance, public support for a U.S. military offensive to liberate Kuwait varied by almost 40 percent depending on whether polling firms used the term "war" or the phrase "military intervention" in the question.[69] For those of us who are interested in what Americans thought about possible war/military conflict in the Persian Gulf, problems like the effects of question wording are admittedly a concern.

Although this is not the place for a full defense of survey research, I wish to make two brief points about the viability of the enterprise in light of its critics. First, it is possible to minimize the impact of potential biases in survey research by simply admitting that biases exist and then specifically identifying those places in the analysis where such biases may lead to a different conclusion. This openness allows readers to draw their own inferences from the results. Second, survey research methodology may not be perfect, but it is pretty darn good. From the infancy of survey research in the 1930s to today, scholars have learned how to draw a more representative sample of the population, how to write less biased questions, and how to elicit more genuine

---

68. Althaus, *Collective Preferences*; Ginsberg, *Captive Public*; Lewis, *Constructing Public Opinion*; Weissberg, *Polling, Policy, and Public Opinion*; Bishop, *Illusion of Public Opinion*.
69. Morin and Dionne, "Vox Populi"; Mueller, *Policy and Opinion*.

responses from the public.[70] As an illustration of the accuracy of public opinion surveys, consider a November 1, 2008, CNN/Opinion Research poll that reported that 53 percent of the public planned to vote for Barack Obama for president while 46 percent planned to cast their ballots for John McCain; the actual 2008 presidential election popular vote results were 52.9 percent for Obama and 45.7 percent for McCain.[71] In my estimation, gauging the opinion of some 130 million voters within a +/- 3 percent margin of error (in this case, a less than 1 percent error) is fairly impressive. In short, although some well-known problems exist in survey research, it is still possible to gain a good understanding of what the public thinks about most issues, most of the time.

If an issue is being covered by television news, it is salient to the American public; if an issue is not being covered by television news, it is not salient to the American public. In this book, the key measure of issue salience is minutes of nightly television news coverage (see appendix A for a more in-depth justification of the measure). There are, however, some obvious concerns with this measure. What if people get their news from other sources? What if the news doesn't cover what people really care about? What about the bevy of other entertainment options—cable television, DVDs and VCRs, the Internet, and video games—that allow people to avoid the news altogether? Although these are valid concerns, considerable research demonstrates that a strong correlation exists between what is covered in the news and what Americans are attentive to.[72] This media attention–public attention link is especially true in foreign policy, as the public depends almost entirely on the media for information. To put it another way, it would be difficult to imagine a scenario in which a vast majority of Americans were up in arms about a foreign policy problem and the issue was *not* covered by the television media.

It is possible to determine a president's true policy preference. Recall that our definition of political responsiveness specifies that presidents abandon their true policy preference for one favored by the public. This definition means, of course, that we must figure out what a president's "true" preference is—a

---

70. For an interesting history of public opinion research, see J. Converse, *Survey Research*.
71. See http://www.pollingreport.com/who8gen.htm (accessed January 12, 2009). Here is one case in which we should be honest about potential biases: not all survey organizations were as accurate as this particular CNN poll. And there have been a number of cases in which surveys have totally blown it (Hillary Clinton and the New Hampshire primary and exit polls in the 2004 election come to mind). Nevertheless, nine out of the ten surveys conducted between November 1 and 3, 2008, predicted Obama's vote margin within +/- 3 percentage points.
72. Graber, *Mass Media and American Politics*; McCombs and Shaw, "Agenda-Setting Function"; McCombs and Shaw, "Evolution of Agenda-Setting"; Neuman, "Threshold of Public Attention"; B. Cohen, *Press and Foreign Policy*.

difficult task indeed. We can often draw evidence from internal political deliberations between a president and his advisors, from presidential memoirs, or from elite interviews (see appendix B for an in-depth discussion of the case study methodology used in this book). Although each source of evidence has its problems (e.g., memoirs may be written so as to place the president in the most favorable light), together they offer glimpses into a president's thought process. A second method is to compare the consistency of presidential decisions throughout the foreign-policy-making process. For example, if a president who has avoided the issue of global warming throughout a term suddenly becomes an environmental advocate on the eve of a tightly contested election, then we might have some evidence that public opinion was at play in producing the change of heart. Admittedly, ascertaining a president's true preference is a difficult job. But if we really want to know how much public opinion influences U.S. foreign policy, it is a task that we simply cannot avoid.

Finally, we can predict whether presidents will respond to public opinion without reference to the specific person who occupies the Oval Office. The theory of political responsiveness offered here assumes that *all* presidents react in a similar fashion to the interplay of issue salience and public preferences. However, an alternative school of thought contends that individual presidents vary in their sensitivity to public opinion.[73] For instance, Douglas Foyle has written persuasively that presidents hold different beliefs about the role that public opinion should play in the policy-making process, and that it is these beliefs that ultimately influence receptivity to the public's views. Jonathan Keller contends that presidents differ in their perceptions of and responses to various political constraints, one of which is public opinion. Stephen Dyson expands on the notion of "constraint challengers" and "constraint respecters" by showing how different leadership styles led British Prime Minister Harold Wilson to refuse to intervene in Vietnam while Prime Minister Tony Blair willingly joined the United States in overthrowing Saddam Hussein.[74] In short, a number of very convincing studies show that it is the style, personality, or beliefs of presidents that determines whether public opinion is heeded or ignored.

So, can we predict presidential behavior without reference to the individual who holds office? This question is the source of an often heated debate between individualist and institutionalist scholars in presidential studies, a debate we need not rehash in full here.[75] In many ways, the divide between

---

73. Thanks to an anonymous reviewer for raising this point.
74. Foyle, *Counting the Public In*; J. Keller, "Constraint Respecters"; Dyson, "Domestic Politics."
75. Moe, "Presidents, Institutions, and Theory"; Greenstein, *Presidential Difference*; Greenstein, "Personality and Politics"; Skowronek, *Politics Presidents Make*.

individualist and institutionalist scholars is much ado about nothing: both approaches are vital in the quest to better understand presidential foreign policy making because each has different strengths and weaknesses. For instance, the relative strength of an institutional theory (like the one found in this book) is that it is, generally, (a) predictive, (b) parsimonious, and (c) broadly applicable. In other words, institutionalist theories bypass all those sticky questions that often plague the more nuanced and descriptive individualist theories, such as, how do we measure personality or leadership style? Does a theory that explains the behavior of one president tell us anything about the behavior of another president? When does leadership style matter? Can we predict a particular outcome from a particular personality or leadership style? Indeed, the "hard core" of the theory presented in this book—i.e., that high issue salience combined with unified public preferences makes political responsiveness more likely—is simple, relies on independent variables that are fairly easy to measure, and yields a priori hypotheses that are testable and falsifiable.

Of course, theories should always be evaluated on how well they stand up to the evidence. The two case studies provided in this book—the 1990–91 Persian Gulf crisis and the Ethiopian famine of the mid-1980s—offer an interesting test of individual vs. institutional theories because of the presidents who occupied the Oval Office. In his individualist theory, Foyle documents that neither Ronald Reagan nor George H. W. Bush was of the normative belief that the public should influence foreign policy making; instead, both felt that it was the role of the president to inform and lead the masses.[76] According to Foyle's theory, therefore, the Persian Gulf crisis and Ethiopian famine represent "least likely" cases for seeing a significant public influence on presidential decision making.[77] If, however, we do see the public's imprint on policy in these two cases, then it suggests that even the most unresponsive presidents must contend with the political implications of a highly attentive and unified public.

Summary

This chapter presented a theory of public opinion and foreign policy making derived from some basic, well-established propositions in the field. We know,

---

76. Foyle, *Counting the Public In.* Foyle does argue that President Bush was a pragmatist and felt that the support of the public might be necessary to accomplish foreign policy goals. Therefore, to a greater extent than Reagan, Bush was willing to incorporate considerations of the public into decision making if necessary for policy success.
77. Eckstein, "Case Study and Theory."

for instance, that presidents make not one but several different choices over the life of a single foreign policy event. We also know that presidents sometimes react to the size of majority opinion and sometimes react to the degree of issue salience. Moreover, we have good ways of predicting (1) what Americans are likely to think and (2) when Americans are likely to be paying attention. Putting it all together, we have a theory that can tell us when to expect presidents to lead, follow, or ignore the American public. The next chapter delves deeper into our expectations of the political context at each of the five stages of decision making.

2

THE FIVE STAGES OF DECISION MAKING

In 1991, Philip Powlick published an article entitled "The Attitudinal Bases for Responsiveness to Public Opinion Among American Foreign Policy Officials," in which he asked sixty-eight U.S. foreign policy officials what they truly thought of the American public. The analysis revealed a number of interesting findings about public opinion from the vantage point of the people who actually make the policy. Most of the officials in the study believed that a successful foreign policy required the support of the American people. As one senior official put it, "If we choose to ignore public opinion, for whatever reason, it comes back to haunt the executive, in the sense that it's [the policy] impossible to sustain. Eventually you start loosing votes; not getting the legislation or funds necessary to implement policy."[1]

Despite their general belief that public support was necessary for the ultimate success of policy, many officials were also skeptical of the public's ability to form educated opinions on the issues. A common problem noted by officials was that the public did not have nearly the same detailed knowledge of the situation that the experts themselves did. A deputy assistant secretary of state provided his thoughts on the public's lack of knowledge about Panama in 1988 (more than a year before a U.S. invasion removed Panamanian president Manuel Noriega from power):

> It's no secret; the U.S. public is not knowledgeable about most foreign policy issues. . . . An example, say Noriega. U.S. public opinion is to go down and grab the little son-of-a-bitch. As an American citizen that's my reaction, but there are an awful lot of complex derivatives of such an action and the American public cannot possibly know about the things

1. Powlick, "Attitudinal Bases for Responsiveness," 624.

having to do with the [Panama Canal] Treaty, the Canal, and our position in Latin America and at the O.A.S. . . . and there's no way the American public can know enough about these things to say, "Yes, I still think we should go and get the bastard."[2]

The officials also found it difficult to get the public to pay attention to foreign affairs. One Foreign Service officer told a story to which many other government officials can likely relate:

> The first time I came back from overseas . . . we had dinner at my mother-in-law's house . . . and a bunch of people were there, and before the dinner, the first five minutes was all, "Oh you're back, how interesting. Tell us all about Italy," and I started to say something about it and then within three minutes someone would say, "Oh yes, I remember that on the Lucy Show she took a trip to Rome," and from then on the conversation was about Lucy, television, taxes, who moved in downstairs. . . . It's a long way of telling you that the great majority of Americans really are more interested in domestic issues, so when you get public opinion polls on foreign policy issues, you really have to question how much thought has gone into that.[3]

A number of fascinating implications flow from Powlick's research, especially when we compare it to other studies in the field. First, the foreign policy officials Powlick interviewed generally believed that public opinion was an important component of a successful U.S. foreign policy. Nevertheless, many (but not all) were pessimistic about the ability of the average American to form cogent opinions. This places decision makers in a bind. Although it is politically advantageous to respond to public preferences, incorporating ill-informed preferences into policy can lead to bad foreign policies. Bad foreign policies lead to bad outcomes. Bad outcomes lead to declining public approval and a short political life. This catch-22 makes it difficult for the policy maker to know exactly how to respond to public opinion.

A second implication is that while decision makers are immersed in the minutia of foreign affairs, the public usually cares little about those details. For instance, U.S. foreign policy experts versed in sub-Saharan African politics know who Robert Mugabe is (president of Zimbabwe), who Paul Biya

---

2. Ibid., 617.
3. Ibid.

is (president of Cameroon), and who Denis Sassou-Nguesso is (president of the Republic of the Congo). In 2007, by contrast, the American public had a difficult time even picking out the current U.S. secretary of defense (21 percent correctly identified Robert Gates), the current Senate majority leader (15 percent correctly identified Harry Reid), and the president of Russia (36 percent correctly identified then president, now prime minister, Vladimir Putin). As a means of comparison, 62 percent of Americans knew of Peyton Manning (quarterback of the Colts) and 64 percent knew of Beyonce Knowles (pop singer).[4] As Michael Delli Carpini and Scott Keeter demonstrate in *What Americans Know About Politics and Why It Matters,* the American public has disturbingly little knowledge of the relevant events of the day.

However, although Americans may not know the details of foreign affairs, they tend to hold reasonable and cogent opinions about U.S. foreign policy *in general.* Some of the seminal works in the field—Benjamin Page and Marshall Bouton's *The Foreign Policy Disconnect,* Page and Robert Shapiro's *The Rational Public,* and Steven Kull and I. M. Destler's *Misreading the Public*—have demonstrated that Americans are far from the provincial foreign policy ignoramuses they are often portrayed to be. Instead, Americans hold sensible "big picture" opinions about which goals and objectives the United States should pursue through its foreign policy, even while knowing very little of the specific details of a situation. So while a majority of Americans could not locate South Africa on a map in 1988,[5] 87 percent knew enough about South Africa's policy of racial apartheid to disapprove of it.[6]

A third implication of Powlick's study is that although certain foreign policies can grab the public's attention, many issues are only periodically salient to the public or escape notice altogether. The Foreign Service officer's story about the dinner party at his mother-in-law's home is a case in point. It seems that the guests at the party were more interested in Lucy Ricardo than they were in the poor officer's discussion of Italian politics. Fair enough. But what if the Foreign Service officer had not been stationed in allied Italy during peacetime,

---

4. Pew Research Center for the People and the Press, "Public Knowledge of Current Affairs Little Changed by News and Information Revolutions: What Americans Know, 1989–2007," April 15, 2007, http://people-press.org/report/319/public-knowledge-of-current-affairs-little-changed-by-news-and-information-revolutions (accessed March 11, 2008).

5. Survey by the Gallup Organization, April 30–May 8, 1988, from LexisNexis, Roper Center for Public Opinion Research, University of Connecticut (accessed April 20, 2004). "(Will you please tell me the number on this [world] map which locates each of the following places or bodies of water?) . . . South Africa."

6. Survey by Louis Harris and Associates, July 18–22, 1986, from LexisNexis, Roper Center for Public Opinion Research, University of Connecticut (accessed April 20, 2004). "Do you approve or disapprove of the system of apartheid in South America?"

but instead had been in the Situation Room of the White House during the Cuban Missile Crisis? I bet that would have grabbed the dinner guests' attention. The point here is that some aspects of U.S. foreign policy are inherently more interesting to the public than others.

The discussion thus far suggests that any theory of the public opinion–foreign policy link must account for the preceding three implications. This chapter takes these implications into account and combines them with the general theoretical model discussed in chapter 1 to generate a number of specific hypotheses on the opinion-policy relationship. The following discussion looks at each of the five decision stages—problem definition, option generation, policy decision, implementation, and policy review—to posit three sets of hypotheses. First, we look at the likely interplay of public preferences and issue salience to predict the political context (i.e., constrained, contested, insulated, or guarded) at each decision stage. The purpose of these hypotheses is to unpack the general thesis that public attention and preferences are predictable (i.e., proposition 5 of chapter 1) into smaller and more testable expectations. A second set of hypotheses examines whether presidents are likely to be more sensitive to the current political context or a future political context. In other words, we will examine whether presidents are responsive to current/active opinion or future/latent opinion (i.e., caveat 1 of chapter 1). Finally, the chapter will present hypotheses about whether presidents will likely lead, follow, or ignore the American public at each decision stage, addressing the question of whether the political context is likely to be endogenous or exogenous to presidential leadership (i.e., caveat 2 of chapter 1).

Problem Definition

There are two types of observations made at the problem definition stage: agenda setting and problem representation.[7] Agenda setting addresses the list of problems the government is working on; problem representation refers to how leaders view those problems. In this sense, agenda setting is captured by the statement "I see that a problem exists," while problem representation is captured by the statement "Here is my interpretation of the problem."

---

7. For some of the classic literature on agenda setting, see Kingdon, *Agendas*; McCombs and Shaw, "Agenda-Setting Function"; Cobb and Elder, *Participation in American Politics*; McCombs, *Setting the Agenda*; and Baumgartner and Jones, *Agendas and Instability*. For literature on problem representation, see Sylvan, Grove, and Martinson, "Problem Representation"; Charlick-Paley and Sylvan, "Use and Evolution of Stories"; Sylvan and Voss, *Problem Representation*; and Sylvan and Thorson, "Ontologies, Problem Representation."

Agenda Setting

Compared to domestic issues, foreign policy has received little attention in the agenda setting literature. The reason for this slight is that foreign crises usually explode onto the agenda when some unexpected international event occurs, such as the Soviets placing missiles in Cuba in 1962. Because crises tend to be episodic and often unpredictable, they are generally not that interesting to agenda setting scholars who endeavor to create generalizable, predictive theories on attention to political problems. What little research has been done has found, as expected, that international crises, and the media's coverage of these crises, largely sets the foreign policy agenda.[8]

Noncrises are a different story since they more closely resemble domestic politics, where politicians, political entrepreneurs, and interest groups all vie to place their pet issues on the agenda. In contrast to crises, presidents may enjoy considerable agenda-setting power in noncrisis situations, as Jeffrey Peake demonstrated in his examination of U.S. policy toward Haitian and Cuban refugees, U.S. trade policy with Japan, and foreign aid to Central America. By examining less salient noncrises instead of focusing exclusively on crises, Peake discovered that presidents are indeed effective foreign policy agenda setters. And if presidents have an ability to place noncrisis issues on the agenda, we might also then expect that they have a considerable ability to keep an issue off the agenda. As Matthew Baum points out, a president has an incentive to keep a low profile on an issue, or "go private," if he feels that the public is opposed to his position.[9] Of course, a president's ability to keep issues off the agenda is not absolute, as other political actors, like special interest

---

8. For the literature on foreign policy agenda setting, see Wood and Peake, "Foreign Policy Agenda Setting"; Edwards and Wood, "Who Influences Whom?"; B. Cohen, *Press and Foreign Policy*; and McCombs and Shaw, "Agenda-Setting Function." There is, however, a large body of scholarship that suggests that presidents manufacture crises to divert public attention away from domestic problems at home, thereby changing the political agenda in the president's favor. For literature on this "diversionary hypothesis of war" (a.k.a. scapegoat theory or "wag the dog" theory), see Simmel, *Web of Group-Affiliations*; Rosecrance, *Action and Reaction*; James and Oneal, "Domestic and International Politics"; Clark, "Strategic Interaction"; Howell and Pevehouse, "Use of Force"; and Belkin, *United We Stand?* Critics, however, charge that there is little evidence for such diversionary tactics. See Levy, "Diversionary Theory of War"; Bueno de Mesquita and Lalman, "Domestic Opposition"; Meernik, *Political Use of Military Force*; Moore and Lanoue, "Domestic Politics"; and Potter, "Does Experience Matter?" With these critics, I contend that if diversionary practices happen at all, they tend to be exceedingly rare because (a) presidents cannot always count on the political use of force to boost approval ratings (wars tend to be unpredictable, and messy wars decrease approval ratings); (b) U.S. casualties can erode support; (c) wars tend to make markets jittery and create economic worries that drive down public approval of the president; and (d) critics and the media may charge that the war was manufactured, thereby dampening public approval.

9. Peake, "Presidential Agenda Setting"; Baum, "Going Private."

groups, may eventually overcome White House recalcitrance and get their issue a public hearing. Still, all things considered, an issue has a better chance of making its way onto the foreign policy agenda if the president *wants* to deal with it than if he does *not* want to deal with it.

This last point deserves clarification. Much of the literature assumes that both the American public and the U.S. government can deal with only a few issues at a time—what is commonly termed "carrying capacity." For the public, the carrying capacity is limited by education, time, interest, and cognitive ability.[10] Similarly, the president and members of Congress have only a finite amount of time to deal with a vast number of issues.[11] Given a limited public and a limited governmental carrying capacity, only a select few issues are dealt with in Washington, D.C., at any one time, and still fewer become important down on Main Street, U.S.A.

Although both the public and the government have a finite ability to deal with issues, we should expect that the government's carrying capacity is significantly larger than that of the public. At any given time, some element of the vast government bureaucracy is behind the scenes working on relatively obscure foreign policy issues, regardless of whether or not the public or press is paying attention.[12] Therefore, presidents have an incentive, and often the capacity, to minimize issue salience in order to pursue policy courses they prefer but the public does not. In other words, sometimes presidents can "go covert" or "go private" to accomplish their goals.[13] So when Congress or the American public suddenly becomes attentive and the U.S. government visibly springs into action, this flurry of activity may not signal agenda setting per se; it may just signify that an increasing number of actors are now openly and publicly working on an issue that has been in the shadows of the White House agenda for some time.[14]

10. Hilgartner and Bosk, "Rise and Fall"; Zhu, "Issue Competition"; McCombs and Zhu, "Capacity, Diversity, and Volatility"; Shaw and McCombs, *American Political Issues*; G. Miller, "Magic Number Seven."

11. Hilgartner and Bosk, "Rise and Fall"; Krehbiel, *Information and Legislative Organization*; Jones, *Reconceiving Decision-Making*; Peake, "Presidential Agenda Setting"; Baumgartner and Jones, *Agendas and Instability*.

12. Consider, for instance, the State Department's Office of Verification Operations (OVO). According to the State Department Web site, the OVO "provides and manages leading-edge information technology and telecommunications for the three bureaus (ISN, PM and VCI) under the Undersecretary for Arms Control and International Security" (http://www.state.gov/t/vci/c23760.htm). Until conducting research for this book, I had no idea that the OVO existed; even after reading the Web site, I am not really sure what the OVO does. The point is that deep inside the bowels of the federal government, somebody somewhere is creating policy on some issue that the public does not even know is an issue.

13. Baum, "Going Private."

14. As one reviewer has noted, if presidents can successfully "go private" in cases where the public is opposed to their position, then we as scholars will ultimately underestimate the role of public opinion

Problem Representation

Public opinion is expected to play little role in the way presidents represent crises. By definition, crises involve threats to the core values of the state and entail a high probability of military force, making it more likely that strategic imperatives will prevail over domestic political considerations. At this stage, I expect the causal process to run top-down, as presidents exercise political leadership by successfully communicating problem representation to the public. In times of crisis, the public usually looks to the White House for leadership and guidance.[15] Therefore, presidents normally have the ability to mold public opinion once a crisis erupts, especially if the event triggers a rally or if the public has little familiarity with the states or stakes involved.[16] As a result, presidents will lead opinion to produce a constrained political context that favors the White House (see table 2). In this case, criticism from the political opposition is often muted, which helps to sustain a public rally for the president. And because presidents are typically the initial shapers of public opinion during crises, political responsiveness, if it comes at all, will occur at a future stage.

By contrast, public opinion is expected to factor more heavily into noncrisis problem representation. As we saw in agenda setting, a president has

---

in foreign policy. The logic is as follows: (a) presidents "go private" when they feel that the public won't support their preferred policy, and (b) these covert activities never show up in our population of cases because, by virtue of being covert, we never know about them; therefore (c) the ultimate effect is that we underestimate the impact of public opinion, which caused the policy to "go covert" in the first place. The magnitude of this bias depends on how well Washington has kept mum about past covert activity: if there are a lot of secrets out there, we will grossly underestimate the role of public opinion in foreign policy; if there are only a few secrets, the bias will be minimal. The problem is that we will never know how many secrets the government is currently keeping, which is what keeps conspiracy theorists in business. To paraphrase Donald Rumsfeld, covert U.S. foreign policies are in the realm of the "known unknowns"—we know that there must be some things we don't know; we just don't know how many things we don't know. Although we may miss several cases by virtue of presidents "going private," the fact that these missed cases constitute a bias of omission (i.e., Type II error) mitigates the distorting effect in the analysis.

15. In certain instances, however, public opinion can play a role in defining an international event as a crisis. One possibility is that the success enjoyed by past presidents in mobilizing public support constrains the behavior of subsequent presidents. For example, much of the origin of the "Red Scare" can be traced to Harry Truman's attempt to secure funds for Greece and Turkey by overselling the threat of communism to Congress and the American people. There is evidence that successive presidents felt compelled by the strong anticommunist sentiment in the American public to take hard-line policy stances despite their preferences for inactivity. Examples involving somewhat reluctant cold warriors include John F. Kennedy's involvement in Cuba, Lyndon Johnson's escalation of the war in Vietnam, and Jimmy Carter's sporadic support of the Somoza regime in Nicaragua and Mobutu in Zaire. See Hampson, "Divided Decision-Maker."

16. Brody, "Crisis, War, and Public Opinion"; Brody, *Assessing the President*; Zaller, *Nature and Origins*; Adam J. Berinsky, "Costs of War"; Baum and Potter, "Mass Media, Public Opinion."

an incentive to put an issue on the political agenda when he thinks that the public agrees with his policy, and an incentive to keep an issue off the agenda when he perceives that the public disagrees with his policy. As a result, presidents will likely view the American public as either a political opportunity or a political constraint. If the president believes that the public will support a preferred policy, he will work to raise the salience of the issue and place it on the political agenda. If the president has reason to believe that the public will not support the policy, he will either abandon it or work to minimize the public visibility of the issue and pursue the policy covertly.

Unlike crises, however, very few noncrisis issues explode onto the scene; instead, they sort of gradually seep into public consciousness over an extended period of time. For instance, U.S. policy toward apartheid South Africa was, at best, a low-salience issue until public outrage finally reached a critical mass in the mid-1980s. Yet the fact that apartheid languished for decades in relative public obscurity did not mean an absence of U.S. policy; it simply meant that U.S.–South African relations were progressing with little citizen oversight. And because issue salience is expected to be low at this initial stage, presidents have little reason to cater to the latent preferences of the moment. Instead, presidents are likely to anticipate a future stage at which latent opinion will become active.

Option Generation

Option generation refers to the array of potential policies that an administration may consider in response to a specific problem. This stage has received considerable scholarly attention from rational choice/expected utility theorists who examine how decision makers rank-order their options, selecting the one that maximizes utility.[17] In bureaucratic models, the options that presidents consider are often shaped by self-interested agencies that advocate tactics that advance their own parochial interests.[18]

In crises, public opinion usually serves to demarcate a region of acceptable policies.[19] For instance, using weapons of mass destruction and targeting

---

17. Bueno de Mesquita and Lalman, *War and Reason*; Morrow, "Rational Choice Approach"; Bueno de Mesquita, *War Trap*; Bueno de Mesquita, "Forecasting Policy Decisions"; Bueno de Mesquita, "War Trap Revisited."

18. Allison, *Essence of Decision*; Vertzberger, *World in Their Minds*; Huntington, "Strategic Planning"; Halperin, *Bureaucratic Politics*.

19. Sobel, *Impact of Public Opinion*; Hinckley, *People, Polls, and Policymakers*; Russett, *Controlling the Sword*; Powlick and Katz, "Public Opinion/Foreign Policy Nexus"; Foyle, *Counting the Public In*.

Table 2 Political context and presidential action at the problem definition stage

	Crises	Noncrises
Political context	Constrained	Guarded or insulated
Future or current context	Future	Future
Presidential action	Lead	Lead (if public support) / Ignore (if public opposition)

civilian populations during war are tactics that now fall outside the boundaries of what most Americans consider morally acceptable behavior. However, within the broad region set by the public, decision makers are likely to have considerable latitude in generating a menu of options. In general, the public is more concerned with getting the job done and much less concerned with exactly how it gets done. As Richard Brody writes, "In the aggregate, the public seems to respond to policy outcomes, not to the means of achieving them; the response is pragmatic rather than ideological."[20] Moreover, the public is often divided in its preferences for alternative options. The media can contribute to this fracture by featuring pundits who conjecture what the president must be thinking and debate his every move. Issue salience is expected to be high at this stage as the public anticipates a presidential decision.

Public ambivalence over policy options and the high degree of issue salience in crises mean that the political context will likely fall into the contested category (see table 3). In this context, presidents usually attempt to lead public opinion, but division in public preferences will make such leadership difficult. Nevertheless, the public's pragmatic take on foreign policy (i.e., concerned with ends, not means) suggests that presidents may simply ignore public opinion as they ponder which option offers the best chance at success. Indeed, while the American public generally pays attention to the option generation stage of crises, the level of salience at this stage pales in comparison to the decision and implementation stages. As a result, presidents may simply discount current preferences and base their choices on what they expect the public will prefer when salience is *really* high—say, for instance, when the bombs start dropping.

Public opinion is also expected to have little influence on the generation of options during noncrises. Issue salience is normally low at this stage, in part because the timeline for considering noncrisis options tends to be comparatively long. While crises demand immediate attention, noncrises can be put off for another day. And because there is always some foreign or domestic crisis

20. Brody, "Crisis, War, and Public Opinion," 210.

going on, Washington often takes a leisurely approach to dealing with non-crises. For instance, the Strategic Arms Limitation Talks (SALT I) negotiations between the United States and the Soviet Union lasted from November 1969 to May 1972. It is certainly unsurprising, given this length of time, that the public eventually lost interest in how the arms talks were going, especially with the Vietnam War in full bloom.

In addition, it is probable that the public will have only weakly formed preferences concerning alternative strategies. Many noncrisis options involve unfamiliar issues of sufficient complexity that a solid understanding of the policy options eludes most Americans. For example, U.S. economic competition with Japan in the 1990s or with China in the 2000s was likely to produce a public concerned with ends (e.g., to increase relative economic strength vis-à-vis Japan and China) rather than with the means to achieve those ends (e.g., a domestic stimulus package versus tariff protection). Given low issue salience and weak public preferences, the political context in such instances will likely be insulated and presidents will generally ignore the inchoate opinions of the American public (table 3). Again, political responsiveness, should it occur, will likely take place at a future stage of decision making.

Policy Decision

The policy decision stage occurs when a president makes a definitive and authoritative decision to resolve some problem. When examining the role of public opinion in U.S. foreign policy, it is only natural that our attention is drawn to the government's most visible policy decision (e.g., deciding to go to war, signing an arms control agreement, or agreeing to a free trade arrangement). However, while the policy decision stage is undoubtedly significant, it is not the only, nor arguably even the most important, aspect of foreign policy making.

The key decision in most foreign policy crises concerns the question of war or peace. The difficulty in making generalizations about the public's preferences regarding war is that those preferences are indelibly tied to the details of each particular case. For instance, scholars have found that the public's preference for the use of force is influenced by geographical proximity to the United States,[21] the objectives of the war,[22] whether other countries support

---

21. Russett, "American Opinion."
22. Jentleson and Britton, "Still Pretty Prudent"; Jentleson, "Pretty Prudent Public"; Oneal, Lian, and Joyner, "Are the American People 'Pretty Prudent'?"; Russett, "American Opinion"; Eichenberg, "Victory Has Many Friends."

Table 3 Political context and presidential action at the option generation stage

	Crises	Noncrises
Political context	Contested	Guarded or insulated
Future or current context	Future	Future
Presidential action	Lead or ignore	Ignore

the United States in the use of force,[23] and whether the public thinks the war will eventually be successful.[24]

Perhaps the strongest predictor of public sentiment is the level of elite agreement or disagreement over the use of military force.[25] It is predictable that most decisions on war or peace will be met with considerable elite debate and a subsequent division in public preferences. This is especially true since the end of the cold war has all but put to rest the old adage "politics stops at the waters edge."[26] Adam Berinsky notes, "When political elites disagree as to the wisdom of intervention, the public divides as well. But when elites come to a common interpretation of a political reality, the public gives them great latitude to wage war."[27] The importance of elite cues in shaping public opinion then begs the question, when exactly are elites united or divided over the question of war? Of course, certain events, such as Pearl Harbor and World War II or 9/11 and the subsequent war in Afghanistan, can produce bipartisan agreement and public consensus. Yet such clear-cut cases are exceedingly rare.

In general, issue salience is expected to be high during the policy decision stage of crises. However, this expectation is complicated by the fact that presidents often decide on war or peace long before the public becomes aware that a decision has been reached. For example, President George W. Bush contemplated ousting Saddam Hussein in the fall of 2001, a time at which the American public was focused on terrorism and Afghanistan, and almost fifteen months before the first shot was fired in Iraq on March 19, 2003.[28] And, as we will see in chapters 4 and 5, the earlier Gulf War followed a similar pattern: President George H. W. Bush decided on war and *then* went to Congress and the UN for authorization. In short, policy decisions are made in private, do

23. Rielly, *U.S. Foreign Policy, 1995*; Kull, "What the Public Knows."
24. Klarevas, "'Essential Domino'"; Eichenberg, "Victory Has Many Friends"; Feaver and Gelpi, *Choosing Your Battles*; Gelpi, Reifler, and Feaver, "Iraq the Vote"; Gelpi, Feaver, and Reifler, "Success Matters."
25. Zaller, "Elite Leadership"; Zaller, *Nature and Origins*; Meernik and Ault, "Public Opinion and Support"; Brody, "Crisis, War, and Public Opinion"; Brody, *Assessing the President*; Berinsky, "Costs of War."
26. Jacobson, *Divider, Not a Uniter*; Knecht, "Benchmarks."
27. Berinsky, "Costs of War," 975.
28. Foyle, "Leading the Public"; Woodward, *Plan of Attack*.

not receive advanced billing, and are not broadcast live on national television. As a result, salience is likely to be high around the time a president decides on a policy course, but not as high as it would be if the public actually knew that a decision was being made.

The political context at the policy decision stage of crises is expected to fall into the contested category as the public becomes divided in its preferences over war and peace and as the threat of war increases salience even more (see table 4). In this context, a president usually attempts to lead the American people to support his decision. However, this decision stage is likely one in which presidents are most concerned with future political contexts. In other words, a crisis decision largely depends on a president's calculations of the probability of success at the implementation stage. Presidents who are confident of policy success may discount the current state of public opinion because there is good reason to expect that the public will rally around a successful war, no matter how divided public opinion was in the prelude to conflict.[29] If, however, the implementation of policy promises to be messy, a president may either opt for covert action to bypass a reluctant public or rely on a weaker means of coercion or compellence, such as economic sanctions. Put another way, presidents making the key decision in a crisis are likely to look ahead to the implementation stage and ask themselves two questions: (a) can we win a military battle, and (b) if so, will the public tolerate the cost of victory? As such, what the American public currently wants matters less in a president's decision than what the voters will think after the fog of war has cleared.

In the case of noncrises, the influence of the public is expected to be strongest at the policy decision stage. Here, high issue salience will likely converge with the widespread public preference to "do something" about a problem, thus creating a constrained political context (table 4). Therefore, at this stage presidents are likely to be responsive to current preferences. However, a popular noncrisis policy announcement is usually enough to placate the American public; decision makers are less concerned about policy actually achieving its goals than they are during crisis situations. This presidential position taking largely results from the fact that most noncrises are long-running issues that have no clear-cut resolution. As such, presidents are generally not held responsible for policy success or failure. For example, the Clinton administration

29. Klarevas, "'Essential Domino'"; Brody, "Crisis, War, and Public Opinion"; Eichenberg, "Victory Has Many Friends"; Eichenberg, Stoll, and Lebo, "War President"; Gelpi, Reifler, and Feaver, "Iraq the Vote"; Gelpi, Feaver, and Reifler, "Success Matters"; Feaver and Gelpi, *Choosing Your Battles*; Jentleson, "Pretty Prudent Public"; Jentleson and Britton, "Still Pretty Prudent."

Table 4 Political context and presidential action at the policy decision stage

	Crises	Noncrises
Political context	Contested	Constrained
Future or current context	Future	Current
Presidential action	Lead or ignore	Follow

entered the 1997 negotiations on the Kyoto Protocol with the demand that developing nations, most notably China and India, also agree to reduction targets in carbon emissions. When it became clear that neither China nor India would be bound to the same standards as the West, President Clinton dropped the demand and signed the protocol anyway, despite believing it to be flawed and despite full knowledge that the treaty would be killed in the U.S. Senate. Nevertheless, over 74 percent[30] of the American public approved of the decision, and the subsequent political blame for the lack of progress in curbing global warming shifted from the White House to the Senate.

Moreover, because public attention typically drops off after a noncrisis policy decision, few Americans monitor whether the policy eventually becomes a success or a failure. In chapters 6 and 7, we will see that the Reagan administration decided to provide massive amounts of food aid to the Marxist Ethiopian government to help alleviate the effects of a devastating famine. Yet public interest in the case dropped dramatically after the policy announcement, allowing the administration to shape the implementation of policy in a manner the public would likely not have approved of had it been paying attention. In sum, presidents can often make popular noncrisis policy decisions because they are rarely held responsible for the ultimate success or failure of those policies.

Implementation

With important exceptions, the implementation phase of foreign policy making has been a neglected topic in the literature.[31] To the extent that this stage

---

30. Survey by Louis Harris and Associates, December 11–15, 1997, from the iPOLL Databank, Roper Center for Public Opinion Research, University of Connecticut (accessed July 12, 2008). "Do you approve or disapprove of the tentative treaty (from the meeting that took place in Kyoto, Japan which discussed what should be done about global warming and so-called greenhouse gases) which would require industrialized countries to reduce their emissions of carbon dioxide and other gases to below the 1990 level of emissions?"

31. For exceptions, see Smith and Clarke, *Foreign Policy Implementation*; Hermann, "Changing Course"; and Zelikow, "Foreign Policy Engineering."

is assessed at all, it is usually only to examine how bureaucratic standard operating procedures can lead to "slippage" between the policy that is decided upon and the policy that is implemented.[32] Here, however, we are interested in a still deeper question: do leaders manipulate the implementation of policy for political purposes?

Before we assess the political context of crises and noncrises, it is necessary to explain what exactly constitutes implementation. Implementation refers to the strategies and tactics involved in carrying out a policy decision. This definition includes an important temporal consideration: *anything* that occurs after a general policy decision falls into the category of implementation. As such, choices made during implementation should not be confused with the option generation or policy decision stages. Steven Smith and Michael Clarke offer a good illustration of implementation in their summation of the ill-fated Operation Eagle Claw rescue of U.S. hostages in Iran. "The decision to attempt the rescue is not the same thing as the plan to employ eight helicopters, train in a certain way, decentralize command, and so on. Decisions on such key aspects of the plan that was to be 'carried out' were themselves decided in the process of implementation."[33]

Thus far in the discussion, our theoretical model has predicted that presidents lead or ignore the American public in foreign policy crises. However, the picture is likely to change during the implementation stage as the confluence of unified public preferences and high issue salience creates a constrained political context, which increases the pressure for political responsiveness (see table 5). As mentioned earlier, the public holds a number of strong preferences concerning the implementation of crisis policy, including an inclination for multilateral military action, a desire that the UN and U.S. Congress be consulted before going to war, and, most of all, a demand for a successful and quick resolution of the conflict with minimal U.S. casualties. Additionally, the implementation stage is typically the most salient aspect of a crisis, especially in the era of twenty-four-hour, real-time television coverage. This interaction of unified preferences and high salience means that the implementation stage is of paramount importance. Indeed, this stage of crises is so crucial that, after military intervention has proven either a success or a failure, the public usually forgets the politics of the prelude.[34]

The overriding importance of the implementation stage has several consequences for presidential decision making. First, as discussed earlier, presidents

32. Halperin, *Bureaucratic Politics*; Allison, *Essence of Decision*.
33. Smith and Clarke, *Foreign Policy Implementation*, 168.
34. Eichenberg, "Victory Has Many Friends."

may simply discount public opinion at previous stages of a crisis (i.e., the problem definition, option generation, and policy decision stages) because they are ultimately held responsible for what occurs during implementation. When implementation goes well, the earlier choices that led to military action tend to fade from our collective memory; it is only when implementation goes poorly—as it did in Vietnam, the Iranian hostage crisis, and the Iraq War— that critics bother revisiting the choices and events that led to the failed policy. In short, because so much rides on implementation, we should expect that presidents will anticipate public opinion at this stage. A second and related implication is that presidents are likely to respond to the public's current preferences during implementation. Because public attention reaches its zenith at this stage, presidents have a political incentive to appear responsive. Finally, presidents at the implementation stage often find themselves facing a difficult trade-off between policies they believe to be militarily or strategically effective and policies that are preferred by the American public. For example, introducing ground troops may be the most effective way of stopping genocide and ethnic cleansing. Yet, because placing ground troops in the midst of a chaotic ethnic conflict promises to produce U.S. casualties, presidents usually avoid that option in favor of a lower-risk, although less effective, aerial bombing strategy. In sum, the importance of the implementation stage increases the probability of political responsiveness, even at the expense of strategic effectiveness.

Conversely, public opinion is expected to play little role in the implementation of noncrisis foreign policy. As mentioned earlier, the actual implementation process is usually long, detailed, bureaucratic, and simply not all that exciting. For instance, few Americans are interested in exactly how weapons are dismantled following an arms control treaty, how the Federal Reserve goes about stabilizing the dollar against foreign currencies, how tariffs and quotas protect U.S. jobs against foreign competition, and whether emergency food aid actually reaches its intended recipients. Instead, the majority of the public assumes that the announced policy decision has solved the problem and then turns its attention elsewhere. The strong tendency for public attention to decline precipitously after a policy decision decreases the pressure on presidents to respond to public opinion at the implementation stage.

It is important to note that while public attention may decrease during the implementation stage of noncrises, preferences are in most cases expected to remain consistent with those of earlier stages. For example, the public is likely to retain its strong preferences to curb global warming, stop the decline of the U.S. dollar, protect American jobs, and feed hungry people in the less developed world. Simply put, people usually do not change their minds unless something dramatic happens. However, because few are attentive to the actual long-term policy implementation, these unified public preferences diminish in importance for policy makers. As an extreme illustration, consider a scenario in which 100 percent of Americans hold the same preference on a noncrisis foreign policy, yet no one is paying attention to what the government is doing. In this case, even in the face of *unanimous* preferences, there would be little cause for political responsiveness (i.e., 100% preferences x 0% issue salience = 0% responsiveness). This assumes, of course, that issue salience will remain low in the future so that latent preferences stay latent. Presidents are sometimes called to account for their policies when the public unexpectedly becomes attentive and finds the White House doing things it shouldn't (e.g., the Iran-Contra affair). Therefore, the game revolves around the benefits that can accrue to presidents and the United States in manipulating implementation to accomplish strategic goals versus the political cost of getting caught doing so. The key variable in this game is the probability that the public will become attentive sometime in the future, and, as we will see in chapter 3, the odds are in the president's favor—the public simply is not interested in the implementation of noncrisis policies.

To summarize, unified public preferences combined with low issue salience create a guarded political context at the implementation stage of noncrises (table 5). In such a context, presidents are expected to ignore the American public. They must, however, be concerned that a previously inattentive public might suddenly turn attentive, and very upset, in the future.

Policy Review

The review of policy is the final stage of the decision-making process and refers to the choice to continue, modify, or abandon a particular policy. If policy is to be judged on whether it ultimately accomplishes its goals, then it is important to examine the endgame. Public opinion is expected to exert a strong influence on presidents at this final stage of crises. Recall that crises tend to

Table 5 Political context and presidential action at the implementation stage

	Crises	Noncrises
Political context	Constrained	Guarded
Future or current context	Current	Future
Presidential action	Follow	Ignore

produce a highly attentive public throughout all stages of the policy-making process. Therefore, the public is interested not only in the selection of policy but also in how that policy is implemented and whether the United States accomplished its goal. The public is also expected to have strong preferences about continuing, modifying, or abandoning a particular course of action. In a sense, the public keeps a scorecard tracking whether the ongoing policy is a success or a failure.[35] In short, the combination of high issue salience and unified preferences creates a constrained political context in which presidents must respond to current opinion (see table 6).

Due to the reelection imperative and/or the need to maintain acceptable levels of political capital, presidents are expected to be highly sensitive to public opinion when reviewing crisis policies. Declining public confidence in the status quo policy can sometimes even force a president to abandon his strategy. This was the case in 1983, for instance, when Ronald Reagan reluctantly decided to pull troops out of Lebanon after 241 marines were killed in a suicide bombing. Similarly, the Clinton administration's escalated troop withdrawal from Somalia in 1993 was likely affected by the drop in public support following the "Black Hawk Down" episode. Alternatively, a long-term erosion of public support can lead presidents to modify their policies, as evidenced in Vietnam as Presidents Johnson and Nixon tried escalation and then Vietnamization to deal with criticism at home. The 2007 "surge" of U.S forces in Iraq represents another modification of existing policy. Although President George W. Bush did not engage in a wholesale reevaluation of his Iraq policy, as many Americans wanted him to do, the surge nevertheless illustrates how declining public confidence can lead a president to revisit and revise the status quo policy.

In noncrisis policy making, public attention tends to decay rapidly after the selection of policy. Accordingly, the autonomy enjoyed by presidents during the implementation phase continues into the review stage. Because the implementation of noncrisis policies typically takes a long time—sometimes years or decades—it is often up to successive presidents to undertake the review of a policy they did not make. And because noncrisis policies involve such long-running issues, the president who made the original decision is generally not held responsible for ultimate policy success or failure. Barring a salient exogenous event or a successful effort by political entrepreneurs to raise public awareness, presidents enjoy considerable freedom in deciding whether to continue with the status quo, make significant policy modifications, or completely

---

35. Johnson and Tierney, *Failing to Win*.

Table 6 Political context and presidential action at the policy review stage

	Crises	Noncrises
Political context	Constrained	Guarded
Future or current context	Current	Future
Presidential action	Follow	Ignore

abandon a particular course of action. However, public preferences are expected to stay fairly consistent, and as such, the decision context will remain guarded (table 6). In this context, presidents will more often than not ignore public opinion. Again, the only concern they may have is that latent opinion will suddenly and unexpectedly become active, which, as we will see in the next chapter, is rather unlikely in noncrises.

Summary

This chapter began by discussing three general facts about public opinion: (1) policy makers often believe that public support is an important component of a successful foreign policy, (2) the public holds sensible "big picture" opinions on foreign policy but cares little for the details, and (3) the public attends to some aspects of foreign policy but not others. With these axioms in mind, we looked at three different hypotheses at each of the five decision stages. First, we explored the likely movement of issue salience and public preferences across the five stages, assessing what their interaction means for the political context. Second, we posited whether presidents are most sensitive to the public's current or future preferences. Finally, we hypothesized about the extent to which presidents create or are prisoners of the decision context.

What follows is the empirical test of these hypotheses. Chapter 3 provides breadth by looking at issue salience in some of the most important foreign policy events over the past forty years. Chapters 4–7 then offer depth through detailed comparative case studies of one foreign policy crisis (the 1990–91 Persian Gulf conflict) and one foreign policy noncrisis (the Ethiopian famine of the mid-1980s). Putting these pieces of the puzzle together offers a more complete picture of how the public's attention affects the White House, and how the White House can affect public attention.

3

PATTERNS OF PUBLIC ATTENTION

Remember the name Michael Fay? In 1994, the American teenager was living in Singapore when police caught him vandalizing cars. Fay was later convicted and sentenced to receive six lashes with a four-foot bamboo rod called a *rotan*. The incident sparked media frenzy in the United States, and over 70 percent of Americans reported following the news about Fay.[1] The unusual nature of the sentence also led to a nationwide debate over corporal punishment and juvenile delinquency, with Americans divided between believing the caning to be too harsh (43 percent) and believing it to be appropriate (51 percent).[2] News of the incident even reached the Oval Office. President Bill Clinton appealed to the Singaporean government to commute Fay's punishment, and U.S. Trade Representative Mickey Cantor later threatened to vote against Singapore in its bid to host the first meeting of the newly created World Trade Organization should the government go through with the caning.[3] (The Singaporean government refused Clinton's request and Cantor's demand, though it did reduce the number of lashes from six to four.) But while the incident

---

1. Survey by Times Mirror/Princeton Survey Research Associates, May 12–15, 1994, from the iPOLL Databank, Roper Center for Public Opinion Research, University of Connecticut (accessed July 25, 2008). "How closely did you follow news stories about . . . the young American who was caned in Singapore for vandalism?" Percent reporting very or somewhat closely.
2. Survey by NBC News/*Wall Street Journal*/Hart and Teeter Research Companies, April 30–May 3, 1994, from the iPOLL Databank, Roper Center for Public Opinion Research, University of Connecticut (accessed July 25, 2008). "As you may have heard, an American teenager in Singapore has been sentenced to six lashes with a cane for vandalism. This punishment, which will be administered by someone who is highly trained in the martial arts, is likely to leave this teenager with permanent physical and emotional scars. Do you think this punishment is too harsh considering the crime, or acceptable and appropriate?" Given such a slanted question (i.e., why state that a highly trained martial arts expert would administer the punishment? How does the survey writer know that the caning will leave emotional scars?), it seems remarkable that a majority of the American public still approved of the caning of Michael Fay.
3. Shenon, "Caned American Says Farewell."

gripped the American public for a short period of time, interest in Michael Fay vanished quicker than the welts on his backside.

In the late 1980s and early 1990s, many Americans were fearful of the apparent rise of Japanese economic power. In 1990, 75 percent of the public even felt that Japan represented a more serious threat to U.S. security than the Soviet Union.[4] Fears intensified when Japanese companies made highly symbolic purchases of American landmarks, such as Rockefeller Center, Columbia Pictures, and Pebble Beach Golf Course.[5] The entertainment world also found in Japan its next great nemesis, replacing the moribund Soviet Union: the Tom Clancy novel *Debt of Honor* and the movie *Rising Sun*, starring Sean Connery and Wesley Snipes, both portrayed Japan as the new evil empire. In academia, American declinism and Japanese ascendancy were hot subjects. In short, many in the United States feared that they would soon play economic second fiddle to Japan. However, after a series of financial stumbles in Japan, coupled with the meteoric rise of the U.S. economy in the mid- to late 1990s, the American public quickly turned its attention away from the "Land of the Rising Sun" and toward the new economic enemy lurking on the eastern horizon: China.

Both the Michael Fay and Japanese cases suggest that public attention to international affairs can be like the wind—here today and gone tomorrow. But is there any way to predict which way the political winds will blow? Is the American public gripped by some foreign policy choices while giving a collective yawn to others? We explore these questions by searching for patterns of public attentiveness to U.S. foreign policy. More to the point, we examine how issue salience ebbs and flows across the five stages of decision making. The purpose of this analysis is to test the proposition that public attention to foreign policy fluctuates in predictable ways (proposition 5 of chapter 1). If we indeed find that issue salience conforms to systematic patterns in foreign policy crises and noncrises, then we have a way to forecast the stage(s) at which presidents are likely to lead, follow, or ignore public opinion. If, however, the movement of issue salience is completely random, then the model has no such predictive capacity. In short, a lot is riding on this evidence.

This chapter offers a wide-ranging look at U.S. foreign policy by examining public attention in thirty-four of the most significant events over the past forty years. The cases include lethal lumberjacks, the rock band Guns N' Roses, a

---

4. Survey by ABC/*Washington Post*, May 17–21, 1990, from LexisNexis, Roper Center for Public Opinion Research, University of Connecticut (accessed April 12, 2004). "Which would you say is a bigger threat to the national security of the United States, the military power of the Soviet Union or the economic power of Japan?"

5. Budner and Krauss, "Newspaper Coverage."

six-year-old boy who became a household name, and a U.S. cruise missile strike against the pharmaceutical industry. We begin by assessing the aggregate movement of issue salience in crises and noncrises before taking a more detailed look at the individual cases in the analysis.

Patterns of Issue Salience in U.S. Foreign Policy

As seen in chapter 1, issue salience is an important mechanism in prompting greater presidential responsiveness to public opinion. For politicians, political costs and benefits increase as more Americans become interested in an issue. In a sense, then, politicians are particularly susceptible to what is called the "observer effect" in the social and natural sciences: the behavior of a subject tends to change when being observed. Politicians under the public microscope know that the choices they make can affect their political future—make a wrong move and your career might be over. But when citizens turn their gaze elsewhere, politicians are relatively free to make any political choice they want, even if that decision cuts against the grain of what the public would have otherwise preferred. In short, policy making in the spotlight is usually very different from policy making in the shadows.

Given the importance of issue salience to political responsiveness, it is important to know when public attention is likely to be high and when it is likely to be low. In other words, uncovering systematic "issue-attention cycles" in foreign policy crises and noncrises allows us to forecast when presidents are likely to be most sensitive to public opinion.[6] Moreover, mapping the issue-attention cycles across our five stages of decision making—problem definition, option generation, policy decision, implementation, and policy review—allows us to precisely identify when the American public might carry more or less weight. In particular, we are looking to test the two hypotheses found in chapter 1 (where the interested reader will also find justifications for each):

H_1: Public attention to crises, while fairly high throughout the decision process, will peak during the implementation of policy.

H_2: Public attention to noncrises, while fairly low throughout most of the decision process, will peak during the policy decision stage.

Again, empirical confirmation of these hypotheses offers some means of predicting the stage at which presidents will likely be most sensitive to public

---

6. Bosso, "Setting the Agenda"; Downs, "Up and Down."

preferences. If the public is found to be most attentive at the implementation stage of foreign policy crises, and found to be most attentive to the policy decision stage of noncrises, we should expect to find more evidence of political responsiveness at those respective stages than during any other juncture in the process.

Methods

There are two methodological hurdles we must clear to identify patterns of issue salience across the five stages of decision making. First, we obviously need to establish a valid indicator of issue salience. This is more a difficult task than it might first appear (for an extended discussion of the methods used in this chapter, see appendix A). This analysis uses network news television coverage as an indicator of public attentiveness. Although it would be a mistake to assume that the American public *always* follows media coverage,[7] solid research evidence shows that the national news heavily influences citizens' attention to political issues and their perception of how important these issues are.[8] This is especially true for foreign affairs because the American public almost entirely depends on the media for information.

The second methodological hurdle to overcome is identifying the stages of decision making in the thirty-four foreign policy crises and noncrises under consideration. Again, this is a difficult task. The beginning and end of a decision stage are not always well defined; identifying the boundary between two stages can sometimes be like identifying the edge of a town. I began my research by undertaking in-depth studies of the two major cases in this book—the Gulf War and the U.S. response to the Ethiopian famine in the mid-1980s—drawing on extensive research in secondary sources, contemporary news media and periodicals, archival research at presidential libraries, and elite interviews. This process is, of course, too costly in time and resources to duplicate for a larger sample of cases. Determining the stages of decision making in the remaining thirty-two cases was accomplished by reviewing the secondary literature and newspaper accounts of the events. Without detailed inside knowledge of these cases, determining the boundaries of the stages is, by nature, a subjective process, and some reasonable readers may disagree with

---

7. Gilboa, "CNN Effect."
8. Iyengar and Kinder, *News That Matters*; McCombs and Shaw, "Agenda-Setting Function"; B. Cohen, *Press and Foreign Policy*; Neuman, Just, and Crigler, *Common Knowledge News*; Page and Shapiro, *Rational Public*; Edwards, Mitchell, and Welch, "Explaining Presidential Approval"; Graber, *Mass Media and American Politics*; Graber, *Processing Politics*; Iyengar, *Is Anyone Responsible?*

the characterization of particular cases presented here. This is especially true of the early stages of noncrises (i.e., problem definition and option generation), as secondary source accounts are often scarce. The good news is that moving the boundary between stages by a day or two would not significantly alter the findings. Indeed, given the sparse media coverage of the early stages of emerging foreign policy issues—particularly noncrisis cases—there is good reason to suppose that even relatively large revisions of the boundaries (say, by a month or so) would be unlikely to alter the gist of the argument, since few news broadcasts would actually shift categories.

Results

So what does the data show? Unsurprisingly, table 7 demonstrates that more television time was devoted to the seventeen crisis cases (22,292 total minutes of coverage) than to the seventeen noncrisis cases (13,182 total minutes of coverage). Given that most crises are sensational and well suited to a visual medium, it should be expected that crises would garner more network airtime. But noncrises were hardly neglected: they received almost 220 hours of television news coverage.

For our purposes, however, the larger question is, does the American public systematically pay attention to some stages of foreign policy decision making more than others? To properly answer this question, we need to take a second look at how we measure public attention at each decision stage. One of the problems in drawing comparisons within and across cases is that the length of the respective decision stages can vary dramatically. For example, the option generation stage of arms control negotiations can last for several years, while some crises flare up and are over in a day or so. If we simply added up the minutes of television coverage per stage, the resulting measure would provide a misleading picture of issue salience; even the occasional broadcasts on arms control negotiations, added up over the course of several years, would give the reader the misleading impression that the option generation stage was more salient than it really was. Instead, what we are after is the *intensity* of public scrutiny at each decision stage. Because the various decision stages differ in length, I normalized the measure of intensity of media coverage in a simple two-step procedure detailed in appendix A. In short, I calculated the average minutes of coverage per day for each of the five stages; by ultimately expressing per-stage coverage as a proportion of the total media coverage for each case, I have allowed for comparability across cases and decision stages.

Table 7 Television news coverage of crisis and noncrisis foreign policy cases

	Total Days	Total Minutes	Average Minutes per Day
Crises			
Gulf War	281	6,721.67	23.91
Kosovo	469	2,517.67	5.08
Afghan I	88	999.00	11.35
Afghan II	138	2,020.32	14.64
Angola	214	260.67	1.22
Desert Strike	25	208.83	8.35
Grenada	45	485.00	10.78
Haiti	167	866.17	29.87
Iran Hostage	509	4,692.00	9.22
Mayaguez	11	171.83	21.48
N. Korea	682	435.17	0.64
Poplar Tree	21	56.00	2.67
UNSCOM	108	531.50	4.92
Desert Fox	180	947.67	5.26
Shaba II	52	311.00	5.98
U.S. Embassy	43	355.50	8.27
Panama	50	517.17	10.34
Total	3,083	22,097.17	10.23
Noncrises			
Ethiopia	2,148	523.67	0.02
Japan Trade	1,905	550.83	0.29
Star Wars	3,653	1,950.33	0.53
ABM, Bush	852	187.83	0.22
Apartheid	2,246	1,076.00	0.48
China Trade	1,736	157.33	0.09
Elián González	219	659.17	3.01
Kyoto, Clinton	2,134	303.83	0.14
Rio	2,679	393.83	0.15
Kyoto, Bush	1,163	174.50	0.19
Gold Standard	1,841	676.83	0.37
Mariel	1,811	599.83	0.33
NAFTA	3,859	694.17	0.18
Panama Canal	1,768	593.00	0.34
SALT II	5,158	3,052.83	0.59
START I & II	6,972	371.83	0.05
Cuba, Clinton	2,480	918.50	0.37
Total	42,624	12,884.31	0.43

Figure 2 shows the percentage of television coverage per decision stage for the thirty-four crises and noncrises in my analysis. For noncrises, there was significantly more media coverage per day during the policy decision stage than in the stages before and after. By contrast, news coverage of crises tended to rise steadily, with media attention peaking during the implementation of policy. Therefore, figure 2 confirms that there is a difference between crises and noncrises in terms of public attention (proposition 5). Moreover, the evidence substantiates both of our specific hypotheses: the trajectory of public attention peaking the implementation of crises (hypothesis 1) and at the policy decision stage of noncrises (hypothesis 2).

Pattern-Conforming and Pattern-Breaking Noncrises

Although the aggregate evidence cited above offers a general confirmation of our hypotheses, it might also obscure subtle differences among the cases. In other words, we should want to know how many of the thirty-four cases in the analysis deviated from the pattern shown in figure 2 and why. For both crises and noncrises, we will examine the cases that conform to the patterns described in figure 2 (i.e., "pattern-conforming" cases) and those cases that deviated from the norm (i.e., "pattern-breaking" cases). Doing so will provide a more nuanced look at the factors that produce the ebbs and flows of public attention.

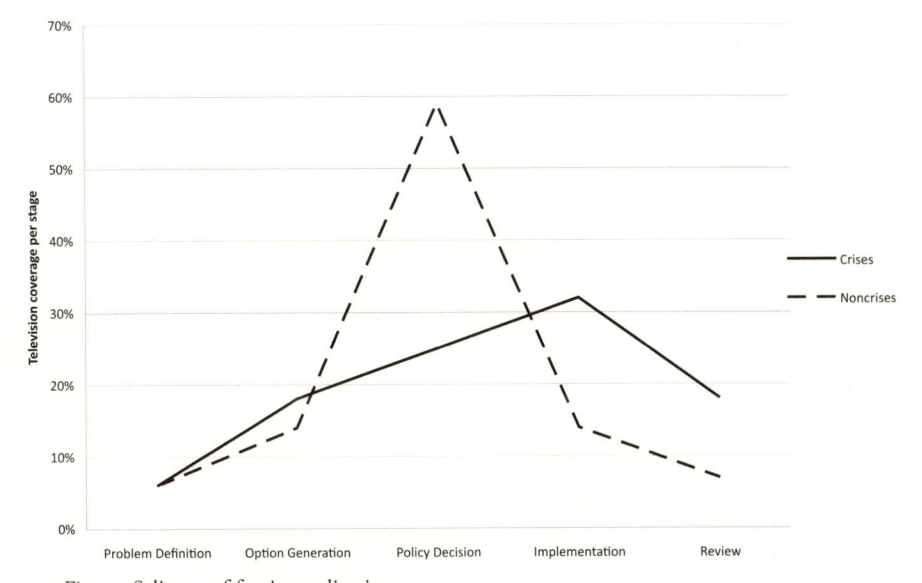

Fig. 2   Salience of foreign policy issues

Pattern-Conforming Noncrises

The vast majority of the noncrises in the analysis (76 percent) featured peak issue salience at the policy decision stage (see figures 3a–b). The list of pattern-conforming cases includes nuclear weapons treaties (i.e., George W. Bush's decision to break the Anti-Ballistic Missile Treaty, and the START and SALT treaties), global warming accords (i.e., George H. W. Bush's decision to sign the Rio Treaty and Bill Clinton's decision to sign the Kyoto Protocol), and international economic issues (i.e., U.S.-Chinese and U.S.-Japanese trade disputes, Richard Nixon's decision to take the United States off the gold standard, and the signing of NAFTA in the early 1990s). Pattern-conforming noncrisis cases also include the Torrijos-Carter Treaty, which abdicated U.S. control of the Panama Canal; Bill Clinton's signing of the Helms-Burton Act in March 1996, which tightened U.S. sanctions against Cuba; public attention to South African apartheid in the 1980s; and the U.S. response to the Ethiopian famine in the mid-1980s (discussed in chapters 6 and 7).

Three factors seem to bind these seemingly diverse noncrisis issues together. First, the sheer length of many of these cases increases the chances of an inattentive public. For instance, the option generation stage of the SALT I treaty (which eventually produced the Anti-Ballistic Missile Treaty) lasted from 1967 to 1972. Likewise, issues such as global environmental protection, bilateral

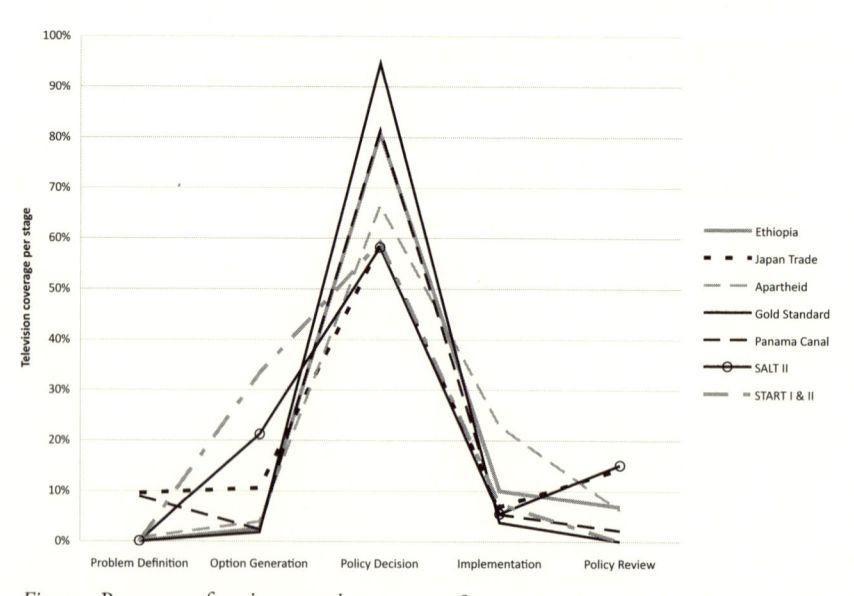

Fig. 3a Pattern-conforming noncrises, 1970s–1980s

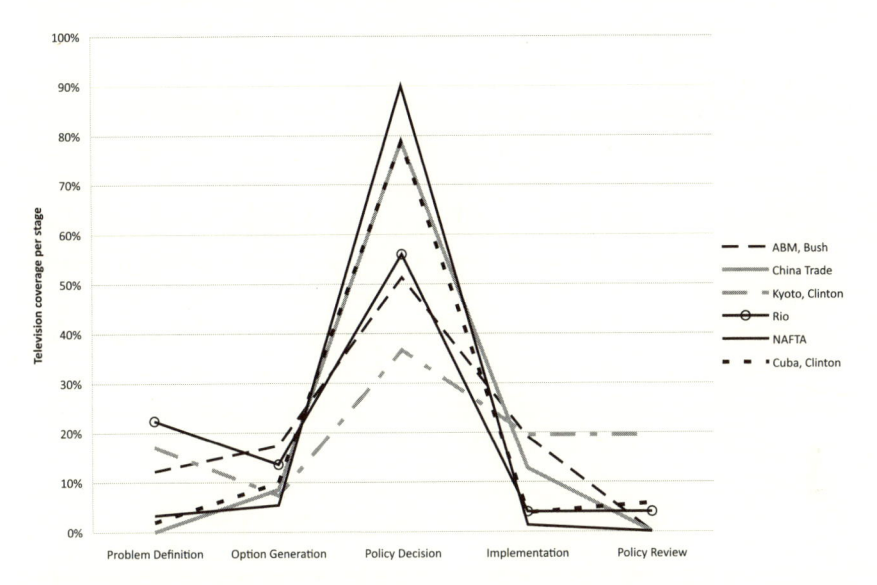

Fig. 3b Pattern-conforming noncrises, 1990s–2000s

trade disputes, and poverty in the less developed world have been on the marginal end of the political and public agendas for decades. Given the glacial pace of decision making for most noncrises, it is little wonder that the media and the public eventually become bored with the issues and turn their attention to more pressing matters.

A second and related point is that while the key decisions of each case were newsworthy, the stages before and after generally were not. The media needs a "peg" or a "hook" to sell a story to the American public, and in most of these cases, such pegs appear rather infrequently.[9] As noted in the previous chapter, the absence of salient events has consistently frustrated environmental activists' attempts to curb global warming. Another example of the absence of a media peg concerns President Richard Nixon's decision to take the United States off the gold standard in 1971. After Nixon allowed the dollar to float in the open market, there was little else for the media to report on. After all, few Americans would be interested in hearing Walter Cronkite announce, "It is day 736, and the dollar is still floating."

Finally, many of these cases feature topics that are unfamiliar to most Americans. From 1989 to 1990, for instance, the United States and Japan attempted

9. Powlick and Katz, "Public Opinion/Foreign Policy Nexus."

to address their economic differences through a series of bilateral negotiations called the Structural Impediments Initiative (SII). The SII talks focused on the domestic roots of the trade imbalance, such as budget deficits and a low national savings rate in the United States, and product distribution, land-use policy, and a high national savings rate in Japan. For most economists, domestic structural impediments lay at the heart of the U.S.-Japanese trade dispute. However, few Americans have the macroeconomic background necessary to understand exactly how these issues affect international trade. Instead, for most of the American public, the issue was simply that Japan was buying up the United States.

In sum, thirteen of the seventeen noncrisis events in the analysis conform to the pattern of a public interested in a noncrisis policy decision but uninterested in the stages before and after. The generally low issue salience throughout most of these cases can be traced to the length of the events, the lack of significant events on which to peg media stories, and the complexity of the issues involved. The next sections look at four exceptions to this general pattern.

Pattern-Breaking Noncrises: Option Generation

Two of the pattern-breaking cases witnessed peak attention during the option generation stage: the Mariel boat lift and President George W. Bush's decision not to send the Kyoto Treaty to the Senate for ratification (figure 4). It is notable that in both cases public attention to the option generation stage was only slightly greater than public attention to the policy decision stage, a near miss for our theory. Nevertheless, it is important to examine why the public seemed so interested in the options being considered by the White House.

In April 1980, Fidel Castro declared that any Cuban citizen who wished to leave the country for the United States could do so, provided they were picked up by boat at the Mariel Harbor. In what became known as the Mariel boat lift, Cuban Americans rushed to find anything that would float in order to get friends and relatives out of Cuba. The sheer number of Cubans entering the United States—an estimated 125,000—coupled with reports that Castro had emptied his jails and mental asylums, sparked widespread public concern about a flood of immigrants swamping America.[10] Indeed, 76 percent of Americans felt that the Cuban refugees should not be allowed into the United States.[11] This placed the Carter administration in a difficult position.

10. Masud-Piloto, *With Open Arms*; Engstrom, *Presidential Decision Making Adrift*.
11. Survey by ABC News/Louis Harris and Associates, May 16–18, 1980, from LexisNexis, Roper Center for Public Opinion Research, University of Connecticut (accessed May 1, 2004). "(Let me read

Promotion of human rights was the defining plank in the administration's foreign policy platform; to then deny asylum to Cubans fleeing a communist regime would seem inconsistent with that humanitarian ideal. On the other hand, public fears about Cuban immigration, combined with high issue salience, increased the political pressure on Carter to close the U.S. border. On June 20, 1980, after months of vacillation, domestic political realities trumped ideology as the Carter administration decided to revoke Cubans' special asylum status in order to stem the tide of refugees flowing into the United States. However, at this point, many of the Cubans with the desire and wherewithal to leave the island had already done so, and the stream of refugees coming into the United States had slowed to a trickle.[12]

The main reason why slightly more attention was given to the option generation stage of the Mariel boat lift than the policy decision stage is that the Cuban refugee problem had somewhat lessened on its own by the time the Carter administration reached its authoritative decision. In the first several weeks of the boat lift, images of thousands of Cuban refugees making the dangerous trek across the Florida Straits made for good television. Because the momentum of Cuban refugees entering the United States slowed prior to the institution of a more forceful policy, the visuals were less dramatic and the story somewhat stale, and consequently the issue received considerably less media coverage. The decline in media coverage inevitably made the issue of Cuban refugees seem somewhat less pressing for the American public. Therefore, Carter's decision became anticlimactic and, for a number of Americans, too late in the game. The end result was that the option generation stage of the Mariel case garnered the greatest public interest, not the policy decision stage.

The second pattern-breaking noncrisis concerned President George W. Bush's global warming policy. In the 2000 presidential campaign, Bush stated that global warming "needs to be taken very seriously" and promised, if elected, to mandate limits on carbon dioxide emissions in the United States.[13] For environmentalists, this campaign pledge offered a glimmer of hope that the new president would make serious progress on climate change.[14] Shortly after Bush's inauguration, administration officials intimated that a more forceful

---

you some statements about the U.S. letting refugees from Cuba into this country. For each, tell me if you tend to agree or disagree.) . . . The United States has always been a place where refugees can come, and we should let the Cubans in, even if as many as 250,000 ended up coming to this country."
    12. Masud-Piloto, *With Open Arms*; Engstrom, *Presidential Decision Making Adrift*.
    13. Kennedy, "Bush Backpedals"; Walsh, "Bush's Toothless Climate Plan."
    14. Lisowski, "Two-Level Game."

U.S. global warming policy was in the works.[15] On March 4, 2001, Christine Todd Whitman, the head of the Environmental Protection Agency, told delegates at the G-8 summit in Trieste, Italy, "Let me just start with the clear and unequivocal statement that the global climate review that's being undertaken by this administration does not represent a backing away from Kyoto."[16] Whitman's comments, along with those from other administration officials, fueled media speculation—hence, coverage—that the new president would soon take steps to curb carbon dioxide emissions in the United States, perhaps even sending the Kyoto Protocol to the Senate. As a result of rampant speculation of what the Bush administration *might* do about global warming, the option generation stage attracted considerable media and public attention.

Soon after the G-8 summit in Trieste, however, it became clear that President Bush had cooled on global warming. On March 15, 2001, Bush wrote a letter to four Senate Republicans informing them that his administration was opposed to the Kyoto Protocol. A few weeks later, Bush publicly stated of the protocol, "I will not accept a plan that will harm our economy and hurt our workers."[17] Under pressure from congressional Republicans, Bush also abandoned his pledge of mandatory carbon caps in the United States in favor of a voluntary compliance system.[18] With that, Bush decided not to address global warming through regulatory policy. Again, the amount of media coverage this decision received was only slightly less than the option generation stage.

It is likely that the option generation stage of the Kyoto case received marginally more coverage than the policy decision stage because the Bush administration's choice of voluntary reductions was, like the Mariel decision, somewhat anticlimactic. For the media, governmental action tends to be more newsworthy than inaction. Therefore, the Bush administration's decision to continue the status quo policy was a less salient story than it would have been had the administration proposed legislation capping carbon emissions or sent the Kyoto Protocol to the Senate and pressed for its ratification.

Pattern-Breaking Noncrises: Implementation

The Reagan administration's strategic defense initiative, better known as the Star Wars program, was a controversial ground and space missile defense system

---

15. *Time*, "Losing the Green Light."
16. Rizzo, "EPA Chief."
17. Seelye, "Facing Obstacles."
18. *Time*, "Losing the Green Light."

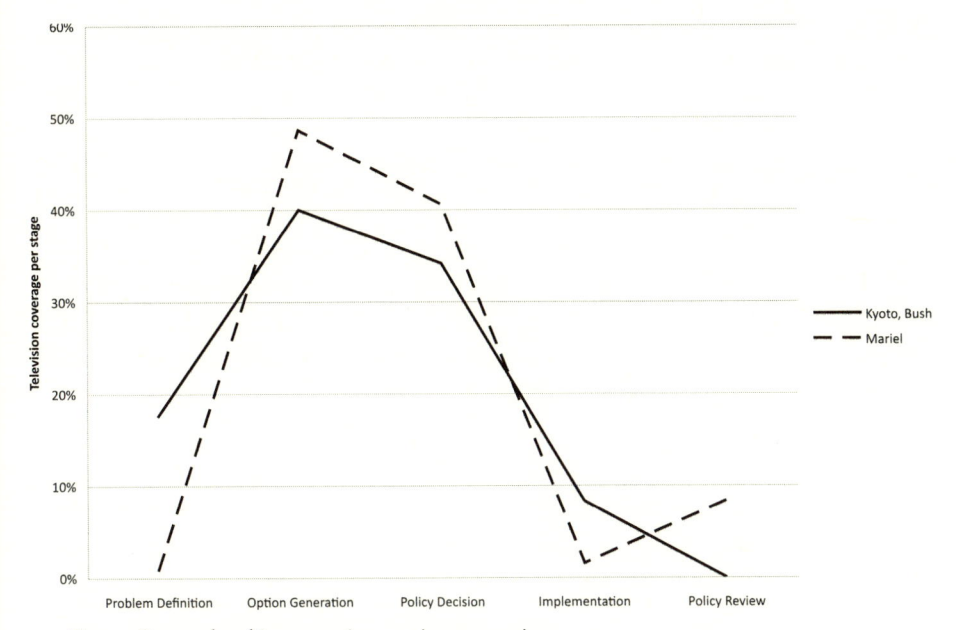

Fig. 4 Pattern-breaking noncrises, option generation

designed to shoot down incoming Soviet intercontinental ballistic missiles. The Star Wars program was unusual in that more media coverage occurred during implementation than at any other stage (figure 5). This postdecision attention to Star Wars stemmed largely from two factors. First, the United States and the USSR held several arms control negotiations that coincided with the implementation of Star Wars. While the ostensive purpose of negotiations was arms reduction, the summits provided the Soviets with a forum to criticize Reagan's Star Wars program as a grave threat to world peace. As a result, Star Wars became a recurring theme each time arms control issues were discussed. Second, domestic political opponents seized the Star Wars program as emblematic of President Reagan's misplaced political priorities, mentioning it in a variety of contexts. Since Star Wars was so controversial both domestically and internationally, the program never experienced the type of media decay typical of most noncrises.

Pattern-Breaking Noncrises: Policy Review

In 1999, six-year-old Elián González, his mother, and twelve others escaped Cuba on a boat bound for the Florida coast. Tragically, the boat capsized in the Florida Straits, and all but Elián and two other refugees were lost at sea.

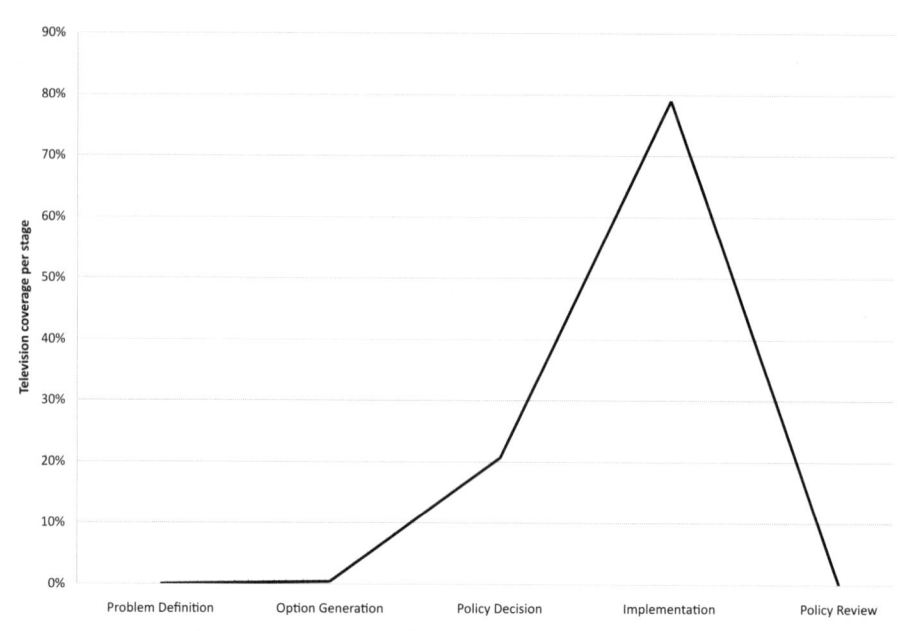

Fig. 5 Pattern-breaking noncrises, implementation (Star Wars)

Elián was rescued by fishermen and eventually transferred to the U.S. Immigration and Naturalization Service (INS), which gave temporary custody of the boy to his great-aunt and great-uncle in Miami. Elián's father, however, still resided in Cuba and demanded custody. After a series of court battles in the United States, the Clinton administration, led by Attorney General Janet Reno, ordered that Elián be returned to his father in Cuba. Elián's relatives in the United States defied the order, setting up a memorable conclusion to the case.

In the early morning of April 22, 2000, federal agents with body armor and semiautomatic machine guns stormed the home in which Elián was staying. A Pulitzer Prize–winning picture captured the image of a frightened Elián screaming as a U.S. agent, with his MP5 submachine gun raised, reached to take the boy from the arms of one of the fishermen who had rescued him. The picture became one of the defining images of 2000, and 81 percent of the American public reported having seen it.[19] Elián was then rushed off to a plane that departed for Cuba. As a result of the considerable postmortem analysis of the case, public attention peaked during the policy review stage (figure 6).

19. Survey by ABC News, April 24, 2000, from LexisNexis, Roper Center for Public Opinion Research, University of Connecticut (accessed May 1, 2004). "Did you happen to see the photograph of a federal agent with a gun just as he was seizing the boy (Elian Gonzalez from his relatives' home in Miami April 22, 2000), or not?"

Pattern-Conforming and Pattern-Breaking Crises

There is somewhat more variation in attention patterns across individual crisis cases than we saw in noncrises. Interest peaked during the implementation stage in a majority (53 percent) of cases, which confirms our hypothesis about crisis attention patterns. Out of the seventeen crises, however, peak attention occurred at the option generation stage in two cases, at the policy decision stage in five cases, and during policy review in one case. This variation from the norm justifies a closer look at the individual cases. By examining the similarities and differences between pattern-conforming and pattern-breaking cases, we can sharpen our understanding of why public attention ebbs and flows in foreign policy crises.

Pattern-Conforming Crises

The common feature of the nine pattern-conforming cases is that they all involved the use of military force. Because wars are high-stakes, high-drama events, is should be expected that peak attention will occur during the implementation stage (figures 7a–b). Four of the nine cases—Grenada, Panama, the 1991 Gulf War, and U.S. intervention in Kosovo—featured large displays of U.S. force. On October 25, 1983, President Ronald Reagan launched Operation Urgent Fury against the small Caribbean island of Grenada. Tensions

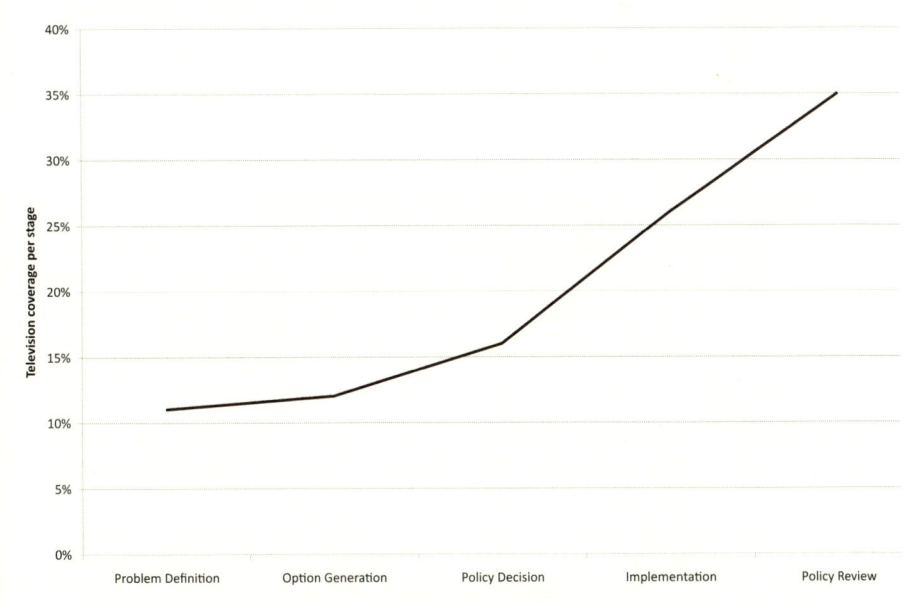

Fig. 6   Pattern-breaking noncrises, policy review (Elián González)

between the United States and Grenada had been mounting over the Reagan administration's claim that Grenada was building an airfield to support Soviet and Cuban forces. A bloody coup in Grenada and the presence of U.S. medical students on the island offered the pretext for American military intervention. More than 4,000 American troops joined forces from the Organization of Eastern Caribbean States (OECS) in what was then the largest display of American force since Vietnam. Although the U.S.-led intervention successfully deposed Grenada's military junta and safely evacuated all U.S. medical students, 18 American soldiers were killed in action with another 116 wounded.[20]

By the late 1980s, it was clear that Panama, under the leadership of Manuel Noriega, had become a haven for drug smugglers and money launderers. President George H. W. Bush attempted to compel Noriega to change his behavior through economic and diplomatic sanctions, but the massive amounts of drug money flowing into Panama made sanctions almost laughable. A failed military coup and the shooting of a U.S. Marine in Panama left Bush with no other viable option but to use military action to resolve the crisis.[21] In December 1989, the Bush administration launched Operation Just Cause to capture Noriega and bring him to the United States for trial.[22] Noriega eluded capture for several days, eventually seeking refuge inside the Vatican embassy in Panama City. Embassies are part of a nation's sovereign territory; to violate that sovereignty is a serious breach of international law. Unable to physically remove Noriega, U.S. forces blared the heavy metal band Guns N' Roses' hit song "Welcome to the Jungle" night and day over loudspeakers in a head-banging bit of psychological warfare. Eventually Noriega surrendered (obviously not a GN'R fan) and was tried and convicted on drug charges in the United States. At that time, the Panama invasion overtook the Grenada intervention as the United States' largest post-Vietnam military excursion, with well over 26,000 American troops participating in the operation.

The 1991 Persian Gulf War is discussed at length in chapters 4 and 5, but suffice it to say here, the war was significant. Operation Desert Storm utilized more than 500,000 U.S. troops; as a means of comparison, there were nearly 160,000 American troops in Iraq *after* the surge of 2007.[23] Another pattern-conforming crisis case was the United States' intervention in Kosovo, a brief description of which was provided in the introduction to this book. A few additional facts here serve to illustrate the substantial U.S. military commitment

20. Rubner, "Reagan Administration."
21. Grant, *Operation Just Cause*.
22. U.S. Army Center of Military History, *Operation Just Cause*.
23. O'Bryant and Waterhouse, *U.S. Forces in Iraq*.

in the Balkans: although the intervention involved no U.S. ground forces, the United States provided a lion's share of the air power, employing 731 different aircraft to drop approximately six thousand tons of munitions on Serbian forces.[24]

The five remaining pattern-conforming crises also featured military action, but in a more limited manner. In May 1975, Khmer Rouge military forces boarded the U.S. merchant ship *Mayaguez* off the Cambodian coast and captured the crew. The Ford administration hastily planned a rescue mission involving a large 430-troop assault on Koh Tang Island, where the *Mayaguez* crew was believed to be held.[25] Unbeknownst to the rescue party, the crew had been moved off the island by the time the U.S. assault began (eventually, the entire crew would be rescued unharmed). When the Marines arrived, Cambodian forces were dug in, and the resulting battle was short but bloody: 41 American soldiers lost their lives in the rescue attempt.

The Iranian hostage crisis also featured peak attention during the implementation stage (discussed earlier in chapter 2).[26] Jimmy Carter's presidency was already in trouble with stagflation, gas shortages, declining public approval, and a primary election challenge from Ted Kennedy. As the Iranian hostage crisis dragged on and images of the standoff played out nightly on television, Chief of Staff Hamilton Jordan warned President Carter that if he did nothing to resolve the standoff, "you can forget about a second term."[27] Concerned about his domestic political standing as well as rescuing the hostages, Carter decided on a risky operation on April 7, 1980.[28] In the immediate aftermath of the failed rescue attempt, television coverage of the crisis spiked and criticism of the president intensified. Massive media coverage continued in the ensuing months, and Walter Cronkite's nightly broadcast sign-off, which reported the number of days Americans had been held in captivity, took on increased significance.[29] All told, the American hostages were held in Tehran for 444 days until their release on the day of Ronald Reagan's presidential inauguration.

In August 1996, 40,000 Iraqi forces illegally moved into a Kurdish safe

---

24. Data on U.S. aircraft from "The Kosovo File: Military Info," *Time.com*, http://www.time.com/time/daily/special/kosovo/military_info.html; data on NATO bombs dropped from "Facts and Figures," *Frontline*, http://www.pbs.org/wgbh/pages/frontline/shows/kosovo/etc/facts.html (both accessed March 14, 2007).

25. American Merchant Marine at War, "Capture and Release of *SS Mayaguez* by Khmer Rouge Forces in May 1975," http://www.usmm.org/mayaguez.html (accessed June 29, 2008).

26. Paterson et al., *American Foreign Relations*; Houghton, *U.S. Foreign Policy*; McDermott, "Prospect Theory."

27. Houghton, *U.S. Foreign Policy*, 102.

28. Ibid.; McDermott, "Prospect Theory."

29. Murphy, "Headlines from Hell."

haven in northern Iraq.[30] In response, the Clinton administration authorized Operation Desert Strike, a U.S. missile strike along the southern Iraqi no-fly zone. The attack, carried out on September 3 and 4, 1996, was quick and hard-hitting, and it degraded Iraqi air defense systems. The operation accomplished its goal, as Hussein's forces soon retreated to Baghdad.

On August 7, 1998, al Qaeda terrorists launched a brazen attack on U.S. embassies in Kenya and Tanzania, killing 301 people and wounding many others.[31] President Clinton responded by ordering a cruise missile strike on suspected al Qaeda sites in Sudan and Afghanistan. The U.S. retaliation in Sudan was particularly controversial. The military target was a pharmaceutical plant that the Clinton administration claimed was an al Qaeda front for producing the chemical agent VX. Thirteen U.S. cruise missiles destroyed the plant on August 20, 1998. In the aftermath, however, critics charged that little evidence existed that the Sudanese plant was making anything other than medicine. "We were not accurate [about the VX intelligence]," a senior Clinton administration official would later say. "That [the missile strike] was a mistake."[32]

Finally, frustrated with Saddam Hussein's repeated defiance of UN resolutions regarding weapons inspections, the Clinton administration decided in late 1998 to use military force to degrade Iraq's arsenal of weapons of mass destruction. In the three-day Operation Desert Fox, the United States launched "strong and sustained" aerial strikes against suspected Iraqi weapon sites.[33] The U.S. attack was controversial at home and abroad. The missile strikes occurred on the eve of Clinton's impeachment proceedings over the Monica Lewinsky scandal. As a result, many critics charged that the president had used military action to divert the public's attention away from his impeachment.

In sum, the pattern-conforming crises presented in this analysis have one thing in common: they all featured the use of American military force. Wars are dramatic, highly visual events that attract considerable media and public attention. High issue salience then raises the political costs and benefits of war.

Pattern-Breaking Crises: Policy Decision

Although a majority of crises conform to the trajectory of attention described in figure 2, a significant number do deviate from this general pattern. The

30. "Operation Desert Strike," GlobalSecurity.org, http://www.globalsecurity.org/military/ops/desert_strike.htm (accessed March 4, 2008).
31. "Attacks on U.S. Embassies in Kenya and Tanzania," GlobalSecurity.org, http://www.globalsecurity.org/security/ops/98emb.htm (accessed March 4, 2008).
32. Weiner and Risen, "Decision to Strike Factory."
33. Paterson et al., *American Foreign Relations*.

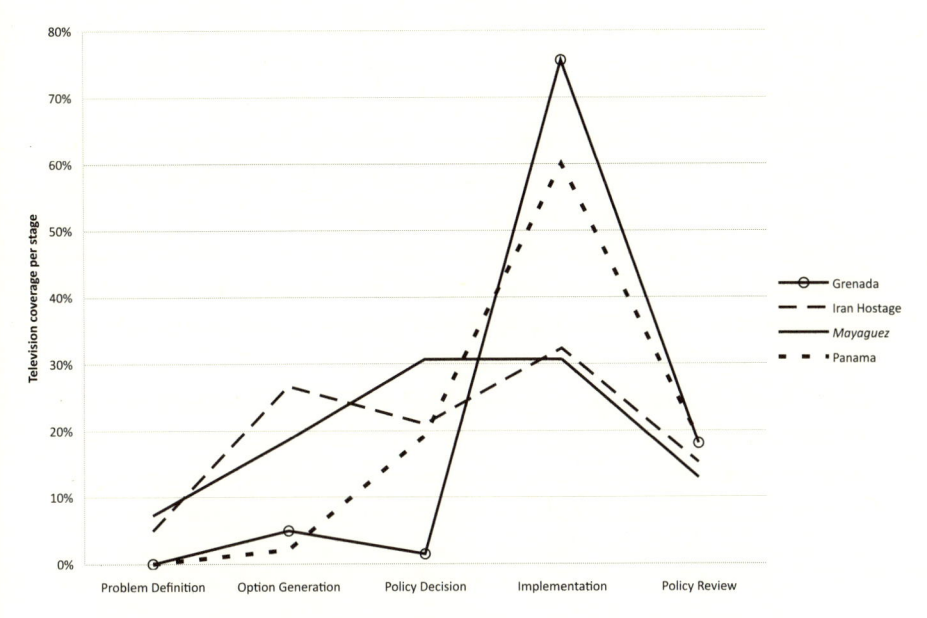

Fig. 7a Pattern-conforming crises, 1970s–1980s

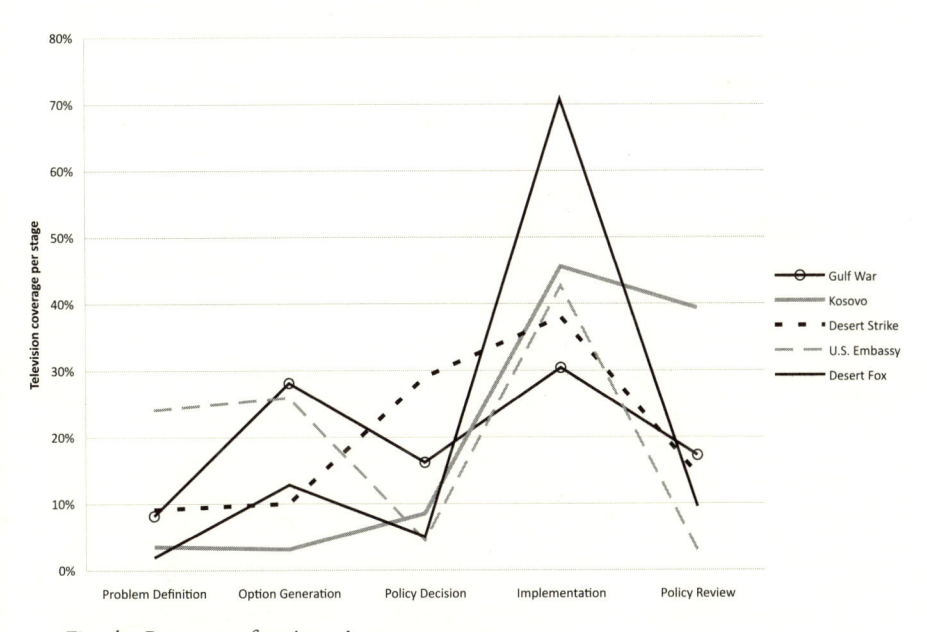

Fig. 7b Pattern-conforming crises, 1990s–2000s

public was most attentive to the policy decision stage in five out of the seventeen crises. In all but one of these cases, presidents stood on the brink of war only to step back at the last moment. This suggests that a slight revision to our hypothesis is in order: public attention tends to peak at the implementation stage of crises that feature military force, *but* public attention tends to peak at the policy decision stage of crises that do not feature military force. This section looks at four cases in which military force was possible but no shots were fired. We then examine one case that is a notable outlier.

The 1991 cease-fire agreement that ended the Gulf War included the provision that UN Special Commission (UNSCOM) weapons inspectors would have unfettered access within Iraq to search for weapons of mass destruction.[34] Throughout the 1990s, however, a recalcitrant Saddam Hussein repeatedly denied inspectors access to suspected weapon sites, including his numerous presidential palaces. On January 13, 1998, Iraq declared that it would no longer comply with UNSCOM, and in response the United States threatened military action. A flurry of diplomatic activity ensued, and military action was averted at the last minute when, in late February 1998, UN Secretary General Kofi Annan convinced Hussein to reopen his country to inspectors.[35]

The Shaba II crisis was sparked when separatist rebels based in Angola invaded the Shaba province of Zaire on May 17, 1978. Zairean president Mobutu Sese Seko claimed that the rebels were communists, funded and trained by the Soviets and Cubans. At the time, the United States had an uneasy relationship with Mobutu. Zaire had long been a U.S. ally, and Mobutu was a fervent anticommunist. However, Mobutu also had an atrocious human rights record. This forced the Carter administration into a difficult position: either prevent a communist takeover of Zaire by supporting an evil dictator or withdraw U.S. support from Mobutu and face the charge at home of being weak on communism. Cold war concerns again trumped human rights as the Carter administration provided weapons and military support to Zaire. Material support, however, was as far as the Carter administration was willing to go, and no Americans troops were introduced in Shaba.

The poplar tree incident is one of the more bizarre cases in American foreign policy history. In August 1976, two American soldiers under the United Nations Command (UNC) were supervising a crew trimming a poplar tree

---

34. "Inspecting the Deal," *The Newshour with Jim Lehrer*, February 25, 1998. Transcript available at http://www.pbs.org/newshour/bb/middle_east/jan-june98/iraq_2-25.html (accessed March 5, 2008).

35. United Nations Special Commission, "Security Council Resolutions," http://www.un.org/Depts/unscom/Chronology/chronologyframe.htm (accessed March 5, 2008).

in the Korean Demilitarized Zone (DMZ). The tree blocked a crucial line of sight between military checkpoints, and the trimming was considered routine. A contingent of North Korean soldiers soon approached the UNC group and demanded that work be stopped. When the American soldiers refused, axe-wielding North Koreans attacked the UN crew, bludgeoning to death U.S. Captain Arthur Bonifas and First Lieutenant Mark Barrett. News of the attack enraged U.S. policy makers; Secretary of State Henry Kissinger said in a private meeting with the Washington Special Action Group, "They [the North Koreans] beat two Americans to death and must pay the price."[36] Three days after the incident, the Ford administration launched Operation Paul Bunyan. In what is undoubtedly the most lethal lumberjack force ever assembled, the UN tree-trimming crew returned to the poplar tree, this time accompanied by 813 troops, three batteries of 105mm howitzers, twenty attack helicopters, twelve AH-1G Cobra gunships, and squadrons of F-4 Phantoms, F-111s, and B-52 bombers.[37] Soon after, 150 to 200 North Korean forces arrived on the scene with machine guns and took up bunkered positions on the north side of the DMZ. The tense standoff between the UNC and North Korean forces had the potential of erupting into a much bigger conflict, yet no shots were fired.

As a candidate in the 1992 presidential election, Bill Clinton repeatedly criticized George H. W. Bush's policy of repatriating Haitian refugees fleeing the brutal military junta that deposed President Jean-Bertrand Aristide in 1991. Upon taking office, however, Clinton became fearful that an open-door Haitian policy might spark a repeat of the 1980 Mariel boat lift.[38] As the Clinton administration vacillated over what to do in Haiti, the stream of Haitian refugees pouring into the United States intensified. After a series of escalating threats and sanctions failed to compel the junta to step down, Clinton, under a UN mandate, ordered a U.S.-led coalition to invade Haiti and forcibly return Aristide to power. Operation Uphold Democracy was authorized in September 1994, but while the troops were en route to the Caribbean island, the junta peacefully relinquished power and allowed Aristide's return. U.S. forces continued on to Haiti, this time in a peacekeeping capacity.

In sum, all four of these pattern-breaking cases—the 1998 UNSCOM crisis, Shaba II, the poplar tree incident, and Operation Uphold Democracy— witnessed presidential brinksmanship. Each president stood at the precipice of war, only to forgo that option at the last moment. As we found earlier, war

36. Oberdorfer, *Two Koreas*, 77.
37. Mobley, "Tree-Trimming Incident."
38. Morley and McGillion, "'Disobedient' Generals."

is usually the most salient aspect of a foreign policy crisis, but when war is averted, we should expect issue salience to peak at the policy decision stage.

A somewhat surprising pattern-breaking case is the current war in Afghanistan, begun in 2001. Figure 8 (see Afghan II) shows that slightly more television news coverage focused on the policy decision than any other juncture. This is a notable exception to our theory: because the war in Afghanistan involved a large and sustained use of military force, we should have expected the American public to focus most intently on the implementation stage. So why did the theory get it wrong in the Afghanistan case? A closer examination reveals three reasons for the high level of attention at the policy decision stage. First, there was only a 1 percent difference in media attention from the policy decision to implementation stage. So while the theory did miss in its prediction, it did not miss by much. Second, the Bush administration decided to strike against Afghanistan only three days after the terrorist attacks on 9/11.[39] As a result, much of the media coverage at the policy decision stage was residual coverage of the 9/11 tragedy.

A final reason is that the war in Afghanistan offered far fewer striking visuals for the media to cover than other conflicts. For the United States, the conflict in Afghanistan was less a conventional war and more a frustrating, high-stakes game of hide-and-seek with the terrorists played out in remote mountain caves. The United States dropped massive amounts of munitions, but it often looked to the American audience like the air force was pounding sand and mountains with little evidence of success or progress. In this respect, the Afghanistan conflict was very different from the 1991 and 2003 wars with Iraq, which featured memorable images of laser-guided smart bombs zeroing in on and demolishing their targets. Indeed, for Secretary of Defense Donald Rumsfeld, the lack of firm indicators of success in Afghanistan was one reason for expanding the War on Terror into Iraq.[40] In short, Afghanistan is a notable outlier for our theory, but for reasons that become clearer once we delve more deeply into the case.

Pattern-Breaking Crises: Option Generation

Two of the pattern-breaking crises featured peak attention during the option generation stage. The first case involved the Carter administration's response to the Soviet invasion of Afghanistan in late 1979. President Carter's initial reaction

---

39. Woodward, *Bush at War*.
40. Woodward, *Plan of Attack*; Woodward, *Bush at War*; Woodward, *State of Denial*.

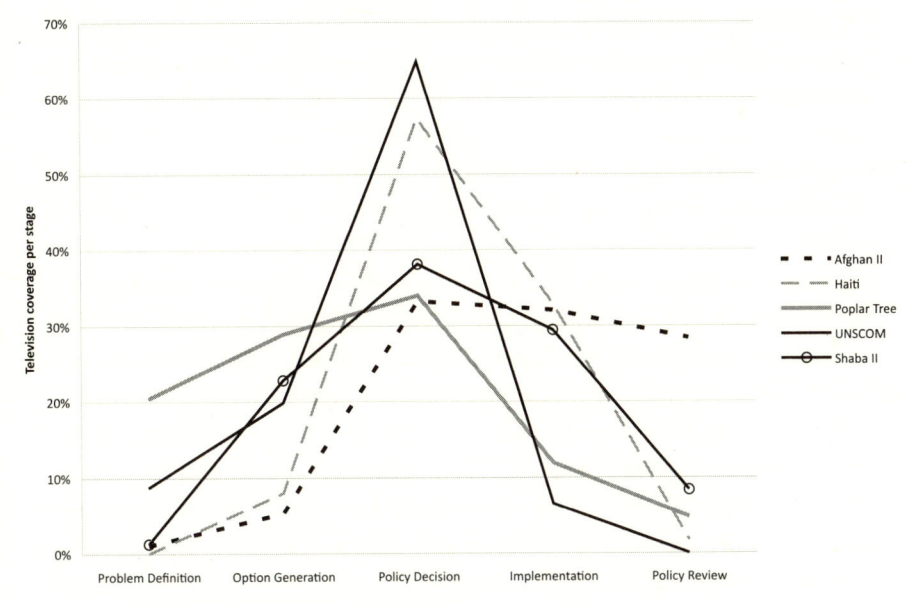

Fig. 8 Pattern-breaking crises, policy decision

to the invasion was surprisingly forceful. In his 1980 State of the Union address, Carter stated that the "Soviet invasion of Afghanistan could pose the most serious threat to peace since the Second World War." The speech articulated what came to be known as the Carter Doctrine: any attempt by foreign powers to gain control of the Persian Gulf would be met with a U.S. military response. There is no evidence that the Carter administration seriously considered using military action in Afghanistan, but strong rhetoric from the White House made the possibility seem real to the American public. Eventually, the Carter administration instituted a laundry list of sanctions against the Soviet Union, covertly funneled U.S. weapons to the mujahedeen, and boycotted the 1980 Moscow Olympic Games. These policy decisions, although certainly significant, did not nearly rise to the magnitude and gravity of decisions for war. As a result, public attention peaked during the option generation stage of the Afghanistan crisis (see Afghan I in figure 9).

The second case with peak attention at option generation involved a standoff between the United States and North Korea during Bill Clinton's first term. By the mid-1980s, the North Koreans had indicated their intention to develop weapons-grade plutonium at the Yongbyon nuclear facility.[41] After

---

41. Gillian Murdoch, "Timeline: North Korea's Nuclear Plant," Reuters, May 1, 2009, http://www.reuters.com/article/reutersEdge/idUSTRE5403TT20090501 (accessed April 14, 2008).

North Korea refused a series of International Atomic Energy Agency (IAEA) inspections, the George H. W. Bush administration negotiated an agreement with Kim Il-sung's government that would open North Korea's weapons program to inspection in return for the removal of U.S. nuclear weapons from South Korea. IAEA officials soon revealed that North Korea had a more vigorous and advanced weapons program than initially expected. Tensions increased further when, in 1993, North Korea announced that it would pull out of the Nuclear Non-Proliferation Treaty (NPT). News that the most secretive and paranoid nation in the world had developed a nuclear weapon sparked widespread concern in the United States. President Clinton weighed his options, even considering a military strike against the Yongbyon nuclear complex.[42] Ultimately, military action was averted and the United States and North Korea entered into an "Agreed Framework" on October 21, 1994. Under the terms of the agreement, the U.S would provide North Korea with light-water nuclear reactors in exchange for North Korea's suspension of plutonium enrichment and full compliance with IAEA inspectors.

In both the Soviet invasion of Afghanistan and North Korean cases, there was a large and tense buildup to a somewhat anticlimactic decision. In some ways, both cases are similar to the concern one feels when waiting to hear from the doctor about the results of a biopsy. The anticipation of what the doctor *might* find is all-consuming, worst-case scenarios are given more attention than they deserve, and it becomes difficult to focus on anything else. When the doctor finally reveals that the biopsy is benign, the patient may feel a sense of relief that is strangely short-lived. He drives away from the doctor's office and resumes his normal routine as if nothing happened, forgetting all of the awful scenarios that consumed his thoughts just hours earlier. In the Afghanistan and North Korean cases, the worst-case scenario was pretty awful—the escalation into nuclear war. So when the policy decisions were made and it appeared that the United States was not going to (nuclear) war after all, there may have been a quick sigh of collective relief and an even quicker shift of attention to the next crisis.

Pattern-Breaking Crises: Policy Review

The 1975 civil war in Angola is an outlier in that peak attention occurred during the policy review stage (figure 10). Soon after gaining independence from

---

42. Banville, "North Korea's Nuclear Program."

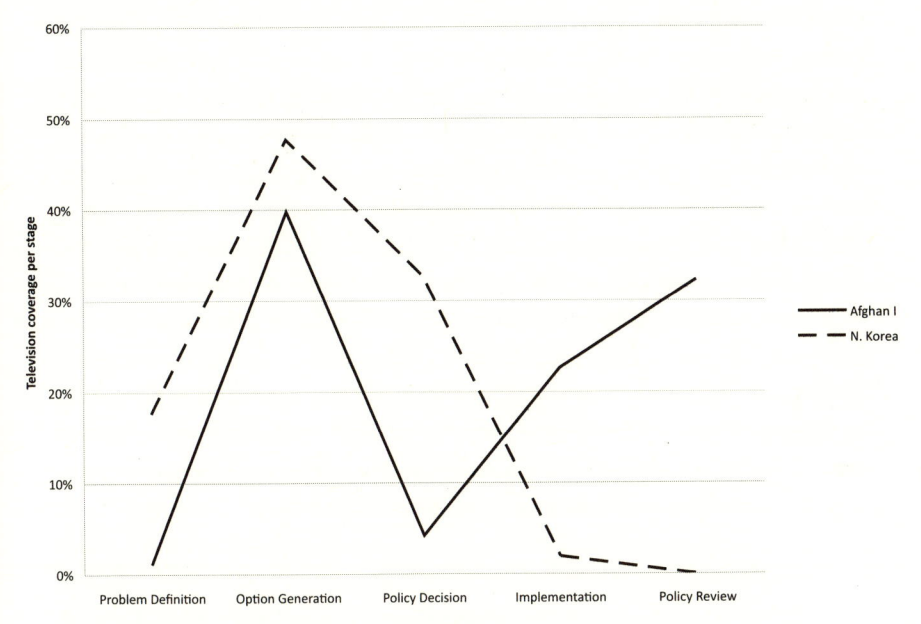

Fig. 9 Pattern-breaking crises, option generation

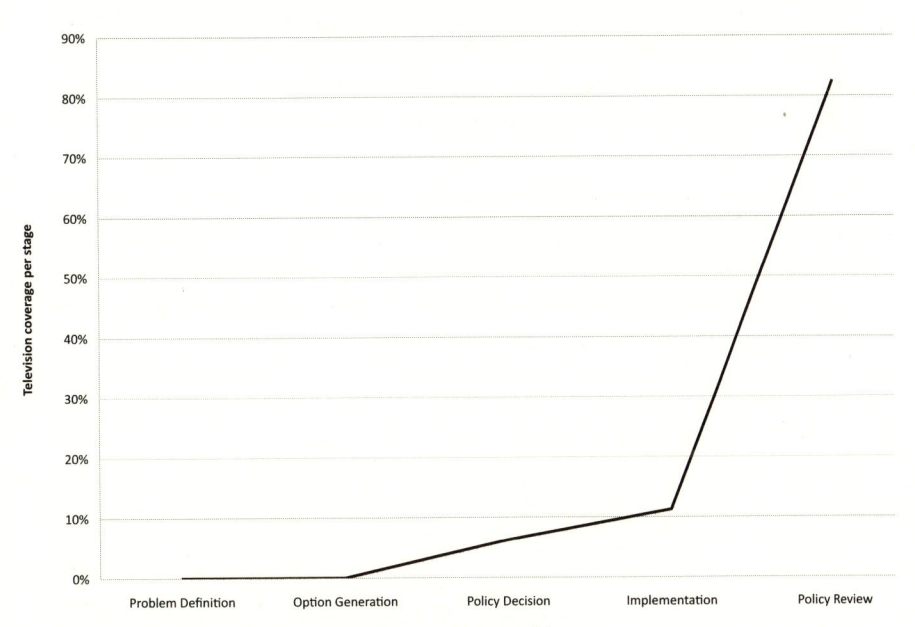

Fig. 10 Pattern-breaking crises, policy review (Angola)

Portugal, the communist political party Popular Movement for the Liberation of Angola (MPLA) and the anticommunist rebel groups National Union for the Total Independence of Angola (UNITA) and National Front for the Liberation of Angola (FNLA) took up arms in a power struggle for control of the country. During the crisis, the media characterized events in Angola as an internal matter that, while of interest to the United States, featured no direct American involvement. Indeed, the Clark Amendment formally barred the United States from providing assistance to belligerents in Angola. Only after the fact was it revealed that the CIA had defied the Clark Amendment and was providing covert aid to UNITA and FNLA. This fait accompli attracted significant media coverage and generated a notable spike in public attentiveness. However, this rise in issue salience coincided with the Ford administration's review and evaluation of its Angola policy. Far from connoting a previously unrecognized fascination on the part of the public with the details of policy evaluation, this attention was focused retrospectively on the policy decision (i.e., the decision months earlier to support covert activities in Angola).

Summary

This chapter offered an empirical test of the proposition that public attention to foreign policy crises and noncrises fluctuates in ways that we can predict. The evidence largely confirms this expectation. In noncrisis foreign policies, issue salience tends to peak as a president announces his policy decision; in crisis foreign policies, the public tends to be most attentive to the implementation of policy. By looking at the individual cases, we are able to deepen still our understanding of why and how public attention ebbs and flows across the five stages of decision making. This evidence offers a way to predict *when* presidents are likely to be more or less sensitive to public preferences. To determine whether presidents actually respond to public opinion requires a deeper look into policy making, which is where we now turn.

4

THE PERSIAN GULF CRISIS
Problem Definition and Option Generation

On August 2, 1990, Iraq invaded the small, oil-rich country of Kuwait and quickly began to amass troops along the Saudi Arabian border. The United States immediately condemned the invasion and froze all Iraqi and Kuwaiti assets. On August 6, the UN authorized economic sanctions and an embargo against Iraq. Two days later, a U.S.-led coalition of states launched Operation Desert Shield to protect Saudi Arabia from Iraqi aggression and to enforce the UN embargo. By October 30, President George H. W. Bush was convinced that sanctions would fail to coerce Iraq in an acceptable time frame and decided to resort to offensive military force to liberate Kuwait. A month later, on November 29, the UN Security Council passed Resolution 678, which authorized the use of force after January 15, 1991, if Iraq did not leave Kuwait. Despite the ultimatum and a flurry of diplomatic activity, Saddam Hussein refused to capitulate to the coalition demands. On January 16, 1991, the coalition began a devastating air war against Iraq. After four weeks of the air campaign, the coalition launched a ground war on February 24. Four days later, and precisely one hundred hours after the start of the ground war, a ceasefire was signed and Kuwait was liberated.

The 1990–91 Persian Gulf conflict provides an empirical test for our conditional theory of presidential responsiveness in foreign policy crises. This chapter examines the first two stages of the crisis—problem definition and option generation. Chapter 5 then discusses the policy decision, implementation, and policy review stages that followed. Our conditional theory of the policy-opinion link contends that early stages of crises are usually marked by presidential leadership of public opinion. Such was the case in the Persian Gulf crisis. The first Bush administration immediately perceived the Iraqi invasion of Kuwait as a threat to vital national interests and quickly communicated that representation to the American public. Because of effective leadership, the political context became constrained (i.e., unified preferences, high issue salience) in a manner that favored the White House and dampened criticism of the president. However, as Iraq refused to leave Kuwait and the stalemate in the Gulf dragged on through the fall of 1990, public interest in the case began to wane and the strong public consensus that initially surrounded the president's policy began to crumble. In this new contested political context (i.e., high, but declining, issue salience; divided public preferences), the Bush administration still attempted to lead the American people, but with much less success than it had enjoyed at the start of the crisis. (An overview of the case study methodology used in the Persian Gulf case can be found in appendix B.)

Problem Definition

Agenda Setting

U.S. policy toward Iraq prior to the Kuwait invasion in the summer of 1990 is best described as one of uncomfortable engagement.[1] Since the late 1970s, the United States had viewed secular Iraq as an important counterbalance to a fundamentalist Iran and had provided military and economic support to Saddam Hussein in his long-running war against Tehran. After the Iran-Iraq war ended in 1988, the United States maintained its support for Hussein's regime through agricultural credits in the hopes that engagement would moderate Iraqi behavior and continue to offer the United States a reliable ally in the Persian Gulf.

In early 1990, however, Saddam Hussein's rhetoric toward neighboring countries became increasingly belligerent and the United States began distancing itself from Iraq. On April 2, Hussein threatened to "burn half of Israel" if there was a repeat of Israel's 1981 air raid on Iraq's Osiraq nuclear reactor. Hussein then accused Kuwait and the United Arab Emirates of "declaring war" on Iraq by violating oil quotas set by the Organization of the Petroleum Exporting Countries (OPEC); he estimated that this had cost his country $89 billion in lost revenue over the past decade. Hussein also charged Kuwait with slant drilling into Iraqi territory to steal oil and demanded a $10 billion grant to cover the cost of the Iran-Iraq war. Kuwait's unwillingness to comply with any of these demands enraged the dictator.

---

1. Much of the following discussion draws on Freedman and Karsh, *Gulf Conflict*; Woodward, *Commanders*.

The tense situation in the Persian Gulf came to a head in late July as Iraqi military forces amassed along the Kuwaiti border. The Bush administration initially believed that the Iraqi troop movement was a bluff designed to intimidate Kuwait into acquiescence.[2] Hussein, however, was not bluffing. The invasion was massive, quick, and brutal; within hours Iraq had gained control of Kuwait, and it installed a puppet regime the next day. Even more disconcerting was that Iraqi forces were now amassed along the Saudi Arabian border and appeared ready to invade that country as well.

Many—perhaps most—crises suddenly explode onto the presidential agenda because of some unanticipated event. Such was the case with the Persian Gulf. Intelligence failures regarding the real and immediate intent of Iraqi troop movements meant that the Bush administration was caught off guard by Iraqi aggression. News of the invasion sent the White House into crisis mode as the principal decision makers in the administration scrambled to formulate the U.S. response.[3]

At the risk of stating the obvious, public opinion had no influence in setting the presidential agenda during the Persian Gulf crisis. Americans had shown little interest in Iraqi or Kuwaiti politics before the invasion, and the decision-making context could best be described as insulated (i.e., low issue salience, divided public preferences). In that political context before the invasion, the Bush administration had responded to an increasingly belligerent Iraq by sending conflicting signals about U.S. intentions. This was most vividly illustrated by a July 25, 1990, meeting between U.S. ambassador April Glaspie and Saddam Hussein. After being lectured by Hussein about the injustice that Iraq had suffered at the hands of the Kuwaitis and the Israelis—and being warned not to interfere in Iraq's affairs—Glaspie told Hussein, "I have direct instructions from the president to seek better relations with Iraq."[4] It is entirely possible that Hussein took Glaspie's comments to mean that the United States was giving a green light to an Iraqi invasion of Kuwait—a misunderstanding of tragic proportions. Without delving too deeply into the counterfactual and the meaning of "better relations," it stands to reason that had the American public and politicians been more attentive to Persian Gulf politics in the months before the invasion, U.S. policy might have been very different in the preinvasion stage.

---

2. One of the few U.S. intelligence experts to believe an Iraqi attack was imminent was Defense Intelligence Agency analyst Walter Lang. Lang's report, however, was given little attention by the decision makers at the Pentagon, the CIA, or the Bush administration. See Woodward, *Commanders*.
3. Ibid.
4. *New York Times*, "Excerpts from Iraqi Document."

While the Iraqi invasion immediately dominated the Washington agenda, it was not a foregone conclusion that it would also occupy a major place on the public agenda. Given most Americans' lack of familiarity with the region, had the Bush administration chosen to issue a muted response to the invasion, it is likely that the public would have paid little heed to events in the Gulf as well. But as we will see, the Bush administration viewed the invasion as a threat to national interests, thereby focusing Americans' attention directly and clearly on the Middle East.

Problem Representation

Our theory of the policy-opinion link contends that public opinion has little influence over the representation of crisis problems. Because crises involve threats to the core values of the state and entail a high likelihood of the use of military force, strategic factors are expected to dominate policy making at this stage. It is also expected that presidents will be capable of communicating to the public which international events are crises that warrant attention. And because the American public typically looks to the White House for guidance in times of crisis, presidents can often lead public opinion in the early stages. As will be demonstrated in this section and the next, the problem representation stage of the Persian Gulf crisis confirms all of these expectations.

As news of the Iraqi offensive reached the White House, the Bush administration faced the task of representing how the invasion affected U.S. interests. The administration formulated its policy objectives in two National Security Council (NSC) meetings held on August 2 and 3, 1990. There is little evidence that public opinion played any role in the policy making at this stage. Rather, declassified transcripts of NSC meetings, decision makers' memoirs, and secondary source interviews all show that strategic considerations dominated these deliberations and shaped the administration's representation of the problem.

After being informed of Iraq's invasion of Kuwait on August 2, the NSC held a meeting that provided participants a chance to air alternative perspectives of the Iraqi invasion. A minority view, one suggested by Treasury Secretary Nicholas Brady, was that the Iraqi invasion was an "Arab problem" to which the United States could easily adapt.[5] Others outside the administration also questioned how vital the situation actually was to the United States.[6]

---

5. Woodward, *Commanders*; Baker and DeFrank, *Politics of Diplomacy*.
6. Friedman, "U.S. Gulf Policy"; Layne, "Not in the National Interest"; Bandow, "Iraq's Oil Stranglehold."

For instance, Iraq's annexation of Kuwait meant that Baghdad controlled 20 percent of the world's proven oil reserves; a successful conquest of Saudi Arabia would increase that share to 40 percent. Although this would be a significant amount by any standard, it is important to distinguish between reserves and production. While Iraq could have gained 40 percent of the world's proven oil *reserves* via a conquest of Saudi Arabia, that share would account for only 15.7 percent of the global *production* of oil.[7] Critics charged that, even with a greater market share, Iraq would still be limited in its ability to control OPEC prices due to a global shift in production and an overall decline in oil consumption throughout the developed world.[8] Furthermore, with a world oil glut and large stocks of reserves providing a temporary price cushion, the United States could weather any short-term disturbance in oil prices. Yet President Bush quickly slammed the door on Brady's "Arab problem" representation: "Let's be clear about one thing: we are not here to talk about adapting. We are not going to plan how to live with this."[9] Bush's statement effectively ruled out the option of doing nothing in the Gulf, thereby ruling in a host of other economic and military options.

The discussion then turned to Iraq's immediate threat to Saudi Arabia. Intelligence showed that Iraqi troops had amassed along Kuwait's southern border and appeared poised for an invasion of Saudi Arabia. Chairman of the Joint Chiefs of Staff Colin Powell suggested that the United States "draw a line in the sand with Saudi Arabia" and spelled out the various U.S. interests involved in protecting the kingdom.[10] Iraq's control of Kuwait would cause some short-term disruptions in the oil market, but these could be offset by the Saudis' ability to increase oil production to stabilize prices. If, however, Hussein captured Saudi Arabia, he would undoubtedly dominate OPEC and the world oil market. The likely result would be a worldwide recession. President Bush agreed with Powell's assessment and stated, "We're committed to Saudi Arabia."[11] The meeting, however, ended on a rather indecisive note. That the United States would defend Saudi Arabia was clear, but the question of whether to attempt a reversal of the invasion had yet to be decided.[12]

At the start of the NSC meeting the next day, President Bush and his most

7. Bandow, "Iraq's Oil Stranglehold."
8. Freedman and Karsh, *Gulf Conflict*; Layne, "Not in the National Interest"; Bandow, "Iraq's Oil Stranglehold."
9. Baker and DeFrank, *Politics of Diplomacy,* 159.
10. Freedman and Karsh, *Gulf Conflict,* 74; Woodward, *Commanders,* 229.
11. Powell and Persico, *My American Journey,* 464.
12. Ibid.; Woodward, *Commanders.*

trusted confidant, National Security Advisor Brent Scowcroft, clearly established the liberation of Kuwait as a goal of U.S. policy.[13] Bush began the NSC meeting by stating, "We need to weigh the implications of taking this [the Iraqi invasion] on directly. The status quo is intolerable." Scowcroft then elaborated on the president's position: "It would be useful to take a minute to look at our objectives. I appreciate the community's opinion and remarks. I detected a note in the end [of the August 2 NSC meeting] that we may have to acquiesce to an accommodation of the situation. My personal judgment is that the stakes in this for the United States are such that to accommodate Iraq should not be a policy option. There is too much at stake."[14] In his memoirs, Scowcroft was less magnanimous about the diversity of opinion at the August 2 meeting and recalled his indignation that the Iraqi occupation of Kuwait could be represented as anything other than a grave threat to vital U.S. interests: "I was frankly appalled at the undertone of the discussion [on August 2], which suggested resignation to the invasion and even adaptation to a *fait accompli*. There was a huge gap between those who saw what was happening as the major crisis of our time and those who treated it as the crisis *du jour*."[15]

Bush's and Scowcroft's statements at the August 3 NSC meeting thus defined the problem for the administration and set as the twin objectives of U.S. policy (a) the protection of Saudi Arabia and (b) the liberation of Kuwait. The remaining questions—how to accomplish these goals and whether to oust Hussein from power—would not be decided for several weeks.

As an aside, readers familiar with the literature on the Persian Gulf crisis will recognize that my characterization of President Bush as firmly committed to the liberation of Kuwait from the start of the conflict stands at odds with alternative accounts. For instance, it is well documented that Colin Powell expressed shock when, on August 5, Bush made his famous "this will not stand" statement, committing the United States to the liberation of Kuwait. At that time, Powell believed that nothing had been decided and felt blindsided to hear of Bush's plans in the news.[16] Powell, in his memoirs, suggested that Bush's meeting with British prime minister Margaret Thatcher in Aspen, Colorado, prompted his change of heart—or, as Jean Edward Smith put it, a "backbone transplant."[17] However, from the minutes of the NSC meetings it seems clear

---

13. Throughout the Persian Gulf conflict, Brent Scowcroft was President Bush's closest and most trusted advisor. In very few instances did the president and his national security advisor disagree over policy direction.
14. Charles, "Minutes from NSC Meeting."
15. Bush and Scowcroft, *World Transformed*, 317.
16. Woodward, *Commanders*, 260–61.
17. Powell and Persico, *My American Journey*, 466–67; J. Smith, *George Bush's War*, 68.

that, from the beginning, Bush and Scowcroft viewed the invasion as "unacceptable" and intended to reverse it. As Richard Haass later remarked about the NSC meetings, "People had their day in court and the military was often asked their views. . . . The policy ought not to have come as a surprise to anyone."[18] Moreover, Haass disputed Powell's and others' contention that Thatcher had to steel a wavering Bush: "The idea that somehow she [Thatcher] gave him an infusion of backbone. . . . I see nothing that supports that thesis."[19] In short, my reading of the NSC documents and alternative accounts of early decision making strongly suggests that Bush was resolutely committed to the liberation of Kuwait from the start of the crisis.

The administration based its representation of the problem on the belief, held by both Bush and Scowcroft, that a return to the status quo in the Persian Gulf was in the national interest of the United States. Scowcroft voiced the case for reversing the invasion at the August 3 NSC meeting: "They [Iraq] would dominate OPEC politics, Palestinian politics and the PLO, and would lead the Arab world to the detriment of the United States." The director of the Office of Management and Budget (OMB), Richard Darman, concurred, saying, "Even without [Saudi Arabia] he [Saddam Hussein] would be in control of world oil prices with Kuwait and Iraq."[20]

There would be several threats to U.S. interests if Iraq were allowed to occupy Kuwait and consolidate its gains. Estimates from the Department of Energy and the Federal Reserve stated that the short-term loss of Iraqi and Kuwaiti oil would increase oil prices to thirty eight dollars a barrel or higher, which would balloon the federal deficit to more than three hundred billion dollars and push the country into recession.[21] Long-term estimates were even more pessimistic. The increased market share that Iraq gained from the seizure of Kuwaiti oil would give it substantially greater power over OPEC politics. Iraq's demonstrated willingness to use force as a means of policy would also likely coerce the oil-producing countries in the Middle East into complying with Hussein's stated preference for lower production quotas and higher prices. The ability to bully OPEC would only increase over time as Hussein translated his economic gains into greater military power to enforce the type of cartel discipline not seen since the early 1970s. As Defense Secretary Richard Cheney said at the August 2 NSC meeting, "[Saddam Hussein] has clearly done what he has to dominate OPEC, the Gulf, and the Arab World. He is

18. Mervin, *George Bush*, 184–85.
19. Ibid., 181.
20. Charles, "Minutes from NSC Meeting."
21. Ibid.

forty kilometers from Saudi Arabia and its oil production is only a couple of hundred kilometers away. If he doesn't take it physically, with his new wealth he will still have an impact and will be able to acquire new weapons. The problem will get worse not better."[22] A memo prepared by the Treasury Department for the president concurred with Cheney's assessment: "The longer-term economic (and other) costs of failing to straighten out the Iraqi situation would be even higher than the short-term costs noted above—hence the 'vital interest.' The practical question is not whether to seek to reduce the long-term risk. That must be done."[23]

The administration was convinced that the situation in the Persian Gulf would be exponentially worse if Hussein invaded Saudi Arabia and captured 40 percent of the world's oil. Even if the United States drew a line in the sand with Saudi Arabia and allowed Iraq to retain control of Kuwait, American forces could not remain in the kingdom forever; at some point, the United States would have to leave and the Saudis would be exposed. A future Iraqi invasion of Saudi Arabia would be even more troublesome for the United States, as Iraq would be stronger militarily by that point and the United States would have to find an alternative country from which to base its military operations against "Greater Iraq." The Iraqi aggression also threatened President Bush's concept of a "new world order." Acquiescing to an old-fashioned land grab would send the wrong message during an era that the Bush administration hoped would be characterized by a global movement toward democracy and market economies.

In sum, the Bush administration arrived at a representation of the problem in the Persian Gulf that was based on a strategic conception of the national interest. As such, considerations of what the American public might think played little role in the decision making.

Leading the American Public

Notably, at the outset of the crisis, the American public did not seem to be itching for a strong U.S. response to the Iraqi invasion. As mentioned earlier, the political context was insulated prior to the invasion, as the American public had little interest in or knowledge of either Iraq or Kuwait. Even during the two days that the Bush administration was formulating its policy objectives, the public paid only a moderate amount of attention to the crisis. Although

22. Bush and Scowcroft, *World Transformed*, 322.
23. U.S. Treasury Department to the president, memorandum, n.d., Bush Presidential Records, John Sununu Files, Persian Gulf War 1991, OA/ID CF00472 (6 of 11).

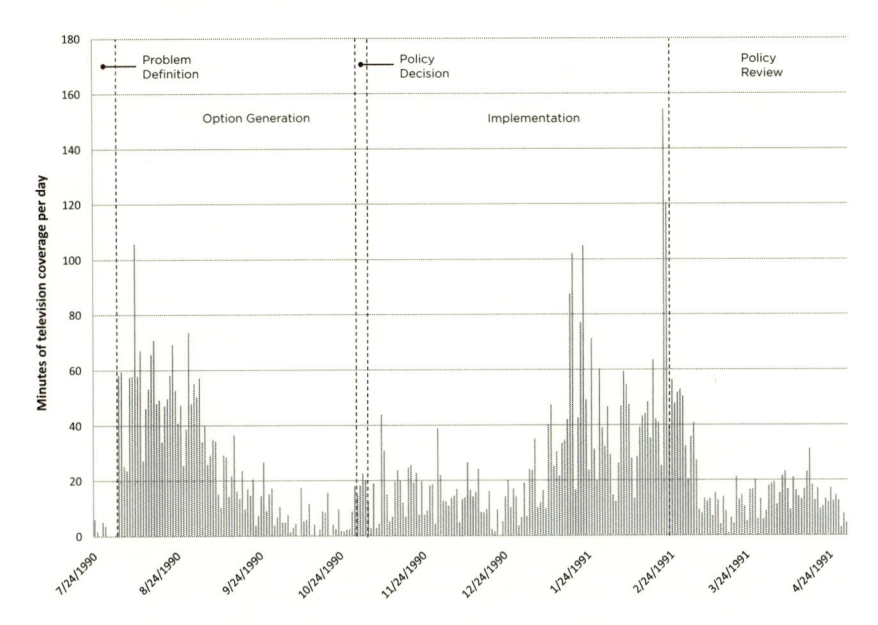

Fig. 11 Television coverage of the 1990–91 Persian Gulf conflict

television news heavily covered the invasion from the start (figure 11), a Gallup poll conducted on August 3–5 found that only 18 percent of the American public was closely monitoring the Iraqi invasion.[24] Further, the public's unfamiliarity with the politics of the region meant that most Americans were highly dependent on elite cues to help make sense of the situation. The public's weakly formed preference and moderate attention to policy making meant that the political context remained insulated throughout the first few days of the crisis. This context provided little motivation for the Bush administration to attempt to divine and respond to the inchoate preferences of the public. As John Zaller put it, "One possible explanation for Bush's actions can be quickly dismissed: He was not responding to any overt pressure from public opinion or the media for a tougher stand."[25]

24. Survey by the Gallup Organization, August 3–5, 1990, from LexisNexis, Roper Center for Public Opinion Research, University of Connecticut (accessed April 12, 2004). "How closely have you followed news about the situation involving the invasion of Kuwait by Iraq? Would you say you have followed it very closely, fairly closely, not too closely, or not at all closely?"

25. Zaller, "Strategic Politicians," 252. However, Zaller does suggest that implicit political pressures may have led President Bush to escalate the crisis with Iraq. Several large-N studies have demonstrated that the United States is more war prone during times of economic downturn—precisely what it was experiencing in 1990–91. Because Zaller points out that there would probably be no "smoking gun"

The Bush administration, having represented the Iraqi invasion and occupation of Kuwait as a threat to U.S. national interests, now faced the task of communicating that to the American public. President Bush presented the administration's case in several public statements from August 2 to August 8. These early comments on the Iraqi invasion had three important effects. First, the statements publicly communicated the administration's policy goals and committed the United States to the liberation of Kuwait.[26] On August 5, Bush issued his strongest public statement on the Iraq situation. Responding to questions from reporters on the White House lawn, an angry Bush promised, "This will not stand. This will not stand, this aggression against Kuwait!" The outburst surprised many political observers and seemed to contradict the president's earlier public statement that "we are not discussing intervention." The statement also added a domestic political component by providing a clear benchmark for the public to evaluate policy success or failure.[27]

The second important effect of the president's early statements was that they focused public attention directly on the Persian Gulf. Had the White House issued a muted response to the Iraqi invasion, it is likely that both the public and media would have soon turned their attention elsewhere. However, Bush's strong comments signaled that the United States viewed the Iraqi invasion of Kuwait as a crisis that threatened vital national interests, which then, of course, implied the possibility of U.S. military involvement. As a result, the conflict in the Persian Gulf shot to the top of the public agenda: over 445 minutes of network television news focused on the crisis during the week after the invasion (figure 11), and the percentage of Americans paying close or very close attention to the crisis rose from 57 percent (August 4) to 72 percent (August 8).[28]

A final outcome of President Bush's public statements was that they helped frame the issue for the American public.[29] Frames act as "mini-stories" that

---

evidence (e.g., internal deliberations, statements to advisors) that President Bush's stance on Iraq was politically motivated, he employs the statistical studies to suggest the possibility. For studies on the political use of force, see James and Oneal, "Domestic and International Politics"; Brace and Hinckley, *Follow the Leader*; and Ostrom and Job, "Political Use of Force."

26. For literature on "audience costs," see Fearon, "Domestic Political Audiences," and A. Smith, "International Crises."

27. Zaller, "Strategic Politicians."

28. Surveys by the Gallup Organization, August 4 and 8, 1990, from LexisNexis, Roper Center for Public Opinion Research, University of Connecticut (accessed April 12, 2004). "How closely have you followed news about the situation involving the invasion of Kuwait by Iraq? Would you say you have followed it very closely, fairly closely, not too closely, or not at all closely?"

29. For literature on framing, see Boettcher and Cobb, "Echoes of Vietnam?"; Iyengar and Simon, "News Coverage"; Iyengar, *Is Anyone Responsible?*; Entman, *Projections of Power*; Kahneman and Tversky, "Choices, Values, and Frames"; Chong and Druckman, "Framing Theory"; Druckman, "Political Preference Formation"; and Neuman, Just, and Crigler, *Common Knowledge News*.

help an audience make sense of a problem by telling them how they should think about an issue and how the problem can be solved.[30] In politics, the side that controls the framing of an issue usually wins.[31] Framing efforts are particularly effective when the audience has little prior familiarity with an issue,[32] when only one frame is presented to the audience,[33] and/or when a frame is presented in easy-to-understand and familiar terms.[34]

The Bush administration enjoyed several advantages in framing the Iraqi invasion for the American public, thus allowing the president to lead mass opinion. Most Americans entered the crisis with little knowledge of Iraq or Kuwait, which gave the White House a virtual blank slate from which to frame the situation. In addition, there were almost no alternative frames to compete with the ones presented by the White House. Congress was in recess, so there were few Democrats around Washington who might have otherwise offered an alternative perspective. The congressional Democrats who did appear in the media either were unwilling to voice their dissent over the president's early handling of the situation or, in fact, agreed with the president's policy.[35] In short, the situation was ripe for presidential leadership of public opinion.

The administration presented the public with several frames to justify a strong U.S. response. The two most important were the *national interest* frame and the *Hussein-as-Hitler* frame, both of which were employed throughout the crisis. The national interest frame closely mirrored the internal deliberations of the Bush administration and stressed that Iraq's invasion of Kuwait, and potential invasion of Saudi Arabia, compromised vital U.S. interests. The Hussein-as-Hitler frame portrayed Saddam Hussein as Adolf Hitler incarnate and likened the Iraqi invasion of Kuwait to the German blitzkrieg of Europe in the late 1930s and early 1940s.[36]

Popular interpretations of the Persian Gulf crisis suggest that the White

---

30. Bennett, "Rethinking Political Perception," 197; Zaller, *Nature and Origins*; Gamson and Modigliani, "Changing Culture."
31. Bennett, "Rethinking Political Perception," 197.
32. Druckman, "Implications of Framing Effects"; Haider-Markel and Joslyn, "Gun Policy."
33. Zaller, *Nature and Origins*; Zaller, "Elite Leadership"; Brody, "Crisis, War, and Public Opinion."
34. Gamson and Modigliani, "Changing Culture"; Druckman, "Implications of Framing Effects"; Ansolabehere, Behr, and Iyengar, *Media Game*; Baum, *Soft News Goes to War*.
35. Brody, "Crisis, War, and Public Opinion."
36. In an August 8 televised address to the nation, Bush announced the deployment of U.S. troops for Operation Desert Shield. In justifying the troop commitment, he made several comparisons between Hussein and Hitler. Calling the Iraqi invasion a "blitzkrieg," Bush went on to state that "appeasement does not work. As was the case in the 1930's, we see in Saddam Hussein an aggressive dictator threatening his neighbors."

House relied primarily on the Hussein-as-Hitler frame to defend U.S. intervention in the Gulf.[37] It is believed that the historical analogy was very influential since it cast the conflict in easy-to-understand terms and vividly illustrated the potential price of inaction. However, an examination of the president's public statements and the newspaper accounts from the first week of the crisis shows that stressing the national interest, not demonizing Hussein, was the centerpiece of the White House's rhetorical strategy. Of all the public comments President Bush made about Iraq from August 2 to August 10—a critical period in which the public was forming its opinions on the situation in the Persian Gulf—less than 1 percent featured the Hussein-as-Hitler frame. During this same period, only 10 percent of the articles in the *New York Times* made use of the analogy. Instead, national interest frames dominated the statements from the White House (59 percent) and the *Times* coverage (50 percent).[38] For instance, stressing the importance of national interests, President Bush stated on August 2, "Needless to say, we view the situation with the utmost gravity. We remain committed to take whatever steps are necessary to defend our longstanding, vital interests in the Gulf. . . . You've heard me say over and over again, however, that we are dependent for close to 50 percent of our energy requirements on the Middle East." He delivered a similar message on August 3: "We view it [the Iraqi invasion] as a matter of grave concern to this country, and internationally as well. . . . The status quo is unacceptable, and further expansion would be even more unacceptable. . . . The integrity of Saudi Arabia, its freedom, are very, very important to the United States. . . . The economic aspects of this are well-known to the American people. And long-run economic effects on the free world could be devastating, and that's one of the reasons I'm as concerned as I am." And on August 8, the president reiterated, "Let me be clear: The sovereign independence of Saudi Arabia is of vital interest to the United States."[39] A common

---

37. Mueller, "American Public Opinion"; Mueller, *Policy and Opinion*; Eastland, *Energy in the Executive*; Mathews, "Road to War"; Woodward, *Commanders*; Mervin, *George Bush*; Freedman and Karsh, *Gulf Conflict*; Dorman and Livingston, "News and Historical Content."

38. These figures are arrived at by using content analysis of the presidential papers (made available by the American Presidency Project at http://www.presidency.ucsb.edu/ws/) and the *New York Times*. For both sources, each individual statement (usually a discrete sentence) was coded via an in-depth rubric. The statements were then broken down into those pertaining to the national interest and those that alluded to Iraq or analogized Iraq to Hitler's Germany. See Knecht and Cass, "Framing Saddam."

39. Quotes taken from the presidential papers: "Remarks and an Exchange with Reporters on the Iraqi Invasion of Kuwait," August 2, 1990, http://www.presidency.ucsb.edu/ws/?pid=18726; "Remarks and an Exchange with Reporters on the Iraqi Invasion of Kuwait," August 3, 1990, http://www.presidency.ucsb.edu/ws/?pid=18738; "Address to the Nation Announcing the Deployment of United States Armed Forces to Saudi Arabia," August 8, 1990, http://www.presidency.ucsb.edu/ws/?pid=18750 (all accessed May 11, 2010).

critique of President Bush is that he personalized the crisis by focusing on Saddam Hussein and did not communicate why liberating Kuwait was in the national interest. The evidence, however, suggests the contrary.

Still, an argument can be made that even though the national interest received more mention, the Hussein-as-Hitler frame was more sensational and therefore more influential and salient to the public. To evaluate this possibility, we need to review the public opinion data on which frame—national interest or Hussein-as-Hitler—resonated more with the American public. Most of the public accepted the Bush administration's position that the Iraqi invasion posed a serious threat to U.S. interests. A *Time*/CNN poll conducted on August 23 asked whether various policy goals were "good reasons" for U.S. involvement in the Persian Gulf crisis. An overwhelming majority of the public believed that U.S. intervention in the crisis was in the national interest: 78 percent agreed that the United States should be involved in the Persian Gulf to deter further aggression by Iraq; 78 percent believed that U.S. involvement was necessary to protect the oil supply in the Middle East; and 73 percent believed that the United States should be involved to force Iraq to remove its troops from Kuwait.[40] The public, it seems, readily followed the president's lead in viewing the occupation of Kuwait as a threat to national interests.

In the early stages of the crisis, a majority of the public also felt that the analogy between Saddam Hussein and Adolf Hitler was apt. A *New York Times* survey conducted on August 9–10 found that 60 percent of the public "accepted Mr. Bush's comparison of Saddam Hussein of Iraq to Hitler."[41] Although 60 percent may have agreed with the analogy, it is also instructive to note that this percentage was significantly lower than the number of Americans who believed that the United States should intervene in the Gulf to protect oil supplies (78 percent). While much has been made of Bush's attempt to personalize the crisis and demonize Hussein, and as compelling as the Hussein-as-Hitler analogy may have been, it appears that the public was more persuaded by the national interest frame.

It is important to understand that the preceding discussion does not suggest that the Hussein-as-Hitler frame had no bearing on public opinion or played little role in the case. Indeed, demonizing Hussein resonated with many

40. Survey by *Time*/CNN, August 23, 1990, from LexisNexis, Roper Center for Public Opinion Research, University of Connecticut (accessed April 2, 2004). "Please tell me if each of the following are good reasons or poor reasons for getting involved in this (Middle East) conflict. . . . To deter further aggression by Iraq . . . to protect the oil supply in the Middle East . . . to force Iraq to remove its troops from Kuwait . . . to protect Saudi Arabia from Iraq . . . to remove Saddam Hussein from power." Percent reporting "good reason."
41. Oreskes, "In a Crisis."

Americans and, as we will see, would later complicate decision making for the administration. But it is equally important to reiterate that the public overwhelmingly agreed with the Bush administration that national interests were at stake in the crisis. It was, therefore, a combination of the national interest and the Hussein-as-Hitler frames that prompted Americans to strongly support U.S. intervention in the Gulf.

In sum, there is little indication that public opinion exerted a significant influence on presidential decision making during the problem definition stage of the Persian Gulf crisis. Instead, this stage reflects how presidents can exercise strong leadership at the beginning of a crisis. Having set the protection of Saudi Arabia and the liberation of Kuwait as the goals of U.S. policy, the Bush administration then effectively communicated its representation of the crisis to the American public. As a result, the Persian Gulf conflict became a highly salient issue and a large majority of Americans approved of Bush's handling of the situation. In the lexicon of our theoretical model, the political context had shifted from insulated (i.e., low attention, nonexistent preferences) to constrained (i.e., high attention, unified preferences). Most important, the political context was constrained *in the president's favor,* largely because of effective leadership.

Option Generation

The Bush administration's representation of the Iraqi problem established the policy objectives and, in the process, circumscribed the appropriate options for dealing with the crisis. Defining the problem as the protection of Saudi Arabia and the liberation of Kuwait meant that the United States would have to rule out some options (e.g., doing nothing) while ruling in others (e.g., use of the U.S. military in some capacity). In addition, President Bush's success in moving from an insulated to a constrained political context eventually added a domestic political component to the crisis: any viable option would have to satisfy both the strategic goals of the administration and the sensibilities of the American public.

The Bush administration was also operating in the lingering shadow of the Vietnam War. The most crucial lesson learned from Vietnam was that public support is the "essential domino" of a successful foreign policy.[42] In order to gain and maintain domestic support, President Bush's Persian Gulf policy

---

42. Klarevas, "'Essential Domino'"; Gelb, "Essential Domino."

needed to meet four conditions. First, the policy would have to achieve its stated objectives of protecting Saudi Arabia and liberating Kuwait. Bush set this benchmark for success when he told the public that the Iraqi invasion "will not stand." Second, any policy would have to achieve its goals in a relatively short period of time. The longer the crisis went unresolved, the more vocal the president's critics would become, and public support would inevitably erode. Third, a successful policy would have to achieve its declared objectives at an acceptable cost. The most salient cost for the public is the amount of U.S. casualties, followed at some distance by the financial cost of the conflict.[43] Finally, the policy would have to remain within the boundaries of what the American public considered to be morally acceptable behavior in times of crisis.

The option generation stage lasted from August 2 to October 29, during which time the administration considered four broad strategies—economic, diplomatic, military, and covert—to compel Iraq to leave Kuwait. Within each of these broad strategies was a vast menu of specific options from which President Bush could select at the policy decision stage. The following two sections provide a chronological view of some of the strategies considered by the administration to resolve the crisis. The first section describes policy making from the start of the crisis on August 2, 1990, to the announcement of Operation Desert Shield on August 8, 1990; the next section looks at the remainder of the option generation stage up to October 29, 1990. Four conclusions are drawn from this analysis: (1) strategic factors played a greater role in the president's choices than did public opinion; (2) the current political context had only a moderate influence on the options under consideration; (3) anticipations of future political contexts had a stronger influence on decision making; and (4) public opinion set a region of acceptability that bound viable options.

August 2–8, 1990

The evidence shows that in the first week of the Persian Gulf crisis, the generation of options was guided primarily by a strategic assessment of which policies were likely to work and which were unlikely to work. Much like the earlier problem definition stage, considerations of the public played only a peripheral role in the administration's deliberations, as most Americans entered the crisis with only weakly formed, or nonexistent, preferences. Moreover, polling organizations had just begun to gather data on American opinion. One of the few surveys taken before the announcement of Operation Desert Shield

---

43. Russett, *Controlling the Sword*; Gartner, "Multiple Effects of Casualties"; Larson, *Casualties and Consensus*; Mueller, *War, Presidents*; Gelpi, Feaver, and Reifler, "Success Matters."

reflects an ambivalent public. On August 3–4, an open-ended question asked, "In your opinion, what, if anything, should the United States do concerning the current situation involving Iraq and Kuwait?" Most Americans opined that they did not know what to do (36 percent); the next highest response was "do nothing" (14 percent).[44] Even if the Bush administration wished to respond to public preferences, and there was no indication that it did, there was little meaningful opinion to which to respond at this point.

Television news covered the crisis from the moment of the invasion, but it is not entirely clear how many Americans were really attentive in those first few days (figure 11). As stated earlier, the Gallup poll conducted August 3–5 found that only 18 percent of the American public was closely monitoring the situation,[45] although the salience of the Persian Gulf crisis dramatically increased when President Bush announced on August 5 that the Iraqi invasion of Kuwait "will not stand." This announcement, and the later introduction of Operation Desert Shield in a televised address on August 8, clearly focused the public's attention on the Gulf.

How should we then describe the political context in the period from the Iraqi invasion on August 2 to the announcement of Operation Desert Shield on August 8? It is clear that, prior to Bush's statements, the public truly did not know what to do in the Gulf situation. At the same time, judging solely by television coverage, issue salience was fairly high. This combination of high salience and divided preferences would usually yield a contested political context in which Democrats and Republicans would battle for control of policy. However, unlike most contested situations, there was little opposition to the president's policy because (a) he had not yet announced what that policy would be, and (b) oppositional leaders in Congress were deferential to the president in the early weeks of the conflict. In a sense, both Congress and the American people seemed to be waiting to see how the White House would respond. In this context, there was little cause for President Bush to divine and respond to public opinion. Although public opinion was discussed in passing, it never became important enough to force the administration to alter its plans.[46] Once again, strategic considerations took precedence.

The option of not responding at all to the Iraqi invasion was eliminated

---

44. Survey by the Gallup Organization, August 3–4, 1990, from LexisNexis, Roper Center for Public Opinion Research, University of Connecticut (accessed April 12, 2004).

45. Survey by the Gallup Organization, August 3–5, 1990, from LexisNexis, Roper Center for Public Opinion Research, University of Connecticut (accessed April 12, 2004). "How closely have you followed news about the situation involving the invasion of Kuwait by Iraq? Would you say you have followed it very closely, fairly closely, not too closely, or not at all closely?"

46. Sobel, *Impact of Public Opinion*, 159.

without deliberation on the first day of the crisis.[47] Upon receiving news of the invasion, President Bush immediately froze Iraqi and Kuwaiti assets, ordered warships in Diego Garcia to head to the Gulf, asked the Saudis to approve a squadron of U.S. F-15 fighters, and publicly demanded Iraq's unconditional withdrawal from Kuwait. These actions were consistent with Bush's representation of the Iraqi invasion as a threat to vital U.S. interests, and there is no evidence that Bush considered public opinion when making these choices.

On August 2, President Bush and his advisors discussed several possible responses to the Iraqi invasion. The commander in chief of the United States Central Command (CENTCOM), General Norman Schwarzkopf, briefed the president on three possible military options for dealing with the crisis.[48] First, the United States could launch an immediate retaliatory air strike against Iraqi targets. Retaliatory strikes would be limited in scope and strategically ineffective, but they could serve a useful purpose by sending a strong message of U.S. resolve to Hussein. Second, the United States could mount a more significant aerial campaign in twenty days. Sustained air strikes might coerce Hussein into leaving Kuwait, but Schwarzkopf felt that this possibility was remote. Finally, the United States could send ground forces into the region. Schwarzkopf outlined the military's only available full-scale option, Plan 90-1002, which was originally developed in the late 1970s to protect Middle Eastern allies against a Soviet or Iranian attack.[49] The plan was a long-term operation that involved sending 200,000 to 250,000 troops into the Gulf over a period of seventeen weeks.

The meeting then turned to a discussion of achieving goals through economic sanctions. Scowcroft remarked, "The most significant option economically is oil. . . . We should mount an embargo of Kuwait and Iraqi oil purchases."[50] Bush replied that he wanted Chapter VII sanctions, referring to a section in the UN charter that obliged all member nations to abide by a sanctions regime. The option of unilateral sanctions was never seriously considered because all of the major oil-consuming states would have to abide by sanctions if they were to be at all effective.

After the meeting, President Bush met with reporters for his first public statement on the Iraqi invasion. He indicated "deep concern" about Iraq's behavior but stated that he "was not contemplating" intervention at that time.

---

47. Much of the following discussion is drawn from Bush and Scowcroft, *World Transformed*, and Woodward, *Commanders*.
48. CENTCOM has the responsibility of overseeing military matters dealing with the Middle East.
49. Bush and Scowcroft, *World Transformed*; Woodward, *Commanders*.
50. Bush and Scowcroft, *World Transformed*, 316–17.

Of course, this message was not exactly true. Bush had already offered U.S. fighter aircraft to Riyadh, had sent carrier groups to the Gulf, and had just been briefed on an extensive array of military options that could be used against Iraq. Bush would later receive criticism for an apparent policy reversal when he declared that the Iraqi "invasion will not stand" on August 5, then ordered troops to the Gulf on August 8.

At the beginning of the August 3 NSC meeting, Bush and Scowcroft defined the Iraqi invasion as "unacceptable." Having set the policy objectives as the defense of Saudi Arabia and the liberation of Kuwait, the discussion again turned to options to resolve the crisis. The participants first considered diplomatic efforts. As it remained throughout the crisis, diplomacy revolved around organizing and maintaining a coalition of allies rather than directly negotiating with Iraq. The NSC staff also contemplated covert action to topple Saddam Hussein. Chairman of the Joint Chiefs of Staff Colin Powell asked, "How individualized is this aggression? If he is gone, would he have a more reasonable replacement?" Scowcroft responded that with Hussein gone, "Iraq could fall apart."[51] President Bush then ordered CIA director William Webster to begin planning a covert operation against Hussein.[52]

The option of using covert action to topple Saddam Hussein was tempting on many levels. If the United States could help orchestrate a military coup or an internal rebellion, it might bring about a quick resolution of the crisis. The consensus within the administration was that Hussein was a megalomaniac and that his recent adventurism did not have the support of either the Iraqi people or his military, which was already worn out from the years of fighting the Iran-Iraq war. Therefore, deposing him would likely result in a pullback of Iraqi forces and the restoration of the Kuwaiti government. More important, a covert operation would likely entail no direct U.S. casualties and only minimal cost. Because the Iraqi military or its citizens would bear the costs of opposing Hussein, the Bush administration could cast the entire matter as an internal dispute and would not have to worry about justifying extensive U.S. involvement to the American people.[53]

Next, the meeting turned to economic sanctions. The most effective economic option to coerce Iraq into withdrawing from Kuwait was to close the

---

51. Charles, "Minutes from NSC Meeting."
52. Woodward, *Commanders*, 237.
53. Little is known of planned or actual attempts to overthrow Saddam Hussein through covert action since national security restrictions prevent scholars from gaining a full view of CIA activity in this respect. One thing can be stated with certainty, however. President Bush never pinned his hopes on covert action. Covert action was always a long-shot policy to be backed up with other options like economic sanctions or military action.

oil pipelines into Turkey and Saudi Arabia and to organize a broad coalition of states to vote for and abide by UN sanctions. Closing off oil would undoubtedly hurt a single-export country like Iraq, but the administration was divided on the ultimate efficacy of sanctions. Secretary of Energy James Watkins indicated that "in 30–60 days, they'll [the Iraqis] try to discount the price and find a market. This is not a long-term fix."[54] In response, Bush quipped that someone would always be willing to take oil for the right price, "like my Texas friends." OMB director Richard Darman also brought up the problem of enforcing sanctions, stating, "The CIA mentioned [that] world attempts at economic sanctions before have had no success."[55]

Powell then led a brief discussion of military options in which he drew a distinction between deterring Iraq from invading Saudi Arabia and liberating Kuwait. Powell felt that Iraq could be deterred from invading Saudi Arabia simply by seeing the U.S. flag on Saudi soil. The liberation of Kuwait was another matter entirely: "Looking at this option, this is harder than Panama and Libya. This would be the NFL [National Football League], not a scrimmage."[56] Powell's NFL comment was a signal to the president that the liberation of Kuwait could be expensive, both militarily and politically.[57] Militarily, defense is generally easier than offense, and a war of liberation would mean attempting to uproot a massive Iraqi army that had time to dig in and fortify defenses. Politically, U.S. casualties would likely erode presidential approval. Bush, however, scoffed at Powell's comment, asking why—if Iraq was so formidable—it had been unable to defeat a relatively weak Iran. "I am not certain he [Saddam Hussein] is invincible," Bush stated. "They [Iraq] tried for five years [in the 1980s], and could not get across a small part of land [the area around Shatt al-Arab, along the Iraqi-Iranian border]."[58]

The exchange between Powell and Bush illustrates the differing opinions about Iraq's military strength that were held by the president and his military staff throughout the crisis. From the start, Bush was convinced that Iraqi military power was overblown and that victory could be achieved swiftly and at minimal cost. As will be shown later in this chapter, the president also believed that a short, successful war would rally public opinion behind his Gulf policy. The military, and Powell in particular, repeatedly attempted to curb the president's enthusiasm for the use of force. Although careful not to oversell

54. Charles, "Minutes from NSC Meeting."
55. Ibid.
56. Charles, "Minutes from NSC Meeting."
57. Ibid.; Powell and Persico, *My American Journey*.
58. Charles, "Minutes from NSC Meeting."

Iraq's strength, both Powell and Schwarzkopf reminded the president that Iraq had a large military with modern weaponry and that war could be costly for the United States.

The August 3 NSC meeting set the foundation for what would be a twin strategy to coerce Iraq: the defense of Saudi Arabia through a large U.S. military presence and the strangulation of Iraq's economy through multilateral economic sanctions. Again, strategic concerns drove decision making, and this policy was formulated with little consideration given to the preferences of the American public. As Scowcroft summarized the plan, "We want to deter him [Hussein] from invading and protect Saudi Arabia so when we begin to clamp down economically, Saddam has no military option."[59]

Within the NSC, there was little opposition to using the U.S. military to protect Saudi Arabia and enforce sanctions. One of the few voices of dissent came from Chief of Staff John Sununu, possibly the most politically astute participant in the NSC meetings. Sununu suggested that the administration consider avoiding the use of the U.S. military, offering that "less than military action could be required for a major response. It is an option to consider."[60] The chief of staff likely raised this point to remind the participants that policy had to be not only strategically effective but also acceptable to the American public; it was not clear at this point whether the public would approve of sending U.S. forces to the Gulf. Sununu's suggestion, however, floated like a lead balloon. The military option was commensurate with Bush and Scowcroft's definition of the crisis as a threat to vital U.S. interests, and consideration of any potential negative political ramifications of that option carried very little weight at this stage. Speaking to reporters later that day, Bush told the press that he would send troops to Saudi Arabia if King Fahd asked for U.S. support.

The next day, the president met with his top advisors at Camp David to further discuss military options, and strategic factors once again dominated. Powell led off the meeting by elaborating on Plan 90-1002, which he called "difficult but doable."[61] There were two dimensions to the plan. First, sending troops to Saudi Arabia would hopefully deter Iraq from further adventurism. Both Powell and Bush were confident that showing the U.S. flag would be enough to convince Hussein that the Americans were serious about defending Saudi Arabia. The second dimension focused on actual fighting. Powell stressed that the United States would be at a tremendous short-term disadvantage if

59. Ibid.
60. Ibid.
61. Bush and Scowcroft, *World Transformed*, 327.

Iraq were to strike against Saudi Arabia in the next few weeks, just as American forces started arriving in the kingdom. Aircraft and light infantry could be in place within two weeks, but a defensive force capable of repelling a full-scale Iraqi invasion would take upwards of four months to assemble. An adequate offensive force that could liberate Kuwait would take even longer—between eight months and a year.[62]

Schwarzkopf then offered his opinion on what the United States was up against: "Iraq is not ten feet tall, but is formidable."[63] The Iraqi strengths included a large army of close to a million men and fairly modern equipment, much of it U.S.-made. However, the Iraqi military had significant weaknesses that could be exploited. Its air force was poorly trained, its command and control was centralized and vulnerable to attack, and the Iraqis were unaccustomed to long supply lines when conducting offensive military operations.[64] The nature of Iraqi weaknesses suggested that U.S. air power should be an important component of any military strategy. However, Schwarzkopf, Powell, Scowcroft, and Cheney were all quick to point out to the president that they were uncomfortable with an "air-power-only" option and felt that, if the United States decided to accomplish its goals by force, ground troops would eventually have to be used to dislodge Iraq from Kuwait.[65]

The limits of air power would be an important and recurring theme throughout the option generation stage. Use of an air-power-only strategy can be tempting to political leaders because it is perceived as surgical and quick, and usually entails minimal U.S. casualties.[66] As such, it is also the military option strongly preferred by the American public. Indeed, the frequent use of an air-power-only strategy in recent U.S. military interventions (e.g., Bosnia, Kosovo, and the responses to terrorist bombings in Tanzania and Kenya) largely reflects a political responsiveness to the public's concerns about U.S. casualties. The military, sensing the lure that air power would have for President Bush, attempted to walk a fine line between advocating its effectiveness and reigning in the temptation to rely solely on the aerial option. Throughout the crisis, Bush leaned repeatedly toward the air-power-only strategy, only to be restrained by the military.[67]

62. Woodward, *Commanders*, 249.
63. Bush and Scowcroft, *World Transformed*, 327.
64. For literature on the domestic roots of Iraq's military weakness, see Belkin et al., "Strategic Bombing," and Biddle and Zirkle, "Technology, Civil-Military Relations."
65. Woodward, *Commanders*, 250; Bush and Scowcroft, *World Transformed*, 328.
66. Powell and Persico, *My American Journey*, 476.
67. This is not to say that Bush was untutored in military matters or that an "air-only" strategy would not have worked. By virtue of his experience at the UN and CIA, Bush had extensive knowledge of the Middle East and more than adequate knowledge of military strategy. His experience as a bomber

As the military briefers (except for Powell) left the room, the discussion turned to the political impact of sending troops to the Gulf. Cheney believed that troops should be introduced only if President Bush was prepared to use them in an offensive capacity: "You must be prepared to defend Saudi Arabia and put the [Kuwaiti] royal family back. The problem is the American people might have a short tolerance for war."[68] Cheney felt that the public might not support a war because it would cost "one hell of a lot of money." Additionally, U.S. interests in the liberation of Kuwait might not be readily apparent to the American public because most of its oil went to Japan. Further complicating matters, Kuwait was ruled by a monarchy with questionable domestic legitimacy; intervening to save a kleptocratic royal family might not play well with an American audience that had just heard Bush extol the virtues of democracy during the fall of the Berlin Wall. Bush and Scowcroft disagreed with Cheney's assessment of public opinion. Bush said, "Lots of people are calling him [Saddam Hussein] Hitler."[69] (It is interesting to note that the Hussein-as-Hitler frame was also used in internal political deliberations. A number of critics charged that demonizing Hussein was a White House rhetorical ploy designed to garner public support for U.S. intervention. But Bush's statement provides some evidence to suggest that he really did think the analogy was fitting. Of course, we cannot know for certain whether Bush entirely believed in its accuracy or if he used it in private deliberations simply to manipulate others in the room, just as he would use it to manipulate the mass public. Nevertheless, it is instructive that the Hussein-as-Hitler analogy was raised in private deliberations, not just devoted to public consumption.)

President Bush's dismissal of the suggestion of an unwilling public was indicative of his general belief about American public opinion throughout the crisis. Bush felt that the public would support military action in the Gulf for two reasons. First, he believed that any U.S.-Iraqi conflict would be relatively short and successful, and cost few American lives. Early in the crisis, the president told Powell, "Colin, these guys [Iraqis] have never been seriously bombed. [Saudi Arabian Prince] Bandar tells me a couple of bombs and they'll fold. Mubarak, Ozal in Turkey, they all tell me the same thing. We can

---

pilot during World War II may have also predisposed him to an air-only strategy. Furthermore, it was certainly possible that the United States could have coerced Iraq into leaving Kuwait by using only air power. The U.S. dominance in the air meant that the United States could operate with relative impunity. The punishment that Iraq would have received, even without ground forces, may have been sufficient to convince Hussein to capitulate to coalition demands.

68. Bush and Scowcroft, *World Transformed*, 328.
69. Ibid.

knock 'em out in twenty-four hours."[70] Later, Bush recalled, "I thought the Defense Department overestimated Iraq's strength and resolve. Despite the size of their army, I just didn't see the Iraqis as being so tough."[71] Even publicly, Bush speculated that a war would be over in a matter of days. If he could orchestrate a short and successful war against a seemingly worthy opponent like Iraq, it would no doubt produce a massive rally in public opinion, erase the Vietnam syndrome that had plagued the country for the past two decades, and restore faith and pride in U.S. military power.

A second and equally important reason why President Bush opted for a military commitment in the Gulf was his firm belief that he had strong moral grounds to justify the use of force before the American public. Bush's invocation of the Hitler analogy when countering Cheney's suggestion of an unwilling public illustrates this conviction.[72] The president argued that the Hitler analogy had already gained widespread acceptance; after he presented his case to the public, Bush felt that even more Americans would come to accept the parallels he saw between Hussein and Hitler. And Bush was convinced that he had ample evidence to make such a case: Hussein had engaged in naked aggression against a defenseless neighbor; had committed atrocities in Kuwait, including rape and murder; had used weapons of mass destruction against his own people; was holding Americans hostage in Kuwait; and threatened to achieve regional hegemony to the detriment of the free world. Believing that the public would support military involvement, the president approved Plan 90-1002, pending Saudi acceptance.

At an NSC meeting on August 5, Bush and Scowcroft ruled out any potential for a negotiated settlement of the crisis. An exchange between NSC participants demonstrates their unwillingness to negotiate with Iraq:[73]

SECRETARY BRADY: Why not get someone to talk to Saddam? Possibly Mitterrand.
THE PRESIDENT: What would he say?
GENERAL SCOWCROFT: We don't want to appear to be negotiating.
SECRETARY BAKER: We could lose any momentum with the Arabs.
THE PRESIDENT: Our solidarity would crumble if we are seen talking to Saddam.
SECRETARY BAKER: Should we ask the Soviets to weigh in?

70. Powell and Persico, *My American Journey*, 476.
71. Bush and Scowcroft, *World Transformed*, 3.
72. For an excellent analysis of the use of analogies in foreign policy decision making, see Khong, *Analogies at War*, and Neustadt and May, *Thinking in Time*.
73. Haass, "Minutes from NSC Meeting, August 5, 1990."

GENERAL SCOWCROFT: We don't want to ask the Soviets. It would send a bad signal.
GOVERNOR SUNUNU: This could slow things down.
GENERAL SCOWCROFT: I am not sure we want things to slow down.
THE PRESIDENT: This is a Catch-22. If he slows down, our side will slow down as well.
SECRETARY BAKER: The only thing that will influence Saddam is our deterrent.

The refusal to negotiate with Iraq was consistent with the administration's definition of the crisis. Bush viewed Iraq's invasion of Kuwait and intimidation of Saudi Arabia as a threat to vital U.S. interests. More important, if Saddam Hussein were allowed to negotiate a settlement and retain some of the spoils of war, the only lesson he would learn was that crime does pay. From the administration's perspective, it would be far better to be uncompromising, deal with the problem now rather than later, and, in the process, hopefully loosen Hussein's grip on power. This choice not to talk directly with Iraq would be revisited later as public pressure on the eve of war prompted a change of heart.

The decision to forgo negotiation was solidified on August 8 when the president announced Operation Desert Shield in a televised speech before the nation. In the speech, Bush stressed the national interests involved in the Gulf and drew several analogies between present-day Iraq and 1930s Germany. Having publicly employed the Hussein-as-Hitler analogy, Bush was then unable to offer any type of diplomatic solution that could be interpreted as appeasement lest he play a latter-day Neville Chamberlain to Hussein's Adolf Hitler.

On August 6, the administration finalized the twin strategy of protecting Saudi Arabia and coercing Iraq into leaving Kuwait through economic sanctions. The Saudis had accepted U.S. troops the night before, so Bush gave the go-ahead for Plan 90-1002, now known as Operation Desert Shield. At the Saudis' request, the Bush administration decided not to inform the Congress or the American public until the first U.S. troops arrived on Saudi soil two days later. Secretary of State James Baker objected to the delay in notification; he thought that the administration would take a beating in the press by presenting a fait accompli.[74] However, Bush was less concerned with public opinion or Congress than with the strategic imperatives of getting U.S. troops into Saudi Arabia safely and placating King Fahd. The economic side of the strategy was realized later that same day when the UN Security Council passed

---

74. Bush and Scowcroft, *World Transformed*, 335–36.

Resolution 661, which imposed Chapter VII economic sanctions against Iraq and Kuwait.

At an NSC meeting also that day, the discussion turned to the effect of sanctions on both the Iraqi and the U.S. economies. Some members of the administration, most notably Powell and Baker, were optimistic about the efficacy of sanctions. Having worked tirelessly to build an international coalition, Baker stated, "We have the potential for effective sanctions."[75] Iraq relied almost exclusively on oil exports for foreign capital and would soon feel the effects of being isolated from the developed world. In addition, Iraq had few allies on which to rely.[76]

Conversely, Bush and Scowcroft doubted that sanctions would work within an acceptable time frame. Over time, the Iraqis would start to discount oil in the attempt to find a market, and the financial benefit gained from cheating on sanctions would tempt many countries to break the embargo.[77] Furthermore, Bush and Scowcroft were skeptical about the coalition's ability to interdict Iraqi and Kuwaiti oil. A naval blockade to prevent shipments would only be partially effective because Iraq could still transport oil over land, and blocking all land routes would be virtually impossible. Finally, Iraq was an autocratic state, and Hussein could pass the costs of sanctions on to disenfranchised segments of the society, such as the Shiites and Kurds, while shielding his military and Ba'athists from the effects.

The anticipated impact of sanctions on the U.S. economy was not encouraging. It was estimated that the loss of Iraqi and Kuwaiti oil would increase the price of oil to as high as thirty to thirty-six dollars a barrel (a high price at the time). Given an already sluggish U.S. economy, higher oil prices would most likely result in a recession. Public approval of the president was bound to follow any downturn in the economy, putting Bush's reelection prospects at risk. The probable effect of a recession on Bush's political future was never an explicit topic of discussion at the NSC meetings, although it was alluded to a number of times. For instance, OMB director Richard Darman noted, "Democracies and market-oriented economies are less prepared to wage this kind of battle [economic warfare] than non-market economies, especially given

---

75. Haass, "Minutes from NSC Meeting, August 5, 1990."

76. There were reports that Jordan was allowing Iraq the use of Jordanian accounts and that Marc Rich, the American fugitive living in Switzerland, had offered to store and move Iraqi oil. In addition to these reports, the administration was unsure if Iran would support the coalition's position. However, after a couple days of intense direct and indirect diplomacy, Jordan and Iran both agreed to abide by UN resolutions. See ibid.

77. Haass, "Minutes from NSC Meeting, August 5, 1990"; Bush and Scowcroft, *World Transformed*, 331.

that modern communications will affect us more than it will them."[78] Although such steps as drawing down the strategic petroleum reserve and gaining increased production from Saudi Arabia might lessen the domestic economic impact, the general consensus from advisors was that the United States had to be prepared for a recession if sanctions were to be given enough time to work.

In his public announcement of Operation Desert Shield on August 8, the president outlined the case for intervention and then described the mission of the U.S. troops as "wholly defensive." The public reaction was overwhelmingly positive. A Gallup poll conducted on August 9–12 showed that 78 percent of the public approved of the decision to send U.S. troops to the Gulf.[79] A major factor in this high approval of the president's policy was a lack of dissension from oppositional elites.[80] Senate Majority Leader George Mitchell (D-Maine) said, "It is important for the nation to unite behind the President in this time of challenge to American interests." House Speaker Thomas Foley (D-Wash.) remarked that President Bush had the "strong support of Congress."[81] The near-consensus bipartisan agreement over policy meant that the American public really only had one elite interpretation of the crisis—that from the White House—resulting in a broad public rally for the president. In fact, support for President Bush's Gulf policy would not decline dramatically until after the number of U.S. troops in the Gulf was doubled in early November, an escalation that was widely interpreted (correctly, as it turned out) as a major shift in policy (figure 12).

August 9–October 29, 1990

By late August, President Bush had begun leaning toward an offensive option to liberate Kuwait despite strong ongoing public support for Operation Desert Shield. On the morning of September 24, Cheney and Powell were preparing for an important briefing with the president on military options, and both had the impression that Bush preferred offensive military action to sanctions. "Dick," Powell said, "the President's really getting impatient. He keeps asking if we can't get the Iraqis out of Kuwait with air strikes." Cheney replied, "Yes. He's concerned that time is running out on him."[82]

78. Haass, "Minutes from NSC Meeting, August 6, 1990."
79. Survey by the Gallup Organization, August 9–12, 1990, from LexisNexis, Roper Center for Public Opinion Research, University of Connecticut (accessed April 12, 2004). "Do you approve or disapprove of the United States' decision to send US troops to Saudi Arabia as a defense against Iraq?"
80. Brody, "Crisis, War, and Public Opinion"; Zaller, "Elite Leadership"; Dorman and Livingston, "News and Historical Content."
81. Michael Kranish, "Congressional Leaders."
82. Powell and Persico, *My American Journey*, 478.

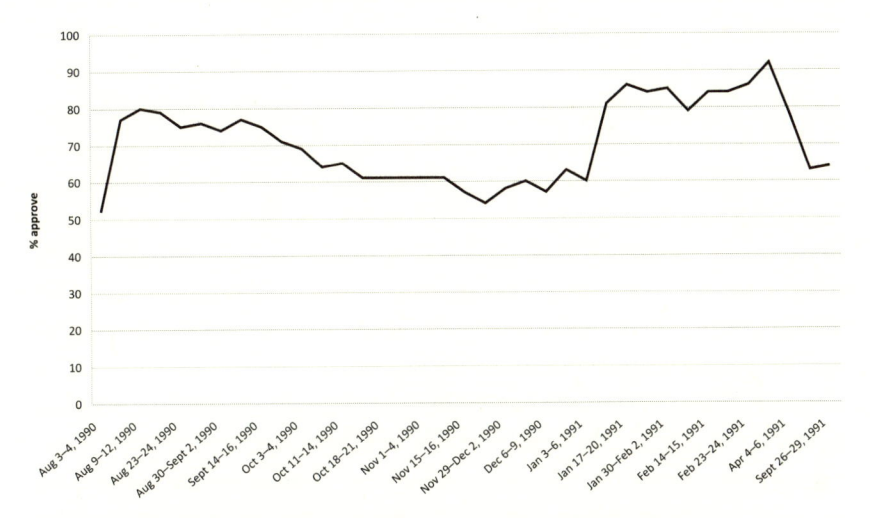

Fig. 12 Public approval of President Bush's handling of the Persian Gulf crisis
Source: Gallup polls, 1990–91.
Note: Before January 15, 1991, the Gallup poll question read, "Do you approve or disapprove of the way George Bush is handling this current situation in the Middle East involving Iraq and Kuwait?" After January 15, it was reworded, "Do you approve or disapprove of the way George Bush is handling the situation in the Persian Gulf region?"

At the briefing, Powell presented two options. The first involved maintaining the status quo and waiting for the sanctions to work. The obvious advantage in relying on economic sanctions was that it would avoid a military confrontation and the resultant loss of life. It was also a policy strongly supported by the American public. The second option involved shifting to the offensive. Powell explained that although the United States could respond to Iraqi provocation in the short term, a more advantageous situation would emerge in January 1991, when the United States would have a sufficient number of ground forces to launch an offensive. Powell informed President Bush that a policy decision did not have to be made until late October; at that point, the flow of troops to the Gulf would have to be capped if the president wanted to continue the policy of economic strangulation, or increased in preparation for the offensive. Bush considered Powell's briefing and replied, "Thanks, Colin. That's useful. That's very interesting. It's good to consider all angles. But I really don't think we have time for sanctions to work."[83]

83. Ibid., 480.

President Bush's reasons for shifting to the offensive will be discussed more fully in the policy decision stage, but suffice it to say here, we can rule out that the public was pressuring Bush to go to war. In September 1990, the president enjoyed strong support (75 percent) for his overall handling of the crisis (figure 12).[84] More important for this discussion, the public strongly approved of the use of economic sanctions over military force to liberate Kuwait: a Gallup poll taken on August 23–24 showed that 80 percent of the public preferred economic sanctions to military action.[85] Strong public support for sanctions, coupled with high issue salience, suggests that the political context was constrained (i.e., high issue salience, unified preference) *against* the shift to an offensive. However, when asked only about the use of military force without being provided with the option of continuing economic sanctions, a slim plurality (45 percent) of the public expressed approval of using U.S. troops to liberate Kuwait.[86] The response to this question suggests that the decision-making context was not constrained, but rather contested (i.e., high issue salience, divided preference). In either case, the emergence of the offensive option ran contrary to the desires of a majority of the American people. As John Mueller states, "Curiously, the military often claims that a central lesson from the Vietnam experience is that forces should not be committed to war unless they go with solid public backing in advance. The troops had that backing in Vietnam, but not in the Gulf War."[87]

That offensive military force became President Bush's preferred option despite a lack of public support does not mean that public opinion was irrelevant at this stage. Contrary to Mueller, the lesson from the Vietnam experience was *not* that decision makers had to have majority support from the public *before* going to war. Rather, the lesson learned was that if war should occur, it had to be quick, it had to accomplish specific objectives, and it had to involve a small number of U.S. casualties.[88] If a war could satisfy these conditions, the public would undoubtedly rally behind the president, and the leanings of

84. Survey by the Gallup Organization, September 14–16, 1990, from LexisNexis, Roper Center for Public Opinion Research, University of Connecticut (accessed April 12, 2004).
85. Survey by the Gallup Organization, August 23–24, 1990, from LexisNexis, Roper Center for Public Opinion Research, University of Connecticut (accessed April 12, 2004). "Should (President) Bush quickly begin military action against Iraq, or should he wait to see if economic and diplomatic sanctions are effective?"
86. Survey by the Gallup Organization, October 18–19, 1990, from LexisNexis, Roper Center for Public Opinion Research, University of Connecticut (accessed April 12, 2004). "Now that the U.S. (United States) forces have been sent to Saudi Arabia and other areas of the Middle East, do you think they should engage in combat if Iraq refuses to leave Kuwait and restore its former government?"
87. Mueller, "American Public Opinion," 205.
88. Gelpi and Mueller, "Cost of War (Response)"; Gelpi, Feaver, and Reifler, "Success Matters"; Eichenberg, "Victory Has Many Friends"; Larson and Savych, *American Public Support*.

public opinion in the prelude to war would become more or less irrelevant. Put another way, the opinion that matters most is the one held by the public after the last bullet has been fired, not the transient preferences in the months leading up to war. Accordingly, President Bush had to seek out options that promised a quick and decisive resolution to the crisis.

In early October, the president ordered the military to present plans for offensive military action. On October 11, Powell and CENTCOM's Major General Robert Johnson briefed the president and his NSC staff in the Situation Room of the White House. The offensive strategy plan had five stages: the first four would rely on air power, followed by a final ground stage that would entail driving an outnumbered U.S. force straight into Iraqi strongholds in Kuwait. Scowcroft was "appalled" with the military's presentation and felt that a ground strategy of meeting force-on-force would needlessly increase U.S. casualties and turn public opinion against the war.[89] Bush agreed with Scowcroft's assessment: "The briefing made me realize we had a long way to go before the military was 'gung ho' and felt we had the means to accomplish our mission expeditiously, without impossible loss of life."[90] Bush and Scowcroft ordered the military to rework the offensive plans.

The scrapping of the first offensive plan was largely due to the influence of public opinion. There was little doubt that the United States would eventually prevail in a force-on-force confrontation. Meeting Iraqi forces head-on also made strategic sense in that it would be a decisive move that would increase the probability of accomplishing the objective and ending the crisis quickly. The casualty rate, however, promised to be high. In an era in which Americans are intolerant, or at least *perceived* to be intolerant, of U.S. casualties, the plan as presented by the military was a political nonstarter. For President Bush, the October 11 plan offered little hope of achieving the strategic objectives while retaining the support of the American public.

As Leslie Gelb remarked about decision making nearly twenty years earlier during the Vietnam War, "Decisions about means ... were based on judgments about both the least risky way to fight the war and the best way to maintain public support at home."[91] The crises in the Gulf and Vietnam differed in many respects, but one similarity was the need to maintain domestic backing for the war efforts. With this goal in mind, the military was ordered back to the drawing board, charged with the responsibility of crafting a strategy that would

89. Bush and Scowcroft, *World Transformed*.
90. Ibid., 381.
91. Gelb, "Essential Domino," 464.

be both militarily effective and acceptable to the public. Later that month, President Bush was presented with a revised plan that offered a high probability of achieving success at a lower cost. On October 30, Bush considered the revamped offensive plan and made his policy decision.

Public opinion placed one additional constraint on the Bush administration's consideration of options: any policy the administration considered would have to be morally justifiable. The moral constraint was first apparent in the discussion of whether to include food in the list of embargoed items.[92] Protocol I of the Geneva Convention (1949) prohibits the "starvation of civilians as a method of warfare." Although neither the United States nor Iraq was a signatory to that protocol, the practice of starving the Iraqi people threatened to erode public support as well as fracture the coalition. Denying food to Iraq was even more problematic given President Bush's frequent statements that the Iraqi people were "innocents" and that the real target of U.S. policy was Hussein and his Republican Guard.[93] Eventually, Bush agreed to exempt food for humanitarian purposes, even though the choice meant the decreased effectiveness of the sanctions.

The operation and conduct of battle also had to be consistent with the broad principles of the "just war" theory, and the Bush administration rejected several options that would have been morally questionable.[94] In mid-October, Dick Cheney asked Powell to prepare a plan for the use of tactical nuclear weapons "just out of curiosity."[95] Powell reluctantly cooperated, although it appears that there was never any serious consideration given to using nuclear weapons in Iraq.[96] The option of using chemical weapons was also briefly considered and rejected.[97]

In addition, the influence of public opinion did shape much of the planning for the air campaign against Iraq. The Bush administration wanted to

---

92. Haass, "Minutes from NSC Meeting, August 6, 1990."
93. Freedman and Karsh, *Gulf Conflict*, 191–94.
94. For literature on just war theory, see Patterson, "Just War"; Walzer, *Just and Unjust Wars*; and Patterson, *Just War Thinking*.
95. Powell and Persico, *My American Journey*, 486. Cheney fueled the speculation that nuclear weapons might be used in Iraq by appearing on a talk show and stating that "were Saddam Hussein foolish enough to use weapons of mass destruction, the U.S. response would be absolutely overwhelming and it would be devastating." Cheney later denied that the comment implied the use of nuclear weapons and said the option was "never on the table." See Freedman and Karsh, *Gulf Conflict*, 289.
96. Powell claims that Cheney shredded the nuclear report upon reading it. Moreover, Freedman and Karsh note that "no effort was made to prepare for nuclear use: some nuclear weapons were removed from warships in order to make room for conventional stores, and Army units with nuclear responsibilities were left behind in Europe." Powell and Persico, *My American Journey*, 486; Freedman and Karsh, *Gulf Conflict*, 289.
97. Powell and Persico, *My American Journey*, 468.

minimize Iraqi civilian casualties and ordered military planners to cut down the amount of collateral damage by using "smart bombs" and laser-guided munitions when targeting heavily populated areas around Baghdad. The concern about the potential effect of Iraqi casualties on the American public was one reason Bush did not follow through with his preference for starting the air war in late September or early October. He later remarked, "I still thought we could simply devastate Iraq's military and strategic facilities with all our air power after a provocation. But Brent [Scowcroft] warned that we might eventually have to follow through with ground troops to liberate Kuwait, and if we pounded from the air too soon, before our forces were ready, there could be public pressure to stop all fighting and turn opinion against ever launching a ground campaign."[98]

Summary

The first two stages of the Persian Gulf crisis—problem definition and option generation—largely reflect presidential leadership of public opinion. The Bush administration premised its choices on strategic considerations and then focused Americans' attention on the Gulf and largely shaped their opinions. Indeed, there is little evidence that public opinion forced a significant policy choice that would not have otherwise been made. As a result, the political context shifted from insulated (i.e., low salience, nonexistent preferences) in the prelude to the conflict, to constrained (i.e., high salience, unified preferences) shortly after the invasion. The key point to remember here is that the political context was constrained in favor of the White House and became so largely because of effective presidential leadership. As we will see in the next chapter, however, the pressure of political responsiveness increased after the policy decision was made.

98. Bush and Scowcroft, *World Transformed*, 382.

5

OPERATION DESERT STORM
Decision, Implementation, and Review

The previous chapter offered a view of presidential leadership in the early stages of a crisis. At the start of the Persian Gulf conflict, President Bush and his advisors represented Iraq's invasion of Kuwait as a serious threat to U.S. interests and made policy choices consistent with this view. There is little indication that public opinion affected these choices or caused the administration to deviate much, if at all, from its preferred course of action. As such, the Bush administration behaved as we would presume in an expected utility model of foreign policy making: the president set a goal and then selected policy options that maximized the chances of achieving that goal. Although the American public had little influence over presidential decision making in the early stages of the crisis, a strong correlation nevertheless existed between the choices made by the Bush administration and mass opinion. The reason for this congruency was that President Bush successfully convinced the American public that the Iraqi invasion of Kuwait was a threat to the United States and, in the process, dramatically increased the salience of the issue. This political leadership resulted in the best situation a president could hope for—a constrained political context that favored the White House.

This chapter presents a different story. Although the Bush administration still attempted to lead the American public at the time of the crucial decision for war, the public was no longer as willing to follow. More important, as the defensive Operation Desert Shield transformed into the offensive Operation Desert Storm, the relationship between public opinion and policy choices also underwent a stunning transformation. At the implementation and review stage of policy, the administration made several policy choices that were consistent with the preferences of a highly attentive public, yet largely inconsistent with the strategic goal of liberating Kuwait and decimating the Iraqi army.

In a sense, the public grabbed the reins of power after the decision for war had been made and forced the administration into several choices that the White House may not have otherwise pursued. In short, we cannot fully understand the 1991 Gulf War without also understanding the role that public opinion played in the case.

The following sections assess policy making from October 30, 1990, when the Bush administration decided to use offensive military force to liberate Kuwait, to the end of the Gulf War on February 28, 1991. Consistent with our theory, President Bush led a reluctant public into a war with Iraq. However, the confluence of unified public preferences and very high issue salience during the subsequent implementation and review stages motivated Bush to become more responsive to mass opinion.

Policy Decision

The Choice for War

President Bush made the decision to liberate Kuwait through military force in a principals' meeting at the White House on October 30. Ostensibly, the purpose of the meeting was to decide whether to cap or increase the flow of troops going into the Gulf. For all intents and purposes, however, the meeting would determine whether offensive military force would be used in the liberation of Kuwait. The president began by offering his evaluation of the current state of the crisis: "The time has come to determine whether we continue to place most of our eggs in the sanctions basket, which would take a good deal more time as things now stand but would possibly avoid the risks and costs of war, or whether we raise the pressure on Saddam by pressing ahead on both the military and diplomatic tracks. I realize that if we do give Saddam some kind of deadline, we are in effect committing ourselves to war." Scowcroft then stated, "We're at a Y in the road," and outlined three options available to the administration: "It seems to me we have three basic choices. First, we can ride out the sanctions and see what happens; second, we could plan on the use of force, which would involve aiming for a specific date, how we deal with the public, and whether we go for a UN Security Council authorization, developing our military strategy and tactics, and choosing a preferred date; and third, how do we react to a provocation or do we create a provocation that would permit military action—for example, our embassy in Kuwait City."[1]

---

1. Bush and Scowcroft, *World Transformed*, 393.

Next, Powell briefed the administration on what an offensive force to liberate Kuwait would require.[2] A shift to offense would necessitate doubling the force size, borrowing VII Corps from Europe, and sending three additional aircraft carriers to the Gulf. The magnitude of this force increase caught Bush and Scowcroft off guard, but they agreed to provide whatever resources the military felt it needed to liberate Kuwait. Powell then presented a revised offensive strategy. The first three stages of the campaign would be devoted to an air war—a plan similar to that presented to the president in the first military briefing back on October 11. The last stage, however, featured a new ground strategy that included a bluff from the south and a flanking maneuver—the so-called left hook—coming from the west. Designed primarily to minimize coalition casualties, the flanking maneuver represented a significant departure from the previous, and more direct, force-on-force strategy. After discussing how the United States might actually initiate the war, President Bush nodded to Cheney and Powell and said, "Defense should go ahead and move its forces."[3] With that comment, the decision had been made to use offensive force to liberate Kuwait.

It is important to pause for a moment here and clarify why the choice made on October 30 is considered *the* decision for war. Indeed, a number of other scholars have placed the decision for war later in the process, such as after Congress approved the war or after negotiations with Iraq failed in January.[4] However, based on the comments of the decision makers involved, it seems clear that the October 30 decision was the key moment. As we will see, very little occurred after this point that could have prevented a war.

Over the next several weeks, the Bush administration would clarify its war objectives. The decision was made to act within the parameters set by the UN resolutions and not attempt to remove Hussein from power. Instead, military force would be used to liberate Kuwait and weaken the Iraqi military to the point that it posed little threat to neighboring countries. Ideally, this strategy would hurt Iraq enough to discourage future adventurism but not enough to create a power vacuum. Powell noted, "We wanted Iraq to continue as a threat and counterweight to Iran." In specifying the objectives of the war, the Bush administration had finally ruled out a regime change. Powell later stated that the removal of Hussein was never a serious objective of U.S. policy. "In none of the meetings I attended was dismembering Iraq, conquering Baghdad, or changing the Iraqi form of government ever seriously considered. We

2. Woodward, *Commanders*, 318.
3. Bush and Scowcroft, *World Transformed*, 395.
4. Foyle, *Counting the Public In*; Sobel, *Impact of Public Opinion*.

hoped that Saddam would not survive the coming fury. But his elimination was not a stated objective. What we hoped for, frankly, in a postwar Gulf region was an Iraq still standing, with Saddam overthrown."[5]

The decision not to overthrow Hussein was made primarily for strategic reasons. But, as we will see at the policy review stage, there would eventually be a strong domestic component to the decision. Through the earlier use of the Hussein-as-Hitler analogy, President Bush helped to mobilize public support for military intervention, but in doing so, he had also implied that regime change was a policy goal of the United States. At the end of the war, it would be difficult for the administration to explain to the American public why Hitler's equivalent was allowed to remain in power. Powell later remarked, "Our plan contemplated only ejecting Iraq from Kuwait.... And I thought it unwise to elevate public expectations by making the man out to be the devil incarnate and then leaving him in place."[6]

Despite the strong rhetoric directed against Hussein, the cost of deposing the dictator promised to be considerably greater than simply liberating Kuwait. Bush believed that marching into Baghdad would mean fighting an "unwinnable urban guerilla war" and would entail a significant number of U.S. casualties.[7] If the war was then allowed to drag on while U.S. forces searched for Hussein, the president would risk declining public support as the death toll mounted. Thus, the administration faced an interesting and difficult tradeoff: continue the war and risk losing public support due to an increasing number of casualties, or narrow the aims of war and risk losing public support for not deposing Hussein. The administration was bound to come under criticism for whatever decision it made, and Bush opted to narrow the war aims in part because limiting the number of U.S. casualties was likely to be more important to the public than ousting Hussein and risking the consequences of doing so.[8]

The Influence of Public Opinion on the Choice for War

President Bush's decision to shift to the offensive was made with only questionable levels of public support. Around the time of the decision, the public was almost perfectly split on the question of war: 46 percent in favor, 45 percent against (figure 13). In addition, the American public strongly preferred

---

5. Powell and Persico, *My American Journey*, 490.
6. Ibid.
7. Bush and Scowcroft, *World Transformed*, 464.
8. Ibid.

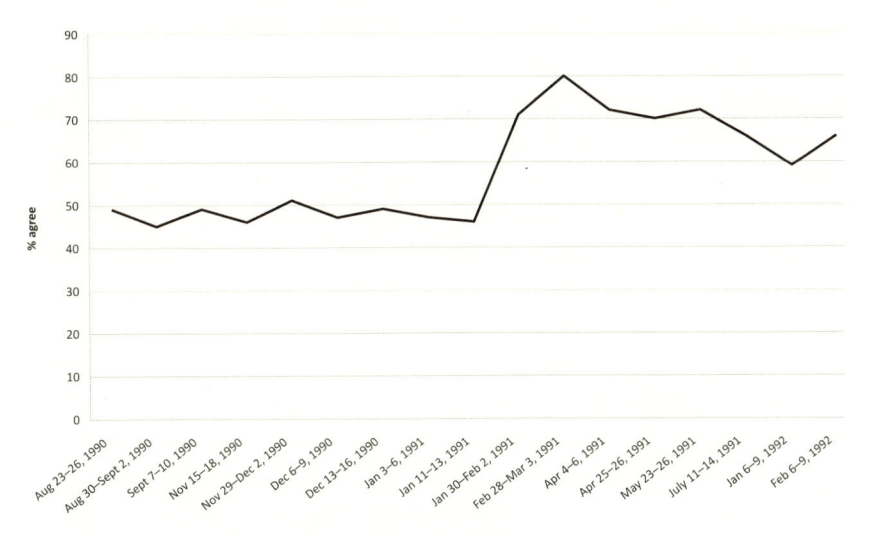

Fig. 13 Public opinion that the situation in the Persian Gulf is/was worth going to war over

Source: Gallup polls, 1990–92.

economic sanctions (73 percent) to the use of military force (21 percent).[9] This division in public preferences on the question of war, as well as mass support for sanctions, indicates that the public was not itching for a fight. Therefore, the politically prudent move at the time might have been a continuation of sanctions.

Assessing the degree of issue salience at the time that the White House reached its decision for war is complicated by the fact that few outside of the Oval Office knew that a decision had been made. Obviously, much presidential decision making occurs outside of the public's purview; such was the case with the October 30 meeting. The decision to escalate the number of troops headed to the Gulf was kept hidden from the public until a few weeks later, and the fact that this decision actually meant war with Iraq was revealed even later still. Moreover, at the time that the administration was reaching its decision, other issues (e.g., the budget stalemate and the upcoming midterm elections)

9. Survey by the Gallup Organization, October 18–19, 1990, from LexisNexis, Roper Center for Public Opinion Research, University of Connecticut (accessed April 12, 2004). "Some people feel that President Bush should quickly begin military action against Iraq. Others say he should wait to see if economic and diplomatic sanctions are effective. Which comes closer to your view?"

were pushing the Gulf War further down on the media agenda (figure 11). Issue salience was still fairly high, but not as high as it would have been if the public knew that a decision for war was to be reached at the October 30 meeting.

Because the conflict in the Persian Gulf was a salient issue and because the public was divided over the use of force to liberate Kuwait, the decision-making context is best classified as contested.[10] And because the Bush administration knew that a massive public and congressional uproar would result from announcing that a decision for war had been reached, it decided to keep the decision quiet for several weeks. Even when it did announce the troop increase, the administration attempted to frame it as a routine choice and not as a final decision for war.

Although President Bush had kept his leanings (and eventually his decision) toward the military option private, members of Congress perceived the president's inclination and cautioned him against rushing into war. Congress had shown rare bipartisan unity during Operation Desert Shield, but a possible shift to the offensive threatened to polarize the parties. In a meeting with Bush held just hours before the decision for the offensive was made, House Speaker Tom Foley (D-Wash.) warned the president, "The country and Congress are not prepared for offensive action." "I agree with my colleagues about the public mood," said Representative Les Aspin (D-Wisc.). "There's no question [the country] has moved away from a more hawkish position within the last month." Senate Majority Leader George Mitchell (D-Maine) pointed out, "It's less than two months since sanctions were put in place. No one expected them to work in a week. The case has not been made that sanctions have failed." Senator Patrick Leahy (D-Vt.) agreed that sanctions should be allowed to continue and noted, "There is no consensus to attack Kuwait."[11]

In light of public and congressional reluctance to resort to a military offensive, it would appear as though domestic opinion was irrelevant to the president. This view, however, is only partially correct. The fact that public opinion was divided over the use of force meant that the president could opt for war while still retaining the support of approximately half of the public, mainly

---

10. A possible objection to the characterization of the decision context is that when the public was presented with a choice between military action and economic sanctions, 73 percent of the public preferred sanctions (ibid.). In this case, the decision context would appear to be constrained. Whether one chooses to represent the political context as constrained or contested is less crucial at this particular stage than it is at others. The important aspect of decision making at this stage was President Bush's anticipations of *future* political contexts, not the current one. Consequently, the nature of preferences at the time of his decision mattered less to Bush than did his expectations of what opinion would look like in the future.

11. Bush and Scowcroft, *World Transformed*, 390.

partisans. But public opinion factored into decision making in a still more crucial respect. It was expected that the most salient aspect of the Persian Gulf crisis would not be the *decision* to go to war, but rather the actual *implementation* of war. So while the current state of public opinion did not factor heavily into the president's decision, what that opinion might look like in the future was influential. Put another way, the president looked ahead to the end game and assessed which policy option—economic sanctions or military force—offered the greater probability of political and strategic success. For President Bush, that choice was clearly the use of offensive military force. The next sections examine why Bush felt that sanctions would not work in an acceptable time frame and why he believed that war with Iraq would be so successful.

The Great Sanctions Debate

Why opt for war at a time when the American public so strongly preferred sanctions? President Bush's decision to give up on sanctions and go on the offensive was actually informed by a mix of strategic and domestic considerations. The president clearly felt that Iraq's occupation of Kuwait constituted a sufficient threat to U.S. interests to warrant military action. National Security Directive 45, written on August 20, 1990, reiterated the Carter Doctrine and clearly specified the U.S. interest in the region: "U.S. interests in the Persian Gulf are vital to the national security. These interests include access to oil and the security and stability of friendly states in the region. The United States will defend its vital interests in the area, through the use of U.S. military force if necessary and appropriate, against any power with interests inimical to our own."[12]

In addition, President Bush chose to shift to the offensive because he lacked confidence that sanctions would work within an acceptable time frame. In a letter to Representative Les Aspin on January 10, Director William Webster summarized the CIA's best estimate on the efficacy of sanctions: "Our judgment remains that, even if sanctions continue to be enforced for an additional six to 12 months, economic hardship alone is unlikely to compel Saddam to retreat from Kuwait or cause regime-threatening popular discontent in Iraq."[13] There were ample reasons to be skeptical of the ability of sanctions to liberate

---

12. National Security Directive 45, August 20, 1990, http://bushlibrary.tamu.edu/research/nsd/index.html (accessed June 15, 2003).
13. William Webster (CIA) to Les Aspin, January 10, 1991, Bush Presidential Records, John Sununu Files, Persian Gulf War 1991, OA/ID CF00472 (8 of 11).

Kuwait: sanctions had not worked well in the past; Saddam Hussein was politically insulated through his vast security network; Iraq had large stores of food and spare military parts; and the economic benefit to industrialized states in defecting from the sanction regime would only increase over time. To make matters worse, the domestic impact of sanctions was helping to push the United States deeper into a recession (figure 14).

Yet a strong case could also be made *for* economic sanctions. The current sanctions against Iraq were the strongest in history, and up to this point, the coalition had demonstrated considerable discipline and resolve.[14] Iraq's ability to export oil was effectively cut off through military enforcement of the embargo and the closing of pipelines into Turkey and Saudi Arabia. Additionally, as sanctions inflicted more pain on the Iraqi military—the elite Republican Guard in particular—it was felt that Hussein might be forced to capitulate to minimize coup risk. But most important, sanctions were an option strongly preferred by the American public. James Baker, one of the most vocal supporters of economic sanctions, cautioned the president about the political impact of going to war: "I know you're aware of the fact that this has all the ingredients that brought down three of the last five Presidents: a hostage crisis, body bags, and a full-fledged economic recession caused by forty-dollar oil."[15] And in congressional testimony, Admiral William Crowe Jr. (Ret.) stated that "if, in fact, the sanctions will work in twelve to eighteen months instead of six months, a tradeoff of avoiding war, with its attendant sacrifices and uncertainties, would in my estimation be more than worth it."[16]

In light of the persuasive arguments on both sides, why did President Bush sense that "time was running out" on the sanction option? Ironically, given the strong public support for sanctions, part of the answer lies with the president's consideration of domestic politics. Bush's "this will not stand" statement provided the public with a benchmark to evaluate his Gulf policy, just as his "read my lips, no new taxes" campaign pledge set the standard for fiscal policy (incidentally, the latter pledge was broken just ten days prior to the decision for war, placing President Bush in the middle of a political firestorm).[17] The longer the crisis went unresolved, the more the political elites on both sides of the aisle would begin to criticize the president. Liberals would attack

14. Elliot, Hufbauer, and Schott, "Big Squeeze."
15. Baker and DeFrank, *Politics of Diplomacy,* 277.
16. Admiral William J. Crowe Jr. Testimony Before the Senate Armed Services Committee, November 28, 1990, in "Crisis in the Persian Gulf Region: U.S. Policy Options and Implications," 95, hearing ID HRG-1990-SAS-0008, LexisNexis Congressional Hearings Digital Collection, http://www.lexisnexis.com/us/lnacademic/ (accessed May 14, 2003).
17. Sobel, *Impact of Public Opinion,* 146.

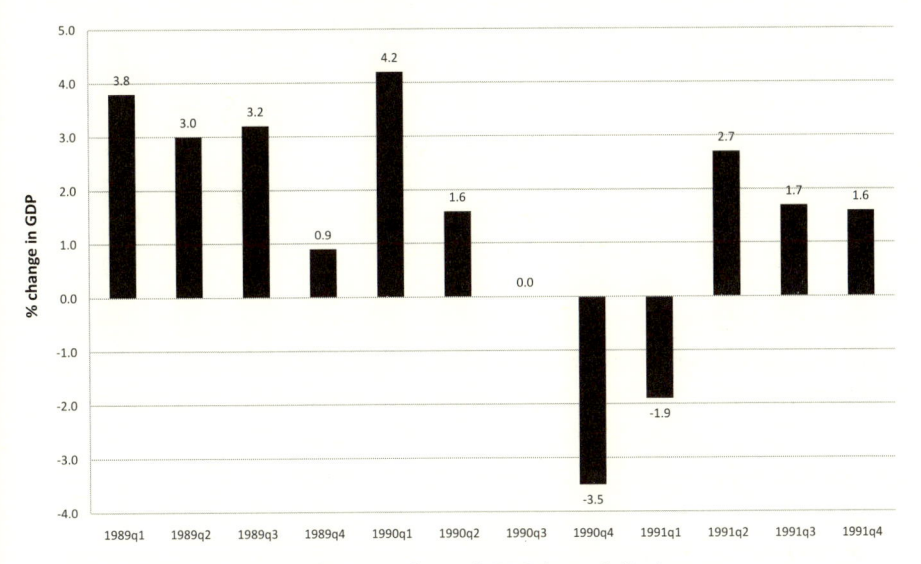

Fig. 14 Change from preceding period in real GDP (2005 dollars)
Source: Bureau of Economic Analysis, http://www.bea.gov/na.

Bush for committing vast resources to a conflict that did not deserve U.S. attention, and conservatives would criticize the president for being "a wimp" when facing Hussein.[18] The chorus of criticism promised to build to a crescendo in the election year of 1992, as ambitious politicians would undoubtedly use the Iraq issue to campaign against the president. Domestic opinion would inevitably follow elite cues, and the broad support once enjoyed by President Bush would steadily erode.

Polls taken in late 1990 provide some empirical support for this very scenario. An NBC/ *Wall Street Journal* poll showed that 72 percent of the public would not favor "waiting for up to two years for sanctions to work with 200,000 troops in Saudi Arabia."[19] In short, President Bush would undoubtedly find

---

18. Some may question the counterfactual that politicians who initially supported economic sanctions would eventually come to criticize President Bush if the crisis dragged on a year or so while sanctions were given time to work. Although some elites might have taken a principled stance and supported continuing sanctions throughout, it is more likely that political expediency would have driven most to have a change of heart. As the stalemate continued and a large number of U.S. troops remained in the Saudi desert, siding with the president would become a political liability. For the rational politician, the best choice would likely be to distance oneself from the White House, no matter what one's original position might have been. Some empirical support for this counterfactual can be found in the behavior of congressional Democrats who initially supported the invasion of Iraq in 2003, yet ran away from that decision and criticized President George W. Bush once it became clear that implementation had gone poorly.

19. Survey by NBC/ *Wall Street Journal,* December 8–11, 1990, from LexisNexis, Roper Center for Public Opinion Research, University of Connecticut (accessed April 12, 2004). "Suppose it takes up to

himself in a bad political situation if the crisis went unresolved into the election year.

The Military Option

The importance of the region to U.S. interests and the belief that sanctions would not compel Iraq to leave Kuwait in an acceptable time frame were necessary reasons to consider a shift to the offensive, but they alone are insufficient explanations of the decision for war. The final and most crucial factor in the decision to take to the offensive was Bush's belief that any U.S.-Iraqi conflict would be relatively short and successful, costing few American lives, and that the American public would rally in response.

There was little doubt in the minds of most knowledgeable observers that the United States would eventually prevail in any military conflict with Iraq; even Saddam Hussein recognized that his forces were no match for those of the United States. Faced with inevitable military defeat, Hussein pinned his hopes for success on turning American public opinion against the war effort by making the conflict as bloody as possible. He communicated this intent to U.S. ambassador April Glaspie, saying, "Yours is a society which cannot accept 10,000 dead in one battle." Accordingly, Iraqi newspapers frequently referred to the coming conflict as America's "second Vietnam."[20] To realize his strategy, Hussein hoped to wait out the coalition's aerial campaign and lure the United States into a protracted ground war, which he promised would be the "mother of all battles." Thus, the question on the minds of both sides was not whether the United States could defeat the Iraqi military, but rather whether the American public would tolerate the costs of victory.

Contrary to Saddam Hussein's promise to deliver the "mother of all battles," President Bush envisioned a relatively easy fight that would be over "in less than a week."[21] Bush's optimistic picture of the coming war was based, in part, on briefings from U.S. military commanders and his discussions with Middle Eastern leaders. The U.S. military had identified significant weaknesses in the Iraqi defense, including a centralized command and control system, incompetent military leaders, a poorly trained air force and inadequate ground-to-air defenses, and low military morale.[22]

---

two years for the economic sanctions against Iraq to work. Would you favor or oppose keeping 200,000 troops in Saudi Arabia while we were waiting for the sanctions to work?"
20. Freedman and Karsh, *Gulf Conflict*, 52–58.
21. Bush and Scowcroft, *World Transformed*, 462.
22. Belkin et al., "Strategic Bombing"; Biddle and Zirkle, "Technology, Civil-Military Relations."

These weaknesses played to U.S. strengths, most notably the unquestioned advantage in high-tech weaponry that promised to achieve air superiority for the United States early on in the war. Having gained control of the skies, the coalition could then set about decimating the Iraqi military through aerial bombing and weaken it to the point that coalition ground troops would face minimal resistance. Bush stated, "From the [military briefing], and what I was hearing back in Washington, the military seemed confident that any war would be a short one—far different from what many in Congress were saying."[23]

It was President Bush's belief in the efficacy of military force and, more to the point, a belief that the public would rally in response to a successful war that made the decision to go on the offensive possible. As long as the United States accomplished specified objectives with minimal loss of life, Bush could be assured of a broad public rally. After the war had succeeded (or failed), the politics of the prelude would be forgotten and it would be essentially irrelevant whether a majority of the public had actually supported the decision for war. Consequently, the president discounted the current state of public opinion—although he frequently worried about his level of public support—and premised his decision on an expectation of what opinion would look like in the future.

The Casualties Concern

Whether the coming war was considered a success or a failure largely depended on the number of casualties the United States would incur.[24] In the months leading up to war, there was rampant speculation over what that number might be. Worst-case scenarios estimated more than twenty thousand American casualties, and an influential report by the Center for Strategic and International Studies estimated that fifteen thousand American troops would be killed in action.[25] By contrast, the Bush administration tended to rely on considerably lower figures. Reluctant to "estimate the inestimable," Schwarzkopf thought that the United States would suffer five thousand killed or wounded, and Powell put the number at three thousand.[26] Both the military and the

---

23. Bush and Scowcroft, *World Transformed*, 412.
24. For literature on perceptions of success and casualties, see Klarevas, "'Essential Domino'"; Eichenberg, "Victory Has Many Friends"; Feaver and Gelpi, *Choosing Your Battles*; Gelpi, Feaver, and Reifler, "Success Matters"; Larson and Savych, *American Public Support*; Gartner, "Multiple Effects of Casualties"; and Gartner and Segura, "War, Casualties."
25. Mueller, "Review"; Mueller, "American Public Opinion"; Powell and Persico, *My American Journey*.
26. Powell and Persico, *My American Journey*, 498.

civilian leadership believed that those numbers could be reduced even further if the air war and the "left-hook" ground attack went according to plan.

On the whole, the public tended to accept the high casualty estimates. A Gallup poll taken on October 18–19 showed that 53 percent of the public thought the United States would suffer more than several thousand casualties, while 38 percent believed that the number would be less than a thousand.[27] Closer to the start of the war, the public became even more pessimistic, with only 15 percent believing that the United States would lose fewer than one thousand soldiers.[28] Furthermore, public support for the war effort tended to decrease as pollsters hypothetically increased casualty rates. An ABC/*Washington Post* poll found that 63 percent of the public favored going to war if Iraq did not withdraw from Kuwait by January 15.[29] Approval dropped to 44 percent when respondents were asked whether they favored war if the United States suffered one thousand casualties, and it further decayed to 35 percent when the casualty rate increased to ten thousand.

The public's acceptance of high casualty estimates proved to be a mixed blessing for the Bush administration. On one hand, the pervasive belief that the war would be costly made the public less willing to fight it. On the other hand, if the war turned out to be less costly than the public imagined, the chances of a broad rally increased. So in a perverse way, the administration actually benefited from the formidable image of Iraq that was constructed in the press. If the war could be won quickly with minimal casualties, the battle would be that much more impressive to the public and would likely produce an even broader rally.

The lessons of the Vietnam War were salient for President Bush as he opted for military force. Bush noted, "I don't think that support would last if it were a long, drawn out conflagration. I think support would erode, as it did in the Vietnam conflict."[30] Although the images of Vietnam were ever-present, an

---

27. Survey by the Gallup Organization, October 18–19, 1990, from LexisNexis, Roper Center for Public Opinion Research, University of Connecticut (accessed April 12, 2004). "If the U.S. takes military action against Iraq, do you think that the number of Americans killed and injured will be . . ." Response includes "several thousand" and "tens of thousands."

28. Survey by ABC/*Washington Post*, January 4–5, 1991, from LexisNexis, Roper Center for Public Opinion Research, University of Connecticut (accessed April 12, 2004). "If the U.S. takes military action against Iraq, do you think that the number of Americans killed and injured will be . . ." Response includes "less than a hundred" and "several hundred."

29. Ibid. "As you may know, the United Nations Security Council has authorized the use of force against Iraq if it doesn't withdraw from Kuwait by January 15th (1991). If Iraq does not withdraw from Kuwait, should the United States go to war with Iraq to force it out of Kuwait at some point after January 15th, or not?"

30. Idelson, "National Opinion Ambivalent," 16.

equally relevant consideration was the outcome of the Iranian hostage crisis during Jimmy Carter's presidency. If Bush relied on economic sanctions and the conflict with Iraq lasted as long as the Iranian hostage crisis, Bush assumed that he would meet the same electoral fate as Carter. As David Mervin put it, "George Bush and his advisers were keenly aware of Johnson's mistakes as well as those made by President Carter during the Iranian hostage crisis of 1979–81. They also assumed that, particularly after the trauma of Vietnam, the American people lacked the stomach for a long drawn-out conflict. If there was to be a war, it needed to be short and sharp and, to accomplish that, a whole-hearted commitment of troops on a massive scale was required."[31]

In a sense, President Bush faced the possibility that if the Persian Gulf crisis went poorly, his presidency would resemble that of either Lyndon Johnson or Jimmy Carter. Obviously, neither possibility appealed to Bush. However, the important aspect in the decision for war was that President Bush attached a low probability that military conflict would turn out poorly (like Vietnam) and a high probability that a less forceful response would fail to produce the desired results in an acceptable time frame (like Iran). In the end, President Bush was willing to gamble that war in the Gulf would not resemble the war in Vietnam, and that his presidency would not resemble that of Johnson or Carter.

In sum, the policy decision stage of the Persian Gulf saw President Bush leading a reluctant public to war. In such a contested political context (i.e., high issue salience, divided preferences), the safe political choice at that time would have been to continue economic sanctions and a defensive posture. However, President Bush was more concerned with future political contexts than the current one. Looking ahead, Bush believed that military force offered a greater chance for strategic and political success than did economic sanctions.

Implementation

The Bush administration, having opted for offensive action to liberate Kuwait, now faced the challenge of carrying out that strategy. While the American public had played a minimal role in the previous stages, mass opinion did factor heavily into the implementation of the policy.[32] From the administration's decision to resort to war to the signing of the cease-fire agreement, much

---

31. Mervin, *George Bush*, 197.
32. Sobel, *Impact of Public Opinion*, 159.

of the U.S. policy appears inconsistent with a purely strategic execution of war, yet entirely consistent with the unified preferences of a highly attentive public.[33] As a result of a constrained political context (i.e., high issue salience, unified public preferences), the Bush administration repeatedly sacrificed military effectiveness in order to placate the American public. In a sense, then, the public took hold of the reins of power as Operation Desert Shield turned into Operation Desert Storm. Obviously, the public did not dictate every White House decision, but Americans collectively exercised more power at this stage than at any other, often leading the Bush administration into political minefields along the path to war.

The Delay in Announcing a Troop Increase

The Bush administration decided to delay announcing the October 30 troop increase until after the midterm elections. Approval ratings for the president had been dropping steadily over the previous month (figure 12), and the administration now felt that such an announcement might jeopardize the Republicans' electoral prospects.[34] The concern was that an increase of U.S. forces in Saudi Arabia would lead to rampant speculation (and, it turns out, accurate speculation) that the administration had made a dramatic policy shift and was now planning for a military offensive without consulting Congress. As Scowcroft put it, "The timing of the decision to reinforce the troops was determined by practical military considerations, but the timing of the announcement of the increase was driven by political ones. The political experts wanted to delay the announcement until after the congressional elections on November 6."[35]

As expected, the announcement of the troop increase brought a chorus of criticism from Congress and the press. Even though the administration attempted to frame the surge as a routine decision, not a fundamental shift in policy, widespread speculation that war was imminent led to a crumbling of the public consensus that had surrounded Operation Desert Shield. Criticism

---

33. I use the phrase "strategic effectiveness" in much the same way as do realist scholars in international relations. Strategic actions are those undertaken by a unitary decision maker, without concern given to domestic or international politics, which maximize the chances of achieving a goal (i.e., security or power). That is, strategic choices ignore what international allies want and what the domestic population prefers, and they are impervious to the normal institutional constraints (e.g., Congress, the UN, elections) that otherwise shape policy outcomes. Strategic effectiveness is therefore almost synonymous with military effectiveness: a strategically effective action is the type of policy that would be made by apolitical generals (think MacArthur in Korea).
34. Bush and Scowcroft, *World Transformed*; Sobel, *Impact of Public Opinion*.
35. Bush and Scowcroft, *World Transformed*, 395.

of the Bush administration became so intense that many within the administration "began to refer to the three-day weekend as the Veterans Day Massacre."[36] Public approval of President Bush's Persian Gulf policy dropped to 54 percent in mid-November—its lowest point in the crisis (figure 12). Having already opted for the offensive, the administration would have to work to ensure that public support did not continue to erode; if baseline public support became too low, it might diminish the size of the rally the president expected to receive after the war achieved its objectives. Moreover, the White House would soon be forced to turn to the UN and the U.S. Congress to authorize war, and a disapproving public could spell political disaster for the White House. The attempt to stop the political bleeding would come to dominate much of the prewar implementation of policy.[37]

The UN Ultimatum

One of the more immediate issues facing the Bush administration was the question of how to initiate hostilities, a dilemma that had been evident since the very beginning of the crisis. In a White House meeting on August 4, President Bush stated, "Our first objective is to keep Saddam out of Saudi Arabia. Our second is to protect the Saudis against retaliation when we shut down Iraq's export capability. We have a problem if Saddam does not invade Saudi Arabia but holds on to Kuwait."[38] The problem was that the United States was on much firmer political ground in responding to Iraqi provocation than it was in initiating actual military conflict.

Bush's intuition about the difference between provocation and initiation was supported by the public opinion data. Figure 15 demonstrates that of the five possible scenarios prompting the United States to engage in combat with Iraq, using U.S. force to liberate Kuwait had the lowest support (56 percent), while using U.S. force to repeal an Iraqi invasion of Saudi Arabia received the highest support (84 percent).[39] The public's reluctance to engage in a war

36. Woodward, *Commanders*, 324.
37. I have argued that prewar opinion was less important to President Bush than anticipations of what opinion would look like after the war. Therefore, it may seem inconsistent with my argument that the president would be concerned with declining public support if he was confident that the war would be a resounding success. However, as we will see in this stage, there were still potential roadblocks to the implementation of the offensive, and maintaining an acceptable level of public support would be crucial to overcoming each obstacle.
38. Bush and Scowcroft, *World Transformed*, 328.
39. Survey by NBC/*Wall Street Journal*, September 4–5, 1990, from LexisNexis, Roper Center for Public Opinion Research, University of Connecticut (accessed April 12, 2004). "I'm going to mention some things that may or may not happen in the Middle East and for each one, please tell me whether

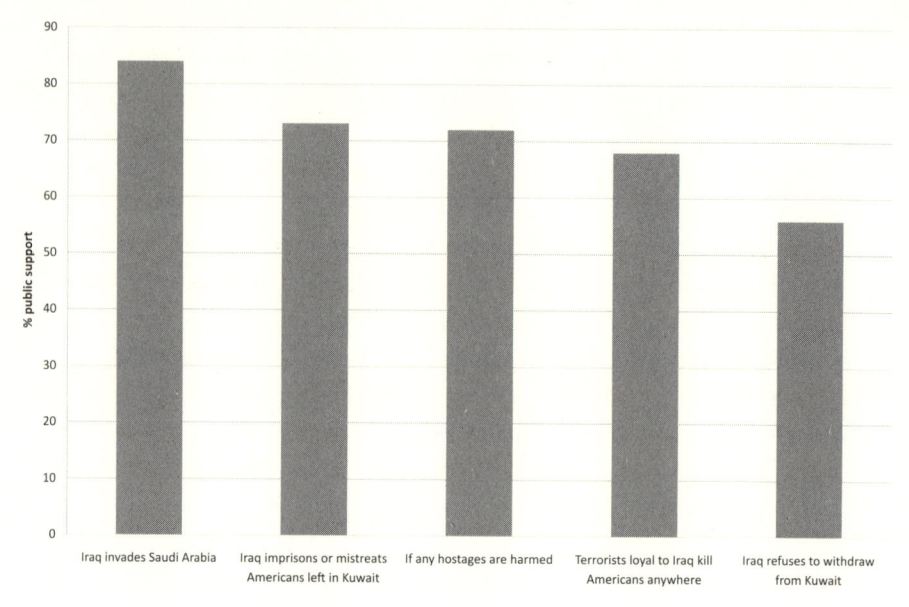

Fig. 15 Reasons for initiating war with Iraq

Bar chart categories (left to right): Iraq invades Saudi Arabia; Iraq imprisons or mistreats Americans left in Kuwait; If any hostages are harmed; Terrorists loyal to Iraq kill Americans anywhere; Iraq refuses to withdraw from Kuwait. Y-axis: % public support (0–90).

of liberation meant that Bush had to find some trigger mechanism to justify hostilities.

The question of how to start hostilities increasingly dominated the president's thoughts in mid-October after he had resigned himself to war. On October 17, Bush wrote in his diary,

> A day of churning. Brent Scowcroft, my trusted friend, comes for dinner. We talk about how we get things moving, and what we do about the [question of] provocation [to justify the use of force]. The news is saying some members of Congress feel I might use a minor incident to go to war, and they may be right. We must get this over with. The longer it goes, the longer the erosion [of public support].... I'm not sure where our own country is. But if they saw a clear provocation, and I think that would include unwillingness to permit us to get our [Embassy] people out of Kuwait, they would be supportive of knocking the hell out of this guy. We can do it from the air.[40]

---

the U.S. should or should not take military action [Dec 8–11: should or should not go to war] in connection with it."

40. Bush and Scowcroft, *World Transformed*, 383.

The October 30 meeting that decided to use military force to liberate Kuwait also focused on three possible scenarios for starting the war with Iraq.[41] First, the United States could implement the offensive with no warning whatsoever. Second, Iraq might be provoked into firing the first shot, which would then justify a massive U.S. counterattack. Finally, the United States could press for a UN ultimatum that would set a deadline for Iraqi compliance. Baker favored an ultimatum, suggesting that it might convince Hussein to capitulate.[42] Cheney disagreed. He felt that an ultimatum would allow Hussein a chance to prepare his defenses and that seeking UN authorization would only tie the administration's hands. British prime minister Margaret Thatcher was also pressuring President Bush not to seek a UN resolution to authorize the use of force.

The ongoing debate about how to initiate the war revolved around the relative importance of political versus strategic concerns. From a military standpoint, implementing the offensive with no warning made the most sense. A preemptive strike would provide an element of surprise—as much as could be had with a large U.S. military force sitting in the desert and CNN faithfully broadcasting U.S. strategy—and was the preferred military strategy. However, a preemptive strike might come with a political price if the public and U.S. allies viewed it as an unprovoked attack against Iraqi forces.

Unlike a preemptive strike, both Iraqi provocation and the issuance of an ultimatum were options that provided political cover. While provocation was preferable from both a strategic and political standpoint, the tactic obviously depended on the Iraqis making the first move, and it did not look like Iraq was willing to fire the first shot. An effort to provoke Iraq into firing first could also backfire if the public and allies saw it for what it was—a ruse to initiate a war, similar to the Gulf of Tonkin incident in the Vietnam War. A UN ultimatum, on the other hand, would appear particularly legitimate both internationally and domestically. However, an ultimatum made little military sense as it would provide Hussein with the precise time of an invasion and afford Iraq additional time to prepare its defenses. Even more troublesome was the possibility that the UN Security Council would veto the use of force.

Faced with these three possible means of starting a war, President Bush chose the least effective military option: a UN ultimatum that set a deadline for Iraqi compliance. On November 29, the UN Security Council passed Resolution 678, requiring Iraq to comply with all previous resolutions and withdraw from

---

41. Ibid., 393.
42. Ibid., 394.

Kuwait by January 15, 1991. Resolution 678 also included a "pause of goodwill," a period in which no hostilities would take place; this held open the possibility, slim as it might be, for a diplomatic solution. Bush would later remark that the decision to seek a UN resolution was equal parts strategic and political maneuvering. "I see two advantages to this approach: diplomacy is only likely to work if Saddam sees we are serious. But if Saddam is not completely out and we must fight, I want to take away from people the argument that we did not give diplomacy a chance."[43] For Scowcroft, the UN resolution was purely political: "As with the vote to back the sanctions, the November UN resolution was a political measure intended to seal international solidarity and strengthen domestic U.S. support by spelling out that we could use force and when."[44]

Thus, the decision to seek a UN resolution authorizing the use of force was essentially a political one made for international and domestic reasons. Working through the UN process would undoubtedly help to rally international support, thus avoiding the perception of Pax Americana in the Middle East. Equally important, the American public overwhelmingly preferred that the United States seek UN approval when dealing with Iraq. While 77 percent of Americans supported the use of force if approved by the UN, only 48 percent supported U.S. force not authorized by a UN resolution.[45] Because the public held a clear preference on when force should be used in Iraq, and because the coming war promised to be highly salient with the American public, the political context regarding the implementation of the offensive was constrained. Taking into consideration the domestic and international contexts, Bush opted for a UN resolution as a trigger mechanism to initiate hostilities, even though doing so made little military sense.

Multinational Force

The U.S. decision to form a multinational military force to defeat Iraq was, in essence, a political decision. The American public strongly favored (88 percent) some burden-sharing arrangement whereby troops from other countries,

43. Ibid., 386.
44. Ibid., 416.
45. Survey by the Gallup Organization, November 8–11, 1990, from LexisNexis, Roper Center for Public Opinion Research, University of Connecticut (accessed April 12, 2004). "To what extent would you support or oppose the use of force against Iraq to make it withdraw from Kuwait if this action was sanctioned by a United Nations resolution?" Percent reporting "strongly support" and "support." "To what extent would you support or oppose the use of force against Iraq to make it withdraw from Kuwait if this action was taken without the support of the United Nations resolution?" Percent reporting "strongly support" and "support."

including Arab nations, would participate in the war effort.[46] This multinational force would also help deflect international criticism that the United States was once again meddling in the Middle East.

Building a coalition of states, however, provided little military advantage to the United States in this particular case.[47] In the event of war, the United States would still shoulder the vast majority of the military burden, and as the only remaining superpower, the U.S. military did not need any support from other countries in order to defeat Iraq. Moreover, integrating troops from other nations would entail considerable costs.[48] Throughout the conflict, much of CENTCOM's time and effort was devoted to the coordination of forces, which usually proved to be more of a political exercise than a strategic task.[49] There were several reasons why a coalition of states decreased military effectiveness: some foreign troops were unreliable, language barriers made centralized command and control difficult, differing degrees of technological sophistication existed among the forces, different training and tactics often made coordination problematic, and the various armies involved often groused about the particular roles they were to play in the upcoming battle. As a member of the elite Navy SEALs told me, "Foreign troops do no good for our forces. They are just window dressing, and actually get in the way. The only group that contributes something of value are the British, especially their special forces."[50] In short, including foreign troops in the campaign to liberate Kuwait, while

---

46. Survey by ABC/*Washington Post*, August 8, 1990, from LexisNexis, Roper Center for Public Opinion Research, University of Connecticut (accessed April 12, 2004). "Bush has said the American troops will join troops from other nations to defend Saudi Arabia from any invasion by Iraq. Is it important or not important that this force include troops from Arab countries?"

47. Observers of the current Iraq War might question this statement given that the lack of a broad coalition has stretched U.S. forces thin since the end of major combat operations in 2003. However, the first Gulf War promised to be a relatively conventional battle, one that the United States is very good at fighting. Since the George H. W. Bush administration had no intention of marching to Baghdad and fighting an urban guerilla war, there was little military need for foreign troops. Likewise, in the second Iraq War there was little need for foreign troops to actually depose Saddam Hussein. However, a broad coalition of nations would have been helpful in the subsequent urban warfare and counterinsurgency battles that have plagued the United States since the end of the main battle for Iraq. Moreover, a broader coalition would have helped George W. Bush politically, both domestic and internationally. And that is precisely the point made here—compiling a multilateral force is often more of a political exercise than a strategic necessity.

48. The one exception to this was financial burden sharing. The United States was keenly interested in gathering financial contributions from coalition members to defray the cost of war. By some estimates, the United States was so successful in its "tin cup" effort that it drew charges of profiteering. Freedman and Karsh estimate that the cost of the war was "$54 billion, of which most—$48.2 billion—was pledged by allies." Freedman and Karsh, *Gulf Conflict*, 358.

49. Woodward, *Commanders*; Gordon and Trainor, *Generals' War*; Freedman and Karsh, *Gulf Conflict*.

50. Interview with Navy SEAL, December 2003.

politically beneficial both domestically and internationally, likely decreased military effectiveness.

Congressional Authorization for War

One of the more important ways in which public opinion exercised its influence during the implementation stage was to prompt the Bush administration to seek congressional approval for the use of force. In early September, members of Congress informed the president that any U.S. military action in the Gulf, even if approved by the UN, would require the consent of Congress. Calls for a congressional vote on the issue intensified after the announced troop increase on November 8. In addition, the American public overwhelmingly believed (82 percent) that President Bush should seek congressional authorization before engaging in military action.[51]

The war powers debate presented a thorny problem for the Bush administration. If Congress voted against the war, the president would be forced to either abandon the offensive or continue and risk impeachment; however, deciding not to go to Capitol Hill also risked impeachment. As Scowcroft remarked, "We were faced with weighing the President's inherent power to use force against the political benefits of explicit support from Congress."[52]

The decision of whether or not to go to Congress was fiercely debated within the administration. Cheney, Scowcroft, Sununu, and Baker all felt that the president was within his constitutional rights as commander in chief to initiate hostilities without congressional approval and that UN Resolution 678 further augmented that authority. More important, the four advisors believed that there was a strong possibility that the president would lose any congressional vote. Conversely, President Bush, Vice President Dan Quayle, and Chief Legal Council C. Boyden Gray believed that, even though the president had the constitutional and international authority to use force against Iraq, he should all the same seek congressional approval for political reasons. In a memorandum prepared at the request of the president, the White House legal staff outlined the constitutional and political considerations involved in seeking congressional approval: "We believe it is legally sufficient to proceed

---

51. Survey by the Gallup Organization, January 11, 1991, from LexisNexis, Roper Center for Public Opinion Research, University of Connecticut (accessed April 12, 2004). "How important do you think it is that President Bush first get the approval of Congress before taking military action against Iraq? Is it very important, somewhat important, not too important or not at all important?" Percent reporting "very" and "somewhat" important.

52. Bush and Scowcroft, *World Transformed*, 416.

with no formal congressional authority at all. However, if U.S. forces will be involved in hostilities or situations where involvement in hostilities is imminent and a congressional endorsement would [be] useful in gaining public support for your action, you should consider seeking a joint resolution approving your action."[53]

On January 6, President Bush sent a letter to Congress asking its members to support UN Resolution 678 and authorize U.S. military action against Iraq. The vote was held on January 12, and military force was approved in the Senate by a narrow margin (52–47) and in the House of Representatives (250–183). In the end, the process of gaining congressional authorization, as strewn as it was with potential roadblocks, was still necessary to ensure domestic political support for the coming war effort.

Going the "Extra Mile for Peace"

In early August, the Bush administration had ruled out a negotiated settlement with Iraq and subsequently made no effort to communicate with Saddam Hussein.[54] However, with war now looming on the horizon, there was increased pressure from the public to seek a diplomatic solution: over 79 percent of Americans believed that the United States should hold talks with Iraq before launching a war.[55] Fearing the domestic and international political fallout that would result from closing the door on diplomacy, President Bush began to consider talks with Baghdad. Bush recalled, "One action I had been contemplating to help strengthen congressional and public support was a direct contact with the Iraqis. I wanted to show that we were going the extra mile for peace and it would help quash some of the charges that I was contemplating war against someone we had not even tried to speak with."[56]

The option of diplomacy with Iraq sparked another contentious debate within the administration.[57] Secretary of State James Baker was still holding out hope that the UN deadline would compel Saddam to leave Kuwait and felt that direct talks with Baghdad would rally flagging domestic support.

53. C. Boyden Gray to the president, memorandum, "Potential Significance of a Declaration of War Against Iraq," August 7, 1990, Bush Presidential Records, John Sununu Files, Persian Gulf War 1991, OA/ID CF00472 (6 of 11).
54. Much of the following discussion is drawn from Bush and Scowcroft, *World Transformed*, 419–21.
55. Survey by ABC/*Washington Post,* January 9, 1991, from LexisNexis, Roper Center for Public Opinion Research, University of Connecticut (accessed April 12, 2004). "Do you think the United States should hold additional talks with Iraq before the January 15th (1991) deadline, or not?"
56. Bush and Scowcroft, *World Transformed,* 419.
57. Ibid.; Baker and DeFrank, *Politics of Diplomacy.*

Scowcroft, on the other hand, felt that diplomacy only weakened the coalition, and he did not want Iraq to withdraw of its own volition and be able to retain its weaponry, giving it the ability to threaten the region for years to come. Like Scowcroft, President Bush had no real interest in a negotiated settlement. However, he also did not see any real chance that U.S.-Iraqi talks would produce such a resolution.[58] The upside of direct talks was that they would take away the opposition's argument that President Bush was rushing into war without giving diplomacy a chance. On November 30, Bush appeared before a nationally televised audience and stated that he would indeed go "the extra mile for peace" by initiating talks with Iraq.

This attempt to go "the extra mile for peace" helped stem a downward slide in public approval. The number of people who believed that Bush had tried hard enough for a diplomatic solution had fallen from 51 percent in August to 38 percent by mid-November; after the talks were announced, the number of Americans who believed that President Bush was serious about diplomacy increased to 44 percent in December and then 47 percent in early January.[59] As far as the public was concerned, these talks represented a final attempt to negotiate a way out of war.

For the Bush administration, however, there was to be no negotiation, and the talks became more public relations than real diplomacy. President Bush had no interest in allowing Saddam Hussein to retain any spoils of his conquest or in providing him with a face-saving way to withdraw from Kuwait. As such, the talks were simply a one-sided reiteration of demands. The United States not only called for Iraq's withdrawal but also demanded that Hussein comply with all UN resolutions, including the stipulation that Iraq leave all its heavy military equipment behind in Kuwait. Because Hussein's rule depended so heavily on his military, there was little chance that he would comply with UN demands—to do so would only loosen his grip on power. Bush would later remark that the diplomacy was designed to increase domestic and international support: "In retrospect, I think he [Saddam Hussein] must have interpreted the first 'home and home' offer in November as a sign of weakness, not recognizing that it was made to show Congress and the European and US publics that we were willing to try for peace."[60]

58. Bush and Scowcroft, *World Transformed*.
59. Surveys by *New York Times*/CBS, August 16–19, 1990; November 13–15, 1990; December 9–11, 1990; and January 5–7, 1991, from Lexis-Nexis, Roper Center for Public Opinion Research, University of Connecticut (accessed April 12, 2004). "In its dealings with the Middle East, do you think the Bush administration had tried hard enough to reach a diplomatic solution, or has it been too quick to get American military forces involved?"
60. Bush and Scowcroft, *World Transformed*, 437.

As expected, the talks held between the United States and Iraq on January 9, 1991, in Geneva failed to resolve the crisis. James Baker presented Iraqi foreign minister Tariq Aziz with a letter from President Bush stating that the UN resolutions were nonnegotiable and that a devastating war would begin shortly after the January 15 deadline. Aziz never looked at the letter. He nervously reiterated the Iraqi position that Kuwait rightfully belonged to Iraq, and he gave no indication that acquiescence to UN demands would be seriously considered in Baghdad. Confirming that the Bush administration had anticipated this outcome, Freedman and Karsh summarized the political nature of the last-minute diplomacy: "The savvy judgment in Washington was that the whole exercise was designed largely to reassure the American people that no avenues were being left unexplored, and to draw the sting out of the Congressional charge that the administration was in a headlong rush to war."[61] With the hopes of a peaceful solution to the crisis dashed, both the coalition and Iraq now braced for war.

Operation Desert Storm

As seen during the option generation stage, the basic military strategy used in the Gulf War was partially shaped by the desire to minimize U.S. casualties to retain domestic political support. The Bush administration had asked the military to revamp its ground attack to avoid U.S. casualties and also instructed the military to minimize Iraqi civilian casualties during the air campaign. Beyond that initial planning, however, there was surprisingly little political input during the actual conduct of the war. With the lessons of Vietnam still prominent, President Bush pledged to the Pentagon not to reenact the scene of Lyndon Johnson leaning over maps and picking military targets.[62] As Cheney would later remark,

> All of Bush's experiences came into play during the course of Operation Desert Storm. He made certain that the U.S. government was given a clear mission and an objective to achieve. After that accomplishment, he left the formulation of plans to the Defense Department and the U.S. military. The Defense Department still had to report to President Bush, but it was free of meddling from Washington. James Baker and Brent Scowcroft sat in on the Defense Department's reports. They were part

---

61. Freedman and Karsh, *Gulf Conflict*, 234.
62. Thompson, *Bush Presidency*, 9.

of the dialogue, but no one second-guessed the Defense Department officials regarding how the operation would be carried out. Much of the credit for that freedom in decision-making should be given to President Bush.[63]

The air war began on January 17 with strikes against military targets in and around Baghdad. According to accounts from Cheney and Powell, President Bush largely kept his word and deferred to the military during the conduct of the war. In contrast to the strong influence of public opinion in shaping the prewar implementation of strategy, this lack of political meddling provides some disconfirming evidence for the hypothesis that presidents will take an unusually active role in the actual conduct of military affairs.

This is not to say, however, that political considerations were absent from the conduct of war. As the coalition effectively destroyed strategic sites in and around Baghdad, the Bush administration began to worry about the impact of the bombing on Iraqi civilians. More to the point, the concern was that pictures of dead Iraqi women and children would turn American opinion against the war effort. As part of his strategy, Saddam Hussein had placed military weaponry in civilian centers in the hope that the deaths of Iraqi citizens would turn American and world opinion against the war. In one notable case, coalition aircraft attacked what was supposed to be a command and control bunker in the Amiriya neighborhood of Baghdad. Although partially a military installation, the Al Firdos bunker also doubled as an air raid shelter, and 314 to 500 Iraqi civilians were reportedly killed in the attack. After the Al Firdos bombing, Cheney asked Powell to review the remaining targets in Baghdad and make a renewed commitment to minimize Iraqi civilian casualties.[64] Powell would later state, "If nothing else, the Al Firdos bunker strike underscored the need to start the combined air/ground offensive and end the war."[65]

News coverage of the effectiveness of the coalition air campaign proved a mixed blessing for the Bush administration. Casualty rates were unexpectedly low, and the public saw a gripping, if antiseptic, picture of war. Equally important was the fact that elite criticism at home was virtually nonexistent. As a result, the public rallied behind the war effort, and approval of President Bush's handling of the war hovered in the mid–80 percent range throughout the war. However, the weak Iraqi resistance also made the coalition air war

63. Ibid.
64. Mathews, "Secret History."
65. Powell and Persico, *My American Journey*, 513.

appear to be a one-sided slaughter. President Bush, anxious to end the war before public support started to decline, repeatedly pushed Schwarzkopf to introduce ground troops, but Schwarzkopf delayed the start of the ground war several times in order to minimize the risk to the ground forces. Despite his eagerness, Bush deferred to his general, and on February 24 the ground war finally began.

Policy Review

Like the air campaign, the ground war phase of Operation Desert Storm went more smoothly than U.S. policy makers had anticipated. Advancing coalition forces encountered little Iraqi resistance, as Saddam Hussein chose not to engage his elite Republican Guard. Poorly trained Iraqi conscripts on the front line surrendered en masse, and journalists began to describe the ground war as "the great prisoner roundup." Despite Hussein's promise of a bloody ground war, only 148 U.S. soldiers were killed in action, 35 of whom were lost to friendly fire.[66]

The success of the ground war presented the administration with a new dilemma. One of the goals of the Gulf War had been to weaken the Iraqi military to a point at which it no longer posed a threat to the region. The coalition had already inflicted considerable damage, but Iraq still retained a significant portion of its weaponry.[67] Especially problematic was that the elite Iraqi Republican Guard had escaped most of the coalition's punishment by retreating to the relative safety of Baghdad. However, although strategic factors suggested that a continuation of the war was warranted, there were political reasons to stop. The lopsided nature of the battle started to bring charges of overkill from the press, as illustrated most vividly by the media coverage of a February 26 U.S. attack on Iraqi forces on the road to Basra. As fleeing Iraqi troops moved in a line along the only highway leading out of Kuwait, coalition air strikes at the front and rear of the convoy created a gridlocked killing zone. The morning papers ran pictures of burned-out tanks under the headline "The Highway of Death," prompting the White House to hold a principals meeting to discuss damage control.[68]

On February 27, Bush met with his closest advisors at the White House.

---

66. Freedman and Karsh, *Gulf Conflict*, 409. Figures on friendly fire casualties from Crenson and Mendoza, "Friendly-Fire Worries."
67. Freedman and Karsh, *Gulf Conflict*; Gordon and Trainor, *Generals' War*.
68. Freedman and Karsh, *Gulf Conflict*.

Powell stated that the military objectives had been realized and suggested that the administration might now consider how and when to end the war. Bush responded, "We're starting to pick up some undesirable public and political baggage with all those scenes of carnage. You say we've accomplished the mission. Why not end it?"[69] With that, the decision was made to stop the war, precisely one hundred hours after the start of the ground campaign.

Clearly, this decision stemmed more from domestic and international political reasons than strategic concerns. Public approval of President Bush's handling of the crisis stood at 86 percent on February 24.[70] If the war had been allowed to continue and U.S. casualty rates had increased, or if more pictures of dead Iraqis had appeared in the media, the president believed that public support would decline and all of the political benefits he gained from leading the most decisive war in U.S. history would be lost. As Cheney would later remark, "From the President's standpoint, the war was less costly than expected. The question was how many additional dead Americans were worth the price of capturing Saddam Hussein; President Bush's answer was, not very many."[71]

However, the decision to end the war was not without its critics. The most stinging critique came from General Schwarzkopf. In an interview with David Frost after the war, Schwarzkopf stated, "Frankly, my recommendation had been, you know, continue the march. I mean, we had them in a rout and we could have continued, you know, to reap a great destruction upon them."[72] Schwarzkopf, who would subsequently back away from his statements, felt that additional time would have allowed the coalition to decimate the Republican Guard and further decrease Saddam Hussein's threat to the region.

Others claimed that the United States should have marched to Baghdad and forcibly removed Hussein from power. Admiral William Crowe (Ret.), who had earlier argued against the use of force in Iraq, now reversed course and argued that the war should have been extended to oust Hussein. This position was supported by a majority of the American public. In February, 84 percent of the public thought that war would not be a success if Hussein remained in power.[73] Surveys after the war also showed that a large majority

---

69. Powell and Persico, *My American Journey*, 521.
70. Survey by the Gallup Organization, February 24, 1991, from LexisNexis, Roper Center for Public Opinion Research, University of Connecticut (accessed April 12, 2004).
71. Thompson, *Bush Presidency*, 23.
72. *New York Times*, "After the War."
73. Survey by the *Los Angeles Times*, February 15–17, 1991, from LexisNexis, Roper Center for Public Opinion Research, University of Connecticut (accessed April 12, 2004). "People have different ideas about what must happen in order for the United States to be successful in the war against Iraq. I'm

of the public believed that the war should have continued until the United States had deposed Hussein.[74]

The difficulty that the American public had in accepting the end of the war without the removal of Saddam Hussein can be traced, in part, to President Bush's earlier attempts to mobilize public support. Throughout the Persian Gulf conflict, Bush had personalized the crisis by employing the Hussein-as-Hitler frame. As noted earlier, the American public tended to be more willing to use military force in Iraq for reasons pertaining to the national interest than because it was persuaded that Hussein was the equivalent of Hitler. Nevertheless, Bush's use of this rhetorical technique did imply that ousting Hussein was a central part of the coalition's war aims. The incongruence between rhetoric and goals now placed the administration in a difficult position. To allow the war to continue with the intent of targeting Hussein was a move fraught with political challenges. Actively seeking a regime change would mean that the United States was violating the terms of the UN resolutions that had authorized force only to liberate Kuwait. As a result, the coalition that had demonstrated such unity in its purpose to liberate Kuwait would likely split.

When the political context is marked by high issue salience and unified public preferences, our theory predicts considerable presidential responsiveness. In this case, issue salience was undoubtedly high at the policy review stage. However, determining the public's preferences is a different and more complex story. The American public held not one, but three very strong preferences: (1) minimize U.S. casualties, (2) act within guidelines set by UN resolutions, and (3) depose Saddam Hussein. The problem for the Bush administration was that it would be impossible to respond to each of these preferences since the goals posed an inherent trade-off. Deposing Hussein would inevitably lead to greater U.S. and Iraqi casualties and would require acting outside of the terms set by UN resolutions; not deposing Hussein would mean defying the 84 percent of Americans who felt that war success hinged on his removal. U.S. policy simply could not be responsive to all three strong, yet incompatible, preferences. As a result, President Bush decided to end the war out of

---

going to read you some things that could happen relating to the war. For each, please tell me if you feel it is necessary or not necessary for this to happen in order for the U.S. to be successful in the war against Iraq. . . . In order for the U.S. to be successful, it is necessary or not necessary for Saddam Hussein to be removed from power."

74. An ABC/*Washington Post* survey asked, "Please tell me if you agree or disagree with this statement: the United States should not have ended the war with Iraqi President Saddam Hussein still in power." On April 2, 1990, 55 percent agreed with the statement; on May 30–June 2, 1991, 63 percent agreed; and on July 25–28, 1991, 73 percent agreed. From LexisNexis, Roper Center for Public Opinion Research, University of Connecticut (accessed April 12, 2004).

the belief that increasing numbers of U.S. casualties would be a more salient concern to the American public than leaving Hussein in power. The decision seemed to help the president shore up domestic support: at the end of the war, 92 percent of Americans approved of the president's Iraq policy.[75]

Summary

This chapter has shown how the relationship between public opinion and presidential foreign policy making can change over the life of a crisis event. While President Bush led the American public through the early stages of the Persian Gulf crisis, including the key decision for war, the pressure for political responsiveness increased in the implementation and policy review stages as unified public preferences converged with high issue salience. In this constrained political context, President Bush made a number of choices—i.e., asking the UN and the U.S. Congress to authorize war, creating a multinational coalition, and going the extra mile for peace—that reflected the preferences of the American people, yet diverged from a single-minded, strategic pursuit of a military goal. This is not to say that domestic public opinion was the *sole* factor that led to these decisions, as many of them were also consistent with the preferences of international allies. It is difficult to fully separate out the relative influence of domestic and international political considerations on these choices, but we can say that public opinion had its greatest influence on presidential decision making at the implementation and review stages of the Gulf War. As such, the Gulf War is only clearly understood if we also understand that presidents can lead the public at some stages only to follow at others.

---

75. Survey by the Gallup Organization, February 28–March 2, 1991, from LexisNexis, Roper Center for Public Opinion Research, University of Connecticut (accessed February 7, 2004).

6

THE ETHIOPIAN FAMINE
Problem Definition and Option Generation

From 1982 to 1986, a devastating famine ravaged the Horn of Africa. The situation was most dire in Ethiopia, a country that had experienced regular famines throughout its history. Hunger and politics are perhaps more closely intertwined in Ethiopia than in any other nation. In the mid-1970s, famine was directly responsible for the collapse of the Ethiopian monarchy when Emperor Haile Selassie, a longtime U.S. ally, attempted to cover up evidence of widespread starvation to insulate his regime from domestic unrest.[1] That decision proved fatal, as peasants and the military conspired in a "creeping coup" that overthrew and imprisoned Selassie.

The successor regime, a military junta known as the Derg, was led by Lieutenant Colonel Mengistu Haile Mariam. Once in power, the Derg announced its commitment to Marxism and within a year had severed ties to the United States, nationalized U.S. property, instituted a command economy, collectivized agriculture, and purchased large amounts of Soviet arms. The United States responded to this loss of its traditional ally by cutting all military and developmental aid, dramatically reducing emergency food aid, and cultivating an alliance with Somalia, a country with which Ethiopia was fighting a low-intensity border war at the time.

The Derg inherited a country rife with political and economic instability. The Ethiopian government was engaged in long-running wars with secessionist rebel groups in the northern provinces of Eritrea and Tigray, as well as with insurgents from Somalia in the south. The incessant conflict led Ethiopia to become the most heavily militarized nation in sub-Saharan Africa. Massive

---

1. Shepherd, *Politics of Starvation*; Shepherd, "Food Aid"; E. Keller, "Politics of Famine"; E. Keller, *Revolutionary Ethiopia*.

defense expenditures acted as a drag on what was already a sluggish economy. Ethiopia possessed little industrial capacity and was largely dependent on the export of coffee for foreign capital. The underdeveloped nature of the Ethiopian economy—coupled with the Derg's commitment to Marxism, high militarization, and rapid population growth—produced little growth in GDP. By most measures, Ethiopia remained the poorest country in the world throughout the 1980s.[2]

It was in this environment that the 1982–86 famine occurred. At its height, an estimated eight to ten million Ethiopians were at risk of starvation. While the estimates on mortality vary, all assume that well over a million Ethiopians died of hunger, prompting one relief expert to call the famine "the worst food crisis of this century."[3] The severity of the famine was the product of an especially pernicious mix of factors inside Ethiopia—drought, war, poverty, land desertification, and government mismanagement—set against the backdrop of the cold war. As such, the famine fell into a category of foreign policy issues aptly termed "complex humanitarian emergencies."[4] Complex humanitarian emergencies are, by nature, political. Although natural disasters (in this case drought) can act as catalysts, social and political factors are the root cause of massive death and human suffering.[5] However, it is important to note that while the situation certainly looked like a crisis from the standpoint of Ethiopian citizens, it was not considered a crisis for the United States according to our definition. Crises are defined by a high probability of military force and threats to the core values of the state. Because neither situation applied for the United States, the famine falls into the noncrisis category.

The case of the Ethiopian famine offers a look at noncrisis foreign policy making. From 1982 to late 1984, few Americans were even aware that there was a famine occurring in Africa. Although there has always been a strong humanitarian current in American public opinion, minimal issue salience in this case meant that the Reagan administration was under little political pressure to respond to the public's still latent preferences. Consequently, the U.S. response to the famine was modest and slow. The political context changed dramatically in October 1984, however, when television and rock stars helped to focus the public's concern on Ethiopia. As a result, consistent, widespread

---

2. Abegaz, *Aid and Reform*.
3. Legum, "Africa's Food Crisis," 25.
4. Natsios, *U.S. Foreign Policy*; Natsios, "NGOs and the UN System"; Natsios, "United States Disaster Response"; Callan, "U.S. Foreign Aid."
5. Sen, *Development as Freedom*; Sen, *Poverty and Famines*; Dreze and Sen, *Hunger and Public Action*.

preferences met with high issue salience for the first time in the case, prompting the Reagan administration to give a record amount of U.S. food aid to the communist nation. However, the new public interest was short lived, and as attention to Ethiopia rapidly declined, so too did the pressure for political responsiveness. When Americans had turned their attention elsewhere, the Reagan administration made several policy choices that, had the public been watching, would have likely have met with widespread disapproval. In short, the Ethiopian case clearly demonstrates how political responsiveness closely tracks the ebbs and flows of public attention.

This chapter assesses the Reagan administration's response to the Ethiopian famine during the policy definition and option generation stages. At these two early stages, there was little indication that public opinion was an important decision premise for the administration. Policy making took place within a guarded political context, as the American public, while expressing a broad preference for humanitarian aid in the general sense, remained inattentive to the specific tragedy in Ethiopia. In terms of our theory of the policy-opinion link, presidents facing a guarded context usually ignore public opinion but must, at the same time, remain cautious about an inattentive public suddenly becoming attentive in the future. As this chapter will show, minimal public interest in the Ethiopian famine from 1982 to 1984 led to a slow U.S. response to a worsening situation.

Problem Definition

Agenda Setting

The Reagan administration first became aware of the famine in Ethiopia in the spring of 1982.[6] Early warning systems indicated that as early as 1979 Ethiopia was beginning to experience drought and the onset of moderate to serious food shortages.[7] By 1982, harvest rains had failed and it was clearly evident that Ethiopia was in the first stage of a potentially massive famine. In response, the Ethiopian government issued several appeals for aid from the international community. These requests were corroborated by reports from nongovernmental organizations (NGOs), intergovernmental organizations (IGOs), and U.S. governmental agencies. In December 1982, the nonprofit Catholic Relief

---

6. General Accounting Office, *United States' Response*, 2.
7. Shepherd, "Food Aid."

Services (CRS) requested emergency food from the U.S. Agency for International Development (USAID), the executive agency charged with administering U.S. emergency foreign assistance. This appeal was endorsed by the U.S. embassy in Addis Ababa, which cabled the State Department with its concerns about an increasing number of Ethiopians flowing into feeding stations. Then, in early 1983, the CIA, the World Food Programme (WFP), and the UN Disaster Relief Organization (UNDRO) all issued findings that indicated that severe famine conditions existed in the Horn of Africa.[8]

As discussed in chapter 2, decision makers often regard the American public as either a potential opportunity or a potential constraint at the agenda setting stage of noncrises. If the White House feels that the public will support its position, it will then seek to raise the salience of an issue and work to place it on the political agenda. If, however, the White House feels that the public is opposed to its position, it will work to minimize issue salience and, in effect, "go private." As will be explained further in the next section, the American public was viewed as a constraint in some quarters of the Reagan administration and an opportunity in others. Therefore, the administration did not work to increase the salience of the Ethiopian famine, nor did it work very hard to keep the issue hidden from the American public. Instead, the famine simply languished in relative public obscurity for several years.

Problem Representation

After becoming aware of the problem in Ethiopia in early 1982, the Reagan administration faced the task of defining what the famine meant in terms of U.S. goals and objectives. This section first examines the guarded political context (i.e., unified public preferences, low issue salience) that characterized the problem definition stage and extended through the option generation stage. It then provides an overview of the various actors involved in U.S. emergency food aid decisions.

THE GUARDED POLITICAL CONTEXT

Assessing public preferences is complicated by the fact that no survey questions specifically referenced the famine in Africa until 1985. Therefore, we must infer preferences by relying on surveys that gauged opinion on foreign aid in more general terms. A common finding in public opinion research is that a strong and persistent anti–foreign aid sentiment runs through the American

8. General Accounting Office, *United States' Response.*

public.[9] This general opposition to foreign aid is reflected in surveys taken during the problem representation stage of the Ethiopian famine. In 1982, 72 percent of the American public believed that the United States was spending too much on foreign aid.[10] Even after dramatic cuts in the foreign aid budget during Reagan's first year in office, 70 percent of Americans still felt that the United States was providing too much international assistance.[11] This widespread belief suggests that Americans may have preferred that little money be spent on relief efforts in Ethiopia.

It is important to point out, however, that preferences regarding foreign aid are highly contingent on policy goals.[12] An overwhelming majority of Americans approve of humanitarian aid to alleviate hunger or poverty, or to respond to some international disaster in the less developed world. By contrast, only a small minority of the public prefers the strategic allocation of foreign aid to advance U.S. interests abroad or to bolster "middle-income" allies, such as Egypt and Israel. Surveys taken in 1982 illustrate that public support for foreign aid is inexorably linked with policy objectives. For instance, 92 percent[13] of the public indicated that the United States should take an active

9. In large part, the public's opposition stems from the pervasive, yet erroneous, belief that the United States devotes a large percentage of its national budget to foreign aid. For instance, a 1995 poll showed that 49 percent of the public favored cuts in U.S. foreign aid. The respondents who favored decreasing foreign aid believed, on average, that the United States spends 18 percent of the federal budget on foreign assistance. When these respondents were informed that less than one percent of the federal budget goes to foreign aid, support for *increasing* U.S. foreign assistance to less developed countries rose to 79 percent. See Kull and Destler, *Misreading the Public,* and Otter, "Domestic Public Support."
10. Survey by the National Opinion Research Center, February–April 1982, from LexisNexis, Roper Center for Public Opinion Research, University of Connecticut (accessed April 12, 2004). "(We are faced with many problems in this country, none of which can be solved easily or inexpensively. I'm going to name some of these problems, and for each one I'd like you to tell me whether you think we're spending too much money on it, too little money, or about the right amount.) Are we spending too much, too little, or about the right amount on . . . foreign aid?"
11. Survey by the Roper Organization, December 3–10, 1983, from LexisNexis, Roper Center for Public Opinion Research, University of Connecticut (accessed April 12, 2004). "(Turning now to the business of the country—we are faced with many problems in this country, none of which can be solved easily or inexpensively. I'm going to name some of these problems, and for each one I'd like you to tell me whether you think we're spending too much money on it, too little money, or about the right amount.) Are we spending too much, too little, or about the right amount on . . . foreign aid?" A few months later, this same preference level was found in a survey conducted by the National Opinion Research Center, February–April 1984, from LexisNexis, Roper Center for Public Opinion Research, University of Connecticut (accessed April 12, 2004).
12. See Program on International Policy Attitudes, *Americans on Foreign Aid.*
13. Survey by the Gallup Organization, October 29–November 6, 1982, from LexisNexis, Roper Center for Public Opinion Research, University of Connecticut (accessed April 12, 2004). "(I am going to read a list of possible foreign policy goals that the United States might have. For each one please say whether you think that it should be a very important foreign policy goal of the United States, a somewhat important foreign policy goal, or not an important goal at all?) . . . Combating world hunger." Percent reporting "very important" or "somewhat important."

interest in alleviating hunger worldwide, while at the same time 72 percent felt that America was spending too much on foreign aid in general.[14] Likewise, a later Pew survey found that while less than 60 percent of Americans ordinarily favored U.S. foreign aid policy, over 87 percent of the public advocated "giving food and medical assistance to people in needy countries."[15] Among the listed reasons for giving foreign aid, assistance to "alleviate hunger and disease in poor countries" was rated the highest, while giving aid "to increase U.S. influence over other countries" received the lowest rating.[16] This evidence implies that assessing American support for foreign aid is meaningless unless a clear reference is made to the goals of that aid. In short, the public draws a distinction between the objectives of foreign aid; it strongly prefers that aid be used to address humanitarian problems, and equally strongly opposes the use of aid to advance U.S. interests abroad.

Americans' almost unanimous humanitarian sentiment provides solid evidence that the public would have expressed a preference that the United States send relief aid to Ethiopia had the question been directly asked in a survey. Even at this early stage, the famine in Ethiopia was a humanitarian tragedy of the first order: almost four million people were affected by acute shortages of food, and mortality rates were climbing rapidly, especially among the children and the elderly. But while there may have been a strong public preference for humanitarian relief, these opinions were latent because Ethiopia received virtually no media or public attention.

Thus, there was little public outcry for a concerted U.S. relief effort at this early stage of the Ethiopian famine. In a span of two years—from August 1982 to August 1984—the television networks ran only eight minutes and seventeen seconds of news coverage on the African famine (figure 16). By comparison, over one hundred fifty minutes of nightly news addressed Iraq's invasion of Kuwait in the *first eleven days* of that crisis. The famine did receive greater mention in newspapers than on television, but here "greater mention" is rather deceiving: only four brief articles appeared in the *New York Times* (figure 17). Nonexistent public interest consequently placed the Reagan administration under little pressure to respond to the Ethiopian famine.

Despite the low salience of the case, public opinion might still have been relevant if decision makers had reason to expect that the public would become

---

14. Survey by the National Opinion Research Center, University of Chicago, February 1982, from the iPOLL Databank, Roper Center for Public Opinion Research, University of Connecticut (accessed July 19, 2008).
15. Program on International Policy Attitudes, *Americans on Foreign Aid*.
16. Ibid.

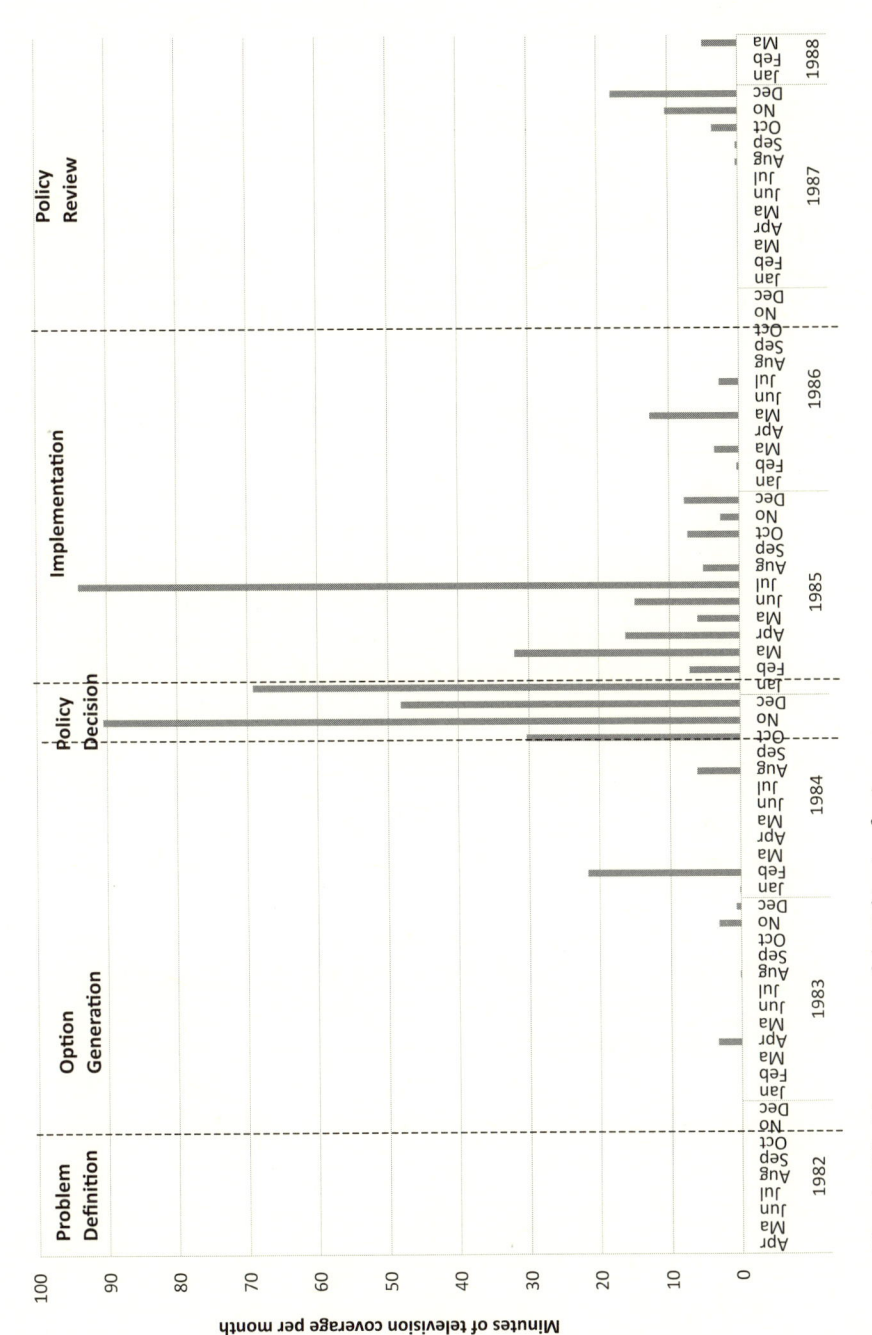

Fig. 16 Television coverage of the Ethiopian famine

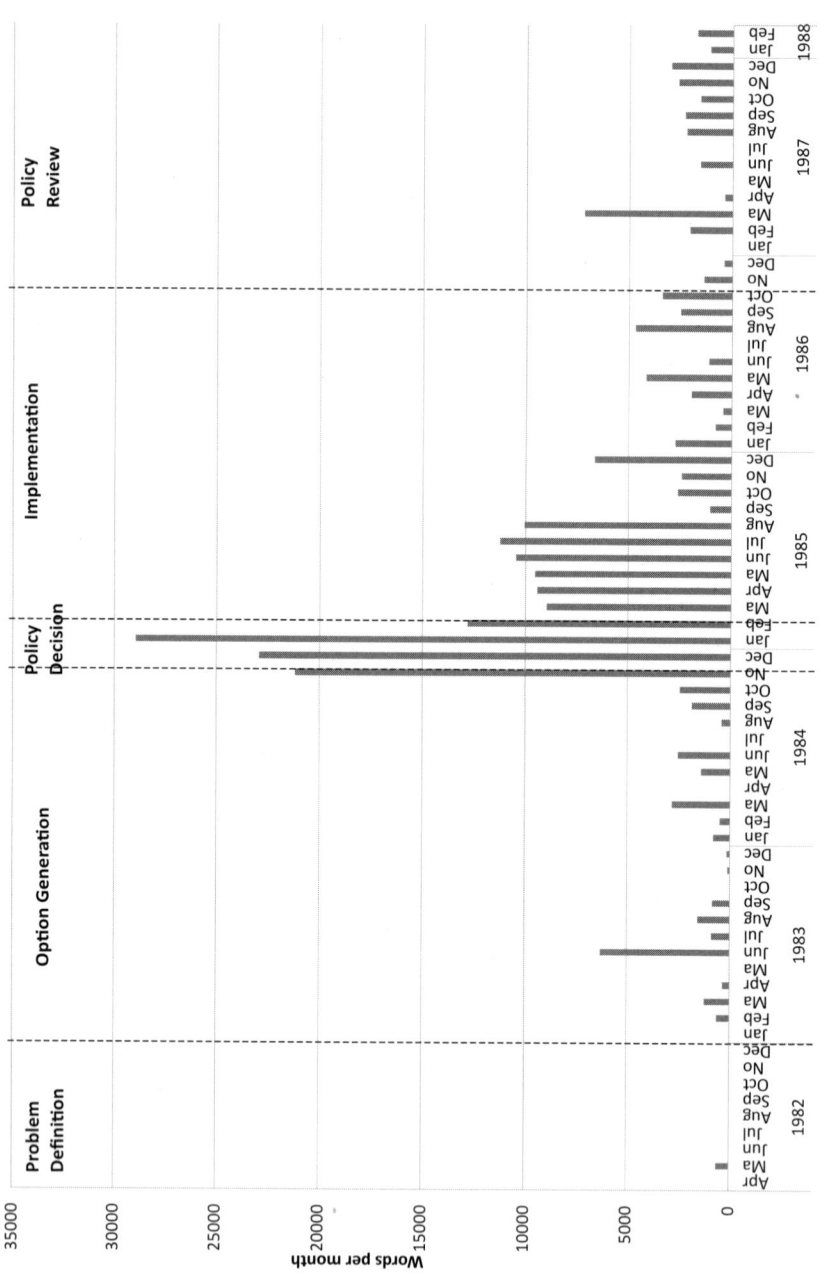

Fig. 17 *New York Times* coverage of the Ethiopian famine

attentive sometime in the future. However, there was little reason at that time to expect that Americans would eventually care about events in Ethiopia. In general, the American public's attention to, and knowledge of, foreign policy issues is low.[17] It is even lower for foreign policy issues that do not potentially involve U.S. military action,[18] and even lower still for regions (like Africa) that are geographically and culturally distant from the United States.[19] Given this already low baseline of public interest, drought and famines typically attract *less* attention than do other types of disasters because of their slow onset and lack of spectacular visuals.[20] In short, at the time it first appeared on the Washington agenda, little about the Ethiopian famine suggested that it was a likely candidate for widespread public concern.

In sum, a widespread, yet still latent, preference for humanitarian assistance coupled with very low issue salience created a guarded political context, giving the White House little incentive to respond to public opinion. This context offered the Reagan administration considerable autonomy in constructing its Ethiopian policy.

U.S. EMERGENCY FOOD AID

Before we examine how the Reagan administration represented the Ethiopian famine, it is important to have a basic understanding of how the U.S. government makes decisions about emergency relief. Unlike crises, which typically concentrate power in the White House, noncrisis issues tend to involve a diverse array of political actors (often with different policy goals) in the decision-making process. Very few humanitarian disasters attract the attention of the president.[21] Instead, policy-making authority typically devolves to the bureaucracy, where problems are dealt with in a complex, convoluted process that involves a number of different agencies. For instance, decisions on

17. Almond, *American People*; Rielly, *U.S. Foreign Policy, 1995*; Graber, *Mass Media and American Politics*; Holsti, "Public Opinion and American Foreign Policy," 283–85; Delli Carpini and Keeter, *What Americans Know*; Gans, *Deciding What's News*; P. Converse, "Nature of Belief Systems," 206–61.
18. Gans, *Deciding What's News*; Benthall, *Disasters, Relief, and the Media*; Eisensee and Stromberg, "News Floods," 722.
19. Gans, *Deciding What's News*, 36; Adams, "Whose Lives Count?"; Eisensee and Stromberg, "News Floods," 722–23; Van Belle, "*New York Times* and Network TV"; Graber, *Mass Media and American Politics*; Power, *Problem from Hell*, 508–9.
20. Drury, Olson, and Van Belle, "Politics of Humanitarian Aid"; Natsios, "United States Disaster Response"; Eisensee and Stromberg, "News Floods." As Eisensee and Stromberg conclude, "For every person killed in a volcano disaster, 40,000 people must die in a drought to reach the same probability of media coverage" (694–95).
21. Drury, Olson, and Van Belle, "Politics of Humanitarian Aid"; Van Belle, "Bureaucratic Responsiveness"; Ruttan, *United States Development*.

emergency food aid during the time of the Ethiopian famine required the *unanimous* consent of USAID, the State Department, the Department of Agriculture, the Office of Management and Budget (OMB), the National Security Council (NSC), and the CIA.[22] The respective mandates of these various agencies meant that "turf wars" over policy occurred frequently.[23] Moreover, because presidents rarely become involved in such decisions, there is little power available to break a bureaucratic deadlock should it occur.[24]

In addition to the myriad of bureaucratic agencies involved in emergency food aid decisions, Congress plays a large role in the food aid policy through its budgetary power and administrative oversight of bureaucratic agencies. Moreover, humanitarian relief is an important issue for many members of Congress. For some, U.S. food aid offers a way to bring pork-barrel projects home to their agricultural districts; others have an ideological or moral interest in problems in the less developed world.[25] Domestic interest groups, particularly farmers, have also been responsible for enlarging the scope of U.S. food aid policy over the years.[26] And NGOs play several very important roles: they lobby the U.S. government for resources, alert members of Congress to ongoing problems, and, most important, implement many of the policy decisions that are made in Washington, D.C. As we will see, much of the U.S. food aid policy is carried out through NGOs in countries where the United States is legally prohibited from dispensing aid. Finally, U.S. food aid policy is shaped by IGOs such as the WFP and UNDRO.

22. General Accounting Office, *United States' Response*.
23. Callan, "U.S. Foreign Aid"; Kissi, "Politics of Food Relief."
24. Shepherd, "Food Aid"; Varnis, *Reluctant Aid*; General Accounting Office, *United States' Response*; Ruttan, *United States Development*; Natsios, *U.S. Foreign Policy*. Initial requests for emergency assistance were directed to USAID's Bureau of Food for Peace and Voluntary Assistance. Most requests for emergency food aid fall under the category of Public Law (PL) 480 Title II, involving either grants of agricultural commodities by the Commodity Credit Corporation directly to a recipient government, or grants by the U.S. government to American NGOs with established in-country feeding programs. In cases in which the U.S. government provides aid to unfriendly states (like Ethiopia), assistance is channeled through NGOs. If the Bureau of Food for Peace deems that the initial request warrants further consideration, it is forwarded to USAID's geographic, policy, and service bureaus for a review. Once all USAID bureaus sign off on a request, it then moves to the PL 480 Title II Working Group of the Food Aid Subcommittee of the interagency Development Coordinating Committee. While USAID administers and funds all PL 480 programs, the approval process at this point involves several executive agencies. The Working Group consists of representatives from USAID and the State Department, Department of Agriculture, Office of Management and Budget, NSC, and CIA. During the Ethiopian famine, participants in the Working Group stated that decision-making was informal and relied on consensus, meaning that each representative agency effectively held a veto over policy. If all agreed on a proposal, USAID would act as the project administrator and fund the project out of its budget. See General Accounting Office, *United States' Response*.
25. Bosso, "Setting the Agenda"; Diven, "Domestic Determinants"; Diven, "Coincidence of Interests."
26. Diven, "Domestic Determinants"; Diven, "Coincidence of Interests."

Competing Representations of the Ethiopian Famine

With so many groups involved in decisions about emergency food aid, it was perhaps inevitable that there would be competing representations of the situation in Ethiopia. Indeed, three main representations of the famine emerged, each stressing different constraints and sometimes even different goals (see table 8). These representations often, although not always, broke down according to bureaucratic agencies and partisan affiliation. The following discussion explores each of the representations in depth.

THE HARDLINERS

The cold war context dominated the hardliner representation of the famine, advanced by some members of the NSC, CIA, USAID, and Congress.[27] This perspective viewed the famine as an opportunity to reclaim an ally that had been lost to the Soviet Union.[28] Access to the Red Sea and the country's close proximity to Saudi Arabia meant that Ethiopia occupied a key strategic position in the Horn of Africa. With the Derg's successful coup, the United States had lost a key communications node while the Soviets had gained several naval bases off Masawa in the Red Sea. A major irritant to the United States was that approximately three thousand Soviet military advisors and twelve thousand Cuban troops trained and fought alongside the Ethiopian army in its various civil wars. To make matters worse, the Derg had formed a close alliance with Libya and was rumored to have provided support to terrorist organizations.

A secondary, but also important, component of the hardliner perspective was that the Marxist policies of the Ethiopian government were actually responsible for the onset and spread of famine. The Mengistu regime had rigidly adhered to a Stalinist-style agricultural policy, with disastrous results.[29] Policies of villagization moved farmers from privately owned plots of land to large collective farms that received few of the modern agricultural inputs needed

---

27. In the Reagan administration, advocates of this representation included then-member of USAID John Bolton and the African affairs advisor to the NSC, Fred Wettering. Members of Congress included Senators Robert Kasten (R-Wisc.) and Ted Stevens (R-Alaska). It should be noted that advocates of the hardliner representation did not respond to my requests for interviews. As a result, I have inferred their representation from secondary sources and from discussions with other decision makers involved in the case. Although this is not ideal evidence—obviously a first-hand account of how hardliners themselves viewed the famine is preferable—the secondary literature and interviewees reflect little disagreement on the essence of the hardliner position.

28. Much of this is drawn from Shepherd, "Food Aid"; Kissi, "Politics of Food Relief"; Callan, "U.S. Foreign Aid"; E. Keller, "Politics of Famine"; and E. Keller, *Revolutionary Ethiopia*.

29. Varnis, *Reluctant Aid*; E. Keller, *Revolutionary Ethiopia*; E. Keller, "Politics of Famine"; Kissi, "Politics of Food Relief."

Table 8 Problem representations in the Ethiopian famine

	Goals	Constraints	Advocates
Hardliners	1) Overthrow the Mengistu regime and reclaim Ethiopia as an ally 2) Coerce or compel Ethiopia to institute a market economy, thereby helping famine victims	1) No viable noncommunist rebel group in Ethiopia 2) Negative public response (low probability)	USAID's John Bolton; African Affairs advisor to the NSC Fred Wettering; Senators Robert Kasten (R-Wisc.) and Ted Stevens (R-Alaska); and Heritage Foundation.
Institutionalists	Help famine victims	1) Civil war 2) Diversion of food aid 3) Marxist policies of Ethiopian government 4) Domestic political pressures from left and right	Administrator of USAID M. Peter McPherson; assistant administrator of USAID's Bureau of Food for Peace Julia Chang Bloch; Assistant Secretary of State for African Affairs Chester Crocker; and Deputy Assistant Secretary of State for African Affairs Princeton Lyman.
Humanitarians	Help famine victims	1) Unwillingness of Reagan administration to respond to needs of a communist country 2) Drought 3) Problems with the Ethiopian government	Chargé d'affaires of the U.S. embassy in Addis Ababa David Korn; CRS's regional director for Africa Kenneth Hackett; Senator John Danforth (R-Mo.) and Representatives Howard Wolpe (D-Mich.), Ted Weiss (D-N.Y.), and Mickey Leland (D-Tex.); and chief of staff for Rep. Wolpe, Steve Weissman.

to produce a sufficient domestic supply of food. To minimize coup risk, the Ethiopian government devoted only 5 percent of its domestic budget to agriculture and set artificially low commodity prices to pacify the urban population and the military.[30] These policies provided few incentives or opportunities for farmers to be productive. As additional insurance against a military coup, Mengistu was believed to be diverting international aid from hungry citizens to feed his army. Thus, for the hardliners, famine and abject poverty would remain a constant condition in Ethiopia as long as Mengistu remained in power.

The primary goal of the hardliners was to replace Mengistu with a regime that was both more amenable to U.S. interests and more benevolent to the Ethiopian people. To accomplish this goal, the United States could (1) withhold food aid and hope that mass starvation would lead to the eventual overthrow of Mengistu, and/or (2) actively support rebel groups in Eritrea and Tigray in their bid to overthrow the Ethiopian government. At first blush, a policy of withholding food to starving people in order to destabilize the Ethiopian government appears "callous at best."[31] Yet consider this representation from another angle. Mengistu was actively using the famine to kill off his political opponents, and any food aid that the United States did provide would likely end up feeding his army, which would do nothing to save starving citizens. Perversely, U.S. food would help ensure the health of Ethiopian soldiers, thereby allowing them the strength to kill more of their countrymen in the rebel-controlled areas of the north. The problem, as seen by the hardliners, was that the United States faced a question of "lifeboat ethics" that meant making a difficult choice.[32] The United States could provide Ethiopia with large amounts of food aid to meet its current needs, and in the process enable a corrupt government to remain in power, virtually ensuring a regular, ongoing occurrence of famine. Alternatively, the United States could withhold food aid to try and topple Mengistu, which might save more lives in the long run but, in the short term, would allow large numbers of Ethiopians to starve. Viewed in this context, U.S. policy was truly between Scylla and Charybdis.

The hardliners recognized two primary constraints. The first was that the two most powerful rebel groups in Ethiopia—the Eritrean People's Liberation Front (EPLF) and the Tigrayan People's Liberation Front (TPLF)—were themselves Marxist. Absent a viable democratic (or, at least, anti-Marxist) alternative, the administration had few options for launching a covert operation. A

---

30. Callan, "U.S. Foreign Aid."
31. Shepherd, "Food Aid."
32. Hardin, "Living on a Lifeboat."

second constraint was that a policy of withholding U.S. food aid to advance a cold war agenda promised to be unpopular with the American public. Nevertheless, at this early stage of the crisis, little suggested that the famine would become a salient issue. While abject poverty and hunger are a constant condition in the less developed world, the American public only rarely attends to these problems. The hardliners could, therefore, attach a relatively low probability to this second constraint becoming an important one in the foreseeable future.

THE INSTITUTIONALISTS

For lack of a better term, the second representation is called the "institutionalist" perspective.[33] Institutionalists focused on the challenges that political factors in Ethiopia and in the United States posed to possible relief efforts. Political appointees at USAID and in the State Department were among the chief advocates of this viewpoint.[34] These appointees obtained their posts in the Reagan administration in part because of their commitment to market-oriented developmental strategies. Nevertheless, these individuals were also, by virtue of their bureaucratic position and/or prior experience, firmly committed to responding to the needs of people in the less developed world.[35]

The primary goal of the institutionalist representation was the alleviation of human suffering in Ethiopia. M. Peter McPherson, the administrator of USAID at the time of the Ethiopian famine, commented in a more recent interview, "When you see that kids are starving, you would have to be pretty hardened to say, 'Well, that kid is starving, but my kids are just fine.'"[36] Julia

---

33. The term "institutionalist" is used here to describe individuals with an overriding concern with the Ethiopian political and economic systems. Ideologically, the institutionalists are probably closest to the neoliberal view in developmental economics. Other possible terms for this viewpoint—structuralist, politicized humanitarians, neoliberal, developmentalists—carry some normative connotations that I felt were unhelpful to the analysis. In short, the term "institutionalists" is my own creation and not meant to refer to some other use of the same term in the literature.

34. USAID is the executive agency charged with administering emergency foreign assistance. Institutionalists interviewed for this project include M. Peter McPherson, Julia Chang Bloch, Chester Crocker, and Princeton Lyman. See below for interviews.

35. For example, M. Peter McPherson and Julia Chang Bloch both served in the Peace Corps. Chester Crocker is an academic with research interests in Africa. Princeton Lyman is a political economist who worked for a number of years with USAID. Ruttan describes McPherson in this way: "A major preoccupation of the [Reagan] administration continued to be using US/AID programming effectively to achieve foreign policy objectives, but success was limited because McPherson was committed to maintaining the humanitarian and development objectives of the agency. The work of McPherson, along with some members of Congress and special interest groups, especially the humanitarian PVOs, enabled the agency to resist many of the more radical reforms on the Reagan agenda." Ruttan, *United States Development*, 136.

36. M. Peter McPherson, interview with the author, Washington, D.C., February 23, 2006.

Chang Bloch, then assistant administrator of USAID's Bureau of Food for Peace, has also since remarked that "when you have a famine and people are dying, you don't have the luxury of arguing about policy. Your first objective is to save lives."[37] And Princeton Lyman, former deputy assistant secretary of state for African affairs, added, "We were not going to play with people's lives [in Ethiopia], even though I had nothing but contempt for Mengistu. We didn't want to let people die for that reason."[38]

Although institutionalists were genuinely concerned with the plight of the Ethiopian people, they were also acutely aware of how political realities, both in the United States and in Ethiopia, could complicate relief efforts. Four constraints dominated the institutionalist representation. First, a civil war in Ethiopia prevented food aid from reaching the vast majority of victims. Of the estimated 7.9 million Ethiopians affected by famine, 5.5 million lived in the rebel-controlled regions of Eritrea, Tigray, and Wollo.[39] International relief efforts were hampered by the Ethiopian government's unwillingness to feed citizens in rebel-controlled areas and its refusal to divert military resources, such as trucks, to assist in the relief effort. As Lyman stated, "The reason you had the threat of massive famine in Ethiopia was because the government was blocking not only knowledge about the depth of the famine but also access to the people who were affected."[40]

A second and related concern was that the Ethiopian government would divert international and U.S. food aid to feed its military or actually sell the food on the open market. Chang Bloch remarked that "there was a legitimate concern that Mengistu would just use the food aid to feed his troops.... That used to be my nightmare: that there would be a front-page story by the *New York Times* or *Washington Post* with pictures of USAID food rotting on the docks. Or worse, in the hands of Mengistu's troops."[41]

Third, much like the hardliners, the institutionalists viewed the Marxist policies of the Ethiopian government as the main culprit of the famine. Unlike the hardliners, however, the institutionalists felt that famine was an inappropriate context in which to push for political change. Chester Crocker, then assistant secretary of state for African affairs, has stated that the famine was

---

37. Julia Chang Bloch, interview with the author, Washington, D.C., February 24, 2006.
38. Princeton Lyman, interview with the author, Washington, D.C., February 24, 2006.
39. General Accounting Office, *United States' Response*, 1. The Ethiopian government claimed sovereignty over the entire country, a claim that legally required relief organizations to seek the permission of the Ethiopian government before conducting feeding operations. In reality, however, the government only controlled a fraction of the region in the north.
40. Lyman, interview.
41. Chang Bloch, interview.

the result of "population pressures on land that was fragile; it was the result of stupid policies by a stupid government that was collectivizing and moving people around in an unconscionable way.... But this was emergency food relief in a humanitarian emergency. If you are going to force broad policy change, you wouldn't use that tool [famine] to try to do it."[42]

Finally, the institutionalists were constrained by political pressures in the United States from both the ideological right and the ideological left. From the right, the institutionalists faced a challenge from hardliners who wanted to overthrow the Mengistu regime, and from the OMB, which held the purse strings tightly during the Reagan era.[43] From the left, the institutionalists were pressured by humanitarians who objected to political considerations clouding U.S. policy. Crocker described this tension by explaining, "Peter McPherson, who was the head of AID, was feeling a lot of political heat from the right . . . and from the critics [of the Reagan administration] who didn't like a cold war framework to be applied in Africa. . . . They wanted a response to be purely and primarily humanitarian."[44]

THE HUMANITARIANS

The humanitarian representation called for a concerted U.S. response despite the failings of the Ethiopian government. Humanitarians stressed that the famine was killing millions of Ethiopians and demanded that the United States provide massive amounts of food, regardless of ideological or political concerns. Advocates of the humanitarian perspective were generally mid-level career bureaucrats and field officers within the State Department and USAID, as well as several members of Congress and all of the NGOs with feeding programs in Ethiopia.[45]

Humanitarians recognized many of the same constraints as the institutionalists but generally assigned them a much-diminished importance. Summarizing the humanitarian position, Kenneth Hackett, CRS's regional director for Africa during the mid-1980s (and now its president), has stated that although the Ethiopian government had demonstrated a "totally inadequate" response to the famine, and Mengistu's rule was "heinous," the U.S. policy of withholding

---

42. Chester Crocker, interview with the author, Washington, D.C., February 24, 2006.
43. Ruttan, *United States Development*; Stockman, *Triumph of Politics*.
44. Crocker, interview.
45. Humanitarians interviewed for this project include David Korn, Kenneth Hackett, and Steve Weissman. See below for interviews. Weissman and Wolpe devoted considerable time to the Ethiopian famine, as did a number of members of Congress, including Senator John Danforth and Representatives Ted Weiss and Mickey Leland.

food aid for political reasons was "unconscionable."[46] Furthermore, in contrast to the other two representations, humanitarians placed greater emphasis on the effect of drought in bringing about the famine. David Korn, chargé d'affaires of the U.S. embassy in Addis Ababa in the mid-1980s, reflected that "the drought was the main thing [that caused the famine].... So little rains fell that by the fall of 1984 even the cactus were dried up."[47] And Steve Weissman, former chief of staff for Representative Howard Wolpe (D-Mich.), has remarked, "The feeling was that a lot of this was the drought, but some of this was undoubtedly the policies [of the Ethiopian government]."[48]

The humanitarians were also more willing than the hardliners or the institutionalists to trust the Ethiopian government to distribute U.S. food aid throughout the country. Korn argued that, contrary to the claims made by the Reagan administration, "there was not a major problem with diversion."[49] Likewise, Weissman contended, "I think people were aware of the problems [with the Ethiopian government], but there was a general feeling that if you use that vehicle [Ethiopia's Rehabilitation and Relief Commission—the major aid organization of the Ethiopian government] it would still be with all the international agencies and private voluntary organizations on the scene watching as well."[50]

Humanitarians may have shunned ideological and political considerations, but they were not ignorant of the centrality that both would play in the case. The primary constraint for humanitarians was the Reagan administration's reluctance to aid a communist country in the midst of the cold war. While humanitarians understood that decisions on foreign aid took place within a political context, they strongly objected to political considerations clouding what they felt should be a compassionate response to true human suffering.

THE AMERICAN PUBLIC AND THE PROBLEM REPRESENTATIONS

Drawing on the public opinion data cited earlier, we might expect that a vast majority of the American public would agree with the humanitarian representation. The power of the humanitarian approach to famine relief—the view that the United States should ignore political considerations and provide massive amounts of aid to help famine victims—was that it framed the problem in relatively simple, apolitical terms: people were starving in Ethiopia, and the

---

46. Kenneth Hackett, phone interview with the author, December 13, 2003.
47. David Korn, phone interview with the author, January 20, 2006.
48. Steve Weissman, interview with the author, Washington, D.C., February 23, 2006.
49. Korn, interview.
50. Weissman, interview.

United States had excess food, so the United States should ship that excess food to Ethiopia.[51] This frame is made even more vivid to the public when starvation in the less developed world is juxtaposed with the lavish lifestyle personally enjoyed by most Americans.

Both the hardliner and institutionalist representations of the problem—the belief that providing food to the Ethiopian government would only make the problem worse—are comparatively more difficult to explain. Appreciation of the institutionalist representation requires a fairly good understanding of the advantages and disadvantages of alternative models of economic development (e.g., problems inherent in socialist developmental models applied to nonindustrialized nations) and the political situation within Ethiopia (e.g., distributional problems resulting from civil war and poor domestic food production resulting from a Stalinist-style agrarian policy). For a public with a limited willingness and/or capacity to understand the details of complex international affairs, convincing the public of the wisdom of the institutionalist and hardliner representations would be a difficult task.

Given the American public's likely acceptance of the humanitarian frame, issue salience came to play a vital role in shaping U.S. policy toward Ethiopia.[52] For the humanitarians, the chances of gaining control over policy rested squarely on raising the salience of the issue, or what E. E. Schattschneider termed in another context "enlarging the scope of conflict."[53] The more people became concerned with the Ethiopian famine (i.e., as the scope of conflict was enlarged), the stronger the humanitarians' position would become. Put differently, the more citizens who were attentive to and concerned about the famine, the more implicit or explicit pressure politicians would feel to respond to the public's strong humanitarian preference.

The situation was reversed for the hardliners. An attentive public would likely object to a policy of denying food to starving people for geopolitical

---

51. Many of us have heard this frame repeated throughout our lives. As a child, I remember my grandfather telling me to eat all my food because "there are starving kids in China." The typical, although probably apocryphal, beauty show contestant's plan for making the world a better place is to end world hunger by "giving up just one meal a day!" Without judging too harshly the validity of such statements—I found it difficult as a child to understand how stuffing myself helped hungry children elsewhere—there is often a tendency for the public to treat complex humanitarian emergencies as really not all that complex. For instance, we often see mass starvation as the total absence of food, when in many cases it is the result of an inability or unwillingness to distribute existing food stocks. We see poor agricultural production in the less developed world as being caused by "bad land," when in many cases it is the result of protectionist agricultural policies in industrialized nations or distorted agricultural problems brought on by governmental mismanagement. In short, the frames of the humanitarian representation are powerful because they usually fit the frames that many Americans have grown up hearing.

52. Bosso, "Setting the Agenda."

53. Schattschneider, *Semi-Sovereign People.*

reasons. Therefore, hardliners had an incentive to "go private" (i.e., minimize issue salience, restrict the scope of conflict) in order to carry out what might be popularly considered a morally objectionable policy. Institutionalists fell somewhere in the middle. They were concerned about the plight of the Ethiopian people and would therefore stand to gain influence if public attention increased. Yet they also had to be concerned with a runaway humanitarian policy that would essentially reward a corrupt and incompetent Ethiopian government while doing little to help those Ethiopian citizens most in need of assistance. In this sense, the prospect of high issue salience was a mixed blessing for the institutionalists.

In sum, there emerged not one, but three different representations of the Ethiopian famine. Hardliners did not want to respond to the famine and preferred an inattentive public; institutionalists wanted to respond to the famine, but in a circumscribed way; humanitarians wanted a massive U.S. response to the famine and needed widespread public concern to succeed. In short, with a constant public preference for humanitarian aid, the key in deciding which view won out was the level of public attentiveness that would accrue to the famine, a point made by Christopher Bosso.[54]

Option Generation

The option generation stage of the Ethiopian famine lasted from December 1982 to October 1984. Throughout this stage, a debate simmered over the aforementioned policy options offered by the hardliners, institutionalists, and humanitarians. Conflict over these representations led to a slow U.S. response to a worsening situation in Ethiopia. Because relief efforts received scant attention from the American media, the public, and the highest ranks of the Reagan administration, there was little impetus to break this bureaucratic deadlock among equals. Because policy makers could not really agree on what to do in Ethiopia, little was done. And because of the lack of public attention toward the situation, doing little became a viable policy option.

The guarded political context (i.e., unified public preferences, low salience) described in the problem representation stage continued throughout the option generation stage. There is no evidence that the public's humanitarian preferences changed throughout this phase, nor is there any evidence that the public's attention to Ethiopia increased in any significant way. (But several times

54. Bosso, "Setting the Agenda."

it did seem possible that an inattentive public might become more attentive. During these times, the Reagan administration became moderately and briefly more responsive to the situation in Ethiopia.) In this context, the Reagan administration made several choices that appeared to be inconsistent with the latent preferences of the American public. These choices reflected more of a bureaucratic deadlock and indecisiveness on how to respond to a very complex situation than a blatant disregard for human suffering. The following section examines several of the administration's choices.

Cutting the Ethiopian Budget for Fiscal Year 1984

In late 1982 and early 1983, the administration began drafting its budget for the 1984 fiscal year (FY).[55] Despite clear knowledge of the famine, the original draft of the FY 1984 presidential budget request included no food aid for Ethiopia. This cut in funding eliminated the approximately two to three million dollars in annual contributions to CRS for its feeding programs for lactating mothers and young children in Ethiopia.[56] Other nations also saw a significant decrease in food aid donations during this time period, yet Ethiopia was the only country singled out for a complete elimination of aid.[57]

Why cut a trivial amount of money from the federal budget during a period of famine, especially since these funds went to feed mothers and their children? The decision to withhold aid to Ethiopia appears diametrically opposed to the American public's preference for U.S. humanitarian assistance to countries facing disasters. The rationale for eliminating these funds from the presidential budget was, however, consistent with both the hardliner and, to a lesser degree, the institutionalist representations of the problem. Both groups felt that the Ethiopian government was largely to blame for the onset and spread of famine. They also believed that the most effective way to respond to the problem would be for the Ethiopian government to devote more of its own resources to famine relief. To this end, both the assistant administrator of USAID's Bureau of Food for Peace, Julia Chang Bloch, and its coordinator, Peggy Sheehan, informed NGOs that the budget cuts were due to the poor efforts of the Ethiopian government in responding to the famine.[58] Sheehan then asked CRS to informally communicate to the Ethiopian government that

---

55. Fiscal year budgets run from October 1 to September 30 of the next year. Planning for the budget often begins a year prior to the start of the fiscal year.
56. General Accounting Office, *United States' Response.*
57. Bosso, "Setting the Agenda."
58. Callan, "U.S. Foreign Aid"; Solberg, *Miracle in Ethiopia*; Shepherd, "Food Aid."

U.S. aid would be reinstated only if the Derg committed more resources to the relief effort.[59] Kenneth Hackett of CRS confirmed to me that the Reagan administration wanted CRS to act as an intermediary, a request that CRS refused because this conflicted with its primary mandate of providing humanitarian assistance regardless of politics.[60]

According to several insiders, the decision to cut all aid to Ethiopia was heavily influenced by hardliners within the Reagan administration. Jason Clay contends that the NSC played the predominate role in the elimination of assistance to Ethiopia: "At a 1982 meeting on the famine, in fact, the NSC reportedly decided to withhold food from Ethiopia even though it was well known that the country was already suffering serious food shortages. According to one council member who attended the meeting, the consensus of those present was to let the famine occur in the hopes of either destabilizing the Mengistu regime or, at the very least, forcing it to make economic reforms more amenable to the US government."[61] According to another Washington insider, U.S. ambassador to the UN Jeanne Kirkpatrick's opposition to relief efforts had "a chilling effect" on U.S. food aid policy to Ethiopia: "No one in the U.S. government wants to do anything [about the Ethiopian famine]. They just want the problem to go away because they don't see any political benefits and they don't want to antagonize the lady in New York [Kirkpatrick]."[62]

Ultimately, the decision to cut U.S. aid to Ethiopia was made possible by low issue salience. Not only is the public generally inattentive to federal budgetary politics, but the specific problem of famine in Ethiopia had yet to hit the headlines. As a result, the public's humanitarian sentiments mattered little at this point.

CRS Food Aid Request

Shortly after the proposed budget cuts, USAID delayed responses to two CRS requests for food: one in December 1982 for 838 metric tons (MT) of food and the other in November 1983 for 16,000 MT. The delays—five and six months, respectively—occurred despite the support of the U.S. embassy, the meager amounts that were being requested, and an average turn-around time of two to three weeks for comparable requests.[63] Stalling on a small request

59. Solberg, *Miracle in Ethiopia*, 26.
60. Hackett, interview.
61. Clay, "Western Assistance," 149.
62. Ross, "Famine, War Threaten Thousands"
63. General Accounting Office, *United States' Response*, 2; Shepherd, "Food Aid."

for food during a period of worsening famine again appears inconsistent with the humanitarian impulse of the public, but very few Americans knew of the famine in Ethiopia, let alone the CRS requests.

There were several reasons behind the delays. First, the initial CRS request sparked what Chang Bloch called "a big, big fight" between institutionalists and hardliners in the Reagan administration over whether the United States should provide Ethiopia with any assistance at all.[64] M. Peter McPherson recalled, "Within the administration, you had the question: Should we be helping communist countries? Aren't we just bolstering or helping to sustain a regime that was hostile to us?"[65]

Second, institutionalists claimed that the delays were due to uncertainty over the extent of the problem in Ethiopia, coupled with a general distrust of humanitarian NGOs. McPherson stated, "I think there was still a debate about the facts. . . . The reports weren't very complete, and were from people [NGOs working in Ethiopia] that seemed to have a history and bias of arguing that there were enormous problems, in part because they needed resources. It is not unusual in disaster relief to state the case in its most embellished form."[66] Princeton Lyman remarked, "There was some dragging of feet, and saying, 'Well, we don't have enough information.' We always go through that with drought. We don't believe the regime, don't believe the World Food Program, don't believe the FAO. And you have to send out your own team. That is an easy way to say we are not sure you need this much or that much."[67] Likewise, Chester Crocker commented more broadly on the relationship between humanitarian NGOs and members of Congress: "They [NGOs] live at the federal trough; they are joined at the hip with the congressional micromanagers that earmark funds for them. And it is a symbiotic relationship that is, in fact, subversive of the public interest."[68]

Third, institutionalists expressed concern about the willingness of the Ethiopian government to feed all of its citizens, especially those living in the north.[69] The Ethiopian government was actively using the famine to weaken its enemies, and it was estimated that only 5 percent of those in rebel-controlled areas

---

64. Chang Bloch, interview.
65. McPherson, interview.
66. Ibid. For the literature on the "iron triangle" of U.S. food policy, see Natsios, *U.S. Foreign Policy*; Ruttan, *United States Development*; Diven, "Domestic Determinants"; and Diven, "Coincidence of Interests."
67. Lyman, interview.
68. Crocker, interview.
69. General Accounting Office, *United States' Response*, 13.

were being fed.[70] Because the Ethiopian government did not supply data on its existing food stocks, the Reagan administration also contended that enough food existed in the country if only the Derg was willing to distribute it.[71] However, the Ethiopian government had refused to divert its military resources, such as trucks and money, to take part in relief efforts. In congressional testimony, McPherson stated that U.S. policy was designed to compel the Ethiopian government to put forth more effort to alleviate famine: "We had made the decision not to advance a number for the ongoing feeding program in Ethiopia, and to informally communicate that we thought the Ethiopians could and should do much more for themselves in light of the question about the military buildup."[72]

Finally, institutionalists and hardliners alike suggested that the delays in relief stemmed from the Ethiopian government's diversion of international relief aid to feed its own army and pay for purchases of Soviet arms. In congressional testimony, Chang Bloch stated that there was evidence of "persistent food divergence and mismanagement in the Ethiopian Program."[73] In light of such allegations, and despite objections from humanitarians who argued that the claims were bogus, USAID came under considerable pressure from the National Security Agency (NSA) and the CIA to conduct a thorough and time-consuming investigation into possible diversion of U.S. aid.[74]

Again, an inattentive public enabled delayed responses to the CRS requests. Indeed, both requests were funded only after events threatened to enlarge the scope of conflict surrounding the famine. For instance, USAID approved the first CRS request shortly after the Reagan administration learned that several American reporters, including a television crew from NBC, had been granted Ethiopian visas to cover the famine.[75] The later CRS request was approved after Congress threatened to hold hearings on the issue. It is possible that the timing of both approvals was purely coincidental, but it is more likely that policy makers were concerned that the American public would suddenly become more attentive to what was going on in Ethiopia, only to find that the Reagan administration had failed to respond to a humanitarian tragedy of the

---

70. G. Smith, "Politics of Famine Relief." A somewhat more optimistic estimate by Duffield and Prendergast was that the Ethiopian government could reach 22 percent of famine victims. See Duffield and Prendergast, *Without Troops and Tanks*, 62–63.
71. U.S. Congress, House Committee of Foreign Affairs, *World Food Situation*, 39.
72. Ibid.
73. U.S. Congress, House Committee on Foreign Relations, *Hunger in Africa*, 52.
74. U.S. Congress, House Committee on Foreign Affairs, *World Food Situation*; General Accounting Office, *United States' Response*, 13; Shepherd, "Food Aid," 92.
75. General Accounting Office, *United States' Response*, 13; Bosso, "Setting the Agenda."

first order. Remember that policy makers can usually ignore the preferences of an inattentive public, but must be sensitive to the possibility that issue salience will increase in the future and thus transform latent opinions into active opinions.

The delay in the CRS request was not an isolated incident, but rather was indicative of a general trend of administration policy making. In late April 1983, the UN Disaster Relief Organization (UNDRO) issued an urgent appeal for 100,000 MT of food and relief supplies.[76] Although the Reagan administration initially provided a token amount of food, it largely ignored the bulk of the UNDRO request for five months. As with the CRS request, the administration responded to the UNDRO appeal only after an increase in media and congressional attention during the summer of 1983 threatened to arouse the public's interest. It would be difficult to imagine these types of delays occurring if the American public had been highly attentive to policy making.

The Cross-Border Operation

One of the more interesting aspects of U.S. policies involved a covert operation by the United States and NGOs to smuggle food and medical supplies across the Sudanese border into Ethiopia. All three representations of the famine—hardliners, institutionalists, and humanitarians—were concerned about getting food into rebel-controlled regions in the north, albeit for different reasons. Moreover, all three groups were concerned with stemming the tide of Ethiopian refugees flowing into U.S.-allied Sudan, a disturbing trend that was creating a humanitarian emergency in that country. To deal with these problems, the Reagan administration created the Interagency Group on Ethiopia and the Sudan (IGETSU), and charged it with formulating a policy to feed the north.

In mid-1983, IGETSU devised a plan whereby U.S. food would enter into rebel-controlled areas of northern Ethiopia through the Sudanese border. Moving food across the border without the Ethiopian government's knowledge constituted a serious violation of legal national sovereignty, so the United States was careful to avoid direct involvement in the operation and directed that the food be channeled through two American NGOs: Lutheran World Relief and Mercy Corps International.[77] Chester Crocker discussed why the cross-border operation was kept covert:

---

76. Shepherd, "Food Aid," 260; General Accounting Office, *United States' Response*, 19.

77. Estimates on the size of the cross-border operation (CBO) vary. Since the CBO was "off the books," funding levels have had to be pieced together from a variety of sources. Shepherd contends

It [the cross-border operation] is obviously a fundamental insult to the sovereignty of the country . . . especially when there is a rebellion going on in which you might be seen as supporting. This was the bipolar world. If you are going to do that [running a cross-border operation], you are sort of inviting the other side to make a federal case out of it in a way that you don't need. You are also inviting a lot of scrutiny by European neutrals . . . when you are dealing in a competitive arena like that, and there are a set of norms, a normative framework with the OAU and the UN and all the rest. . . . There were a combination of diplomatic considerations, as well as not wanting to rub the Ethiopians' nose in it before it was up and running.[78]

The cross-border operation was also a compromise solution that partially, though not entirely, satisfied all of the bureaucratic factions involved in the emergency relief process. For the hardliners, the policy provided a means of pressuring the Mengistu regime by feeding rebel groups; for the institutionalists and humanitarians, the operation provided a means of circumventing the Ethiopian government and ensuring that food reached those in greatest need. As Princeton Lyman stated,

> That issue [the cross-border operation] bounced around for a long time. . . . There were people, one in particular, the African advisor of the NSC, who thought that this was the way of further working against the Mengistu regime. And he was not happy with us sending food to one side and not the other. . . . [The decision to go ahead with the cross-border operation] eliminated the opposition of the NSC to the rest of the program and satisfied two things: it satisfied the political problem we were having with the NSC, and it satisfied the humanitarian side because a lot of people who were suffering couldn't be reached by Mengistu. To say that we are only to go through the [Ethiopian] government either was to back their desire to conquer those areas or not to have people reached.[79]

---

that by mid-1984 the United States was moving 10,000 MT of food a month over the Sudanese border; by 1985 at least 200,000 MT of food and 225 trucks were moving into rebel-controlled regions. Other scholars have found a more modest U.S. contribution to the CBO. For instance, Duffield and Prendergast contend that the CBO received one 5,000 MT donation from USAID in April 1984 before a modest increase to 23,000 MT in October. Varnis finds that in addition to the 5,000 MT April donation, AID gave 17,000 MT of food to the CBO from June 1983 to March 1984 before the size of the operation began to increase by late 1984. Shepherd, "Food Aid," 407–10; Duffield and Prendergast, *Without Troops and Tanks*; Varnis, *Reluctant Aid*, 128.

78. Crocker, interview.
79. Lyman, interview.

It is important to note here that the cross-border operation was kept covert not out of a desire to conceal a dubious policy from the American public, but rather to avoid both antagonizing the Ethiopian government and running afoul of international law.[80] Indeed, it is likely that the American public would have approved of the idea of smuggling food to starving people.

Congressional Attention

In the summer of 1983, the Reagan administration's Ethiopian policy came under greater scrutiny in Congress. On June 1, 1983, seventy-four members of the House of Representatives wrote to USAID's M. Peter McPherson to urge a quicker response to future requests for aid to Ethiopia.[81] On June 29, 1983, the Senate passed Resolution 168, which called for immediate emergency assistance to Ethiopia, and the House soon followed with a similar resolution.[82] In August, a congressional delegation from the House Foreign Affairs Committee made a fact-finding trip to Ethiopia and subsequently issued another urgent request for more U.S. assistance.[83]

From July 17 to 26, the House Foreign Affairs Committee held several contentious hearings on the African famine, providing a forum for NGOs and humanitarians in Congress to voice their displeasure with administration policy. Stephen Coats, issue director for the nonprofit group Bread for the World addressed the delays in responding to the CRS and UNDRO requests and the Reagan administration's cuts to the Ethiopian budget: "As far as we can determine, the United States has turned aside requests for aid from the Ethiopian government because of its politics and a desire for that government to implicitly or explicitly renounce its actions in seizing U.S. property."[84] Among the more vocal congressional critics of administration policy were Representatives Howard Wolpe (D-Mich.), Mickey Leland (D-Tex.), and Ted Weiss (D-N.Y.). Wolpe began the hearings by stating, "The United States, usually the major source of humanitarian aid, has been particularly slow in its response with respect to Ethiopia where they are experiencing famine conditions far worse

---

80. By contrast, Shepherd ("Food Aid") argues that the cross-border operation was an attempt by the U.S. to help overthrow the Mengistu regime. Although the Reagan administration did not like the regime, there is little evidence to support that the operation was designed to be anything other than a humanitarian mission. See Varnis, *Reluctant Aid*, and Duffield and Prendergast, *Without Troops and Tanks*.
81. General Accounting Office, *United States' Response*.
82. Ibid.
83. U.S. Congress, House Committee on Foreign Affairs, *World Food Situation*.
84. U.S. Congress, House Committee on Foreign Affairs, *Impact of U.S. Foreign Policy*, 123.

than any other drought-affected country on the continent. . . . Specifically disquieting is the failure of the administration to reinstate the Public Law 480 title II program for Ethiopia in fiscal 1984 which was eliminated in the administration's fiscal 1984 budget request or otherwise respond to the Catholic Relief Services request for this funding which has been pending since May."[85]

Now placed on the defensive, institutionalists in the Reagan administration were forced to equivocate on the role that politics played in the formulation of policy. The administration was eager to communicate its representation of the famine and justify using humanitarian assistance as a means of compelling the Ethiopian government to put forth more of its own effort in famine relief. To this end, McPherson repeatedly stressed that the root cause of famine lay with Ethiopia's failed collectivist agriculture policies, the poor relief effort by the Ethiopian government, and the militaristic nature of the Mengistu regime. Despite the centrality of these considerations in shaping policy, the administration was also keen on framing that policy in purely humanitarian terms. McPherson stated, "Our position is that we are going to respond without regard to political considerations. The hungry child knows no politics. We think we have done that."[86] The attempt to frame the problem in Ethiopia as the result of Marxist policies, while characterizing the U.S. response as purely humanitarian, was emblematic of the administration's rhetorical strategy throughout the entire famine.

McPherson's statement—"the hungry child knows no politics"—struck a nerve with congressional critics. Wolpe remarked that while he was glad to hear the administration's philosophy, he doubted that humanitarian considerations were really driving their policy making: "I think that is also a terribly important statement. I do stress at this point in time, because with all respect to your testimony today, I do not believe it is an accurate reflection of what administration policy has been up to this point in time."[87]

The congressional hearings were accompanied by a modest increase in newspaper coverage. In mid-June 1983, a series of front-page articles in the *Washington Post* focused on the famine and were especially critical of the administration's response. *Post* reporter Jay Ross wrote, "Tens of thousands of Ethiopians, mostly women and children, are threatened with starvation in the next few months in a famine that could become one of the most catastrophic in African history. Despite urgent appeals for international assistance while

85. Ibid., 3.
86. Ibid., 38.
87. Ibid., 56.

there is still time to save thousands of lives, the United States, the world's largest source of surplus food, has virtually turned its back on the potential disaster."[88]

The Reagan administration responded to congressional agitation and the increased media coverage by becoming more attentive to the situation in Ethiopia. On July 6, CRS requested another 4,500 MT for its feeding programs in Makelle. Unlike the previous request, which took five months to approve, this request was granted by USAID in nine days.[89] The administration also announced on July 24 that it was reversing its earlier decision to cut U.S. food aid to Ethiopia from the budget. A USAID team then toured Ethiopia in August and concluded that 15,000 MT of food should be sent immediately. Finally, after a five-month delay, USAID granted UNDRO's request for eight hundred thousand dollars to help cover the transport of food in Ethiopia.

The administration's summer response illustrates once again the effect that a *potentially* attentive public can have on policy making. As congressional and media attention threatened to enlarge the scope of conflict, the administration's tendency to drag its feet in Ethiopia became increasingly risky politically. Faced with the possibility that greater public interest would change the political context, the administration was forced to provide enough aid to justify its rhetoric of "the hungry child who knows no politics."

The November 1983 CRS Request

As congressional and media attention to the famine began to wane in the fall of 1983, so too did the political pressure on the Reagan administration to respond quickly to Ethiopia. In this context, CRS found its request for food again delayed by USAID in a manner similar to the earlier appeals. In November 1983, the situation in Ethiopia was becoming more desperate as thousands of famine victims flowed into relief stations. To meet this growing need, CRS requested from USAID 16,000 MT of food and $1.5 million in logistical support to feed fifty-five thousand families in Makelle and to expand its feeding operation in Eritrea and Tigray.[90]

The apparent shift in the administration's responsiveness to Ethiopia over the summer provided CRS with a modicum of confidence that this new request would be quickly granted. Its optimism was soon dashed as David Korn,

---

88. Ross, "Famine, War Threaten Thousands."
89. General Accounting Office, *United States' Response.*
90. Ibid.

U.S. chargé d'affaires in Addis Ababa, regretfully suggested that CRS cut its request in half "since 'signals' from Washington indicated that 16,000 was unlikely to be approved."[91] Believing 16,000 MT to be the bare minimum needed to sustain its operations, CRS refused to compromise and forwarded the full amount to USAID. In December 1983, a USAID team toured Ethiopia and recommended to Washington that the CRS request be granted immediately. In January 1984, USAID provided a verbal assurance to CRS that it would fund the request, but for only half of the requested amount.[92] Finally, in May 1984, a full six months after the initial submission, USAID granted CRS half of its original 16,000 MT request.[93]

Part of the administration's rationale for cutting the CRS request in half was that USAID was overextended worldwide and there was simply not enough money to go around.[94] In later interviews, key policy makers noted the importance of budget constraints in shaping the Reagan administration's Ethiopian policy but disagreed on the severity of the constraint imposed by the Office of Management and Budget (OMB) and its director, David Stockman. Steve Weissman, then chief of staff for Representative Wolpe, believed that budget concerns, even more than antipathy for the Ethiopian government, guided the Reagan administration's policy:

> The problem we [humanitarians in Congress] experienced was, throughout this whole period, that they [the Reagan administration] were not giving enough. They never said "we can't give any." They just weren't giving enough. . . . But we thought that, at a certain point, we don't know when, they kind of said, "Okay, we'll give you emergency food aid," . . . but that in Ethiopia and the rest of Africa they were more worried about the budget priorities. That [budget concerns] is what was dominating. Now where does my perception come from? It comes from long discussions with AID officials. . . . McPherson was the guy who was kind of on the other side, but kind of knew they should be helping. He was pushed by budget constraints. . . . I'm sure there were certain quarters that didn't like Ethiopia . . . but in terms of food aid, emergency food aid, I felt that budget constraints were the most important. The OMB in particular.[95]

91. Cennerazzo, CRS, internal memo, November 13, 1984, 1, quoted in Shepherd, "Food Aid," 270.
92. Shepherd, "Food Aid," 269.
93. General Accounting Office, *United States' Response*, 17.
94. Ibid.
95. Weissman, interview.

M. Peter McPherson has a slightly different recollection. McPherson claimed that he was constantly pressured by Director Stockman to justify expenditures. But McPherson also noted that he was usually granted the funds he asked for and that the USAID budget during his tenure was significantly higher than that of his predecessor during the Carter administration:

> My good friend from Michigan, David Stockman . . . guarded the gate on money, and necessarily so. I remember that George Shultz told me that the worst job he ever had in government was the head of OMB. You have to say no to everybody. Anyway, Stockman was always pushing up justification, which I viewed to be his job. . . . We got a huge increase [in the USAID budget]. . . . Under my tenure, I had more family planning money for the six and a half years than in previous administrations. A lot of the money went to Central America. . . . Overall the AID budget went up very significantly. . . . There is always the issue with Stockman on everything. But there was always the issue of Stockman with everybody. So I won't blame David; I think that the nature of his job is to question anyone who wants money.[96]

In addition to budget concerns, the November 1983 CRS request prompted many of the same rationales from the Reagan administration that were seen earlier. The Ethiopian government was again accused of diverting international food aid. USAID also contended that food existed in Ethiopia to satisfy demand if only the government was willing to distribute it.[97] Furthermore, the Reagan administration wanted to expand its cross-border feeding operation, a policy that in a zero-sum budgetary environment inevitably came at the expense of the CRS request.[98]

Jack Shepherd has argued that an additional reason for the delay, and one that was not made public until after the famine, involved the capture of a CIA

---

96. McPherson, interview.

97. Initially, there were independent reports that supported the contention that Ethiopia did not need much international food aid. In January 1984, the WFP announced that there was enough food in Ethiopia to last all of 1984. A donor community meeting in March also confirmed an ample supply of food. These optimistic reports, however, provided a misleading picture of conditions in Ethiopia and were soon challenged by increasing evidence of the severity of the famine. In March 1984, the U.S. Embassy cabled the State Department, stating that the spring rains had failed and that the potential for widespread famine was high. A few weeks later, an UNDRO team reported that Ethiopia would run out of food by May. Finally, in April the Food and Agriculture Association (FAO) of the UN stated that a food deficit of 372,000 MT would exist in Ethiopia throughout 1984. See General Accounting Office, *United States' Response*.

98. Ibid.; Shepherd, "Food Aid," 270.

agent in Ethiopia.[99] In December 1983, the Israeli Mossad informed the United States that Ethiopian security forces had detained and were torturing a CIA agent in Addis Ababa.[100] On February 4, 1984, President Reagan sent U.S. ambassador-at-large Vernon Walters to negotiate the agent's release. Two days later, the Ethiopian government expelled four U.S. diplomats, including the CIA officer. With the agent's release secured, the 8,000 MT CRS request was, according to an internal CRS memo, "lost in Washington."[101] Although USAID attributed the delayed response to the CRS request to concerns about diversion and distribution, Shepherd argued that an equally plausible reason is that it was retribution for the brutal treatment of the CIA officer in Ethiopia.[102] The story is certainly interesting, and seems plausible, but there is little hard evidence to suggest that the CRS donation was linked to the CIA officer.

Ultimately, in a manner similar to that regarding the earlier CRS request, the Reagan administration had once again engaged in a policy of delay in order to extract concessions from the Ethiopian government. And, like the politics behind the earlier request, a disinterested American public helped to make this delay possible.

The 1984 Budget Supplemental Debate

In late 1983, it became apparent that USAID was running out of money. Overall cuts to the food aid budget would have made for difficult funding decisions at USAID during normal times; however, the growing famine, coupled with a 50 percent cut in aid to sub-Saharan Africa, produced an alarming situation in which relief organizations were required to make triage decisions about who received aid and who did not.[103] Such a depletion of funds forced the Reagan administration to go to Congress to request a supplemental appropriation for the 1984 fiscal year. By turning to Congress, the administration opened the door for competing proposals, provided humanitarians with a forum to critique administration policy, and invited increased public scrutiny of policy.

The administration's decision to request a supplemental appropriation from Congress was prompted in part by the efforts of Senator John Danforth

99. Shepherd, "Food Aid."
100. Tyler and Ottaway, "Ethiopian Security Police"; Shepherd, "Food Aid."
101. Shepherd, "Food Aid," 418.
102. Ibid.
103. "BFW Report on the U.S. Response to the African Famine," May 1984, 7, quoted in Shepherd, "Food Aid," 278.

(R-Mo.). In late 1983, Danforth toured sub-Saharan Africa and was deeply troubled by the devastation caused by the famine. Upon his arrival back in the United States, Danforth was granted a private meeting with President Reagan, where he presented a slide show of starving Ethiopians and their "emaciated bodies, sticklike limbs and distended bellies."[104] The senator then urged Reagan to provide food aid to countries in Africa regardless of any ideological considerations. A few days later, Danforth appeared on *The Today Show*, where he discussed his visit to Ethiopia and stated that "no systematic effort is being made to feed these people."[105]

By many accounts, President Reagan was deeply moved by Senator Danforth's presentation and expressed a genuine desire to help end starvation in Africa. Remember that decisions on emergency food aid rarely reach the president's desk. Therefore, Danforth's visit with the president may have been one of the first times that Reagan was fully briefed on the Ethiopian situation. In addition to humanitarian compassion, however, the president had to consider political factors. The senator's appearance on *The Today Show* offered the potential for greater public attention to the famine and, by extension, to the administration's Ethiopian policy. The specter of a wider public audience was especially important given that 1984 was an election year. As Shepherd writes, "Senator Danforth's timing was excellent. The run-up to the 1984 presidential election had begun. Although President Reagan was virtually unchallenged, the first primaries were less than six weeks away. Inaction in the face of widening starvation across sub-Sahara Africa would appear, at best, callous."[106]

President Reagan's increased involvement with food aid policy, as well as the growing potential for greater public attention to the situation in Ethiopia, spurred the bureaucracy into action. On January 21, 1984, Secretary of State George Shultz cabled USAID missions in Africa: "As you are aware, last week's fact-finding trip by Sen. Danforth has stirred considerable interest in the Africa food crisis, and we have been asked for best estimates for questions given below. . . . African emergency food requirements are receiving considerable, repeat considerable, attention."[107]

Despite the urgency explicit in Secretary Shultz's cable, the Reagan administration did not wait for the USAID assessments to be compiled before issuing its supplemental request to Congress. On January 30, 1984, President Reagan

---

104. Meszoly, "Africa Drought," 3042.
105. Shepherd, "Food Aid," 280.
106. Ibid.
107. "Food Production/Deficit Information for Africa," Department of State cable to mission directors and representatives, January 21, 1984, cited in Shepherd, "Ethiopia."

requested $90 million in emergency food aid for the entire African continent. The president also requested another $500 million in long-term developmental aid as an inducement for the less-developed countries to adopt market-oriented policies. As it turned out, the president's $90 million request for emergency aid looked woefully inadequate once the USAID assessments were finally compiled a few weeks later. USAID concluded that sub-Saharan Africa required 1.1 million tons of food for 1984 at an estimated cost of $520 million.[108] Given the Reagan administration's stated goal of providing for half of Africa's food needs, the president's supplemental request was $170 million short.

The administration's supplemental proposal was widely criticized in Congress. On February 9, the House introduced its own initiative, House Joint Resolution (HJR) 492, which sought to increase the president's request by providing $150 million in emergency food. On March 6, HJR 492 passed the House and the bill was sent to the Senate. There, Robert Kasten (R-Wisc.) and Ted Stevens (R-Alaska) attached riders to the bill that linked the supplemental appropriation for Africa to $93 million in funds for El Salvador and Nicaraguan Contras.[109] Congressional Democrats assumed that the Reagan administration was behind these amendments. Speaker of the House Tip O'Neill (D-Mass.) called the amendments "a lousy, mean thing to do."[110] In addition, O'Neill charged that the linkage of African aid with the Contras demonstrated that Reagan was "unfit to be President of the United States."[111] Representative Wolpe called the riders "obscene . . . shabby at best." However, these seemingly very newsworthy quotes by congressional critics were largely ignored in the press.[112] A handful of editorials in the *New York Times* and *Washington Post* were critical of the administration's Ethiopian policy, but by and large, the flap over supplemental appropriations failed to make any real headlines. Consequently, the American public remained inattentive to the policy-making process.

Realizing that aid to the Contras was a "killer amendment," Senator Danforth saved the supplemental to Africa by attaching the $90 million in food aid (President Reagan's initial proposal) to a domestic heating subsidy bill that easily passed Congress on March 27, 1984.[113] The remaining $60 million—part of the original $150 million in HJR 492—continued to be stalled in the

---

108. Shepherd, "Food Aid," 283. This estimate is still significantly lower than the $1.75 million estimate by the FAO in January.
109. Meszoly, "Africa Drought," 3043.
110. Ayres, "Senate Unit Backs Aid."
111. *Washington Post*, "Some Aid to Africa Freed."
112. Bosso, "Setting the Agenda."
113. Meszoly, "Africa Drought."

Senate. Eventually, humanitarians in Congress found enough support to defeat the "Contra Amendments," and the $60 million was signed into law on July 2, 1984. Yet the delay in the passage of HJR 492 had an important effect on a very crucial period of famine relief. The $90 million in supplemental appropriations that had passed on March 27 was spent quickly, and the additional three months it took to authorize the remaining $60 million meant that an entire month went by in which no U.S. food was shipped to Africa.[114]

The 1984 supplemental budgetary dustup also reflected some of the issues discussed earlier in this chapter. The specter of increased public attention that stemmed from Senator Danforth's actions played a significant role in spurring the bureaucracy into action. The actual supplemental request, however, was largely shaped by budgetary concerns and was widely considered by humanitarians in Congress to be "inadequate" in addressing the growing problem. Finally, and most important, the supplemental reflected a continued ambivalence toward Ethiopia and interbureaucratic conflict. Very little of the appropriations was earmarked for Ethiopia, the country most affected by famine; instead, the bulk of the funding went to U.S. allies like Kenya, Zaire, and Somalia, despite the fact that these countries were experiencing famine to a far lesser degree.[115] These allocation decisions, based primarily on politics rather than need, suggest that hardliners in the Reagan administration were still driving policy making. The allocation decisions also appear inconsistent with the American public's united preference both *for* humanitarian aid and *against* strategic aid. However, low public attention to the politics of foreign aid meant that the Reagan administration was able to ignore the public's preference in deciding which countries received U.S. food and which did not.

The Ethiopian Government's Tenth Anniversary Celebration

By early fall of 1984, the famine in Ethiopia had grown to unprecedented levels. In a move reminiscent of Emperor Selassie a decade earlier, the Ethiopian government attempted to cover up the famine as it prepared for the tenth anniversary of the Marxist revolution.[116] The anniversary celebration, which took place from September 6 to 10, provided Mengistu with the opportunity to showcase the "miracle of Ethiopian socialism." Preparations for the event

---

114. Shepherd, "Food Aid."
115. Callan, "U.S. Foreign Aid"; Shepherd, "Ethiopia"; Omang, "Anti-Hunger Drive"; Omang, "Film of Emaciated Children."
116. Shepherd, *Politics of Starvation*; Shepherd, "Food Aid"; E. Keller, *Revolutionary Ethiopia*; E. Keller, "Politics of Famine."

lasted longer than a year and involved massive construction and beautification projects throughout Addis Ababa. At Ethiopian ports, priority was given to Soviet ships carrying construction materials, while Western ships containing food often had to wait for weeks at sea before unloading their cargo. On Mengistu's orders, all mentions of famine were forbidden beginning in May of 1984. The Ethiopian government was so successful in censoring the domestic and international media that many Ethiopians living in urban areas were surprised to learn, months later, that a famine actually existed in their country.

The cost of the anniversary celebration is a matter of some debate.[117] M. Peter McPherson estimated the cost at $100 million, while others believe it was half that amount, with the Soviet Union paying the majority of the expense.[118] Regardless of the true cost, the celebration was, at the very best, indulgent during a period of famine.

The Ethiopian government's preoccupation with the anniversary provided the Reagan administration with a foil from which to frame U.S. policy. The State Department released a memo stating that the Ethiopian government's "response to the drought and famine [has] been disappointing" and that this reflected its preference for "providing massive resources for the festivities celebrating the 10th anniversary of the Ethiopian revolution" rather than famine relief.[119] In congressional testimony, McPherson justified U.S. policy by again contrasting the vices of Marxism with the virtue of U.S. humanitarianism: "It wasn't altogether popular in this [Reagan] government to get food to Ethiopia where the [Ethiopian] government has a celebration costing millions of dollars . . . and where they gave priority in their ports to Soviet cement which delayed our getting food through the ports. It is not very popular in some quarters to give people in that country food. But we have said we don't care what the politics are."[120]

While the Ethiopian government's tenth anniversary celebration did provide good rhetorical fodder, it also modestly increased the American media coverage of the famine. Despite the Ethiopian censorship, which prevented reporters from traveling to relief stations, several newspaper reporters did file famine stories based on interviews with NGO workers and second-hand accounts of famine victims. These stories—most notably by David Ottaway of the *Washington Post* and Judith Miller of the *New York Times*—not only juxtaposed

---

117. Meszoly, "Africa Drought," 3043.
118. Harden, "Ethiopia Scolds Aid Donors"; Boffey, "U.S. Will Provide $45 Million."
119. U.S. Department of State, Bureau of Public Affairs, "GIST," October 1984, cited in Shepherd, "Food Aid," 361.
120. U.S. Congress, House Committee on Foreign Relations, *World Food and Population*, 97.

the famine with the lavish celebration conducted by the Ethiopian government but also threatened to increase the American public's awareness of the famine in general and of U.S. policy in particular.[121] During this time, McPherson called a meeting with NGOs and promised that the United States would soon begin augmenting its assistance to Ethiopia.[122]

Summary

This chapter examined the early stages of the Ethiopian famine. In a guarded political context marked by low issue salience and unified public preferences, there was little pressure to resolve the bureaucratic conflict that raged between the hardliners, institutionalists, and humanitarians. Instead, internal political disagreements over policy led to a slow U.S. response to a worsening situation. When the Reagan administration did act quickly, it was usually in response to events that could potentially increase issue salience.

It is also important to point out that during these early stages, the United States did provide assistance to Ethiopia. This suggests that public attention is not the only factor that motivates the bureaucracy. Nevertheless, the amount of aid given by the United States was minuscule compared to the depth of the problem. In short, the U.S. response did not have to be large in part because public interest was, at the time, so minimal. This situation, however, was about to change.

---

121. Ottaway, "Ethiopia Squeezed"; J. Miller, "Famine Engulfs Ethiopia Again."
122. Solberg, *Miracle in Ethiopia.*

7

THE ETHIOPIAN FAMINE
Decision, Implementation, and Review

As we saw in the previous chapter, a guarded political context allowed the Reagan administration to ignore public opinion when dealing with Ethiopia. As a result, U.S. policy became gridlocked, vacillating, and often dilatory. However, in late 1984, television and rock stars united to make the Ethiopian famine one of the most salient events of the 1980s. The Reagan administration responded to an explosion of public concern by doing an about-face and suddenly flooding Ethiopia with U.S. food. But as public attention began to wane in 1985, so too did the pressure for political responsiveness. With Americans' gaze once again turned elsewhere, U.S. policy began deviating from the humanitarian impulse of the public in several important ways.

This chapter assesses the U.S. response to the Ethiopian famine during the policy decision, implementation, and policy review stages. The Ethiopian case study shows how a highly attentive public can suddenly grab the wheel and guide U.S. foreign policy. It also demonstrates that the public does not hold onto power for very long and that, when it does let go, policy can drift in unexpected directions.

Policy Decision

Our theory of the policy-opinion link assumes that the American public is most attentive at the policy decision stage of noncrises. Such was the case during the Ethiopian famine. From late October 1984 to January 1985, famine in Ethiopia became one of the top news stories, if not *the* top story, in the United States. The convergence of high issue salience with the already widespread humanitarian sentiment of the American public produced a constrained political context in which the pressure for political responsiveness increased dramatically, and as a result, the Reagan administration followed the public's mandate.

Television and Rock Stars

On October 23, 1984, the BBC ran a documentary on the massive starvation and death occurring at the Ethiopian feeding camps. The next day, NBC News rebroadcast the footage for an American audience. The heart-wrenching documentary showed in graphic detail men, women, and children dying of hunger. That NBC ran the documentary at all illustrates how policy outcomes are often contingent on seemingly small factors.[1] Originally, the producers at NBC decided not to air the Ethiopia footage, contending that it was not newsworthy. Tom Brokaw happened to be in the studio at the time the producers were previewing the tape and demanded that the footage be shown that night. Had Brokaw not been in the studio and the film not been aired, the public's interest in famine might have come at a much later date, if at all.

The Ethiopian documentary set off media frenzy. Journalists engaged in a mad scramble to get into Ethiopia, descending on Addis Ababa in droves and making hasty arrangements to visit relief stations.[2] In November, CBS's *60 Minutes* had compiled its own footage of the famine, which attracted an audience of thirty-four million viewers. After years of public and media neglect, the African famine suddenly shot to the top of the agenda—238 television minutes were devoted to the famine in the three months following the NBC broadcast, compared to just 14 minutes over the *previous two years* (see figure 16).

Television coverage also set the newspaper agenda. As figure 17 shows, the *New York Times* coverage of the famine was spotty at best in the years prior to the NBC broadcast. After the broadcast, the *New York Times* coverage of the famine increased to almost twenty-five thousand words per month. This change suggests an interesting finding: television coverage of famine set the newspaper agenda, but newspaper coverage of famine did not set the television agenda. As a visual medium, television had the advantage in capturing public attention by providing graphic images of the suffering in Ethiopia that produced a visceral response in the American public.[3] The combined television and newspaper coverage also had a compounding effect on public attention.

1. Solberg, *Miracle in Ethiopia*; Bosso, "Setting the Agenda"; Shepherd, "Food Aid."
2. Bosso, "Setting the Agenda."
3. Graber, *Processing Politics*.

As Christopher Bosso writes, "There seems little doubt that newspaper editors used Americans' reaction to pictures of tragedy to set their agendas. And it would be this multiplier effect, the crescendo of coverage by a wide array of media, that proved most critical to making the Ethiopian famine a national concern. The sheer *repetition* of the problem, be it by local television stations or non-elite periodicals, made the famine familiar to most Americans."[4]

Furthermore, the media coverage attracted the attention of celebrities. In December 1984, Bob Geldof, lead singer of the Boomtown Rats, organized Band Aid, a collaborative group of British musicians who recorded the song "Do They Know It's Christmas?" Not to be outdone by their British counterparts, a group of American pop stars organized USA for Africa and recorded "We Are the World" in January 1985. Both songs became pop hits and received massive airtime on radio and MTV. The proceeds from album sales and related concerts and contributions raised approximately $326 million for famine relief in Africa.

The importance of celebrities in drawing the public's attention to the African famine is hard to overestimate. Not since Vietnam had so many pop cultural icons (Michael Jackson, Mick Jagger, Tina Turner, and Bruce Springsteen, to name a few) taken such an active interest in an international issue. This star power contributed to the "magnifier effect" of media attention and made the issue salient to young people—the notoriously apathetic MTV generation.[5] As a result, the famine in Ethiopia was viewed not only as a human tragedy but also as a pop cultural phenomenon and one of the defining events of the 1980s.

The Constrained Political Context

As demonstrated earlier, a strong humanitarian sentiment courses deeply through the American public. The public holds a unified, almost unanimous, preference for U.S. humanitarian assistance to help those suffering from extreme poverty or natural disasters. This opinion has changed little over the years. But while the public's humanitarian preferences are consistently high, issue salience surrounding global poverty is usually quite low. Simply put, the American public only rarely notices problems in the less developed world. Given an inattentive public, U.S. policy makers often feel little domestic pressure to pursue a vigorous human rights or basic human needs agenda in the third world. However, this scenario would change in the mid-1980s.

4. Bosso, "Setting the Agenda," 167.
5. Ibid.

In the weeks following the NBC broadcast, the American public's response to the famine was nothing short of extraordinary. The phone lines of charitable organizations were flooded by calls from citizens wanting to help. "Many of them are in tears when they call," said James Sheffield, president of the U.S. Committee for UNICEF. "They've seen television footage, and they say it's horrible and something must be done."[6] Private donations to NGOs skyrocketed to more than $40 million in the two months after the broadcast.[7] The Catholic Relief Services (CRS), which had received $80,000 in contributions for all of 1983, collected $23 million in donations by Christmas.[8] Stories of remarkable individual generosity abounded. An elderly man on food stamps donated his entire life's savings to famine relief, accompanied by a note apologizing that it wasn't more. Schoolchildren from across the country started classroom donations and sent in their nickels and dimes to relief organizations. And, in a break with usual broadcast policy, nightly news programs publicized phone numbers that viewers could call if they wanted to donate funds.

As a measure of the public's interest, a *Los Angeles Times* survey showed in January 1985 that more Americans were following the Ethiopian famine than any other current event, including the upcoming Super Bowl.[9] Over 86 percent of the public remarked that the famine had had an impact on their "mood."[10] And by the end of 1985, the Ethiopian famine was recalled as one of the top three news stories of the year.[11] In short, public concern was overwhelming.

6. Berger, "Offers of Aid."
7. Teltsch, "2-Month U.S. Total."
8. Pezzulo, "Catholic Relief Services," 218; Solberg, *Miracle in Ethiopia*, 71.
9. Survey by the *Los Angeles Times*, January 19–24, 1985, from LexisNexis, Roper Center for Public Opinion Research, University of Connecticut (accessed April 12, 2004). "Which one of these stories in the news have you been paying the most attention to recently? Have you been following more closely stories about: the bombing of abortion clinics . . . or nuclear arms limitation talks with the Russians . . . or stories about children being molested . . . or the famine in Ethiopia . . . or the federal budget deficit . . . or the Super Bowl . . . or the administration's plans for income tax reform . . . or the weather . . . or something else—or haven't you been following closely many stories in the news?"
10. Survey by Gordon S. Black, *USA Today*, February 1985, from LexisNexis, Roper Center for Public Opinion Research, University of Connecticut (accessed April 12, 2004). "(Major national and international news events can sometimes have an impact on people—sometimes directly and sometimes simply on how they feel. I would like to read a list of some of the major stories during the past several months, and I would first like you to tell me whether the event had any impact on you at all, either directly or on your mood or how you feel.) . . . The mass starvation in Ethiopia in which 300,000 people are reported to have died."
11. Survey by the Roper Organization, December 7–14, 1985, from LexisNexis, Roper Center for Public Opinion Research, University of Connecticut (accessed April 12, 2004). "1985 is now drawing to a close. Looking back over the things that have happened during this year, which two or three of these events or developments would you say were the most important events or developments of the year?"

Policy Making in a Constrained Political Context

There is little doubt that the confluence of high issue salience and unified public preferences exerted considerable pressure on the Reagan administration to "do something" about the famine in Ethiopia. As such, the administration's tendency toward bureaucratic inertia during the option generation stage now became politically untenable. During the peak of public attention to the famine from late October 1984 to January 1985, the Reagan administration made a series of decisions that were consistent with the public's preference for humanitarian aid, yet inconsistent with the administration's overriding concern with the Ethiopian government. Massive amounts of U.S. emergency relief flooded Ethiopia with very few strings attached. Thanks to intense public interest, long-suffering humanitarians finally enjoyed considerable influence over U.S. policy.

One of the most important effects of increased public attention was that it effectively eliminated the hardliners from the policy-making process. The spike in public attention had caused senior administration officials, including President Reagan, to step in to break the bureaucratic deadlock that had previously stymied U.S. policy. With public scrutiny clearly focused on Ethiopia, "doing nothing"—the preferred hardliner policy—was no longer a viable political option. As Princeton Lyman stated,

> No question about it [public attention influenced policy]. It [famine relief] then became one of the major programs of the United States government. Heavy involvement of very senior people and public attention to the drought made an enormous difference. Because it cut through all the political angst about should we be helping the Mengistu regime.... It cut through all that. The question was how to do it, and how to deal with a recalcitrant and negative regime, and all of those issues persisted. But there was no question that what we were answering to was an enormous amount of public attention. Live Aid and all of that attention.... So there is no question that public reaction had a major impact on policy.... I think it is a fascinating case of how the public opinion drives policy ... how it reinforced those in the government that wanted to do relief.[12]

With the hardliners out of the picture, two views of the famine remained: the institutionalist and the humanitarian representations. In many ways, the

12. Lyman, interview.

institutionalists and humanitarians shared the same policy goal—to alleviate human suffering in Ethiopia. They also agreed that Mengistu's regime was "particularly bad."[13] They differed, however, on the lengths to which the United States should go to avoid directly or indirectly assisting the Ethiopian government. The institutionalists often fixated on the Ethiopian government and went to great pains to ensure that U.S. aid circumvented the Mengistu regime. By contrast, the humanitarians were much less concerned about such matters and, consequently, advocated massive U.S. assistance for Ethiopia, regardless of political considerations. (With the hardliners no longer involved in decision making, the institutionalist representation really became *the* position of the Reagan administration. Therefore, for clarity's sake, "Reagan administration" is used instead of "institutionalists" from this point forward in our discussion.)

For the humanitarians, the timing of public attention could not have been better. The close proximity of the NBC broadcast to the 1984 presidential election meant that the Ethiopian famine now became heavily politicized. The Democratic presidential candidate, Walter Mondale, quickly incorporated President Reagan's food aid policy into his campaign. In a stump speech, Mondale stated that "instead of planning a trillion dollar Star Wars scheme, instead of running an illegal war in Nicaragua, I would be mobilizing an international air and sea-lift for food for our fellow beings starving in sub-Saharan Africa."[14] Even though the issue of food aid to Ethiopia was unlikely to erode President Reagan's significant lead in the presidential race, the prominence of the famine among the American electorate demanded a response from the president. As Jack Shepherd writes,

> It is difficult with the passage of time since 1984 to recall the enormous public outcry and generosity that followed the television news films of Ethiopia. In retrospect, ignoring that awakening might have cost President Reagan a significant share of the electorate, although probably not the election. But in late October, with the election near, no candidate should take chances. Continuing to turn his back to the pleas of hungry Africans, especially in the face of the BBC films and the response of other donors, would have made the president appear heartless and perhaps cruel. It was not a risk worth taking.[15]

13. During my interviews, institutionalists described Mengistu as a "dog," "thug," "murderer," and "clown." The humanitarians were only slightly less disdainful of the Mengistu regime, calling it "heinous," "corrupt," and "particularly bad."
14. Joyce, "Northwest Visit Delights Mondale."
15. Shepherd, "Food Aid," 307.

Other politicians seized upon the spike in issue salience and scrambled to get to Ethiopia. A congressional delegation, as well as the Reverend Jesse Jackson, applied for visas to tour Ethiopia in the days after the NBC broadcast. USAID administrator M. Peter McPherson also made hurried plans to visit Ethiopia. According to State Department records, McPherson was in such a rush to get to Africa that he "left for Ethiopia with a seven-person team, even before his arrival schedule or any appointments in Ethiopia had been confirmed."[16] While the desire to be the first to arrive in Ethiopia might have been partially motivated by political concerns, McPherson's trip seemed to have made a genuine impact on him. He called it "one of the most meaningful, powerful experiences in my life."[17]

Two days after the October 23 NBC broadcast, the Reagan administration pledged $45 million in aid to Ethiopia.[18] McPherson characterized the amount as "frankly enormous" and used the announcement as an opportunity to contrast U.S. generosity with the paltry amount of aid the USSR had donated to its own ally.[19] On November 1, 1984, the Reagan administration chartered two Hercules transport planes to aid in the relief efforts. The planes were symbolic of the administration's newfound concern with Ethiopia but were of little practical value since only a small amount of food can be transported by air.[20]

The most shocking moment of the policy decision stage came on November 2, 1984, when the Reagan administration declared Marxist Ethiopia a "friendly government." That declaration enabled the administration to bypass legal restrictions in the United States that prevented direct donations of food to the Ethiopian government. The administration subsequently announced that it was providing 50,000 MT of food to the Mengistu regime—the first and last time a direct government-to-government donation was made in the case.[21]

Why would the Reagan administration, once so convinced of the ineptitude and utter corruptness of the Ethiopian government, now make a U-turn and donate food directly to that very same regime? One possibility is that the NGOs working in Ethiopia—the medium through which the United States channeled assistance to unfriendly countries—were at their absorptive capacity

16. Solberg, *Miracle in Ethiopia*, 73.
17. Meszoly, "Africa Drought," 3039.
18. Shepherd, "Food Aid," 299–300.
19. The Warsaw Pact provided 1 percent (24,933 MT) of the total international contribution to Ethiopia during the famine. By contrast, the United States provided 46 percent (779,748 MT). See Varnis, *Reluctant Aid*, 118.
20. Cuny, "Politics and Famine Relief."
21. Varnis, *Reluctant Aid*.

and could no longer handle additional food. This calculation likely played a role in the decision, but an even more plausible reason is that the government-to-government food grant was politically expedient. The donation eliminated, or at least temporarily suspended, critics' argument that the administration was denying food to Ethiopia on the basis of ideology. The government-to-government donation was also highly visible. Unlike the cross-border operation, which functioned in secrecy, the 50,000 MT grant made headlines for which the administration could claim credit.[22]

The decision to declare Ethiopia a friendly state, although politically beneficial, was inconsistent with the Reagan administration's (read, institutionalist) representation of the problem. The administration still believed that the Ethiopian government was not providing enough resources to the famine relief and that Mengistu would most likely mismanage the American food. Furthermore, if the concern was about getting assistance to those in the greatest need, the 50,000 MT of food might have been better used in the cross-border operation in the north, where more people were at risk of starvation and where the Ethiopian government was unwilling to provide assistance. In short, it is highly unlikely that the administration would have declared Ethiopia a "friendly" nation if not for the massive public interest in the famine.

Issue salience remained high into November, and the decision-making frenzy continued. Upon his return from Ethiopia, McPherson announced another U.S. donation of 130,000 MT of food.[23] An additional 80,000 MT of food was granted to Ethiopia on November 28 when President Reagan ordered that a U.S. supply ship full of grain and bound for India be rerouted to Ethiopia.[24] That same day, President Reagan authorized, for the first time ever, the tapping of the wheat reserve.[25] Since the enactment of the Wheat Reserve Act of 1980, the United States has kept in abeyance 4 million MT of wheat, 300,000 MT of which the president can release for "unanticipated" need in foreign countries.[26] The tapping of the reserve was significant in that, just eight

---

22. Relief efforts in the north were opaque for a number of reasons discussed later in this chapter. One study showed that of the 572 newspaper articles on the famine from January 1984 to June 1986, less than 1 percent mentioned the relief operations of the rebel groups. G. Smith, "Politics of Famine Relief," 35.

23. Shepherd, "Food Aid," 300.

24. Meszoly, "Africa Drought," 3043. The rerouting of the ship bound for India was indicative of the zero-sum game in food aid appropriations. Presumably, the 80,000 MT of food would have helped a number of needy people in India. In one of the tragic ironies of food aid, the massive public attention to Ethiopia was accompanied by diminished attention (both public and private) to hunger and famine in other parts of the world. See Bosso, "Setting the Agenda," 167–68, and Shepherd, "Food Aid."

25. Bosso, "Setting the Agenda"; Shepherd, "Food Aid."

26. Meszoly, "Africa Drought," 3039.

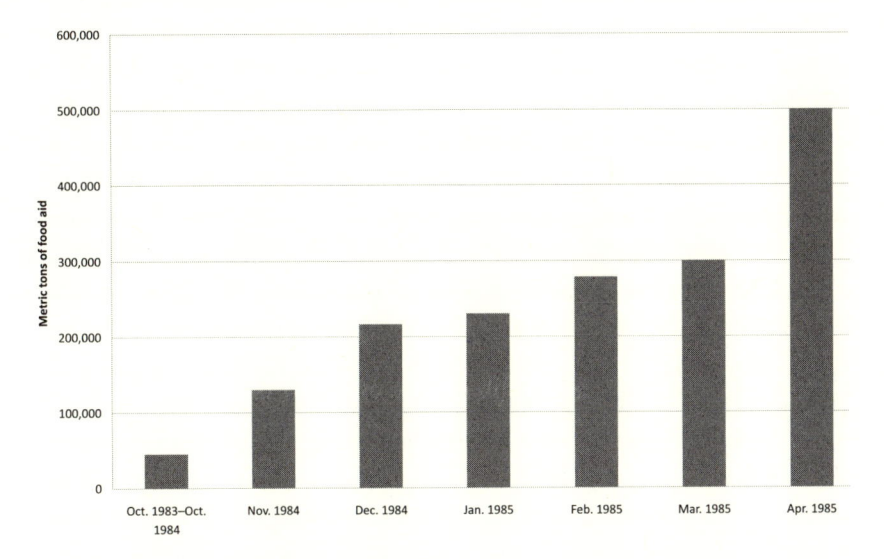

Fig. 18 Increases in U.S. food aid to Ethiopia
Source: Shepherd, "Food Aid."

months prior, the administration had refused a congressional request to do so by arguing that Africans did not eat wheat.[27]

In the first forty-five days of fiscal year 1985, USAID approved roughly $200 million for emergency relief for sixteen African countries.[28] Approximately half of this money went to Ethiopia. Figure 18 demonstrates the incredible shift in administration policy following the NBC broadcast. While the United States donated 45,000 MT of food in the entire fiscal year of 1984, USAID appropriated almost three times this amount *in the month of November alone.*

Overview of the Policy Decision Stage

The U.S. response to the Ethiopian famine from late October 1984 to January 1985 was impressive and unprecedented. In the three months after the NBC documentary, the United States donated twelve times the amount of food it had sent to Ethiopia in the *entire previous year.* The policy seems even more remarkable when we consider that it was President Reagan, a staunch anti-communist and fiscal conservative, who approved a record amount of food

27. Shepherd, "Food Aid."
28. Meszoly, "Africa Drought," 3037.

aid to a communist nation. There is little question that the spike in issue salience caused the dramatic shift in policy. In later interviews, several decision makers in the Reagan administration remarked on the importance of public attention. According to Chester Crocker, former assistant secretary of state for African affairs, "Once you get the major media into it [famine relief], obviously it means that the next morning it isn't just on your desk, it's on the Secretary's [of State] desk. It's at the noon briefing. That escalates everything. It may not lead to better policies, but it sure escalates everything. Your phones ring a lot more: 'What the hell are we doing about this?'"[29] Likewise, McPherson recalled, "I think it [public attention] did make a big difference. Well before that [the October 23, 1984, NBC documentary], we had gone through the political struggles of the decisions, and the food numbers were going up. But the media coverage, as so often happens, moved the political process much faster. . . . I always mentioned it [media attention at internal policy meetings]. But it was self-evident to everyone anyway. The decision to move food was already made, but the decision to augment dramatically was enormously enhanced by the media focus."[30]

Even the die-hard congressional critics of the Reagan administration were forced to acknowledge that the U.S. response in late 1984 and early 1985 was outstanding. This praise, however, was usually tempered with a criticism of the administration's prior response to famine. As Representative Ted Weiss (D-N.Y.) remarked, "I think that the response of the administration during the last 3 months of 1984 has been nothing short of magnificent. . . . It must be said [however] that until the last quarter of fiscal year 1984, AID staff has consistently for the last 2 years severely underestimated what the needs are."[31] Representative Mickey Leland (D-Tex.) echoed, "I have commended the President for his actions on many occasions, both publicly and privately. . . . However, we as a nation cannot abrogate our responsibility for what we knew was happening in Ethiopia many months previously."[32] And Representative Howard Wolpe (D-Mich.) stated,

> There is no question whatsoever that the response of the United States and American people, once there was a full public recognition of this through the medium of television . . . has been absolutely extraordinary; has been magnificent; is in the finest humanitarian tradition of this

29. Crocker, interview.
30. McPherson, interview.
31. U.S. Congress, House Committee on Foreign Affairs, *African Famine Situation*, 6.
32. Ibid., 23.

country.... If we continue to insist that somehow we did [not] know what was happening 2 years ago, that is simply deception. That is simply deception at that point, because the Ethiopian government in October 1982, came before the international community. The Catholic Relief Services came before the administration in November 1982, the international relief agencies in the field were pleading for a response back in 1982, so let us all understand very clearly that 2 years ago we knew— the governments of this world knew—the relief community knew, the government in Ethiopia knew.[33]

The humanitarians' tendency to praise and criticize in the same breath likely reflected a very deep political frustration over the probability that the Reagan administration, by virtue of its massive response *after* the public became attentive, would emerge from the Ethiopian case smelling like a rose. An NGO lobbyist summed up this irritation: "I'll be really outraged if they [the Reagan administration] come out of this looking like humanitarians. That's the farthest thing from the truth."[34]

In sum, the confluence of strong public preferences and high issue salience led to this dramatic shift in U.S. policy. With the hardliners dropping their objection to U.S. assistance in Ethiopia, the hesitation and vacillation that once had characterized U.S. policy was now replaced by a rush of policy making and a record amount of U.S. food aid. Even more astounding, the Reagan administration largely set aside its preoccupation with the Mengistu regime, even going so far as to declare the communist Ethiopian government "friendly." And yet the political context was about to change once again.

Implementation

All of the humanitarian decisions made in late 1984 and early 1985 would have been meaningless if policy was not implemented in a rational, coherent manner. The nature of international food aid—characterized by long delays between decision and implementation—meant that policy decisions were not immediately translated into tangible assistance for famine victims.[35] The way in which the Reagan administration approached the implementation of policy was therefore of vital importance to millions of at-risk Ethiopians.

33. Ibid., 101.
34. Boffey, "U.S. Will Provide $45 Million."
35. Cuny, "Politics and Famine Relief"; Cuny, *Disasters and Development*, 277; Ruttan, *United States Development*.

Our theory predicts that the decline in public attention after a noncrisis policy decision affords presidents and their administrations considerable freedom to implement that policy in whatever manner they choose. As we will see, public interest in the Ethiopian famine quickly faded by February 1985. As issue salience decreased, the Reagan administration turned its attention back to the Ethiopian government.

Was There Still a Problem in Ethiopia?

Determining the congruence between opinion and policy during the implementation stage requires that we assess the conditions that existed in Ethiopia. Recall that most Americans believe that the United States spends too much in foreign aid, but that they also favor emergency humanitarian relief to meet basic human needs.[36] Had the situation in Ethiopia improved dramatically during the implementation stage, then it is likely that Americans would have also approved of a commensurate decrease in U.S. foreign aid. Put more simply, most Americans don't want to give any more foreign aid than is absolutely necessary. Therefore, determining whether policy choices were consistent or inconsistent with public preferences requires assessing the degree to which the situation in Ethiopia did or did not improve over time.

Figure 19 shows the number of Ethiopians affected by famine. Although the number of famine victims began to decline after 1985, the total affected population was still large by any standard. From 1985 to 1987, the number of at-risk Ethiopians never dipped below five million—an amount greater than the number of victims during both the problem representation and option generation stages. By late 1985, Ethiopia was still on the Food and Agriculture Association's (FAO's) list of the world's neediest countries, and the UN estimated that Ethiopia would require 1.2 million MT of food for 1986.[37]

Considering the political environment within Ethiopia, famine remained especially acute in the war-torn northern providences. In June 1985, a Red Cross representative stated that the "relief effort here [northern regions of Ethiopia] has not been commensurate with the need. The situation has become

---

36. Surveys taken during the implementation stage reflect this trend: while 64 percent of Americans believed that the United States should cut its foreign aid budget, over 63 percent felt that combating world hunger should be a very important foreign policy goal for the United States. Surveys by the National Opinion Research Center, February–April 1985, and the Gallup Poll, October 30–November 12, 1986, from LexisNexis, Roper Center for Public Opinion Research, University of Connecticut (accessed April 7, 2004).

37. Harden, "Famine's Grip Loosened."

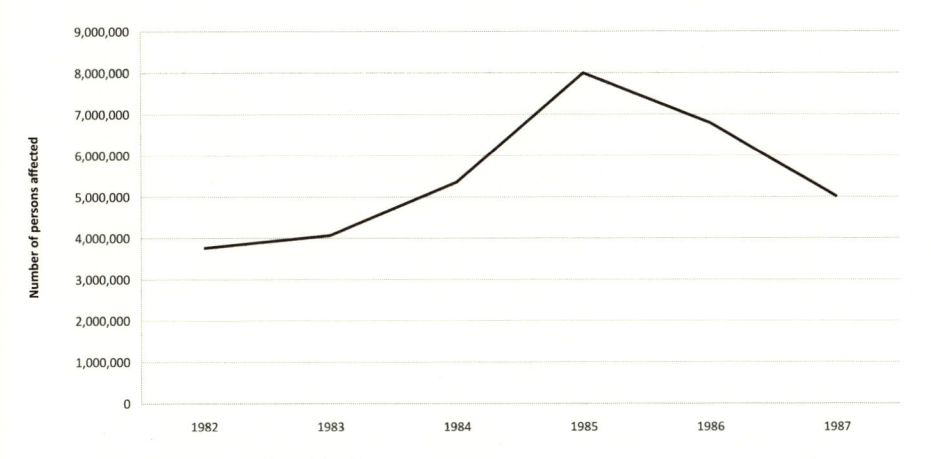

Fig. 19   Ethiopians affected by famine, 1982–87
Source: Varnis, *Reluctant Aid,* 80; Harden, "Ethiopia Faces Famine Again."

much worse."[38] Unlike many other sub-Saharan African countries, Ethiopia had an especially difficult time pulling out of the grips of famine. The combination of civil war, more infrequent rains than anywhere else in the region, and farmers too weak to plant resulted in a 13 percent lower crop yield than normal. In short, a serious problem still existed during the implementation stage.

The Guarded Political Context

The evidence cited above indicates that Ethiopia still needed emergency assistance well into 1985 and 1986. How did the American public view this situation? Because most survey organizations stopped asking questions about Ethiopia early in 1985, we have to again assess Americans' preferences for foreign aid in more general terms. Surveys taken during the implementation stage continued to reflect the general humanitarian sentiment of the American public. In 1986, over 94 percent of Americans believed that combating world hunger should be an important foreign policy goal for the United

38. May, "Northern Ethiopia Crisis."

States.[39] The public also continued to rank the alleviation of hunger and poverty as the number one reason for providing foreign aid.[40] These humanitarian preferences, coupled with the fact that emergency conditions existed well into 1985 and 1986, suggest that most Americans would have likely supported a continued U.S. commitment to Ethiopia if asked for their opinion.

Even though the American public may have actually preferred a sustained response to Ethiopia, few remained interested in famine by this stage in the policy-making process. While the major television networks devoted almost seventy minutes of coverage to famine in January 1985, coverage had dropped to a little over seven minutes in the month of February (see figure 16). During the same time period, the number of words devoted to famine in the *New York Times* was cut in half (see figure 17). In short, the American public had begun to exhibit signs of "donor fatigue" or "compassion fatigue," as the pictures of starving Africans no longer stimulated the type of urgent response they once had. Save for the brief period during the summer of 1985 when the Live Aid concerts were held, the Ethiopian famine rapidly slid off the public's agenda.

The American public's widespread preference for humanitarian aid combined with low attention to Ethiopia once again produced a guarded political context. In this context, the Reagan administration carried out its earlier policy decisions with an eye on the Ethiopian government. In particular, the administration shaped implementation in a way that attempted to pressure the Mengistu regime into devoting more of its own resources to famine relief. In addition, the Reagan administration drew a sharp line between emergency relief (which it would provide) and developmental assistance (which it would not provide). Although these policies made perfect sense from an institutionalist perspective, they were inconsistent with what humanitarians, and by extension the American public, preferred. But the fact that few Americans were attentive to Ethiopia at this stage meant that policy could now safely diverge from public opinion.

---

39. Survey by the Gallup Organization, October 30–November 12, 1986, from LexisNexis, Roper Center for Public Opinion Research, University of Connecticut (accessed April 12, 2004). "(I am going to read a list of possible foreign policy goals that the United States might have. For each one please say whether you think that it should be a very important foreign policy goal of the United States, a somewhat important foreign policy goal, or not an important goal at all?) . . . Combating world hunger." Percent responding "very important" or "somewhat important" foreign policy goal.

40. Survey by Interaction and Overseas Development Council/Strategic Information Research Corporation, April 7–May 6, 1986, from the iPOLL Databank, Roper Center for Public Opinion Research, University of Connecticut (accessed August 14, 2008). "What is the most important reason to you for favoring foreign aid?"

Inland Transportation

By early 1985, the problem in Ethiopia had largely shifted from an insufficient supply of food to an inadequate distribution of available food.[41] Fewer than half of the trucks needed to ensure a clean pipeline of food were in the country, resulting in a massive backlog of aid at Ethiopian ports. In April, an estimated 60 percent of the 332,000 MT of food in Ethiopia remained undelivered and rotting on docks.[42]

After months of haggling with NGOs, USAID announced in late June 1985 that it would provide four hundred trucks to help unclog the bottleneck in Ethiopian ports, and international relief organizations began making plans based on the assumption that a greater capacity to transport food would soon be forthcoming. By late September, however, only forty-eight of the four hundred pledged trucks were in Ethiopia.[43] This delay sparked another heated congressional hearing, in which Representative Wolpe began by questioning the administration's willingness to implement its earlier policy decisions: "But the issue right now is not whether we have been generous in our response; the issue is whether the United States has used clearly available funds which have already been authorized, for which appropriations have already been made, in a timely way so as to address, in conjunction with host governments and other donors, the continuing critical transportation bottlenecks that are preventing hundreds of thousands of tons and millions of U.S. dollars and food from reaching those people who are starving and suffering so severely."[44]

This congressional challenge placed USAID on the defensive. McPherson claimed that the United States had indeed provided close to four hundred trucks and that any discrepancy in the numbers was due to accounting differences. For instance, USAID argued that it had never intended to provide four hundred trucks itself, but rather was counting vehicles donated by American NGOs as part of that commitment. Members of Congress quickly rejected this rationale. Wolpe argued, "The problem, very frankly, is the massaging of the numbers to create an impression . . . that we are making a commitment that I think we are not. That's the problem."[45]

Realizing that Congress was unlikely to be persuaded on the basis of a technicality, McPherson offered more substantive insight into the administration's

---

41. Solberg, *Miracle in Ethiopia*; Varnis, *Reluctant Aid*; Shepherd, "Food Aid"; Callan, "U.S. Foreign Aid."
42. Harden, "Strings on U.S. Aid."
43. U.S. Congress, House Committee on Foreign Affairs, *Emergency Famine Relief Needs*, 2.
44. Ibid., 3.
45. Ibid., 37.

decision making. He reiterated to the Committee on Foreign Affairs the administration's position that the root of distribution problems in Ethiopia lay with Mengistu's unwillingness to divert trucks from the war effort to aid in famine relief. The delay in the U.S. commitment of trucks was, therefore, an attempt to pressure the Ethiopian government into devoting more of its own resources to distribute the donated food. McPherson noted, "I think the only way there is going to be enough trucks to take the food that I think should be delivered in the next few weeks is if the Ethiopian government themselves put in substantial vehicles."[46]

The Reagan administration had a good reason for wishing to compel the Ethiopian government to cooperate. Mengistu had at his disposal the means to move the massive amount of U.S. and international food from Ethiopian ports to the relief stations in the north. Indeed, the Ethiopian military, not the United States or the NGOs operating in the area, was best positioned to provide the transportation so vital to effective relief operations. But while the Ethiopian government had the capacity to transport the food, it certainly exhibited little willingness to do so. As McPherson told me, "Mengistu's point of view was that the [famine] would weaken the north anyway so the more they starved, from his point of view, would be just fine. The pressure on Mengistu to deliver the trucks was reduced if we committed to deliver the trucks."[47]

Nevertheless, there is little doubt that the image of food rotting on Ethiopian docks while people starved in feeding camps would have been disturbing to many Americans. And it is likely that, if asked, most Americans would have preferred that the United States supply the trucks to move the food, regardless of what the Ethiopian government was or was not doing. By this time, however, donor fatigue had largely set in and the American public had turned its attention elsewhere. In this guarded political context, delaying transportation assistance in order to pressure the Ethiopian government into making reforms became a viable policy for the Reagan administration.

Thus, the key factor explaining the reemergence of ideological conflict during policy implementation in this case was the decline of issue salience. Just a few months earlier, the intense public concern over Ethiopia had forced the administration to make policy choices consistent with the humanitarian preferences of the American public and against its own better judgment. With famine off the headlines, the administration now had little reason to consult public opinion when carrying out that policy.

46. Ibid., 38.
47. McPherson, interview.

Development Projects

A second example of the reemergence of ideological conflict concerned development projects. For institutionalists, providing resources for economic development was especially problematic because it would ultimately bolster the Mengistu regime. McPherson remarked, "We felt strongly that this government wouldn't use development assistance to have a long-term impact."[48] Julia Chang Bloch, then assistant administrator of USAID's Bureau of Food for Peace, stated, "When you are talking about long-term development assistance, there is no sense in throwing money down a rat hole."[49] Chester Crocker said, "We didn't want to do development for those clowns. . . . We were trying to back winners by focusing our regular development and ESF [Economic Support Fund] on countries that were either doing the right thing economically, or the right thing politically, or hopefully both. But not doing the wrong thing on both."[50]

Officials in the Reagan administration, who had little interest in providing developmental support to Ethiopia, could also cite amendments to the Foreign Assistance Act that legally prevented them from doing so. The Hickenlooper Amendment stipulated that no developmental aid could be provided to foreign governments that had nationalized U.S. property. The Brooke Amendment banned developmental projects in countries whose governments had defaulted on military loans. And the Gonzalez Amendment required that the United States use its influence in the World Bank to veto developmental projects in countries with poor human rights records.[51] When it came to these amendments, Ethiopia had three strikes against it. It is important to note, however, that it was possible for a president committed to providing developmental assistance to circumvent each of these legal restrictions. For instance, the language of the Hickenlooper Amendment stated that its terms could be nullified if a president found that a country was taking "appropriate steps" in making reparations to the United States. In early 1985, State Department lawyers issued a ruling that stated that "appropriate steps" could be "whatever President Reagan decides. Hickenlooper could be waived by the president this afternoon." The only way to waive the Brooke Amendment was for the president to cite national security concerns. As one State Department official commented, "We have had meetings around this building [the State

48. Ibid.
49. Chang Bloch, interview.
50. Crocker, interview.
51. Duffield and Prendergast, *Without Troops and Tanks*; Callan, "U.S. Foreign Aid," 340–44.

Department] about Hickenlooper and Brooke, but there is no feeling around Washington that it [the Ethiopian famine] is a crisis."[52]

The ban on developmental projects stands in sharp contrast with the generous emergency relief provided by the United States. The resulting policies awkwardly tried to address current needs in Ethiopia without providing assistance for the future. Three examples illustrate the tension between development and emergency relief. First, USAID helped Oxfam dig wells in the northern province of Wollo.[53] While USAID did not consider the act of digging to be a developmental project, it did consider providing the expertise and equipment needed to pump water to be developmental and, therefore, banned. Second, many NGOs proposed programs in which food rations would be exchanged for work on developmental projects.[54] USAID banned all NGOs receiving U.S. money from engaging in food-for-work projects because of the developmental focus of the indigenous labor. Finally, USAID refused to provide seeds to Ethiopian farmers because seeds were also considered developmental. As Princeton Lyman stressed, "It's a terrible situation to be in, because one of the things you would like to do is get seeds to farmers so they can plant for the season. But there was a big debate: were seeds developmental aid? We were constantly dealing with these lines."[55]

By contrast, humanitarians argued that developmental projects were an indispensable part of addressing famine. As Oxfam spokesperson Hugh Goyder put it, "So many people [in Ethiopia] will have become dependent on handouts and the infrastructure of the country will not have been improved. . . . The U.S. delusion is that if you throw a lot of food at this problem it will go away. It won't. The drought will come again. And I believe that if nothing is done in agriculture development, health and water, it could be worse in Ethiopia in five years' time."[56] Niels Nikolasen, chief representative of the nonprofit Lutheran World Federation, strongly objected to the administration's veto of food-for-work projects: "We can only give American food to people who are sitting on their ass. . . . You keep people alive only to starve. We appreciate very much the American food, but in the long term, what good does it do?"[57]

Like the issue of inland transportation of food, the sharp distinction between emergency relief and developmental programs in Ethiopia revealed the

52. Harden, "Strings on U.S. Aid."
53. Ibid.
54. Ibid.
55. Lyman, interview.
56. Harden, "Strings on U.S. Aid."
57. Ibid.

fault lines between the Reagan administration and the humanitarians. The administration considered providing developmental assistance both wasteful and counterproductive in helping to bolster an incompetent and dangerous regime. Humanitarians, much less concerned with the nature of the Ethiopian government, found little logic in providing relief aid without providing assistance for the future. As U.S. chargé d'affaires in Ethiopia James Cheek stated, "We signed on here only to do fireman's relief, to get them back to where they were. That means millions of Ethiopians will be malnourished when we pull out. But that is not a problem we came here to address."[58]

Pursuing a no-development policy again depended on low issue salience. During the period when policy was being implemented, over 76 percent of the American public favored giving U.S. money for developmental projects such as health care, agriculture, and education.[59] However, erosion of public interest in Ethiopia created a context in which the administration could implement what promised to be unpopular policies in America—like digging wells but not pumping water—without the fear of political retribution.

Fiscal Year 1986 Budget

In the spring and summer of 1985, USAID began preparing its budget for fiscal year (FY) 1986. A consensus among NGOs was that, while rains and massive amounts of emergency aid had stabilized the situation in Ethiopia, crisis conditions would still be in effect throughout late 1985 and 1986. The number of persons affected by serious food shortages in 1986 was estimated to be at 6,788,000, down from 7,995,000 in 1985 (see figure 19). While this figure represented an 18 percent decrease in the number of Ethiopians affected by famine, U.S. aid to Ethiopia decreased by 58 percent from FY 1985 to FY 1986. The decline in funding to Ethiopia raises the question of whether the administration was responding to an improved situation in Ethiopia or whether the cuts were driven by political and ideological considerations.

In September 1985, the Reagan administration finalized its FY 1986 budget. The administration justified budget cuts to Ethiopia by citing a dramatically

58. Harden, "Famine's Grip Loosened." It is likely that Cheek's statement was made tongue-in-cheek. David Korn, Cheek's predecessor, often expressed exasperation with the Washington decision makers' slow response to the Ethiopian famine. Indeed, the situation often looks different to field officers in-country, like Korn and Cheek, than it does to the bureaucrats back in D.C.

59. Survey by Interaction and Overseas Development Council/Strategic Information Research Corporation, April 7–May 6, 1986, from the iPOLL Databank, Roper Center for Public Opinion Research, University of Connecticut (accessed August 14, 2008). "Thinking about the issues we have discussed, can you tell me whether you tend to favor or oppose U.S. giving of foreign aid for development projects such as health care, education, and agriculture to countries in Asia, Africa, and Latin America?"

improved situation. USAID's Julia Chang Bloch contended that increased rain fall would translate into improved crop production. Chang Bloch also argued that the United States should stem its flow of food to Ethiopia to avoid creating dependencies: "We are now at that critical stage of our food assistance programs where we must assure that our food assistance does not create dependencies nor act as a disincentive to agricultural production."[60] As a result, USAID decreased the amount of food delivered to Ethiopia by 170,000 MT and imposed a 50 percent across-the-board cut to all NGO programs.

USAID was certainly correct in stating that the situation in Ethiopia had stabilized. Mortality rates were down, the number of Ethiopians in feeding stations had decreased dramatically, and rains had improved the prospects for crop harvests. In addition, there were large stocks of food in the country, and the problem was largely one of distribution rather than supply. Finally, there was a genuine concern, both inside and outside the administration, that U.S. food aid would create dependencies within Ethiopia and depress the already poor domestic production of agriculture.

On the other hand, the Reagan administration's FY 1986 budget seems inconsistent with many of these beliefs.[61] If the administration had been concerned about dependencies created by U.S. food in Ethiopia, then the FY 1986 budget should have seen an even more dramatic decrease in U.S. food aid. USAID's FY 1986 budget included 340,000 MT of food for Ethiopia, down only 106,000 MT from the previous year. Christopher Bosso points out that the decision to donate this amount of food was driven by the desire to provide relief for American farmers.[62] Food aid is a way of dealing with surplus production at home; thus, the problems of domestic farmers provided an incentive to continue participating in famine relief efforts.[63]

Perhaps more important, as table 9 shows, the appropriations for nonfood assistance (e.g., health care, transportation, developmental projects) actually *decreased* from the previous year, both in aggregate terms (from $44.05 million in FY 1985 to $15.06 million in FY 1986) and as a percentage of total aid to Ethiopia (from 15 percent in FY 1985 to 8 percent in FY 1986). This decrease in nonfood aid appears inconsistent with the administration's contention that

---

60. Solberg, *Miracle in Ethiopia*, 136.
61. Shepherd, "Food Aid"; Varnis, *Reluctant Aid*.
62. Bosso, "Setting the Agenda." See also Diven, "Domestic Determinants," and Diven, "Coincidence of Interests."
63. This was especially true for members of Congress from farming states, but less so for the Reagan administration. In fact, the administration had threatened to veto any foreign aid bill that became a "Christmas tree" for domestic farming interests. Bosso, "Setting the Agenda."

Table 9 U.S. food and nonfood aid to Ethiopia, 1984–86

Fiscal Year	Food Aid Value ($ million)	Nonfood Aid Value ($ million)	Total ($ million)
1984	23.09	0	23.09
1985	249.06	44.05	293.11
1986	156.54	15.06	171.60
Total	428.69	59.11	480.80

Source: Varnis, Reluctant Aid, 119.

the problem in Ethiopia was no longer a lack of food, but rather the lack of adequate transportation and health care.

Moreover, the FY 1986 budget apparently relied on an overly optimistic picture of the situation in Ethiopia. In a manner reminiscent of policy making during the option generation stage, USAID formulated its budget projections before any data on the current harvest were available.[64] The small amount of proposed funds led congressional critics to argue that the administration held unrealistic expectations and that the budgetary process was driven more by domestic fiscal considerations than a rational attempt to deal with the problems in Ethiopia.[65]

Taken alone, the decline in the FY 1986 budget did not necessarily mean that the Reagan administration was making policy contrary to the preferences of the American public, especially given the pervasive belief that the United States spends too much in foreign aid. On the other hand, budget cuts were dramatic and most severe in areas that needed the most attention (e.g., transportation, health care, etc.), suggesting a policy that was inconsistent with the public's humanitarian preferences.

Policy Review

The policy review stage lasted from November 1985 to September 1986. In contrast to the Gulf War, there was no clear delineation that marked the beginning of policy review in the Ethiopian case. Rather, as the famine in Ethiopia stabilized, the Reagan administration gradually began to reconsider its Ethiopian policy. As our theory predicts, the public had little interest in the famine during this stage, affording the administration considerable decision-making autonomy.

64. Solberg, *Miracle in Ethiopia*, 137.
65. U.S. Congress, House Select Committee on Hunger, *Africa*, 35–36.

Minimal Public Attention

Public interest in Ethiopia, which had been in decline since mid-January 1985, had all but disappeared by the policy review stage. From November 1, 1985, to September 1, 1986, only 29 minutes of nightly news telecasts were devoted to Ethiopia, compared to 383 minutes the previous year (figure 16). During the same period, coverage in the *New York Times* decreased almost sixfold from the previous year (figure 17). The meager coverage tended to feature "good news" stories of how U.S. assistance had helped save millions of lives. For most Americans, the problem in Ethiopia had been dealt with long ago, and attention now turned to more pressing matters.

The decline in public attention troubled many humanitarians who believed both that public interest was an integral part of famine relief and that the situation in Ethiopia, while improved, was still dire. Representative Howard Wolpe stated, "I think there is a false feeling in the world that the problem of the African famine has been solved by the world's relief effort so far. That is a false sense of optimism."[66] Many NGOs noted the difficulty in sustaining the public's attention to the famine as the issue turned from emergency relief to rehabilitation and development. William Schaufele, director of African operations for Catholic Relief Services (CRS), pointed out, "People are very generous when they see dying children. But when you want to strike at the basic problems—seeds, hand tools, water supply—it's very hard to get the money."[67]

This low level of public attention meant that the Reagan administration had little reason to consult public opinion at this stage. However, determining whether the decision-making context was guarded or insulated, and assessing whether policy choices were consistent or inconsistent with the public's preference, requires a closer examination of policy making.

Fiscal Year 1987 Budget for Ethiopia

Beginning in late 1985 and continuing into the summer of 1986, the Reagan administration prepared its FY 1987 budget for Ethiopia. Assessing the factors that actually influenced the Ethiopian budget is a difficult task. Unlike earlier presidential budget requests during the famine, there were no hearings, newspaper articles, or public comments on the FY 1987 budget for Ethiopia. That the FY 1987 budgetary process was so opaque while past budgets

---

66. Jenkins, "Reagan Gets Appeal."
67. *New York Times*, "Famine Relief Shifts to Permanent Solutions."

were so public illustrates the extent to which Ethiopia had dropped off the political agenda. As a result, conclusions drawn from the budgetary process have to be tentative.

USAID budgeted $6.1 million to Ethiopia in FY 1987, down nearly 92 percent from the previous year (figure 20).[68] This cut reflected a near return to the pre-decision levels of funding. Although the decline of U.S. assistance was dramatic, it is debatable whether this cut reflected an improved situation in Ethiopia or whether it resulted from the Reagan administration's unwillingness to continue its support of the communist regime. As with the implementation stage, the rationale behind the budget cuts has implications here for assessing the congruence between policy choices and the public's preference. If the decrease in aid was commensurate with the degree to which the situation in Ethiopia had improved, then the public likely would have supported the budget cuts. If, however, the cuts were made *despite* a continuing need for external assistance in Ethiopia, then that policy would appear inconsistent with the now latent preferences of the American public.

The first possibility is that the decline in U.S. assistance to Ethiopia was a calibrated response to an improved situation. As discussed earlier, there was evidence that Ethiopia no longer faced as great a need for external support in 1986 and 1987. Rains had returned to the region, and the United States estimated that the domestic shortfall of food within Ethiopia would dramatically decrease from previous years. Large stockpiles of donated food were awaiting distribution. The general consensus among aid workers and donor governments was that the emergency phase of the famine was over and the situation had stabilized. As McPherson stated, "The skeleton-like people, the kids with bloated bellies, you hardly see that now. There are still people dying, of course, but the contrast is dramatic."[69]

An alternative perspective is that, while the famine had abated, the situation was still dire. The Ethiopian government estimated that in 1986, 1.2 million MT of food would be needed to feed 5.8 million people then threatened by starvation. Estimates for 1987 were only slightly lower, with 5 million at-risk Ethiopians. According to an FAO report, Ethiopia was one of five African

---

68. Note that these figures are normal budgetary allotments to AID for PL 480 programs and do not reflect supplemental expenditures or allocations from other departments. As a result, total U.S. aid to Ethiopia is greater than the figures expressed in this graph. However, examining normal budgetary allotments is valuable because they tend to be more closely correlated with the presidential budget request and therefore provide a better indication of the degree of support the administration had planned on devoting to Ethiopia prior to congressional involvement.

69. May, "Ethiopian Suffering Eases."

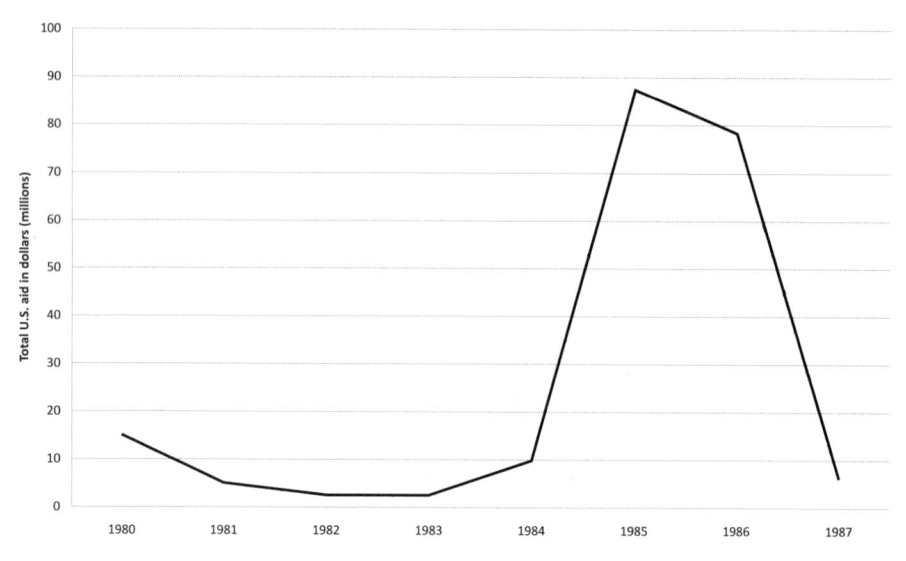

Fig. 20 USAID economic assistance to Ethiopia

countries still in the grips of famine. In fact, both the food requirements and the number of at-risk people were greater in Ethiopia than in *all other African countries combined.* While the U.S. government arrived at significantly lower estimates than did the Ethiopian government, the United States still believed that Ethiopia would need 500,000 MT of food for 1987—a figure twice as great as the amount the United States had provided at the height of the famine.[70]

As mentioned earlier, the situation in Ethiopia failed to improve as quickly as it did in other African countries. Despite increased rainfall, Ethiopia faced much lower than average crop production, and Ethiopian farmers were often too weak to plant crops. Nevertheless, USAID frequently relied on overly optimistic projections of crop yields that assumed both a continuation of the harvest rains and Ethiopian farmers' ability to work at prefamine levels. Finally, inadequate health care in the country led some experts to estimate that deaths from diseases associated with malnutrition and unsanitary conditions would rival the number of deaths from actual starvation. Projections for 1986 stated that Ethiopia would produce 5.8 million MT of food, about 1 million MT less than the 1981–83 average.[71]

---

70. Harden, "Ethiopia Faces Famine Again."
71. Gargan, "Old Specter."

This evidence suggests that while the situation in Ethiopia had stabilized, a large need for international assistance remained. Therefore, we have some basis here to reject the claim that budget cuts were consistent with the latent public preference for U.S. humanitarian assistance to needy countries. However, the lack of public interest in policy making regarding Ethiopia helped to make these cuts possible. In short, the guarded political context during the review stage allowed the Reagan administration to dramatically cut funding to Ethiopia by 92 percent.

The policy review stage ended in late August 1987 as it became evident that a new famine was beginning in Ethiopia. Thus, the decision-making process started over again with the problem definition stage. This time, however, the administration responded quickly to the first indication of famine and was widely praised by humanitarians for having averted another potential catastrophe. The administration's rapid response to the deteriorating situation occurred even though the American public remained largely inattentive to conditions in Ethiopia. It seems likely that decision makers learned a valuable lesson from the earlier case: the American public can suddenly and unexpectedly become attentive to humanitarian tragedies. As James Cheek, chargé d'affaires at the U.S embassy, remarked, "There won't be a GAO [General Accounting Office] report on this one."[72]

Summary

The U.S. response to the mid-1980s famine in Ethiopia offers an interesting look at the role of public opinion in noncrisis foreign policy making. Throughout the event, the American public was unified in its preference for emergency humanitarian aid but was only periodically attentive to the tragedy in Ethiopia. From 1982 to late 1984, a guarded political context allowed the Reagan administration to safely ignore the latent preferences of the American public. That situation changed as television and rock stars focused public attention on Ethiopia and, for the first time, the public's unified humanitarian preferences intersected with high issue salience. The Reagan administration responded to this new constraint by following the lead of public opinion: it set aside its misgivings about Mengistu and donated a record amount of U.S. aid to the communist regime. But the decline in public attentiveness decreased

---

72. Blaine, "Ethiopia Faces Famine Again."

the pressure for political responsiveness. Now back in a guarded political context, the Reagan administration carried out its policy decisions in a manner that, had the public been attentive, would likely have met with widespread disapproval. In short, the Ethiopian case study clearly shows how the pressure for political responsiveness closely tracks the level of issue salience.

CONCLUSION

An environmentalist friend recently spoke with me at length about how the looming threat of global climate change is closer than we think. His discussion of global warming included some pretty dire predictions of aquifers drying up, massive desertification, and eventual global famine—all in an alarmingly brief time frame. Of course, I am familiar with global warming and know of its likely consequences, but this new information was even worse than I had imagined. Thoroughly panicked, I asked him what else I should be afraid of. What about acid rain? Should we add acid rain to the list of imminent apocalyptic plagues? We both sat quietly for a moment, he in contemplation and me in dread. Finally, he answered, somewhat bewilderedly, "I don't know what happened to acid rain." Shocked, I responded, "Me either."

Acid rain was perhaps the most salient and scary environmental threat in the 1980s. When factories discharge pollutants into the atmosphere, especially sulfur dioxide, the result is increased acidic levels in precipitation. Acid rain kills fish, plants, and animals, causes cancer in humans, and is known to melt away gravestones and statues. This is not the kind of drizzle that makes you want to go singing in the rain. Acid rain is also an international environmental issue that has no respect for boundaries on a map. For example, about 50 percent of the acid deposits in Canada come from the United States, and pollution in the UK has destroyed large swaths of forest in Sweden.[1] During the 1980s, acid rain seemed to dominate the environmental news. I was particularly attuned to the issue because I lived in the always-rainy Pacific Northwest and was convinced that acid rain would soon melt my umbrella.

So there we sat, my friend the expert on all things environmental, and me the erstwhile-concerned citizen and periodic environmentalist, both trying

---

1. Alm, "Acid Rain Policy," 353.

to recall what had become of acid rain. Was the problem solved? Had it been overblown to begin with? Are there currently news stories on acid rain that we are missing? If acid rain is still wreaking havoc, is someone covering up the problem? We just didn't know. Yet acid rain was certainly salient to me back in the 1980s, as it was for a large number of Americans. Moreover, I was part of the 80 percent of Americans who felt that restrictions on sulfur dioxide emissions were necessary to curb acid rain, even if that meant I would pay higher electric bills.[2] Given this political context of high issue salience and unified preferences, it is of little surprise that President George H. W. Bush acted to limit the emissions of sulfur dioxide in the United States by signing the Clean Air Act of 1990. But for me, what happened next is a mystery. My interest in acid rain abruptly ended with the last stroke of Bush's pen—the Clean Air Act solved the problem, didn't it?—and thus began my admittedly all-too-episodic concern with global warming. Indeed, for almost two decades, acid rain was relegated to the foggy recesses of my mind, only to be suddenly called forth by a conversation with my environmentalist friend.

The point of this story is that issue salience rises and falls in ways that are predictable. The simple fact is that Americans find some aspects of foreign policy inherently interesting and other aspects insufferably boring. When we, the American public, are attentive to foreign affairs, presidents have good reason to listen to our opinions, especially if the public is of one mind. However, when we turn our attention elsewhere—usually ignoring those devilish little details of politics that seem dull yet are so very important—there is little reason for presidents to care what we think. In short, the regular ebbs and flows of public attention affect foreign policy making in deep and meaningful ways.

The Theory and Evidence: A Recap

This book offers a theory of conditional political responsiveness to examine when presidents lead, follow, or simply ignore the American public. The model is based on five simple propositions. First, presidents make a number of choices during a foreign policy event that may be influenced by public opinion. By conceptualizing foreign policy making as a five-stage process consisting of problem definition, option generation, policy decision, implementation, and policy

---

2. Survey by ABC News/ *Washington Post,* June 1989, from the iPOLL Databank, Roper Center for Public Opinion Research, University of Connecticut (accessed April 29, 2010). "As you may know, sulphur dioxide emissions from coal-burning power plants are a major cause of the acid rain that destroys forests and lakes. Do you approve or disapprove of requiring electric companies to cut back drastically on sulphur dioxide emissions even if that means higher electric bills?"

review, we can begin to better understand the potentially varying influence of public opinion throughout the life of a single case. Second, presidents are partially sensitive to the public's preferences. Although there is little meaningful opinion to respond to when the preferences are evenly split (i.e., 50–50 percent), a significant majority opinion (i.e., 60 percent or higher) is very difficult for presidents to ignore. Third, presidents are partially sensitive to the degree of public issue salience. Simply put, policy making under the glare of public scrutiny is very different from policy making when no one is looking. Fourth, presidential responsiveness is influenced by the confluence of preferences and issue salience. Given that they both act as partial mechanisms for responsiveness, it is reasonable to assume that presidents respond more to their interaction than to either factor in isolation. Finally, both public preferences and issue salience move in predictable ways across the five decision stages, allowing us to anticipate when political responsiveness is likely to occur.

According to this conditional theory, in foreign policy crises, the public tends to hold unified preferences and pays the most attention to the implementation of policy. By contrast, the public is typically interested in "doing something" about noncrisis issues but is relatively inattentive throughout the rest of the process. The three empirical tests of the conditional theory presented in this book, briefly summarized in the following sections, have demonstrated that issue salience does indeed ebb and flow predictably across the decision stages. Thus, the evidence suggests that it is possible to forecast when public attention might converge with unified public preferences to produce presidential responsiveness.

Forty Years of Issue Salience in U.S. Foreign Policy

Chapter 3 examined the patterns of issue salience in some of the most notable foreign policy issues over the past forty years. True to the conditional theory, clear and identifiable patterns emerged for both crises and noncrises: the public tended to be most attentive to the implementation of crisis policy, and public interest concentrated on the main policy decision in noncrises. Although there were a few deviations from this pattern in noncrises, crises exhibited somewhat more variation, largely depending on whether or not they involved U.S. military force. For those crises that featured a large and sustained military action, public attention tended to focus on that action. By contrast, in those cases where presidents either avoided the use of force or used force in a covert manner, public attention was less systematic.

Importantly, the results of this empirical test complement the vast literature on public preferences. A wealth of studies has shown that Americans' foreign policy opinions are stable and rational, and move predictably in relation to events and policy outcomes. Taken together, the patterns of issue salience and public preferences allow us to predict trends in political responsiveness. In the case of crises, strong public preferences are most likely to converge with high issue salience at the implementation stage of crises, suggesting that presidents who have decided to use military force as a means of policy have an incentive to be responsive when carrying out their decision. Alternately, the pressure for political responsiveness will likely be most acute at the decision stage of noncrises, yet minimal throughout the rest of the case.

The 1990–91 Persian Gulf Crisis

The broad look at issue salience and public preferences in chapter 3 provided context for the book's two in-depth case studies, which sought to uncover how, if at all, public opinion actually influenced a president's policy choices. The first case study, the 1990–91 Persian Gulf crisis, tested the conditional theory of presidential responsiveness in foreign policy crises. The early stages of the conflict offered a clear example of presidential leadership of the American public. Within the matter of a week, the public went from knowing and caring very little about the politics of the Gulf region to believing that Iraq's invasion of Kuwait represented a grave threat to U.S. interests. The White House, having molded public opinion in its favor, then set about considering how to deal with Iraq. Although President George H. W. Bush still led the American public at the option generation stage, public opinion became a more frequent subject of internal political deliberations and did serve to limit viable policy options. Presidential leadership of opinion continued through the crucial decision to use offensive military force to liberate Kuwait. Despite evidence of a reluctant public, Bush opted for war because he felt that the U.S. military would achieve its objectives quickly with minimal loss of life, and he believed that the public would rally in response to a successful conclusion to the case.

However, the confluence of high issue salience and unified public preferences at the implementation stage dramatically increased the pressure for political responsiveness. As a result, President Bush made a series of decisions that were consistent with public preferences but inconsistent with a purely strategic pursuit of the administration's objectives in Kuwait. Even the timing of the cease-fire with Iraq reflected the president's sensitivity to domestic opinion at the policy review stage. In short, President Bush led the American public in the early stages of the Persian Gulf conflict, only to follow the public after the decision for war had been made.

The Ethiopian Famine

The second major case study in this book, the Ethiopian famine of the mid-1980s, explored the role of public opinion during noncrisis foreign policy making. Despite the widespread humanitarian sentiment of the American public, problems in the less developed world rarely attract much attention in the United States. Such was the political context from 1982 to late 1984 as the Reagan administration deliberated over what to do about Ethiopia. With public attention to the famine virtually nonexistent, the Reagan administration felt little external pressure to act quickly, and conflicting views about how to respond to the famine led the administration into a deadlock.

When television coverage and celebrity efforts turned public attention toward Ethiopia in late 1984, the public's humanitarian preferences finally intersected with high issue salience. This pressured the Reagan administration to respond to public opinion and, by extension, to the needs of starving Ethiopians. And respond it did—with huge amounts of U.S. food aid with few political strings attached. However, when Americans' interest in Ethiopia died down, the Reagan administration was again free to pursue the policies it wished. In short, the Ethiopian famine demonstrates that what the public pays attention to, and, sometimes more important, what the public doesn't pay attention to, ultimately affects the direction of U.S. policy.

Implications

There are a number of implications that derive from our conditional theory of political responsiveness. The following looks at five of those implications before turning to a discussion of what role the American public should play in U.S. foreign policy.

Success, Not Decisions, Matters in Crises

When assessing the influence of public opinion on foreign policy in crisis situations, it is perhaps only natural that we focus primarily on the decision for war or peace. Yet this book has suggested that the actual policy decision is among the last places we should find the public's imprint. For the American public, the paramount consideration is *not* the decision for war, but whether the subsequent military action is successful or not.

We often forget that some of the recent military interventions generally considered "successes" had less than majority support going in: Grenada (46 percent),[3] Panama (28 percent),[4] the 1991 Persian Gulf War (46 percent),[5] and Kosovo (46 percent).[6] After these military actions proved to be relatively successful, public approval jumped dramatically in each case: Grenada (70 percent),[7] Panama (81 percent),[8] the 1991 Persian Gulf War (92 percent),[9] and Kosovo (68 percent).[10] Ironically, two of the most controversial wars in U.S. history—Vietnam and Iraq—enjoyed initial high levels of public support, only to succumb to a subsequent erosion as evidence of policy success became increasingly infrequent. For instance, only 24 percent of the public thought it was a mistake to send U.S. troops to Vietnam in the fall of 1965, compared to 60 percent who thought it was a mistake in 1973.[11] In Iraq, 70 percent of the public felt that the war was worth fighting in late April 2003, compared to just 34 percent in June of 2008.[12] General George C. Patton, it seems, was right when he growled, "Americans love a winner and will not tolerate a loser."

One of the implications of a success-minded public is that it essentially eliminates the need for presidents to consult the public before going to war. If Americans *always* approve of a successful war and *always* disapprove of an unsuccessful war, then there is little motivation for presidential responsiveness in the crucial decision to use military force as a means of policy. Put differently, presidents can safely ignore public opinion at the time they make

3. Survey by CBS News/*New York Times,* October 26, 1983, from the iPoll Databank, Roper Center for Public Opinion Research, University of Connecticut (accessed July 8, 2008).
4. Survey by *Time*/CNN/Yankelovich Clancy Shulman, October 1989, from the iPoll Databank, Roper Center for Public Opinion Research, University of Connecticut (accessed July 8, 2008).
5. Survey by the Gallup Organization, January 11–13, 1991, from LexisNexis, Roper Center for Public Opinion Research, University of Connecticut (accessed April 12, 2004).
6. Surveys by the Harris Organization, March 19–23, 1999, and January 11–13, 1999, from LexisNexis, Roper Center for Public Opinion Research, University of Connecticut (accessed April 12, 2004).
7. Survey by *Time*/CNN/Yankelovich Clancy Shulman, October 1989, from the iPoll Databank, Roper Center for Public Opinion Research, University of Connecticut (accessed July 8, 2008).
8. Survey by ABC News/ *Washington Post,* January 1990, from the iPoll Databank, Roper Center for Public Opinion Research, University of Connecticut (accessed July 8, 2008).
9. Survey by the Gallup Organization, February 28–March 3, 1991, from LexisNexis, Roper Center for Public Opinion Research, University of Connecticut (accessed April 12, 2004).
10. Survey by Princeton, June 9–13, 1999, from LexisNexis, Roper Center for Public Opinion Research, University of Connecticut (accessed April 12, 2004).
11. Surveys by the Gallup Organization, August 27–September 1, 1965, and January 12–15, 1973, from the Roper Center for Public Opinion Research, University of Connecticut, http://www.ropercenter.uconn.edu/education/examples/historical_context_vietnam_war.html (accessed July 11, 2008).
12. Survey by ABC News/ *Washington Post,* June 12–15, 2008, http://pollingreport.com/iraq.htm (accessed July 11, 2008).

their decision because they are secure in their knowledge that their choice will ultimately be judged on whether the subsequent military action is a success or a failure. As a result, presidents become forward-looking when making the key decision for war; they are more concerned with what the public might think after the fog of war has cleared than they are with the transient preferences of the moment. The upshot is that the American public has become, and may always have been, largely irrelevant in the decision for war or peace.

Consequences of Political Responsiveness in Crises

Although presidents may have little incentive to respond to public preferences when deciding on war or peace, they usually are quite sensitive to public opinion during the implementation of such a policy—if by implementation, we mean war. The combined pressures of high issue salience and unified public preference can force presidents into difficult trade-offs between maximizing strategic effectiveness and maximizing political support.

In the Gulf War, for instance, President George H. W. Bush opted for political support over strategic effectiveness in seeking UN and congressional authorization for war, deciding to form a multilateral coalition, and going the extra mile for peace by holding talks with Iraq. An "at-a-distance" review of other post-Vietnam conflicts reveals similar patterns of public influence at the implementation and review stages. The public's imprint on policy is certainly evident in the zero-casualty military strategies of both the Bosnian and Kosovo interventions, the hasty withdrawal of U.S. forces from Lebanon and Somalia, and President George W. Bush's decision to mirror his father's actions by seeking congressional and UN authorization long *after* the decision for war with Iraq had been made.

Given the public's seemingly tight grip on the implementation of crisis policies, we might ask, is that not a good thing? Should wars not be fought in a manner that the public finds morally justifiable? Should not the political leadership try to avoid U.S. casualties? Should not the UN and the U.S. Congress be consulted in the decision for war? Should we not want other nations to share in the terrible burden of war? In general, the answer to each question is a qualified "yes," but with an important forewarning: we must be careful of what we wish for.

Consider four unintended consequences of the public's strong influence at the implementation stage. First, the pervasive concern with minimizing U.S. casualties inevitably transfers the risks of war from soldiers to civilians.[13]

13. Shaw, *New Western Way of War.*

Attempting to shield U.S. forces from casualties requires the U.S. military to adopt tactics that are necessarily inefficient. In Kosovo, for instance, U.S. warplanes were required to fly at altitudes higher than those called for by standard operating procedures so as to avoid Serbian surface-to-air (SAM) missiles.[14] Although this tactic helped ensure that no U.S. pilots lost their lives in the combat, it also decreased the accuracy of the bombing raids, thereby placing innocent civilians at risk. Even in the era of "smart" weaponry, a zero-casualty mind-set increases the risk of collateral damage.

A second implication of a heavy public imprint on the implementation of policy is that trying to achieve success while minimizing U.S. casualties may actually prolong a conflict, increase casualties, and decrease the chances of achieving political and military goals. Indeed, when surveyed during the Kosovo case, the American public expressed a preference for a longer and less effective war (57 percent) over a quick and decisive, yet bloody, war (34 percent).[15] The 2003 Iraq War and its lingering aftermath is another case in point. In the rush to declare victory in Iraq in 2003, Secretary of Defense Donald Rumsfeld ignored his military commanders, who advised that the United States should target the groups who would soon emerge to form the core of the Iraqi insurgency, the Ba'athists and the Fedayeen.[16] For the Bush administration, expanding the war to go after these would-be insurgents would only prolong the major combat operation stage and would entail even more U.S. casualties. So in a rush to proclaim victory in Iraq and seal public support, President George W. Bush declared "mission accomplished" on May 1, 2003, aboard the aircraft carrier *USS Abraham Lincoln*. But as events over the next several years came to show, the mission had not yet been accomplished, and more American soldiers have died in Iraq during the insurgency than during major combat operations. Following through with the counterfactual, had the United States entered Iraq with massive amounts of military force (i.e., the Powell Doctrine instead of the Rumsfeld Doctrine), it is possible that the current situation would be very different. The recent success of the "surge" of U.S. forces in Iraq provides evidence for this counterfactual: had the surge been made years earlier, the situation in Iraq might have stabilized and we might not have witnessed a decline of public support for President Bush's Iraq

14. Lyon, "Operation Allied Force."
15. Survey by CBS/*New York Times*, April 5–6, 1999, from LexisNexis, Roper Center for Public Opinion Research, University of Connecticut (accessed April 12, 2004). "What about ground troops in Kosovo? Is it better to restrict the use of ground troops even if it means a longer war or is it better to use ground troops even if it means risking American and NATO (North Atlantic Treaty Organization) casualties in order to bring the war to a quick end?"
16. Gordon and Trainor, *Cobra II*; Woodward, *State of Denial*.

policy. Yet, ironically, a concern with minimizing casualties and demonstrating success to the American public ultimately led to military mistakes, a longer war, and a resultant erosion of popular support.

Third, the perception that the American public is casualty phobic and success crazed can lead presidential administrations toward a "drunkard's search" in U.S. military interventions.[17] In the aftermath of 9/11, for instance, Donald Rumsfeld repeatedly pushed the administration toward war with Iraq. At least part of Rumsfeld's desire to target Iraq stemmed from the fact that evidence of U.S. success in Afghanistan, a country of mountainous terrain with few hard military targets, was so difficult to come by.[18] By contrast, a victory in Iraq, with its desert terrain and conventional military, seemed a fairly easy task for the U.S. military. As a consequence of the political need to demonstrate success to the American public, decisions about military interventions might be based on which job is easiest, not which job is most important.

A final and related problem regarding the public and implementation is that concerns over casualties may lead presidents to not intervene in situations where perhaps they should. If the United States is to live up to its lofty political ideals, it must be steadfastly intolerant of human rights abuses around the globe. This means that the United States cannot sit idly by and allow genocide to happen in places like Cambodia, Somalia, Rwanda, and Darfur. The American public is usually hesitant to intervene militarily in these situations, and rightfully so. Internal political conflicts are not easily resolved, and U.S. intervention likely means that American soldiers will lose their lives. Yet in preserving the lives of American soldiers, the United States has tacitly allowed the slaughter of millions of innocent people. This situation must change. The United States must be the global leader in human rights, and this leadership must include a readiness to act militarily to protect innocent civilians when peaceable options have failed. Hopefully, when the United States does intervene to prevent genocide or ethnic cleansing, it will be with other countries on board, but it also must be willing to act alone when others are unwilling.

The U.S. political leadership thus has an obligation to expand its view of the national interest to include the protection of innocent civilians from genocide and ethnic cleansing, and communicate that policy stance to the American public. For its part, the American public needs to become more attentive to these world crises and be willing to use U.S. force if needed, even tolerating

---

17. The drunkard's search is the story of a drunk looking for his keys at night under a street lamp. His buddy asks him, "Why are you looking for your keys there?" The drunk replies, "Because I can see here."
18. Woodward, *Bush at War*; Woodward, *Plan of Attack*; Woodward, *State of Denial*.

American casualties in the process. Losing brave American soldiers is a tragedy and should never be taken lightly. Yet American soldiers are warriors who volunteer to place themselves in harm's way to defend America and her interests. Innocent civilians in places like Darfur, Somalia, and Bosnia are not warriors. When these citizens cannot rely on their own nation for safety, or when it is indeed the nation that is committing the slaughter, protection must come from elsewhere. As the only remaining military superpower, this job often falls upon the United States. While U.S. military intervention should always be a last resort, it must remain an option in the minds of both presidents and the public.

Decisions, Not Results, Matter in Noncrises

This book has shown that the American public tends to be singularly concerned with a noncrisis policy decision and pays little attention to policy making throughout the rest of the case. Because of the length and complexity of noncrises, presidents are generally not held responsible for the ultimate outcome of policy, but instead are judged on their decision. An inattentive public throughout the majority of a noncrisis case affords presidential administrations the freedom to shape the details of a policy in a manner that can diverge from the spirit, if not the letter, of that policy decision.

In the case of the Ethiopian famine, for instance, the Reagan administration responded to public opinion in late 1984 and early 1985 by donating a record amount of U.S. food. For most Americans, the decision to flood Ethiopia with food solved the problem, and their attention soon turned elsewhere. At the implementation stage, however, the Reagan administration delayed the provision of trucks, refused to provide developmental assistance, and cut the Ethiopian emergency aid budget. Although there may have been sound reasons behind each of these choices, they certainly appear inconsistent with the public's latent preferences and incongruent with the spirit of the early policy decisions.

We might look at global warming as another example in which decisions, not results, have been the most important consideration for politically savvy presidents. The introduction to this book opened with a short discussion of the George H. W. Bush administration's 1992 decision to sign the Rio Treaty on global warming despite a belief that it was detrimental to U.S. interests. In this case, lax enforcement and a weak treaty allowed the administration to gain political benefits from appearing to fulfill a campaign pledge to "do something" about global warming, while at the same time protecting the U.S.

economy by actually doing very little to curb greenhouse gas emissions. Later in the decade, the Clinton administration believed that the Kyoto Protocol was flawed because China and India were not bound by the same reduction targets in carbon emissions as were developed nations. The administration signed the treaty anyway, knowing that it could pass the buck to the Senate, which declared it "dead on arrival" in a unanimous 95–0 vote. Finally, although President Barack Obama has signed the new Copenhagen Accord, the real test of U.S. commitment to curb global warming will come from Senate ratification (at present, there is no word on when the Senate might pick it up) and, eventually, effective implementation.

Consider as well other Western democratic countries that have signed and ratified the Kyoto Protocol. For the citizens of these nations, ratification offers hope that something is being done about global warming. However, simply ratifying the Kyoto Protocol does nothing to actually curb global warming. It is only the *implementation* of that agreement that can reduce greenhouse gas emissions. To examine the implementation of Kyoto, we must look at the Marrakesh Accords, which provide the compliance system for the protocol. These accords are so weak, with so many loopholes, that the Kyoto Protocol has essentially become a self-governed framework. While there are international agencies that monitor countries' greenhouse gas emissions, they have no real enforcement power. Therefore, it is up to concerned citizens to apply sanctions—usually through the electoral mechanism—if and when their governments are found to be in noncompliance. If citizens fail in this personal responsibility, the Kyoto regime will ultimately do little to curb global warming. Unfortunately, monitoring compliance with emission standards is one of those nuanced policy details that the public typically ignores. So while European, and now American, publics applaud themselves and their governments for having signed global warming accords, the battle has just begun.

Manipulation of Issue Salience

Given the importance of issue salience as a trigger for political responsiveness, some politicians, groups, and individuals have an incentive to enlarge the scope of conflict (i.e., take a low-salience issue and make it a high-salience issue), while others have an incentive to contract the scope of conflict (i.e., ensure that issue salience stays low).

As we have seen in the analysis of the Ethiopian famine, the humanitarians gained a strong voice in policy making only when television and rock stars combined to raise public awareness of the issue. We can probably think of many private and public actors who find their fortunes indelibly tied to issue salience. For instance, the nuclear freeze movement operated for years in relative obscurity until the early 1980s.[19] The issue of South African apartheid languished for many years in the United States until activists at home and abroad raised the salience of the issue by emulating many of the tactics of the early civil rights movement.[20] Broad coalitions of antiglobalization activists (e.g., labor unions, environmentalists, and anarchists) have used protests at WTO meetings to raise the salience of global trade and finance.[21] And recent television ads featuring unlikely pairings (e.g., Speaker of the House Nancy Pelosi and former Speaker Newt Gingrich) have tried to focus more public attention on global warming. For these groups, probability of winning does not entail changing people's opinions—most of the public already agrees with their position. Instead, winning becomes possible only when the salience of the issue is raised, thus transforming latent public opinion into active public opinion.

There are also times when politicians or groups wish to minimize issue salience and restrict the scope of conflict. Many rent-seeking interest groups thrive in a low-salient environment.[22] The domestic sugar industry, for instance, has successfully lobbied the U.S. government for protection against foreign sugar producers at an annual cost of $2 billion to the American consumer. But sugar is trivial compared to the corn industry, which, according to the Environmental Working Group, received more than $50 billion in subsidies from 1995 to 2005.[23] For such groups, low issue salience is a blessing, not a curse. Presidents and their administrations may also seek to restrict the scope of conflict when the public appears opposed to their preferred policies. Covert actions, such as those undertaken in Cuba, Chile, Peru, Nicaragua, and Iran, allow presidents to pursue their favored policies outside the glare of public attention and the glower of public disapproval.

Ineffective Public Oversight of Foreign Policy

A key tenet of democratic theory is that it is the role of citizens to monitor the political process and hold elected officials accountable for their actions.

19. Wittner, *Toward Nuclear Abolition.*
20. Solop, "Public Protest."
21. O'Brien et al., *Contesting Global Governance.*
22. In economics, a "rent" is anything above what the market would normally bear. Rents are often gained from government protect, such as subsidies, tariffs, quotas, tax exemptions, etc.
23. Environmental Working Group, Farm Subsidy Database, http://farm.ewg.org/farm/progdetail.php?fips=00000&progcode=corn (accessed April 29, 2010).

This study suggests that the American public usually falls short of that ideal. Noncrisis foreign policy poses a difficult test for the public. Noncrises tend to involve seemingly routine and long-running issues, and it is perhaps unreasonable to expect a highly attentive public throughout all stages of decision making. Yet, insofar as important policy choices are made at each decision stage, monitoring governmental behavior is vital to ensure congruence between the public's preferences and policy output. The abdication of this oversight responsibility can lead to outcomes that the public, if it were attentive, might find highly undesirable. We saw this in both the option generation and implementation stages of the Ethiopian famine, as well as the Rio and Kyoto global warming cases.

Crises also pose a special problem for citizen oversight of government. Americans tend to be highly attentive throughout all stages of a crisis and, in this way, fulfill their democratic responsibility to be active participants in the political process. However, the national security concerns intrinsic to crises mean that the public is not privy to the same information that is possessed by the White House. Presidents' ability to selectively disseminate information increases the potential of political manipulation and decreases the capacity of the public to hold politicians accountable for their actions. This was certainly true in the first Gulf War, as the George H. W. Bush administration concealed the October 30, 1990, troop increase until after the midterm elections and then framed the surge as routine choice instead of the actual decision to go to war. And many critics have charged the George W. Bush administration with playing up the intelligence on Iraq in the prelude to that war.

What Role Should the American Public Play in U.S. Foreign Policy?

As we conclude our examination of the role that the American public *has* played in U.S. foreign policy, let's contemplate for a moment a different question: what role *should* the American public play in U.S. foreign policy? Shifting the focus from the empirical to the normative is difficult because how we answer such a question is indelibly tied to our own policy views, the views held by our fellow citizens, and the views of the person currently sitting in the Oval Office. In other words, we usually want the president to respond to the wisdom of public opinion when we are in the majority, but want him to ignore the irrational public when we are in the minority. When reflecting further on this question, we need to set aside our own policy inclinations, forget about the current occupant of the White House (whomever it may be), and think in general about which of two extreme alternatives we find preferable: either presidents should always follow public opinion or always ignore public opinion.

The first perspective—that presidents should follow public opinion—is often termed the *delegate* model of representation. In the delegate model, a politician assesses the preferences of his or her constituency, usually through public opinion polls, and faithfully turns these preferences into policy. The key to the delegate model is that the politician exercises no independent judgment on policy choices, but rather slavishly follows whatever the constituency wants. For many people, the delegate view of representation is really what a republican form of democracy is all about. After all, a democracy is, in the words of Abraham Lincoln, a system of "government of the people, by the people, and for the people." We may particularly want presidents to act as delegates in foreign policy since it is ultimately the American people who must bear the costs of war or see their jobs outsourced to other nations.

Thus, the delegate view places the control of U.S. foreign policy firmly in the hands of the public. But is the American public capable of making sound foreign policy decisions? A wealth of scholarship claims that, indeed, Americans hold foreign policy preferences that are reasonable, stable, and prudent. In this view, U.S. foreign policy has been led astray by politicians who are out of touch with the masses but in touch (some would say in bed) with the CEOs of multinational corporations and powerful economic interest groups. Not only would U.S. foreign policy become more democratic if presidents followed public opinion, but it would become more effective and efficient as well.

The delegate view of representation also holds that politicians should *act as if* the public is closely following their every move. It is perhaps unreasonable to expect the American public to attend to every policy choice made in Washington. However, some issue public or interest group is usually paying attention and acts as a proxy for the rest of us. Therefore, the rational politician knows that today's vote made in relative obscurity could be used by interest groups as campaign fodder in the next election. Consequently, the safest bet for politicians is to act within the strictures of public opinion to avoid being thrown out of office at the next election or avoid losing precious political capital as public approval declines.

In the delegate view, political responsiveness occurs when politicians anticipate and then meet the opinions of their constituents in between elections. This process has become increasingly easier over the years with the growth of public opinion surveys. Not only do surveys allow the public to transmit its opinions to representatives in between elections, but some argue that surveys are more democratic than other forms of political participation. Nationwide surveys are designed to cull the opinions of a representative cross-section of Americans (within +/- 3 percent). In this way, groups who are regularly disenfranchised in elections (i.e., unequal voter turnout), unable to make monetary political donations (i.e., unequal wealth), or kept from communicating with politicians (i.e., unequal skill) all have an equal chance of being heard in Washington, D.C. As Sidney Verba states, "Surveys produce just what democracy is suppose to produce—equal representation of all citizens."[24]

The second view—that presidents should ignore public opinion—is often termed the *trustee* model of representation. In the trustee model, citizens elect the politician who most closely mirrors their own political preferences. That politician then goes to Washington and makes decisions that he or she thinks are in the best interest of the public (without, we might add, consulting the public). If, when the next election rolls around, the constituents approve of the politician's actions, they reelect that person; if not, they throw the rascal out of office. In this case, responsiveness to public opinion occurs through periodic elections, not through public opinion polls.

Most people initially reject the trustee model of representation because it smacks of government paternalism. However, consider the trustee model from another angle. Unlike the delegate model, this view argues that citizens' foreign policy preferences are ill informed and ill considered. For instance, on March 25, 1999, one day into NATO's bombing campaign in Kosovo, a *Los Angeles Times* national poll reported that 79 percent of the public had read a "great deal or some" about the conflict.[25] The results of the poll were fairly encouraging, suggesting that Americans were fulfilling their citizen duty by being informed observers of foreign affairs. But in a follow-up question, the *Times* found that only 40 percent of the public knew that the United States was opposing Serbia in the conflict.[26] In another survey taken around the same time, 57 percent of American could not identify Kosovo as the province where the conflict was taking place.[27] The public's lack of knowledge about Kosovo

24. Verba, "Citizen as Respondent," 3.
25. Survey by the *Los Angeles Times*, March 25, 1999, from LexisNexis, Roper Center for Public Opinion Research, University of Connecticut (accessed April 12, 2004). "How much have you heard or read about the conflict in Kosovo? . . . A great deal, some, not much, nothing?"
26. Survey by the *Los Angeles Times*, March 25, 1999, from LexisNexis, Roper Center for Public Opinion Research, University of Connecticut (accessed April 12, 2004). "Do you know which side the United States is opposing (in Kosovo) or haven't you heard enough about it yet to say? (If yes, ask:) Which group is the US opposing?"
27. Survey by Princeton University, March 24–28, 1999, from LexisNexis, Roper Center for Public Opinion Research, University of Connecticut (accessed April 12, 2004). "I would like to ask you a few questions about some things that have been in the news. Not everyone will have heard about them. Do you happen to know the name of the province in Yugoslavia where there is conflict between Serbians and ethnic Albanians? (If yes, ask:) Which province?"

is troubling enough, but it is even more disconcerting when we consider that the event was a *highly salient issue!* In other words, the issue at hand was not an obscure bilateral dispute over corn subsidies or sugar tariffs, but rather a *war* that was splashed all over the news.

In addition, the trustee model argues that public opinion surveys, instead of being a boon for democracy as the delegate model suggests, have created a weekly referendum that subverts the power of governance by forcing elected representatives to become hyperresponsive to public opinion in order to maximize electoral prospects.[28] If a representative is forced to only do the bidding of her constituency, she is little more than a conduit through which the transient, and oftentimes irrational, opinions of the masses are expressed. As a result, deliberation—that thoughtful discussion of competing ideas that should be the hallmark of a competent democracy—is all but lost in governance. As James Fishkin writes of public opinion, "The giant who rules America may stand over presidents and senators, but it is constructed from the most ineffable of materials—the casual impressions of ordinary citizens."[29] Proponents of the trustee position argue that the basis of a sound government must reside in the freedom of elected officials to base their decisions on their own judgment rather than simply echoing the whims of their constituency. As Walter Lippmann put it, "The people have acquired power which they are incapable of exercising, and the governments they elect have lost powers which they must recover if they are to govern. . . . When mass opinion dominates the government, there is a morbid derangement of the true functions of power. The derangement brings about enfeeblement, verging on paralysis."[30]

Whether you prefer the delegate or a trustee model of representation as a guiding principal for American foreign policy depends, in large part, on where you place your faith: in the public or in the politicians. Do you believe your fellow citizens are attentive and informed enough about international affairs to make rational foreign policy decisions? If so, you just might be a delegate. Do you believe that politicians and bureaucrats make foreign policy decisions with the public's best interest in mind? If so, you just might be a trustee.

Regardless of which model you think is best, American foreign policy can

---

28. Lippmann, *Essays in the Public Philosophy*; Brace and Hinckley, *Follow the Leader*.
29. Fishkin, "Voice of the People," 76.
30. Lippmann, *Essays in the Public Philosophy*, 15. Ole Holsti notes that Lippmann had a change of heart concerning public opinion during the Vietnam War. As Lippmann became increasingly frustrated by Lyndon Johnson's escalation of the war, he also revised his lifelong pessimistic view about American public opinion. Indeed, Lippmann found that it was the American public, not the political leadership, that held the more rational view on Vietnam. See Holsti, "Public Opinion on Human Rights," 131.

only benefit if more of the public is attentive to and informed about international affairs. As it stands now, the American public is only periodically interested in U.S. foreign policy and only moderately informed on some of the key issues of the day. A healthy democracy requires citizens who understand the issues and are attentive to policy making, even to the things that seem somewhat boring. To neglect this duty is to let go of the reins of power. When we loosen our grip on power, it should come as no surprise to us that presidents chart their own foreign policy course. If we object to being led or ignored, the solution is to become more attentive and informed. The choice is ours to make. As Cassius said to Brutus, "The fault, dear Brutus, is not in our stars, / But in ourselves, that we are underlings."[31]

---

31. William Shakespeare, *Julius Caesar*, act 1, scene 2, lines 140–41.

Appendix A: Quantitative Methods

The quest to identify patterns of issue salience in crises and noncrises inevitably confronts several thorny methodological questions. Which foreign policy cases should be included in the analysis? How do we measure issue salience? How do we know when one decision stage ends and the next one begins? The following explanation gives the interested reader an in-depth look into the research methods that were used to track the ebbs and flows of public attention in chapter 3.

Case Selection

The first step of the research project entailed compiling a list of relevant crisis and noncrisis foreign policy events. The population from which I selected the thirty-four cases in chapter 3 consists of highly visible U.S. foreign policy events over the past forty years. The International Crisis Behavior Project database provided the population of crisis cases.[1] I am unaware of a comparable dataset for noncrises; therefore, I compiled a population drawn from Charles Kegley and Eugene Wittkopf's chronology of foreign policy events, supplementing their work with a list of congressional hearings on foreign policy issues taken from Frank Baumgartner and Bryan Jones's Policy Agendas Project.[2] These procedures ensured a population of crisis and noncrisis cases that includes virtually all of the more visible U.S. foreign policy cases. Put differently, the population includes those cases that were sufficiently familiar to the American public that mass opinion could have been a plausible premise for presidential decision making, while it excludes persistently low-visibility cases in which presidents would have had little cause to consider public opinion. This allows us to focus the pattern, duration, and intensity of public attentiveness.

Measuring Issue Salience

Issue salience is a surprisingly difficult concept to operationalize. The literature employs three common indicators of salience. The first technique is to examine

---

1. The International Crisis Behavior Project data can be accessed at http://www.icpsr.umich.edu.
2. Kegley and Wittkopf, *American Foreign Policy*. Baumgartner and Jones provide a wealth of valuable data at http://www.policyagendas.org.

the open-ended "most important problem" (MIP) question asked by many survey organizations.[3] The advantage of this measure is its directness—it literally asks people what issue they are most concerned about. The disadvantage of using the MIP question is that it conflates importance with salience in ways that complicate the analysis.[4] For instance, the public may believe that the economy is the most important problem, but might then be more attentive to the latest Paris Hilton scandal.[5]

A second method of measuring attentiveness is to examine public opinion polls that ask respondents how closely they have been following the news about various issues.[6] Like the MIP question, the advantage to this measure is its directness. However, there are several reasons why survey responses may not necessarily be the most valid indicator of the public's attention.[7] National polls typically take the public's pulse only when a particular issue has already reached a sufficient degree of salience. Moreover, response categories for questions on public attentiveness usually feature vague quantifiers that are particularly susceptible to variation in respondent interpretation.[8] What is, after all, the difference between following the news "fairly closely" and "somewhat closely"? Finally, questions addressing attentiveness are prone to "social desirability effects," as a respondent may attempt to conceal ignorance in order to convey the impression of an informed citizen to the interviewer.[9] This particular bias increases if the respondent has little reason to expect follow-up questions assessing factual knowledge.

The final method, and the one ultimately employed in this analysis, is to use network television news coverage as a proxy for issue salience. There are a number of advantages to this particular measure. The main benefit is that television, unlike surveys, offers a daily running indicator of what issues Americans

---

3. See McCombs and Zhu, "Capacity, Diversity, and Volatility," and Jones, *Reconceiving Decision-Making*. An example of the most important question is "What do you think is the most important problem facing the country today?" Survey by CBS News/*New York Times*, March 28–April 2, 2008, http://www.pollingreport.com/prioriti.htm (accessed August 8, 2006).

4. Edwards, Mitchell, and Welch, "Explaining Presidential Approval"; Wlezien, "Salience of Political Issues."

5. See Baum and Jamison, "Oprah Effect"; Baum, "Going Private"; and Baum, *Soft News Goes to War*.

6. Survey questions on attentiveness generally take the following form: "How closely have you followed news about . . . ? Would you say you have followed it very closely, fairly closely, not too closely, or not at all closely?" (Gallup, CBS); or "Overall, how closely have you followed the situation in . . . ? Very closely, somewhat closely, not too closely, or not at all?" (Gallup).

7. Edwards and Wood, "Who Influences Whom?"; Edwards, Mitchell, and Welch, "Explaining Presidential Approval"; Wood and Peake, "Foreign Policy Agenda Setting."

8. See Moxey and Sanford, *Communicating Quantities*; Tourangeau, Rips, and Rasinski, *Psychology of Survey Response*; and Bradburn and Miles, "Vague Quantifiers."

9. See Tourangeau, Rips, and Rasinski, *Psychology of Survey Response*.

are potentially attentive to. This then allows for a fine-grained tracking of public attentiveness over the foreign-policy-making process. Moreover, a significant body of research shows that national news coverage heavily influences citizens' perceived salience of political issues.[10] As Bernard Cohen writes, the press may not tell the public what to think, "but it is stunningly successful in telling its readers what to think about."[11] According to Stuart Soroka, this is especially true for foreign policy: "If we learn about these [foreign policy] events, it is almost surely the product of media coverage."[12]

Nevertheless, it is important to consider a couple of threats to validity that can come from using television coverage as a measure of issue salience. Of course, the American public might be informed of foreign policy news by other sources. Indeed, more people get their news from local television coverage (59 percent), newspapers (41 percent), and cable news networks (38 percent) than they do from network broadcasts (34 percent).[13]

As a partial test of the similarity or difference in forms of news coverage, I compared television news and the *New York Times* coverage of two crisis cases (the Gulf War and Kosovo) and two noncrisis cases (the Ethiopian famine and U.S.-Japanese economic relations).[14] For each case, I searched the *New York Times* historical archive, identifying relevant stories and then calculating word counts per day of coverage. The television and print coverage of these key foreign policy stories covaries quite strongly, ranging from 60 percent to above 90 percent of the maximum correlation.[15] This evidence suggests that while there is a difference between what is covered by the network news and what appears in the *New York Times,* that difference is not large.

The indirectness of our indicator of public attentiveness is also a valid source of concern. After all, just because an issue is covered by the network news does

---

10. Iyengar and Kinder, *News That Matters*; Page, Shapiro, and Dempsey, "What Moves Public Opinion?"; Soroka, "Media, Public Opinion,"; Stanley and Niemi, *Vital Statistics*; Graber, *Mass Media and American Politics*; B. Cohen, *Press and Foreign Policy*; McCombs and Shaw, "Agenda-Setting Function."

11. Cohen, *Press and Foreign Policy,* 13.

12. Soroka, "Media, Public Opinion," 43.

13. Pew Research Center for the People and the Press, "News Audiences Increasingly Politicized," June 8, 2004, http://people-press.org/report/?pageid=834 (accessed April 9, 2008).

14. Knecht and Weatherford, "Public Opinion."

15. To establish a baseline for comparing day-to-day coverage between print and television outlets, we first calculated how closely the amount of a given medium's coverage of the story on day zero correlated with its previous coverage of the same story, using lags of one, three, and seven days. For television coverage of the Gulf War, for instance, the average correlation across these three lags is 0.567; for newspaper coverage the average is 0.604. The correlation between television coverage and newspaper coverage of the Gulf War is 0.5, approximately 85 percent of the correlation of the media's coverage with its own earlier coverage. The corresponding percentage for the Ethiopian famine case is 62 percent, and for the Kosovo case and the Japan trade case above 95 percent.

not mean that the public is actually attentive to it.[16] In fact, the public may not be attentive to the news at all. Today there is a wealth of other entertainment options—cable, DVDs, video games, and the Internet—that allow the militantly apolitical to avoid the news altogether. Nevertheless, we must approach the question of issue salience through the eyes of the political actors who participate in the decision-making process. Presidents and their advisors know that, in general, media attention and public concern covary, and that intense media attention represents the *potential* for greatly increased public scrutiny.[17] As Philip Powlick and Andrew Katz state, "In essence, policy makers gauge the degree to which there is debate on their issues and assume (usually correctly) that the absence of debate means the absence of active public opinion."[18] Therefore, whether the public is actually attentive or not matters less to decision makers than the potential for public attention. News coverage of an issue gives the public the chance to be attentive, and as a result, presidents are apt to use media coverage as a proxy for issue salience in the same way it is used in this study.

Tracking Television Coverage by Decision Stage

To measure media coverage, I compiled minutes of nightly television news coverage for each foreign policy case. Using the Vanderbilt Television News Archives, I searched for relevant news stories, read the abstracts of the broadcasts to ensure that the stories dealt with the case in question, and recorded the length of the coverage.[19] To gain a per-day measure of coverage, I added up the minutes of nightly news devoted to the foreign policy issue by the three major networks: ABC, CBS, and NBC. (CNN and Fox were excluded because these networks were not in existence throughout the entire time period covered by this study, and CNN's twenty-four-hour format complicates the analysis.) Each of the three major networks carries approximately twenty-two minutes of nightly news, for a combined total of sixty-six minutes of potential per-day coverage of an issue.[20]

As mentioned in chapter 3, the varying lengths of the decision stages required that I normalize the measure of intensity of media coverage using a

16. Gilboa, "CNN Effect."
17. Powlick and Katz, "Public Opinion/Foreign Policy Nexus"; Powlick, "Sources of Public Opinion."
18. Powlick and Katz, "Public Opinion/Foreign Policy Nexus," 45.
19. The Vanderbilt Television News Archive can be accessed at http://tvnews.vanderbilt.edu.
20. Wood and Peake, "Foreign Policy Agenda Setting."

two-step procedure. First, to adjust for the different lengths of the decision stages, I calculated the average minutes of coverage per day for each of the five stages (this is simply total coverage in a decision stage divided by the length of the stage). Then, to adjust for differences in the length of the cases, I express per-stage coverage as a proportion of the total media coverage for that case. The resulting media coverage indicator is thus normalized for comparability across cases and decision stages.

Appendix B: Case Study Methods

This appendix describes the methods used in the case studies of the 1990–91 Persian Gulf crisis and the Ethiopian famine in the mid-1980s (chapters 4–7). The following details how the cases were selected, the qualitative methods used to draw causal inferences, and the data used in the studies.

Case Selection

The selection of cases was based in part on Harry Eckstein's criteria of "least likely" cases.[1] A least likely case is one in which the researcher's theory is expected to have significantly less explanatory power than rival hypotheses. The value of selecting least likely cases is that if a theory is confirmed in this difficult test, it is more likely to be valid in other cases that provide a less strenuous test.[2]

The first Gulf War presents a difficult test for the proposition that public opinion can influence foreign policy. Many scholars assume that public opinion plays little role in situations that involve threats to vital national interests and large-scale military conflict. At first blush, the Gulf War seems to conform to this expectation. In many academic and journalistic circles, the rationale for war was attributed to President George H. W. Bush's conception of the national interest, in which the need to maintain a cheap and stable supply of oil from the Middle East was paramount. In addition, John Mueller has pointed out that President Bush's decision to opt for offensive military action to liberate Kuwait was made without broad public support.[3] Consequently, the Persian Gulf crisis provides a case in which we might have expected to find little influence of public opinion.

My noncrisis case study assesses the U.S. response to famine in Ethiopia during the mid-1980s. We might have again expected public opinion to play little role in U.S. policy making during this case for three reasons. First, Ethiopia was governed by a Marxist regime and was the Soviet's largest client state in sub-Saharan Africa. Given President Reagan's anticommunist reputation, it might have seemed unlikely that the United States would mount a concerted

---

1. Eckstein, "Case Study and Theory."
2. Odell, "Case Study Methods."
3. See chapter 4 of Mueller, *Policy and Opinion*.

effort to help rescue an avowed enemy. Second, the Reagan administration was not known for its globalist outlook in the provision of humanitarian assistance, preferring to concentrate 72 percent of its foreign aid in seven allied countries with geostrategic importance.[4] Although Ethiopia occupied an important position within the Horn of Africa, its commitment to Marxism and close alliance with the Soviet Union meant that the United States had little *strategic* interest in providing humanitarian assistance. The Ethiopian famine also occurred during a period of severe budget deficits in the United States, which the administration managed through cuts in nonmilitary programs, including foreign aid. Finally, much of the famine overlapped Reagan's second term in office, a period in which the absence of electoral considerations might be expected to decrease presidential responsiveness to public opinion.

Additionally, both the Gulf War and the Ethiopian famine present difficult tests for my model because of the presidents who occupied the office. An alternative theory advanced by Douglas Foyle is that the influence of the American public depends on whether the president in question believes that public opinion *ought* to play a role in foreign policy. As Foyle documents—and as I discussed in chapter 1—neither Ronald Reagan nor George H. W. Bush believed that the public should influence foreign policy making; in their view, the president should inform and lead the masses.[5] Considering the persuasiveness of Foyle's argument, the extent to which I can show that public opinion did exert influence over policy decisions suggests that my model is robust.

Case Study Methodology

In order to assess the opinion-policy link, I employ the qualitative methods of the *congruence procedure* and *process tracing*. Both methods were developed by Alexander George and employed with great skill in Yuen Foong Khong's *Analogies at War* and Douglas Foyle's *Counting the Public In*.[6] The congruence procedure is used as a "first-cut" approach to determining the plausibility of my hypotheses. Process tracing is then employed to provide additional evidence of a causal relationship. The methods are complementary and are designed to increase the validity of the findings.

---

4. See Shepherd, "Food Aid," 144, and Lancaster, "U.S. Aid," 65. These countries were Israel (30.4 percent), Egypt (23.7 percent), Turkey (7.2 percent), Greece (5 percent), Pakistan (4.7 percent), South Korea (3.3 percent), and Portugal (2 percent).

5. Foyle, *Counting the Public In*.

6. George and McKeown, "Theories of Organizational Decision Making"; George, "Case Studies and Theory Development"; George, "'Operational Code.'"

The Congruence Procedure

In a congruence procedure, the researcher specifies which values of the dependent variable are theoretically consistent with given values of the independent variables. This requires that the researcher list the dependent variable (the real-life outcome) along with potential values (counterfactual outcomes) that the dependent variable could take. The researcher then indicates which causal relationships are consistent or inconsistent with theory. Foyle provides a summary of the congruence method: "The congruence procedure requires first specifying the predicted theoretical relationship between the independent and dependent variables. Then, the values of the observed independent and dependent variables are determined and evaluated according to the theory's predictions. If the findings agree with the theory, a causal relationship may exist."[7]

In this analysis, the congruence procedure is used at each stage of the decision process in order to determine the plausibility of the hypotheses.[8] Consider for the moment what the congruence procedure would look like in the 1999 U.S. intervention in Kosovo. The theory presented here argues that an attentive public that prefers few U.S. casualties might influence decision makers to implement a low-risk aerial bombardment strategy rather than the more risky, but potentially more effective, strategy of introducing ground troops (see figure 21). While the strategy of aerial bombing is theoretically consistent with a hypervigilant and casualty-phobic public, a risky strategy of employing ground troops is theoretically inconsistent with the given value of the independent variable. If, counterfactually, the Clinton administration decided to send U.S. ground forces into Kosovo, the incongruence of that decision with the hypothesized independent variable would provide disconfirming evidence toward our theory.

In some cases, the congruence procedure alone is an inadequate means of determining whether a causal relationship exists. The congruence procedure is a "second-best" method of determining causality for two reasons. First, there may be other values of the dependent variable that are theoretically consistent with a given value of the independent variable. In the Kosovo example, the options of aerial bombing and doing nothing are both theoretically consistent with a highly attentive and concerned public. If there is no compelling justification for why one option is more consistent than another, the researcher cannot claim to have provided evidence of a causal relationship.

---

7. Foyle, *Counting the Public In*, 294.
8. For similar models, see Khong, *Analogies at War*, and George, "Causal Nexus."

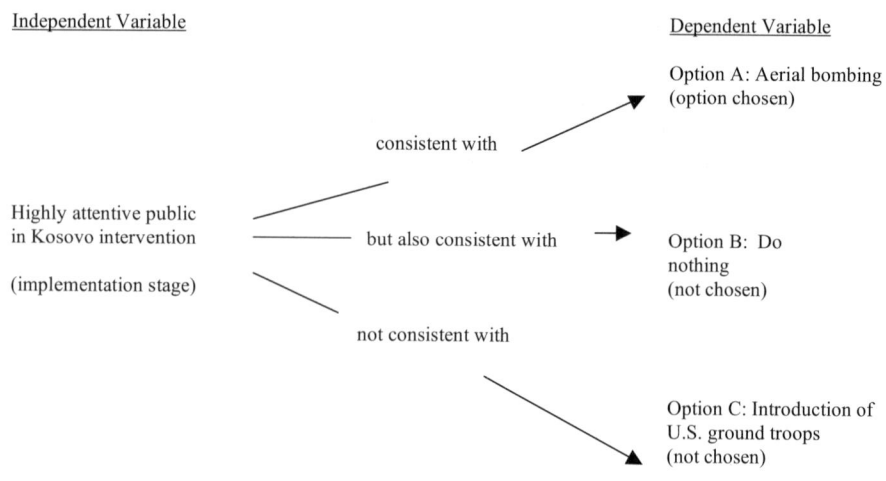

Independent Variable		Dependent Variable
	consistent with →	Option A: Aerial bombing (option chosen)
Highly attentive public in Kosovo intervention (implementation stage)	—— but also consistent with →	Option B: Do nothing (not chosen)
	not consistent with	Option C: Introduction of U.S. ground troops (not chosen)

Fig. 21 The congruence procedure

Second, in most cases the dependent variable is overdetermined. This means that several different independent variables could potentially account for a given outcome. Without additional evidence, the researcher has little basis to claim the superiority of one theoretical relationship over another. Again turning to the Kosovo example, it is possible that the option of aerial bombing was chosen *not* because of a highly attentive public (the researcher's independent variable) but because of policy makers' beliefs in the *effectiveness* of aerial bombing (an omitted independent variable). In this case, what appears to be a causal relationship between a concerned public and the strategy of aerial bombing is spurious, and the real relationship is found between beliefs about strategic effectiveness and aerial bombing. Due to these two factors, congruence procedure is often more valuable in falsifying hypotheses than in providing conclusive evidence that a causal relationship exists.

Process Tracing

In light of the inherent difficulties of using a congruence procedure to determine causality, I also employ process tracing whenever possible. Process tracing involves an in-depth analysis of the stimuli that presidents respond to when making a decision.[9] Alexander George and Timothy McKeown describe process tracing as a "decision process by which various initial conditions are translated

---

9. King, Keohane, and Verba, *Designing Social Inquiry*; George and McKeown, "Theories of Organizational Decision Making"; George, "Case Studies and Theory Development"; George, "'Operational Code.'"

into outcomes."[10] In my research, process tracing involves examining the relative importance of public opinion as a decision premise compared to strategic and other domestic decision-making factors.

The drawback in process tracing is that it requires that the researcher have considerable insight into presidential decision making. The most straightforward means of assessing the influence of opinion on policy is uncovering instances in which the president and his administration discussed the American public when making a policy choice. Evidence of this sort is best revealed through archival records of meetings, memoirs, and elite interviews. This research strategy is complicated by the secrecy involved in foreign policy making and the reluctance of the U.S. government to declassify many documents pertaining to recent cases.

One benefit of using the congruence procedure and process tracing is that both methods complement my theoretical framework of decision stages. This analysis treats each foreign policy case as though it were a series of interrelated, yet analytically distinct, decisions. Each stage of the decision process, therefore, provides a separate observation in which the relationship between the independent and dependent variables can vary. According to Gary King, Robert Keohane, and Sidney Verba, process tracing is an appropriate method for this type of research: "Instead of treating the ultimate outcome (for example, of an international crisis) as the dependent variable, new dependent variables are constructed; for instance, each decision in a sequence, or each set of measurable perceptions by decision-makers of others' action and intentions, becomes a new variable."[11]

Sources of Evidence for Case Studies

This study draws evidence from a variety of sources to test the proposition that the public's attention to foreign policy issues can influence presidential decision making. In the case of the Persian Gulf crisis, I surveyed the vast secondary literature to provide background information and to substantiate my conclusions. Much evidence used in the case study was also drawn from archival research that I conducted at the George Bush Presidential Library in June 2003 and June 2005.[12] Although only a small portion of the archives are

---

10. George and McKeown, "Theories of Organizational Decision Making," 35.
11. King, Keohane, and Verba, *Designing Social Inquiry,* 227.
12. I wish to extend special thanks to employees of the Bush Presidential Library for their hospitality and assistance.

open to researchers, several recently declassified files provided considerable insights into the decision-making process. Particularly valuable were transcripts of three National Security Council (NSC) meetings held in early August. These transcripts constitute the bulk of the evidence used in chapter 3.

Due to national security concerns that continue to restrict access to much of the archives, I supplemented my research at the Bush Library with the memoirs of the principal decision makers within the Bush administration—George Bush and Brent Scowcroft's *A World Transformed*, James Baker's *The Politics of Diplomacy*, and Colin Powell's *My American Journey*. The Bush and Scowcroft volume was particularly useful in this respect; it not only provided a first-hand account of policy making but also incorporated many of the still classified documents of the Bush Presidential Library. Of course, scholars must be vigilant about potential biases when utilizing autobiographic material. Therefore, whenever possible, I attempted to corroborate the accounts in memoirs with alternative perspectives.

The Ethiopian famine proved a more difficult case to research. Despite the fact that this was a defining event of the 1980s, there is surprisingly little scholarly work on the U.S. response to famine in Africa. Although the secondary literature is sparse, my research makes use of several exemplary works on the subject, including dissertations by Jack Shepherd, Edward Kissi, and Timothy Callan; books by Stephen Varnis, Richard Solberg, and Mark Duffield and John Prendergast; and a book chapter by Christopher Bosso.[13] In addition, I incorporated numerous newspaper accounts drawn from a comprehensive LexisNexis search for the years 1981 to 1987.

Attempts to access archival documents from the Reagan administration proved to be a frustrating process. None of the files pertaining to famine in Ethiopia held at the Reagan Presidential Library are currently open to researchers, and I was informed that the Freedom of Information Act queue was four years long. Efforts to obtain documents from executive agencies were met with a similar response. In addition, it appears as though the Interagency Working Group—an ad hoc committee that made many of the important food aid decisions regarding Ethiopia—kept no formal records of meetings or decisions.[14]

Due to an inability to access original documents, my research relies heavily on interviews. On February 23–24, 2006, I conducted open-ended interviews

---

13. Shepherd, "Food Aid"; Kissi, "Politics of Food Relief"; Callan, "U.S. Foreign Aid"; Varnis, *Reluctant Aid*; Solberg, *Miracle in Ethiopia*; Duffield and Prendergast, *Without Troops and Tanks*; Bosso, "Setting the Agenda."

14. General Accounting Office, *United States' Response*.

with many of the key decision makers during the Ethiopian famine. I also conducted two phone interviews at different times. I appreciate these individuals' willingness to take the time to offer valuable and illuminating insights into the case. Granted, the obvious concern in using secondary sources and elite interviews to infer the problem representations of decision makers is that statements made for public consumption may differ sharply from those expressed in private. Moreover, the interviews occurred more than twenty years after the event, prompting concerns about memory effects. Nevertheless, the interviewees seemed quite candid in their discussions with me, and I attempted to corroborate their statements with other accounts whenever possible.

Bibliography

Abegaz, Berhanu. "Aid and Reform in Ethiopia." In *Aid and Reform in Africa: Lessons from Ten Case Studies,* edited by Shantayanan Devarajan, David Dollar, and Torgny Holmgren, 167–226. Washington D.C.: World Bank, 2001.

Adams, William C. "Whose Lives Count? TV Coverage of Natural Disasters." *Journal of Communication* 36, no. 2 (1986): 113–22.

Adler, David Gray, and Larry N. George, eds. *The Constitution and the Conduct of American Foreign Policy.* Lawrence: University Press of Kansas, 1996.

Aldrich, John H. *Why Parties? The Origin and Transformation of Political Parties in America.* Chicago: University of Chicago Press, 1995.

Aldrich, John H., Christopher Gelpi, Peter Feaver, Jason Reifler, and Kristin Thompson Sharp. "Foreign Policy and the Electoral Connection." *Annual Review of Political Science* 9, no. 1 (2006): 477–502.

Aldrich, John H., John L. Sullivan, and Eugene Borgida. "Foreign Affairs and Issue Voting: Do Presidential Candidates 'Waltz Before a Blind Audience'?" *American Political Science Review* 83, no. 1 (March 1989): 123–41.

Allison, Graham T. *Essence of Decision: Explaining the Cuban Missile Crisis.* Boston: Little, Brown, 1971.

Alm, Leslie R. "Scientists and the Acid Rain Policy in Canada and the United States." *Science, Technology, and Human Values* 22, no. 3 (1997): 349–68.

Almond, Gabriel Abraham. *The American People and Foreign Policy.* New York: Praeger, 1960.

Althaus, Scott L. *Collective Preferences in Democratic Politics: Opinion Surveys and the Will of the People.* New York: Cambridge University Press, 2003.

American National Election Studies. *The ANES Guide to Public Opinion and Electoral Behavior.* Ann Arbor: University of Michigan, Center for Political Studies. http://www.electionstudies.org/nesguide/nesguide.htm (accessed April 7, 2008).

Ansolabehere, Stephen, Roy Behr, and Shanto Iyengar. *The Media Game: American Politics in the Television Age.* New York: Macmillan, 1993.

Arnold, Douglas R. *Logic of Congressional Action.* New Haven: Yale University Press, 1990.

Arterton, Christopher F. *Media Politics: The News Strategies of Presidential Campaigns.* Lexington, Mass.: Lexington Books, 1984.

Ayres, B. Drummond, Jr. "Senate Unit Backs Aid for Salvador." *New York Times,* March 15, 1984, A1.

Baker, James Addison, and Thomas M. DeFrank. *The Politics of Diplomacy: Revolution, War, and Peace, 1989–1992.* New York: Putnam's Sons, 1995.

Bandow, Doug. "The Myth of Iraq's Oil Stranglehold." *New York Times,* September 17, 1990, A23.

Banville, Lee, comp. "North Korea's Nuclear Program." *PBS Newshour,* October 19, 2006. http://www.pbs.org/newshour/indepth_coverage/asia/northkorea/nuclear.html (accessed April 14, 2008).

Bartels, Larry M., and John Zaller. "Presidential Vote Models: A Recount." *PS: Political Science and Politics* 34, no. 1 (June 2002): 9–20.

Bauer, Raymond A., Ithiel de Sola Pool, and Lewis A. Dexter. *American Business and Public Policy: The Politics of Foreign Trade.* New York: Atherton, 1963.

Baum, Matthew A. "Going Private: Public Opinion, Presidential Rhetoric, and the Domestic Politics of Audience Costs in U.S. Foreign Policy Crises." *Journal of Conflict Resolution* 48, no. 5 (2004): 603–31.

———. "How Public Opinion Constrains the Use of Force: The Case of Operation Restore Hope." *Presidential Studies Quarterly* 34, no. 2 (2004): 187–226.

———. *Soft News Goes to War: Public Opinion and American Foreign Policy in the New Media Age.* Princeton: Princeton University Press, 2003.

Baum, Matthew A., and Angela S. Jamison. "The Oprah Effect: How Soft News Helps Inattentive Citizens Vote Consistently." *Journal of Politics* 68, no. 4 (November 2006): 946–59.

Baum, Matthew A., and Philip B. K. Potter. "The Relationship Between Mass Media, Public Opinion, and Foreign Policy: Toward a Theoretical Synthesis." *Annual Review of Political Science,* no. 11 (2008): 39–65.

Baumgartner, Frank R., and Bryan D. Jones. *Agendas and Instability in American Politics.* Chicago: University of Chicago Press, 1993.

Beasley, Ryan. "Collective Interpretations: How Problem Representations Aggregate in Foreign Policy Groups." In *Problem Representation in Foreign Policy Decision Making,* edited by Donald A. Sylvan and James F. Voss, 80–115. Cambridge: Cambridge University Press, 1998.

Beasley, Ryan K., Juliet Kaarbo, Charles F. Hermann, and Margaret G. Hermann. "People and Processes in Foreign Policymaking: Insights from Comparative Case Studies." *International Studies Review* 3, no. 2 (2001): 217–50.

Belkin, Aaron. *United We Stand? Divide-and-Conquer Politics and the Logic of International Hostility.* Albany: State University of New York Press, 2005.

Belkin, Aaron, Michael Clark, Gulriz Gokcek, Robert Hinckley, Thomas Knecht, and Eric Patterson. "When Is Strategic Bombing Effective? Domestic Legitimacy and Aerial Denial." *Security Studies* 11, no. 4 (2002): 51–88.

Bennett, W. Lance. "Rethinking Political Perception and Cognition." *Micropolitics* 2 (1982): 175–202.

———. "Toward a Theory of Press-State Relations in the United States." *Journal of Communication* 40, no. 2 (1990): 103–27.

Bennett, W. Lance, Regina G. Lawrence, and Steven Livingston. *When the Press Fails: Political Power and the News Media from Iraq to Katrina.* Chicago: University of Chicago Press, 2007.

Benthall, Jonathan. *Disasters, Relief, and the Media.* London: IB Tauris, 1993.

Berger, Joseph. "Offers of Aid for Stricken Ethiopia Are Pouring into Relief Agencies." *New York Times,* October 28, 1984, A1.

Berinsky, Adam J. "Assuming the Costs of War: Events, Elites, and American Public Support for Military Conflict." *Journal of Politics* 69, no. 4 (November 2007): 975–97.

———. *Silent Voices: Public Opinion and Political Participation in America.* Princeton: Princeton University Press, 2004.

Biddle, Stephen, and Robert Zirkle. "Technology, Civil-Military Relations, and Warfare in the Developing World." *Journal of Strategic Studies* 19 (1996): 171–212.

Billings, Robert S., and Charles F. Hermann. "Problem Identification in Sequential Policy Decision Making: The Re-representation of Problems." In *Problem Representation in Foreign Policy Decision Making,* edited by Donald A. Sylvan and James F. Voss, 53–66. Cambridge: Cambridge University Press, 1998.

Bishop, George F. *The Illusion of Public Opinion: Fact and Artifact in American Public Opinion Polls.* Lanham, Md.: Rowman and Littlefield, 2005.

Boettcher, William A., III, and Michael D. Cobb. "Echoes of Vietnam?" *Journal of Conflict Resolution* 50, no. 6 (December 2006): 831–54.
Boffey, Philip M. "U.S. Will Provide $45 Million for Famine Relief in Ethiopia." *New York Times*, October 26, 1984, A12.
Bosso, Christopher J. "Setting the Agenda: Mass Media and the Discovery of Famine in Ethiopia." In *Manipulating Public Opinion: Essays on Public Opinion as a Dependent Variable,* edited by Michael Margolis and Gary A. Mauser, 153–74. Pacific Grove, Calif.: Thomson Brooks/Cole, 1989.
Brace, Paul, and Barbara Hinckley. *Follow the Leader: Opinion Polls and the Modern Presidents.* New York: Basic Books, 1992.
Bradburn, Norman M., and Carrie Miles. "Vague Quantifiers." *Public Opinion Quarterly* 43, no. 1 (Spring 1979): 92–101.
Brecher, Michael, and Jonathan Wilkenfeld. *International Crisis Behavior Project, 1918–2004.* College Park: University of Maryland (producer); Ann Arbor, Mich.: Inter-University Consortium for Political and Social Research (distributor), 2007. http://dx.doi.org/10.3886/ICPSR09286 (computer file ICPSR09286-v7).
Brody, Richard A. *Assessing the President: The Media, Elite Opinion, and Public Support.* Stanford: Stanford University Press, 1991.
———. "Crisis, War, and Public Opinion: The Media and Public Support for the President." In *Taken by Storm: The Media, Public Opinion, and U.S. Foreign Policy in the Gulf War,* edited by Lance W. Bennett and David L. Paletz, 210–27. Chicago: University of Chicago Press, 1994.
Brossard, Dominique, James Shanahan, and Katherine McComas. "Are Issue-Cycles Culturally Constructed? A Comparison of French and American Coverage of Global Climate Change." *Mass Communication and Society* 7, no. 3 (2004): 359–77.
Budner, Stanley, and Ellis S. Krauss. "Newspaper Coverage of U.S.-Japan Frictions: Balance and Objectivity." *Asian Survey* 35, no. 4 (April 1995): 336–56.
Bueno de Mesquita, Bruce. "Forecasting Policy Decisions: An Expected Utility Approach to Post-Khomeini Iran." *PS: Political Science and Politics* 17, no. 2 (Spring 1984): 226–36.
———. *The War Trap.* New Haven: Yale University Press, 1981.
———. "The War Trap Revisited: A Revised Expected Utility Model." *American Political Science Review* 79, no. 1 (March 1985): 156–77.
Bueno de Mesquita, Bruce, and David Lalman. "Domestic Opposition and Foreign War." *American Political Science Review* 84, no. 3 (September 1990): 747–65.
———. *War and Reason: Domestic and International Imperatives.* New Haven: Yale University Press, 1992.
Burstein, Paul. *Discrimination, Jobs, and Politics: The Struggle for Equal Employment Opportunity in the United States Since the New Deal.* Chicago: University of Chicago Press, 1998.
———. "The Impact of Public Opinion on Public Policy: A Review and an Agenda." *Political Research Quarterly* 56, no. 1 (March 2003): 29–40.
———. "Public Opinion and Congressional Action on Labor Market Opportunities, 1942–2000." In *Navigating Public Opinion: Polls, Policy, and the Future of American Democracy,* edited by Jeff Manza, Fay Lomax Cook, and Benjamin I. Page, 86–105. New York: Oxford University Press, 2002.
———. "Why Estimates of the Impact of Public Opinion on Public Policy Are Too High: Empirical and Theoretical Implications." *Social Forces* 84, no. 4 (June 2006): 2273–89.
Bush, George H. W., and Brent Scowcroft. *A World Transformed.* New York: Knopf, 1998.
Callan, Timothy Charles. "U.S. Foreign Aid in Complex Humanitarian Emergencies:

Motivations Behind Aid in Western Europe, Cambodia, Ethiopia, and North Korea." Ph.D. diss., State University of New York at Buffalo, 2000.

Canes-Wrone, Brandice. *Who Leads Whom? Presidents, Policy, and the Public.* Chicago: University of Chicago Press, 2006.

Canes-Wrone, Brandice, Michael C. Herron, and Kenneth W. Shotts. "Leadership and Pandering: A Theory of Executive Policymaking." *American Journal of Political Science* 45, no. 3 (July 2001): 532–50.

Canes-Wrone, Brandice, and Kenneth W. Shotts. "The Conditional Nature of Presidential Responsiveness to Public Opinion." *American Journal of Political Science* 48, no. 4 (October 2004): 690–706.

Charles, Sandra. Sandra Charles to Brent Scowcroft (through Richard N. Haass). Memorandum, "Minutes from NSC Meeting, August 3, 1990, on the Persian Gulf," 1990. Bush Presidential Records, Richard Haass Files, Working Files Iraq 8/2/90–12/90, FOA/ID CF01518 (8 of 8).

Charlick-Paley, Tanya, and Donald A. Sylvan. "The Use and Evolution of Stories as a Mode of Problem Representation: Soviet and French Military Officers Face the Loss of Empire." *Political Psychology* 21, no. 4 (December 2000): 697–728.

Chong, Dennis, and James N. Druckman. "Framing Theory." *Annual Review of Political Science* 10, no. 10 (2007): 103–26.

Clark, David H. "Can Strategic Interaction Divert Diversionary Behavior? A Model of U.S. Conflict Propensity." *Journal of Politics* 65, no. 4 (November 2003): 1013–39.

Clay, Jason. "Western Assistance and the Ethiopian Famine: Implications for Humanitarian Assistance." In *The Political Economy of African Famine,* edited by R. E. Downs, Donna O. Kerner, and Stephen P. Reyna, 147–75. Philadelphia: Gordon and Breach Science Publishers, 1991.

Cobb, Roger W., and Charles D. Elder. *Participation in American Politics.* Boston: Allyn and Bacon, 1972.

Cohen, Bernard C. *Democracies and Foreign Policy: Public Participation in the United States and the Netherlands.* Madison: University of Wisconsin Press, 1995.

———. *The Press and Foreign Policy.* Princeton: Princeton University Press, 1963.

———. *The Public's Impact on Foreign Policy.* Boston: Little, Brown, 1973.

Cohen, Jeffrey E. *Presidential Responsiveness and Public Policy-Making: The Public and the Policies That Presidents Choose.* Ann Arbor: University of Michigan Press, 1997.

Converse, Jean M. *Survey Research in the United States: Roots and Emergence, 1890–1960.* Berkeley and Los Angeles: University of California Press, 1987.

Converse, Philip E. "The Nature of Belief Systems in Mass Publics." In *Ideology and Discontent,* edited by David Apter, 206–61. New York: Free Press, 1964.

Cook, Fay L., Tom R. Tyler, Edward G. Goetz, Margaret T. Gordon, David L. Protess, and Harvey L. Molotch. "Media and Agenda Setting: Effects on the Public and Interest Group Leaders." *Public Opinion Quarterly* 47, no. 1 (Spring 1975): 16–35.

Crenson, Sharon L., and Martha Mendoza. "Friendly-Fire Worries Still Plague Military 12 Years After Persian Gulf War." Associated Press, March 5, 2003. http://www.globalsecurity.org/org/news/2003/030305-friendly01.htm (accessed July 14, 2008).

Cuny, Frederick C. *Disasters and Development.* New York: Oxford University Press, 1983.

———. "Politics and Famine Relief." In *The Moral Nation: Humanitarianism and U.S. Foreign Policy Today,* edited by Bruce Nichols and Gil Loescher, 278–87. Notre Dame: University of Notre Dame Press, 1989.

deLeon, Peter. "The Stages Approach to the Policy Process: What Has It Done? Where Is

It Going?" In *Theories of the Policy Process,* edited by Paul A. Sabatier, 19–32. Boulder, Colo.: Westview Press, 1999.
Delli Carpini, Michael X., and Scott Keeter. *What Americans Know About Politics and Why It Matters.* New Haven: Yale University Press, 1996.
Destler, I. M. *American Trade Politics.* Washington, D.C.: Institute for International Economics, 2005.
Diven, Polly J. "A Coincidence of Interests: The Hyperpluralism of U.S. Food Aid Policy." *Foreign Policy Analysis* 2, no. 4 (2006): 361–84.
———. "The Domestic Determinants of U.S. Food Aid Policy." *Food Policy* 26, no. 5 (2001): 455–74.
Dorman, William A., and Stephen Livingston. "News and Historical Content: The Establishing Phase of the Persian Gulf Policy Debate." In *Taken by Storm: The Media, Public Opinion, and U.S. Foreign Policy in the Gulf War,* edited by Lance W. Bennett and David L. Paletz, 63–81. Chicago: University of Chicago Press, 1994.
Downs, Anthony. "Up and Down with Ecology: The Issue-Attention Cycle." *Public Interest* 28 (1972): 38–52.
Dreze, Jean, and Amartya K. Sen. *Hunger and Public Action.* Oxford: Clarendon Press, 1990.
Druckman, James N. "The Implications of Framing Effects for Citizen Competence." *Political Behavior* 23, no. 3 (September 2001): 225–56.
———. "Political Preference Formation: Competition, Deliberation, and the Irrelevance of Framing Effects." *American Political Science Review* 98, no. 4 (November 2004): 671–86.
Druckman, James N., and Justin W. Holmes. "Does Presidential Rhetoric Matter? Priming and Presidential Approval." *Presidential Studies Quarterly* 34, no. 4 (2004): 755–78.
Druckman, James N., and Lawrence R. Jacobs. "Lumpers and Splitters: The Public Opinion Information that Politicians Collect and Use." *Public Opinion Quarterly* 70, no. 4 (Winter 2006): 453–76.
Druckman, James N., Lawrence R. Jacobs, and Eric Ostermeier. "Candidate Strategies to Prime Issues and Image." *Journal of Politics* 66, no. 4 (November 2004): 1180–1202.
Drury, A. Cooper, Richard Stuart Olson, and Douglas A. Van Belle. "The Politics of Humanitarian Aid: U.S. Foreign Disaster Assistance, 1964–1995." *Journal of Politics* 67, no. 2 (May 2005): 454–73.
Duffield, Mark R., and John Prendergast. *Without Troops and Tanks: Humanitarian Intervention in Ethiopia and Eritrea.* Lawrenceville, N.J.: Red Sea Press, 1994.
Dyson, Stephen B. "Alliances, Domestic Politics, and Leader Psychology: Why Did Britain Stay Out of Vietnam and Go into Iraq?" *Political Psychology* 28, no. 6 (2007): 647–66.
Eastland, Terry. *Energy in the Executive: The Case for the Strong Presidency.* New York: Free Press, 1992.
Eckstein, Harry. "Case Study and Theory in Political Science." In *Handbook of Political Science,* vol. 7, *Strategies of Inquiry,* edited by Fred I. Greenstein and Nelson W. Polsby, 79–137. New York: Addison-Wesley, 1975.
Edwards, George C., III. *On Deaf Ears: The Limits of the Bully Pulpit.* New Haven: Yale University Press, 2003.
Edwards, George C., III, William Mitchell, and Reed Welch. "Explaining Presidential Approval: The Significance of Issue Salience." *American Journal of Political Science* 39, no. 1 (February 1995): 108–34.
Edwards, George C., III, and B. Dan Wood. "Who Influences Whom? The President, Congress, and the Media." *American Political Science Review* 93, no. 2 (June 1999): 327–44.
Eichenberg, Richard C. "Victory Has Many Friends: U.S. Public Opinion and the Use of Military Force, 1981–2005." *International Security* 30, no. 1 (Summer 2005): 140–77.

Eichenberg, Richard C., Richard J. Stoll, and Matthew Lebo. "War President." *Journal of Conflict Resolution* 50, no. 6 (December 2006): 783–808.
Eisensee, Thomas, and David Stromberg. "News Floods, News Droughts, and U.S. Disaster Relief." *Quarterly Journal of Economics* 122, no. 2 (2007): 693–728.
Eisinger, Robert M. *The Evolution of Presidential Polling.* Cambridge: Cambridge University Press, 2003.
Elliot, Kimberly, Gary Hufbauer, and Jeffrey Schott. "The Big Squeeze: Why the Sanctions on Iraq Will Work." *Washington Post,* December 9, 1990, K1.
Engstrom, David W. *Presidential Decision Making Adrift: The Carter Administration and the Mariel Boatlift.* Lanham, Md.: Rowman and Littlefield, 1997.
Entman, Robert M. *Projections of Power: Framing News, Public Opinion, and U.S. Foreign Policy.* Chicago: University of Chicago Press, 2004.
Erikson, Robert S., Michael MacKuen, and James A. Stimson. *The Macro Polity.* New York: Cambridge University Press, 2002.
Eulau, Heinz, and Paul D. Karps. "The Puzzle of Representation: Specifying Components of Responsiveness." *Legislative Studies Quarterly* 2, no. 3 (August 1977): 233–54.
Everts, Philip. "Public Opinion After the Cold War: A Paradigm Shift." In *Decisionmaking in a Glass House: Mass Media, Public Opinion, and American and European Foreign Policy in the Twenty-first Century,* edited by Brigitte L. Nacos, Robert Y. Shapiro, and Pierangelo Isernia, 177–94. Lanham, Md.: Rowman and Littlefield, 2000.
Fearon, James D. "Domestic Political Audiences and the Escalation of International Disputes." *American Political Science Review* 88, no. 3 (September 1994): 577–92.
Feaver, Peter, and Christopher Gelpi. *Choosing Your Battles: American Civil-Military Relations and the Use of Force.* Princeton: Princeton University Press, 2004.
Fiorina, Morris P. *Congress: Keystone of the Washington Establishment.* New Haven: Yale University Press, 1977.
Fisher, Louis. *Politics of Executive Privilege.* Durham, N.C.: Carolina Academic Press, 2004.
———. *Presidential War Power.* Lawrence: University Press of Kansas, 1995.
Fishkin, James S. *The Voice of the People: Public Opinion and Democracy.* New Haven: Yale University Press, 1995.
Foyle, Douglas C. *Counting the Public In: Presidents, Public Opinion, and Foreign Policy.* New York: Columbia University Press, 1999.
———. "Leading the Public to War? The Influence of American Public Opinion on the Bush Administration's Decision to Go to War in Iraq." *International Journal of Public Opinion Research* 16, no. 3 (Autumn 2004): 269–94.
Freedman, Lawrence, and Efraim Karsh. *The Gulf Conflict, 1990–1991: Diplomacy and War in the New World Order.* Princeton: Princeton University Press, 1993.
Friedman, Thomas L. "U.S. Gulf Policy—Vague 'Vital Interests.'" *New York Times,* August 12, 1990, A1.
Gamson, William A., and Andre Modigliani. "The Changing Culture of Affirmative Action." *Research in Political Sociology* 3, no. 2 (1987): 137–77.
Gans, Herbert J. *Deciding What's News: A Study of CBS Evening News, NBC Nightly News, "Newsweek," and "Time."* New York: Pantheon Books, 1979.
Gargan, Edward A. "Old Specter for Ethiopia's New Year: Famine." *New York Times,* December 27, 1985, A1.
Gartner, Scott Sigmund. "The Multiple Effects of Casualties on Public Support for War: An Experimental Approach." *American Political Science Review* 102, no. 1 (March 2008): 95–106.

Gartner, Scott Sigmund, and Gary M. Segura. "War, Casualties, and Public Opinion." *Journal of Conflict Resolution* 42, no. 3 (June 1998): 278–300.

Geer, John G. *From Tea Leaves to Opinion Polls: A Theory of Democratic Leadership.* New York: Columbia University Press, 1996.

Gelb, Leslie H. "The Essential Domino: American Politics and Vietnam." *Foreign Affairs* 50, no. 3 (April 1972): 459–75.

Gelpi, Christopher, Peter D. Feaver, and Jason Reifler. "Success Matters: Casualty Sensitivity and the War in Iraq." *International Security* 30, no. 3 (Winter 2005–6): 7–46.

Gelpi, Christopher, and John E. Mueller. "The Cost of War (Response)." *Foreign Affairs* 85 (2006): 139–44.

Gelpi, Christopher, Jason Reifler, and Peter Feaver. "Iraq the Vote: Retrospective and Prospective Foreign Policy Judgments on Candidate Choice and Casualty Tolerance." *Political Behavior* 29, no. 2 (June 2007): 151–74.

General Accounting Office. *The United States' Response to the Ethiopian Food Crisis.* Washington, D.C.: General Accounting Office, 1985.

George, Alexander L. "Case Studies and Theory Development: The Method of Structured, Focused Comparison." In *Diplomacy: New Approaches in History, Theory, and Policy,* edited by Paul Gordon Lauren, 43–68. New York: Free Press, 1979.

———. "The Causal Nexus Between Cognitive Beliefs and Decision-Making Behavior: The 'Operational Code' Belief System." In *Psychological Models in International Politics,* edited by Lawrence S. Falkowski, 95–124. Boulder, Colo.: Westview Press, 1979.

———. "The 'Operational Code': A Neglected Approach to the Study of Political Leaders and Decision-Making." *International Studies Quarterly* 13, no. 2 (June 1969): 190–222.

George, Alexander L., and Timothy J. McKeown. "Case Studies and Theories of Organizational Decision Making." *Advances in Information Processing in Organizations,* no. 2 (1985): 21–58.

Gilboa, Eytan. "The CNN Effect: The Search for a Communication Theory of International Relations." *Political Communication* 22, no. 1 (January–March 2005): 27–44.

Ginsberg, Benjamin. *The Captive Public: How Mass Opinion Promotes State Power.* New York: Basic Books, 1986.

Gordon, Michael R., and Bernard E. Trainor. *Cobra II: The Inside Story of the Invasion and Occupation of Iraq.* New York: Pantheon Books, 2006.

———. *The Generals' War: The Inside Story of the Conflict in the Gulf.* Boston: Little, Brown, 1995.

Graber, Doris A. *Mass Media and American Politics.* 7th ed. Washington, D.C.: CQ Press, 2006.

———. *Processing Politics: Learning from Television in the Internet Age.* Chicago: University of Chicago Press, 2001.

Graham, Thomas W. "The Politics of Failure: Strategic Nuclear Arms Control, Public Opinion, and Domestic Politics in the United States, 1945–1980." Ph.D. diss., Massachusetts Institute of Technology, 1989.

———. "Public Opinion and U.S. Foreign Policy Decision Making." In *The New Politics of American Foreign Policy,* edited by David A. Deese, 190–214. New York: St. Martin's Press, 1994.

Grant, Rebecca L. *Operation Just Cause and the U.S. Policy Process.* Santa Monica, Calif.: RAND, 1991.

Greenstein, Fred I. "Can Personality and Politics Be Studied Systematically?" *Political Psychology* 13, no. 1 (March 1992): 105–28.

———. *The Presidential Difference: Leadership Style from Roosevelt to Clinton.* New York: Free Press, 2000.

Haass, Richard N. Richard N. Haass to William F. Sittmann. Memorandum, "Minutes from NSC Meeting on Iraqi Invasion of Kuwait, August 5, 1990, 5:00 P.M.–6:30 P.M., Cabinet Room," 1990. Bush Presidential Records, Richard Haass Files, Working Files Iraq 8/2/90–12/90, FOA/ID CF01518 (8 of 8).

———. Richard N. Haass to William F. Sittmann. Memorandum, "Minutes from NSC Meeting on Iraqi Invasion of Kuwait, August 6, 1990, 5:05 P.M.–6:00 P.M., Cabinet Room," 1990. Bush Presidential Records, Richard Haass Files, Working Files Iraq 8/2/90–12/90, FOA/ID CF01518 (8 of 8).

Haider-Markel, Donald P., and Mark R. Joslyn. "Gun Policy, Opinion, Tragedy, and Blame Attribution: The Conditional Influence of Issue Frames." *Journal of Politics* 63, no. 2 (May 2001): 520–43.

Hallin, Daniel C. *The Uncensored War: The Media and Vietnam.* Berkeley and Los Angeles: University of California Press, 1986.

Halperin, Morton H. *Bureaucratic Politics and Foreign Policy.* Washington, D.C.: Brookings Institution Press, 1974.

Hampson, Fen Osler. "The Divided Decision-Maker: American Domestic Politics and the Cuban Crises." *International Security* 9, no. 3 (Winter 1984–85): 130–65.

Harden, Blaine. "Ethiopia Faces Famine Again, Requests Massive Food Relief." *Washington Post,* September 14, 1987, A1.

———. "Ethiopia Scolds Aid Donors; Backing Sought for Plan to Relocate Famine Victims." *Washington Post,* December 12, 1984, A1.

———. "Famine's Grip Loosened in Ethiopia: Morgue at Feeding Station Empty After International Drive." *Washington Post,* November 27, 1985, A1.

———. "Strings on U.S. Aid Complicate Ethiopian Relief." *Washington Post,* April 26, 1985, A1.

Hardin, Garrett. "Commentary: Living on a Lifeboat." *BioScience* 24, no. 10 (October 1974): 561–68.

Heith, Diane. *Polling to Govern: Public Opinion and Presidential Leadership.* Stanford: Stanford University Press, 2004.

Henry, Gary T., and Craig S. Gordon. "Tracking Issue Attention: Specifying the Dynamics of the Public Agenda." *Public Opinion Quarterly* 65, no. 2 (Summer 2001): 157–77.

Herman, Edward S., and Noam Chomsky. *Manufacturing Consent: The Political Economy of the Mass Media.* New York: Pantheon Books, 1988.

Hermann, Charles F. "Changing Course: When Governments Choose to Redirect Foreign Policy." *International Studies Quarterly* 34, no. 1 (March 1990): 3–21.

Hibbs, Douglas A. *The American Political Economy: Macroeconomics and Electoral Politics.* Cambridge: Harvard University Press, 1987.

———. "Bread and Peace Voting in U.S. Presidential Elections." *Public Choice* 104, no. 1 (2000): 149–80.

Hilgartner, Stephen, and Charles L. Bosk. "The Rise and Fall of Social Problems: A Public Arenas Model." *American Journal of Sociology* 94, no. 1 (July 1988): 53–78.

Hill, Kim Quaile. "The Policy Agendas of the President and the Mass Public: A Research Validation and Extension." *American Journal of Political Science* 42, no. 4 (October 1998): 1328–34.

Hinckley, Ronald H. *People, Polls, and Policymakers: American Public Opinion and National Security.* New York: Lexington Books, 1992.

Holsti, Ole R. *Public Opinion and American Foreign Policy.* Rev. ed. Ann Arbor: University of Michigan Press, 2004.

———. "Public Opinion and Foreign Policy: Challenges to the Almond-Lippmann Consensus. Mershon Series: Research Programs and Debates." *International Studies Quarterly* 36, no. 4 (December 1992): 439–66.

———. "Public Opinion on Human Rights in Foreign Policy." In *The United States and Human Rights: Looking Inward and Outward,* edited by David P. Forsythe, 131–94. Lincoln: University of Nebraska Press, 2000.

Houghton, David Patrick. *U.S. Foreign Policy and the Iran Hostage Crisis.* New York: Cambridge University Press, 2001.

Howell, William G., and John C. Pevehouse. "Presidents, Congress, and the Use of Force." *International Organization* 59, no. 1 (Winter 2005): 209–32.

Huntington, Samuel P. "Strategic Planning and the Political Process." *Foreign Affairs,* no. 28 (1960): 285–99.

Hutchings, Vincent L. *Public Opinion and Democratic Accountability: How Citizens Learn About Politics.* Princeton: Princeton University Press, 2003.

Idelson, Holly. "National Opinion Ambivalent as Winds of War Stir Gulf." *Congressional Quarterly Weekly,* April 20, 1991, 14–17.

Iyengar, Shanto. *Is Anyone Responsible? How Television Frames Political Issues.* Chicago: University of Chicago Press, 1991.

Iyengar, Shanto, and Donald R. Kinder. *News That Matters: Television and American Opinion.* Chicago: University of Chicago Press, 1987.

Iyengar, Shanto, and Adam F. Simon. "News Coverage of the Gulf Crisis and Public Opinion: A Study of Agenda-Setting, Priming, and Framing." *Communication Research* 20, no. 3 (June 1993): 365–83. Reprinted in *Taken by Storm: The Media, Public Opinion, and U.S. Foreign Policy in the Gulf War,* edited by Lance W. Bennett and David L. Paletz, 167–85. Chicago: University of Chicago Press, 1994.

Jacobs, Lawrence R. "The Recoil Effect: Public Opinion and Policymaking in the U.S. and Britain." *Comparative Politics* 24, no. 2 (January 1992): 199–217.

Jacobs, Lawrence R., and Benjamin I. Page. "Who Influences U.S. Foreign Policy?" *American Political Science Review* 99, no. 1 (March 2005): 107–23.

Jacobs, Lawrence R., and Robert Y. Shapiro. "Issues, Candidate Image, and Priming: The Use of Private Polls in Kennedy's 1960 Presidential Campaign." *American Political Science Review* 88, no. 3 (September 1994): 527–40.

———. *Politicians Don't Pander: Political Manipulation and the Loss of Democratic Responsiveness.* Chicago: University of Chicago Press, 2000.

———. "Politics and Policymaking in the Real World: Crafted Talk and the Loss of Democratic Responsiveness." In *Navigating Public Opinion: Polls, Policy, and the Future of American Democracy,* edited by Jeff Manza, Fay Lomax Cook, and Benjamin I. Page, 54–75. New York: Oxford University Press, 2002.

———. "The Rise of Presidential Polling." *Public Opinion Quarterly* 59, no. 2 (Summer 1995): 163–95.

Jacobson, Gary C. *A Divider, Not a Uniter: George W. Bush and the American People.* New York: Longman, 2007.

James, Patrick, and John R. Oneal. "The Influence of Domestic and International Politics on the President's Use of Force." *Journal of Conflict Resolution* 35, no. 2 (June 1991): 307–32.

Jann, Werner, and Kai Wegrich. "Theories of the Policy Cycle." In *Public Policy Analysis: Theory, Politics, and Methods,* edited by Frank Fischer, Gerald J. Miller, and Mara S. Sidney, 43–62. New York: CRC Press, 2007.

Jenkins, Loren. "Reagan Gets Appeal on Famine Transport." *Washington Post,* August 22, 1985, A35.
Jenkins-Smith, Hank C., and Paul A. Sabatier. "The Study of Public Policy Processes." In *Policy Change and Learning: An Advocacy Coalition Approach,* edited by Paul A. Sabatier and Hank C. Jenkins-Smith, 1–6. Boulder, Colo.: Westview Press, 1993.
Jentleson, Bruce W. "The Pretty Prudent Public: Post Post-Vietnam American Opinion on the Use of Military Force." *International Studies Quarterly* 36, no. 1 (March 1992): 49–73.
Jentleson, Bruce W., and Rebecca L. Britton. "Still Pretty Prudent: Post–Cold War American Public Opinion on the Use of Military Force." *Journal of Conflict Resolution* 42, no. 4 (August 1998): 395–417.
Johnson, Dominic D. P., and Dominic Tierney. *Failing to Win: Perceptions of Victory and Defeat in International Politics.* Cambridge: Harvard University Press, 2006.
Jones, Bryan D. *Reconceiving Decision-Making in Democratic Politics: Attention, Choice, and Public Policy.* Chicago: University of Chicago Press, 1994.
Joyce, Fay S. "Northwest Visit Delights Mondale." *New York Times,* October 30, 1984, A22.
Kahneman, Daniel, and Amos Tversky. "Choices, Values, and Frames." *American Psychologist* 39, no. 4 (1984): 341–50.
Karol, David, and Edward Miguel. "The Electoral Cost of War: Iraq Casualties and the 2004 U.S. Presidential Election." *Journal of Politics* 69, no. 3 (August 2007): 633–48.
Kegley, Charles W., and Eugene R. Wittkopf. *American Foreign Policy: Pattern and Process.* 4th ed. New York: St. Martin's Press, 1991.
Keller, Edmond J. "Drought, War, and the Politics of Famine in Ethiopia and Eritrea." *Journal of Modern African Studies* 30, no. 4 (December 1992): 609–24.
———. *Revolutionary Ethiopia: From Empire to People's Republic.* Bloomington: Indiana University Press, 1988.
Keller, Jonathan W. "Constraint Respecters, Constraint Challengers, and Crisis Decision Making in Democracies: A Case Study Analysis of Kennedy Versus Reagan." *Political Psychology* 26, no. 6 (2005): 835–67.
Kelman, Herbert C. "Social-Psychological Approaches to the Study of International Relations: The Question of Relevance." In *International Behavior: A Social-Psychological Analysis,* edited by Herbert C. Kelman, 565–607. New York: Holt, Rinehart and Winston, 1965.
Kennedy, Robert F., Jr. "Bush Backpedals on Environment." *Seattle Post-Intelligencer,* August 4, 2004, B8.
Key, V. O. *Public Opinion and American Democracy.* New York: Knopf, 1961.
Khong, Yuen Foong. *Analogies at War: Korea, Munich, Dien Bien Phu, and the Vietnam Decisions of 1965.* Princeton: Princeton University Press, 1992.
King, Gary, Robert O. Keohane, and Sidney Verba. *Designing Social Inquiry: Scientific Inference in Qualitative Research.* Princeton: Princeton University Press, 1994.
Kingdon, John W. *Agendas, Alternatives, and Public Policies.* Boston: Little, Brown, 1984.
Kiousis, Spiro. "Explicating Media Salience: A Factor Analysis of *New York Times* Issue Coverage During the 2000 U.S. Presidential Election." *Journal of Communication* 54, no. 1 (2004): 71–87.
Kissi, Edward. "Famine and the Politics of Food Relief in United States Relations with Ethiopia, 1950–1991." Ph.D. diss., Concordia University, 1997.
Klarevas, Louis. "The 'Essential Domino' of Military Operations: American Public Opinion and the Use of Force." *International Studies Perspectives* 3, no. 4 (November 2002): 417–37.
Knecht, Thomas. "Benchmarks in American Foreign Policy Opinion." Paper presented at

the Annual Conference of the Midwest Political Science Association, Chicago, Ill., April 23–25, 2010.
Knecht, Thomas, and Jordan Cass. "Framing Saddam: Rhetorical Analysis, the National Interest, and the Persian Gulf War." Unpublished manuscript, n.d.
Knecht, Thomas, and M. Stephen Weatherford. "Public Opinion and Foreign Policy: The Stages of Presidential Decision Making." *International Studies Quarterly* 50, no. 3 (September 2006): 705–27.
Kollman, Ken. *Outside Lobbying: Public Opinion and Interest Group Strategies.* Princeton: Princeton University Press, 1998.
Kranish, Michael. "Congressional Leaders Back Sending of Troops to the Gulf." *Boston Globe,* August 9, 1990, 18.
Krehbiel, Keith. *Information and Legislative Organization.* Ann Arbor: University of Michigan Press, 1992.
Kriner, Douglas L., and Francis X. Shen. *The Casualty Gap: The Causes and Consequences of American Wartime Inequalities.* New York: Oxford University Press, 2010.
———. "Iraq Casualties and the 2006 Senate Elections." *Legislative Studies Quarterly* 32, no. 4 (2007): 507–30.
Krosnick, Jon A., and Laura A. Brannon. "The Impact of the Gulf War on the Ingredients of Presidential Evaluations: Multidimensional Effects of Political Involvement." *American Political Science Review* 87, no. 4 (December 1993): 963–75.
Kull, Steven. "What the Public Knows That Washington Doesn't." *Foreign Policy,* no. 101 (Winter 1995): 102–15.
Kull, Steven, and I. M. Destler. *Misreading the Public: The Myth of a New Isolationism.* Washington, D.C.: Brookings Institution Press, 1999.
Kull, Steven, and Clay Ramsay. "Elite Misperceptions of U.S. Public Opinion and Foreign Policy." In *Decisionmaking in a Glass House: Mass Media, Public Opinion, and American and European Foreign Policy in the Twenty-first Century,* edited by Brigitte L. Nacos, Robert Y. Shapiro, and Pierangelo Isernia, 95–110. Lanham, Md.: Rowman and Littlefield, 2000.
Kuperman, Ranan D. "A Dynamic Framework for Analyzing Foreign Policy Decision Making." *International Studies Review* 8, no. 3 (2006): 537–44.
Lancaster, Carol. "U.S. Aid, Diplomacy, and African Development." *Africa Report,* July–August 1984, 62–66.
Larson, Eric V. *Casualties and Consensus: The Historical Role of Casualties in Domestic Support for U.S. Military Operations.* Santa Monica, Calif.: RAND Corporation, 1996.
Larson, Eric V., and Bagdan Savych. *American Public Support for U.S. Military Operations from Mogadishu to Baghdad.* Santa Monica, Calif.: RAND Corporation, 2005.
Layne, Christopher. "Why the Gulf War Was Not in the National Interest." *Atlantic (02769077)* 268, no. 1 (July 1991): 55–81.
Legum, Colin. "Ethiopia Dramatizes Africa's Food Crisis." *New African,* December 1984, 25–26.
Levy, Jack. "The Diversionary Theory of War." In *Handbook of War Studies,* edited by M. Midlarsky, 259–88. Boston: Unwin Hyman, 1989.
Lewis, Justin. *Constructing Public Opinion: How Political Elites Do What They Like and Why We Seem to Go Along with It.* New York: Columbia University Press, 2001.
Light, Paul C. *The President's Agenda: Domestic Policy Choice from Kennedy to Carter (with Notes on Ronald Reagan).* Baltimore: Johns Hopkins University Press, 1982.
Lindsay, James M. *Congress and the Politics of U.S. Foreign Policy.* Baltimore: Johns Hopkins University Press, 1994.

Lippmann, Walter. *Essays in the Public Philosophy.* Boston: Little, Brown, 1955.

Lisowski, Michael. "Playing the Two-Level Game: U.S. President Bush's Decision to Repudiate the Kyoto Protocol." *Environmental Politics* 11, no. 4 (Winter 2002): 101–19.

Lyon, Charlie. "Operation Allied Force: A Lesson on Strategy, Risk, and Tactical Execution." *Comparative Strategy* 20, no. 1 (January–March 2001): 57–75.

Manza, Jeff, and Fay Lomax Cook. "A Democratic Polity? Three Views of Policy Responsiveness to Public Opinion in the United States." *American Politics Research* 30, no. 6 (November 2002): 630–67.

Manza, Jeff, Fay Lomax Cook, and Benjamin I. Page, eds. *The Impact of Public Opinion in Public Policy: The State of the Debate.* New York: Oxford University Press, 2002.

Masud-Piloto, Felix R. *With Open Arms: Cuban Migration to the United States.* Lanham, Md.: Rowman and Littlefield, 1995.

Mathews, Tom. "The Road to War." *Newsweek,* January 28, 1991, 34–45.

———. "The Secret History of the War." *Newsweek,* March 18, 1991, 28–33.

May, Clifford D. "Northern Ethiopia Crisis Said to Worsen." *New York Times,* June 16, 1985, A3.

———. "U.S. Official Says Ethiopian Suffering Eases." *New York Times,* August 30, 1985, A6.

Mayhew, David R. *Congress: The Electoral Connection.* New Haven: Yale University Press, 1974.

McCombs, Maxwell E. *Setting the Agenda: The Mass Media and Public Opinion.* Malden, Mass.: Blackwell, 2004.

McCombs, Maxwell E., and Donald L. Shaw. "The Agenda-Setting Function of Mass Media." *Public Opinion Quarterly* 36, no. 2 (Summer 1972): 176–87.

———. "The Evolution of Agenda-Setting Research: Twenty-five Years in the Marketplace of Ideas." *Journal of Communication* 43, no. 2 (1993): 58–67.

McCombs, Maxwell E., and Jian-Hua Zhu. "Capacity, Diversity, and Volatility of the Public Agenda: Trends from 1954 to 1994." *Public Opinion Quarterly* 59, no. 4 (Winter 1995): 495–525.

McDermott, Rose. "Prospect Theory in International Relations: The Iranian Hostage Rescue Mission." *Political Psychology* 13, no. 2 (June 1992): 237–63.

Mearsheimer, John J., and Stephen M. Walt. "The Israel Lobby and U.S. Foreign Policy." *Middle East Policy* 13, no. 3 (September 2006): 29–87.

Meernik, James David. *The Political Use of Military Force in U.S. Foreign Policy.* Burlington, Vt.: Ashgate, 2004.

Meernik, James David, and Michael Ault. "Public Opinion and Support for U.S. Presidents' Foreign Policies." *American Politics Research* 29, no. 4 (July 2001): 352–73.

Mervin, David. *George Bush and the Guardianship Presidency.* New York: St. Martin's Press, 1996.

Meszoly, Robin. "Africa Drought Poses Major Aid Challenge." *Congressional Quarterly Weekly,* December 1, 1984, 3037–42.

Miller, George A. "The Magic Number Seven, Plus or Minus Two: Some Limits on Our Capacity for Processing Information." *Psychological Review* 63, no. 2 (1956): 81–97.

Miller, Judith. "Famine Engulfs Ethiopia Again; Death Toll Rises." *New York Times,* September 18, 1984, A1.

Mobley, Richard A. "Revisiting the Korean Tree-Trimming Incident." *Joint Force Quarterly,* Summer 2003, 108–15. http://www.dtic.mil/doctrine/Jel/jfq_pubs/2035.pdf (accessed April 28, 2010).

Moe, Terry M. "Presidents, Institutions, and Theory." In *Researching the Presidency: Vital*

Questions, New Approaches, edited by George C. Edwards III, John H. Kessel, and Bert A. Rockman, 337–85. Pittsburgh: University of Pittsburgh Press, 1993.

Monroe, Alan D. "Public Opinion and Public Policy, 1980–1993." *Public Opinion Quarterly* 62, no. 1 (Spring 1998): 6–28.

Moore, Will H., and David J. Lanoue. "Domestic Politics and U.S. Foreign Policy: A Study of Cold War Conflict Behavior." *Journal of Politics* 65, no. 2 (May 2003): 376–96.

Morgenthau, Hans J. *Politics Among Nations: The Struggle for Power and Peace.* New York: Knopf, 1978.

Morin, Richard, and E. J. Dionne Jr. "Vox Populi: Winds of War and Shifts of Opinion." *Washington Post,* December 23, 1990, C1.

Morley, Morris, and Chris McGillion. "'Disobedient' Generals and the Politics of Redemocratization: The Clinton Administration and Haiti." *Political Science Quarterly* 112, no. 3 (Autumn 1997): 363–84.

Morrow, James D. "A Rational Choice Approach to International Conflict." In *Decision-Making on War and Peace: The Cognitive-Rational Debate,* edited by Nehemia Geva and Alex Mintz, 11–32. Boulder, Colo.: Lynne Rienner, 1997.

Moxey, Linda M., and Anthony J. Sanford. *Communicating Quantities: A Psychological Perspective.* Hove, UK: Lawrence Erlbaum Associates, 1993.

Mueller, John E. "American Public Opinion and the Gulf War." In *The Political Psychology of the Gulf War: Leaders, Publics, and the Process of Conflict,* edited by Stanley A. Renshon, 199–226. Pittsburgh: University of Pittsburgh, 1993.

———. *Policy and Opinion in the Gulf War.* Chicago: University of Chicago Press, 1994.

———. "A Review: American Public Opinion and the Gulf War: Some Polling Issues." *Public Opinion Quarterly* 57, no. 1 (Spring 1993): 80–91.

———. *War, Presidents, and Public Opinion.* New York: Wiley, 1973.

Murphy, Jarrett. "Headlines from Hell." *CBSNews.com,* January 19, 2001. http://www.cbsnews.com/stories/2001/01/19/iran/main265565.shtml (accessed March 4, 2008).

Murray, Shoon Kathleen. "Private Polls and Presidential Policymaking." *Public Opinion Quarterly* 70, no. 4 (Winter 2006): 477–98.

Murray, Shoon Kathleen, and Peter Howard. "Variation in White House Polling Operations." *Public Opinion Quarterly* 66, no. 4 (Winter 2002): 527–58.

Mutz, Diana C., and Joe Soss. "Reading Public Opinion: The Influence of News Coverage on Perceptions of Public Sentiment." *Public Opinion Quarterly* 61, no. 3 (Autumn 1997): 431–51.

Natsios, Andrew S. "NGOs and the UN System in Complex Humanitarian Emergencies: Conflict or Cooperation?" *Third World Quarterly* 16, no. 3 (September 1995): 405–20.

———. "The Politics of United States Disaster Response." *Mediterranean Quarterly* (1995): 46–59.

———. *U.S. Foreign Policy and the Four Horsemen of the Apocalypse: Humanitarian Relief in Complex Emergencies.* Westport, Conn.: Praeger, 1997.

Neuman, W. Russell. "The Threshold of Public Attention." *Public Opinion Quarterly* 54, no. 2 (Summer 1990): 159–76.

Neuman, W. Russell, Marion R. Just, and Ann N. Crigler. *Common Knowledge News and the Construction of Political Meaning.* Chicago: University of Chicago Press, 1992.

Neustadt, Richard E. *Presidential Power: The Politics of Leadership.* New York: Wiley, 1960.

Neustadt, Richard E., and Ernest R. May. *Thinking in Time: The Uses of History for Decision-Makers.* New York: Free Press, 1986.

New York Times. "After the War; Excerpts from the Schwarzkopf Interview." March 28, 1991, A18. http://www.lexisnexis.com/us/lnacademic/ (accessed April 28, 2010).

---. "Excerpts from Iraqi Document on Meeting with U.S. Envoy." September 23, 1990. http://www.chss.montclair.edu/english/furr/glaspie.html (accessed June 29, 2008).

---. "Famine Relief Shifts to Permanent Solutions." November 3, 1985, A13.

Nincic, Miroslav. "U.S. Soviet Policy and the Electoral Connection." *World Politics* 42, no. 3 (April 1990): 370–96.

Nisbet, Matthew C., and Teresa Myers. "The Polls Trends: Twenty Years of Public Opinion About Global Warming." *Public Opinion Quarterly* 71, no. 3 (Autumn 2007): 444–70.

Oberdorfer, Don. *The Two Koreas: A Contemporary History.* New York: Basic Books, 2001.

O'Brien, Robert, Anne Marie Goetz, Jan Aart Scholte, and Marc Williams. *Contesting Global Governance: Multilateral Economic Institutions and Global Social Movements.* Cambridge: Cambridge University Press, 2000.

O'Bryant, JoAnne, and Michael Waterhouse. *U.S. Forces in Iraq.* CRS Report for Congress, May 8, 2008.

Odell, John S. "Case Study Methods in International Political Economy." *International Studies Perspectives* 2, no. 2 (May 2001): 161–76.

Omang, Joanne. "Anti-Hunger Drive Smoother, but Far from Goals." *Washington Post,* August 11, 1984, A10.

---. "TV Film of Emaciated Children Ended Apathy on Ethiopian Famine." *Washington Post,* November 21, 1984, A14.

Oneal, John R., Brad Lian, and James H. Joyner Jr. "Are the American People 'Pretty Prudent'? Public Responses to U.S. Uses of Force, 1950–1988." *International Studies Quarterly* 40, no. 2 (June 1996): 261–79.

Oreskes, Michael. "In a Crisis, Support with Reservations." *New York Times,* August 12, 1990, A1.

Ostrom, Charles W., Jr., and Brian L. Job. "The President and the Political Use of Force." *American Political Science Review* 80, no. 2 (June 1986): 541–66.

Ottaway, David B. "Ethiopia Squeezed Between East and West." *Washington Post,* September 23, 1984, A1.

Otter, Mark. "Domestic Public Support for Foreign Aid: Does It Matter?" *Third World Quarterly* 24, no. 1 (March 2003): 115–25.

Ozkececi-Taner, Binur. "Reviewing the Literature on Sequential/Dynamic Foreign Policy Decision Making." *International Studies Review* 8, no. 3 (2006): 545–54.

Page, Benjamin I. "Toward General Theories of the Media, Public Opinion, and Foreign Policy." In *Decisionmaking in a Glass House: Mass Media, Public Opinion, and American and European Foreign Policy in the Twenty-first Century,* edited by Brigitte L. Nacos, Robert Y. Shapiro, and Pierangelo Isernia, 85–94. Lanham, Md.: Rowman and Littlefield, 2000.

Page, Benjamin I., and Jason Barabas. "Foreign Policy Gaps Between Citizens and Leaders." *International Studies Quarterly* 44, no. 3 (September 2000): 339–64.

Page, Benjamin I., and Marshall M. Bouton. *The Foreign Policy Disconnect: What Americans Want from Our Leaders but Don't Get.* Chicago: University of Chicago Press, 2006.

Page, Benjamin I., and Robert Y. Shapiro. "Changes in Americans' Policy Preferences, 1935–1979." *Public Opinion Quarterly* 46, no. 1 (Spring 1982): 24–42.

---. *The Rational Public: Fifty Years of Trends in Americans' Policy Preferences.* Chicago: University of Chicago Press, 1992.

Page, Benjamin I., Robert Y. Shapiro, and Glenn R. Dempsey. "What Moves Public Opinion?" *American Political Science Review* 81, no. 1 (March 1987): 23–43.

Paterson, Thomas G., J. Garry Clifford, Shane J. Maddock, Deborah Kisatsky, and Kenneth

J. Hagan. *American Foreign Relations: A History.* Vol. 2, *Since 1895.* 6th ed. New York: Houghton Mifflin Company, 2005.
Patterson, Eric. "Just War in the Twenty-first Century: Reconceptualizing Just War Theory After September 11." *International Politics* 42, no. 1 (2005): 116–34.
———. *Just War Thinking: Morality and Pragmatism in the Struggle Against Contemporary Threats.* Lanham, Md.: Lexington Books, 2008.
Peake, Jeffrey S. "Presidential Agenda Setting in Foreign Policy." *Political Research Quarterly* 54, no. 1 (March 2001): 69–86.
Peterson, Paul E. "The President's Dominance in Foreign Policy Making." *Political Science Quarterly* 109, no. 2 (Summer 1994): 215–34.
Pezzulo, Lawrence A. "Catholic Relief Services in Ethiopia: A Case Study." In *The Moral Nation: Humanitarianism and U.S. Foreign Policy Today,* edited by Bruce Nichols and Gil Loescher, 213–31. Notre Dame: University of Notre Dame Press, 1989.
Potter, Philip B. K. "Does Experience Matter? The Link Between American Presidential Experience, Age, and International Conflict." *Journal of Conflict Resolution* 51 (2007): 351–78.
Powell, Colin L., and Joseph E. Persico. *My American Journey.* New York: Random House, 1995.
Power, Samantha. *A Problem from Hell: America in the Age of Genocide.* New York: Basic Books, 2002.
Powlick, Philip J. "The Attitudinal Bases for Responsiveness to Public Opinion Among American Foreign Policy Officials." *Journal of Conflict Resolution* 35, no. 4 (December 1991): 611–41.
———. "The Sources of Public Opinion for American Foreign Policy Officials." *International Studies Quarterly* 39, no. 4 (December 1995): 427–51.
Powlick, Philip J., and Andrew Z. Katz. "Defining the American Public Opinion/Foreign Policy Nexus." *Mershon International Studies Review* 42, no. 1 (May 1998): 29–61.
Program on International Policy Attitudes. *Americans on Foreign Aid and World Hunger.* February 2, 2001. http://www.pipa.org/OnlineReports/BFW/finding3.html (accessed May 12, 2004).
Rielly, John E. *American Public Opinion and U.S. Foreign Policy, 1995.* Chicago: Chicago Council on Foreign Relations, 1995.
———. *American Public Opinion and U.S. Foreign Policy, 1999.* Chicago: Chicago Council on Foreign Relations, 1999.
Rizzo, Alessandra. "EPA Chief: Washington Reviewing Global Warming Policy." Associated Press, March 3, 2001. http://www.lexisnexis.com/us/lnacademic/ (accessed April 28, 2010).
Rose, Richard. *The Postmodern President: George Bush Meets the World.* Chatham, N.J.: Chatham House, 1991.
Rosecrance, Richard N. *Action and Reaction in World Politics: International Systems in Perspective.* Boston: Little, Brown, 1963.
Rosenau, James N. *National Leadership and Foreign Policy: A Case Study in the Mobilization of Public Support.* Princeton: Princeton University Press, 1963.
———. *Public Opinion and Foreign Policy.* New York: Random House, 1961.
Ross, Jay. "Famine, War Threaten Thousands in Ethiopia." *Washington Post,* June 26, 1983, A1.
Rottinghaus, Brandon. "Rethinking Presidential Responsiveness: The Public Presidency and Rhetorical Congruency, 1953–2001." *Journal of Politics* 68, no. 3 (August 2006): 720–32.
Rubner, Michael. "The Reagan Administration, the 1973 War Powers Resolution, and the Invasion of Grenada." *Political Science Quarterly* 100, no. 4 (Winter 1985–86): 627–47.

Russett, Bruce M. "American Opinion on the Use of Military Force Abroad." *Political Science Quarterly* 91, no. 3 (1976): 411–31.

———. *Controlling the Sword: The Democratic Governance of National Security.* Cambridge, Mass.: Harvard University Press, 1990.

Ruttan, Vernon W. *United States Development Assistance Policy: The Domestic Politics of Foreign Economic Aid.* Baltimore: Johns Hopkins University Press, 1996.

Sabatier, Paul A. "The Need for Better Theories." In *Theories of the Policy Process,* edited by Paul A. Sabatier, 3–17. Boulder, Colo.: Westview Press, 1999.

Sabatier, Paul A., and Hank C. Jenkins-Smith, eds. *Policy Change and Learning: An Advocacy Coalition Approach.* Boulder, Colo.: Westview Press, 1993.

Schattschneider, E. E. *The Semi-Sovereign People.* New York: Holt, Rinehart and Winston, 1960.

Schlesinger, Arthur M., Jr. *The Imperial Presidency.* New York: Popular Library, 1974.

Schuman, Howard, and Stanley Presser. *Questions and Answers in Attitude Surveys: Experiments on Question Form, Wording, and Context.* Thousand Oaks, Calif.: Sage, 1996.

Seelye, Katharine Q. "Facing Obstacles on Plan for Drilling for Arctic Oil, Bush Says He'll Look Elsewhere." *New York Times,* March 30, 2001, A13.

Sen, Amartya K. *Development as Freedom.* New York: Knopf, 1999.

———. *Poverty and Famines.* New York: Oxford University Press, 1981.

Shapiro, Robert Y., and Benjamin I. Page. "Foreign Policy and Public Opinion." In *The New Politics of American Foreign Policy,* edited by David A. Deese, 216–37. New York: St. Martin's Press, 1994.

———. "Foreign Policy and the Rational Public." *Journal of Conflict Resolution* 32, no. 2 (1988): 211–47.

Shaw, Donald L., and Maxwell E. McCombs. *The Emergence of American Political Issues: The Agenda-Setting Function of the Press.* St. Paul, Minn.: West, 1977.

Shaw, Martin. *The New Western Way of War: Risk-Transfer War and Its Crisis in Iraq.* Cambridge, UK: Polity, 2005.

Shenon, Philip. "Caned American Says Farewell to Singapore." *New York Times,* June 22, 1994, A10.

Shepherd, Jack. "Ethiopia: The Use of Food as an Instrument of U.S. Foreign Policy." *Issue: A Journal of Opinion,* no. 14 (1985): 4–9.

———. "Food Aid as an Instrument of U.S. Foreign Policy: The Case of Ethiopia, 1982–1984." Ph.D. diss., Boston University, 1989.

———. *The Politics of Starvation.* Washington, D.C.: Carnegie Endowment for International Peace, 1975.

Simmel, Georg. *Conflict and the Web of Group-Affiliations.* Translated by Kurt H. Wolff. New York: Free Press, 1964.

Skowronek, Stephen. *The Politics Presidents Make: Leadership from John Adams to George Bush.* Cambridge: Harvard University Press, 1993.

Smith, Alastair. "International Crises and Domestic Politics." *American Political Science Review* 92, no. 3 (September 1998): 623–38.

Smith, Gayle. "Ethiopia and the Politics of Famine Relief." *Merip Middle East Report,* no. 145 (March–April 1987): 31–37.

Smith, Jean Edward. *George Bush's War.* New York: H. Holt, 1992.

Smith, Steve, and Michael Clarke, eds. *Foreign Policy Implementation.* London: Allen and Unwin, 1985.

Sobel, Richard. *The Impact of Public Opinion on U.S. Foreign Policy Since Vietnam.* New York: Cambridge University Press, 2001.

———. "To Intervene or Not to Intervene in Bosnia: That Was the Question for the United States and Europe." In *Decisionmaking in a Glass House: Mass Media, Public Opinion, and American and European Foreign Policy in the Twenty-first Century,* edited by Brigitte L. Nacos, Robert Y. Shapiro, and Pierangelo Isernia, 111–32. Lanham, Md.: Rowman and Littlefield, 2000.

Solberg, Richard W. *Miracle in Ethiopia: A Partnership Response to Famine.* New York: Friendship Press, 1991.

Solop, Frederic I. "Public Protest and Public Policy: The Anti-Apartheid Movement and Political Innovation." *Policy Studies Review* 9, no. 2 (Winter 1990): 307–26.

Soroka, Stuart N. "Media, Public Opinion, and Foreign Policy." *Harvard International Journal of Press/Politics* 8, no. 1 (2003): 27–48.

Stanley, Harold W., and Richard G. Niemi. *Vital Statistics on American Politics, 2005–2006.* Washington, D.C.: CQ Press, 2006.

Stimson, James A., Michael B. Mackuen, and Robert S. Erikson. "Dynamic Representation." *American Political Science Review* 89, no. 3 (September 1995): 543–65.

Stockman, David A. *The Triumph of Politics: How the Reagan Revolution Failed.* New York: HarperCollins, 1986.

Sullivan, Terry. "The Bank Account Presidency: A New Measure and Evidence on the Temporal Path of Presidential Influence." *American Journal of Political Science* 35, no. 3 (July 1991): 686–723.

Sylvan, Donald A., Andrea Grove, and Jeffrey D. Martinson. "Problem Representation and Conflict Dynamics in the Middle East and Northern Ireland." *Foreign Policy Analysis* 1, no. 3 (2005): 279–99.

Sylvan, Donald A., and Stuart J. Thorson. "Ontologies, Problem Representation, and the Cuban Missile Crisis." *Journal of Conflict Resolution* 36, no. 4 (December 1992): 709–32.

Sylvan, Donald A., and James F. Voss, eds. *Problem Representation in Foreign Policy Decision Making.* Cambridge: Cambridge University Press, 1998.

Teltsch, Kathleen. "2-Month U.S. Total to Help Ethiopians Reaches $40 Million." *New York Times,* January 1, 1985, A1.

Thompson, Kenneth W. *The Bush Presidency: Ten Intimate Perspectives of George Bush.* Lanham, Md.: University Press of America, 1997.

Tiefer, Charles. *Semi-Sovereign Presidency: The Bush Administration's Strategy for Governing Without Congress.* Boulder, Colo.: Westview Press, 1994.

Time. "Book Excerpt: Losing the Green Light." February 8, 2005. http://www.time.com/time/magazine/article/0,9171,1025722,00.html (accessed June 2, 2008).

Todorov, Alexander, and Anesu N. Mandisodza. "Public Opinion on Foreign Policy: The Multilateral Public That Perceives Itself as Unilateral." *Public Opinion Quarterly* 68, no. 3 (Autumn 2004): 323–48.

Tourangeau, Roger, Lance J. Rips, and Kenneth A. Rasinski. *The Psychology of Survey Response.* New York: Cambridge University Press, 2000.

Towle, Michael J. *Out of Touch: The Presidency and Public Opinion.* College Station: Texas A&M University Press, 2004.

Tuchman, Gaye. *Making News.* New York: Free Press, 1978.

Tyler, Patrick E., and David B. Ottaway. "Ethiopian Security Police Seized, Tortured CIA Agent; Captivity Ended After Envoy Intervened." *Washington Post,* April 25, 1986, A1.

U.S. Army Center of Military History. *Operation Just Cause: The Incursion into Panama.* CMH pub. no. 70-85-1. http://www.history.army.mil/brochures/Just%20Cause/JustCause.htm (accessed July 7, 2008).

U.S. Congress. House. Committee on Foreign Affairs. *African Famine Situation.* 99th Cong., 1st sess., January 30 and February 19, 1985.
———. Committee on Foreign Affairs. *Emergency Famine Relief Needs in Ethiopia and Sudan.* 99th Cong., 1st sess., September 19, 1985.
———. Committee on Foreign Affairs. *The Impact of U.S. Foreign Policy on Seven African Countries.* 98th Cong., 2nd sess., August 6–25 and 24–27, 1983.
———. Committee on Foreign Affairs. *The World Food Situation.* 98th Cong., 1st sess., July 26–27, 1983.
———. Committee on Foreign Relations. *Hunger in Africa.* 98th Cong., 2nd sess., March 1, 1984.
———. Committee on Foreign Relations. *World Food and Population Issues/Emergency Assistance to Africa.* 98th Cong., 2nd sess., August 2 and September 13, 1984.
———. Select Committee on Hunger. *Africa: Famine Relief and Rehabilitation.* 99th Cong., 1st sess., July 25, 1985.
U.S. Congress. Senate. Committee on Foreign Relations. *Famine in Africa: Hearing Before the Committee on Foreign Relations.* 99th Cong., 1st sess., January 17, 1985.
Van Belle, Douglas A. "Bureaucratic Responsiveness to the News Media: Comparing the Influence of the *New York Times* and Network Television News Coverage on U.S. Foreign Aid Allocations." *Political Communication* 20, no. 3 (July–September 2003): 263–85.
———. "*New York Times* and Network TV News Coverage of Foreign Disasters: The Significance of the Insignificant Variables." *Journalism and Mass Communication Quarterly* 77, no. 1 (Spring 2000): 50–70.
Varnis, Steven. *Reluctant Aid or Aiding the Reluctant? U.S. Food Aid Policy and Ethiopian Famine Relief.* New Brunswick, N.J.: Transaction, 1990.
Vasquez, John A. "Domestic Contention on Critical Foreign-Policy Issues: The Case of the United States." *International Organization* 39, no. 4 (Autumn 1985): 643–66.
Vasquez, John A., and Richard A. Mansbach. "The Issue Cycle: Conceptualizing Long-Term Global Political Change." *International Organization* 37, no. 2 (Spring 1983): 257–79.
Verba, Sidney. "The Citizen as Respondent: Sample Surveys and American Democracy. Presidential Address, American Political Science Association, 1995." *American Political Science Review* 90, no. 1 (March 1996): 1–7.
Vertzberger, Yaacov Y. *The World in Their Minds: Information Processing, Cognition, and Perception in Foreign Policy Decision Making.* Stanford: Stanford University Press, 1990.
Voeten, Erik, and Paul R. Brewer. "Public Opinion, the War in Iraq, and Presidential Accountability." *Journal of Conflict Resolution* 50, no. 6 (December 2006): 809–30.
Walsh, Brian. "Bush's Toothless Climate Plan." *Time,* April 16, 2008. http://www.time.com/time/health/article/0,8599,1731550,00.html (retrieved July 2, 2009).
Waltz, Kenneth N. *Theory of International Politics.* New York: McGraw-Hill, 1979.
Walzer, Michael. *Just and Unjust Wars: A Moral Argument with Historical Illustrations.* New York: Basic Books, 2006.
Washington Post. "Some Aid to Africa Freed." March 16, 1984, 6.
Weiner, Tim, and James Risen. "Decision to Strike Factory in Sudan Based Partly on Surmise." *New York Times,* September 21, 1998. http://partners.nytimes.com/library/world/africa/092198attack-sudan.html?Partner=PBS&RefId=Eutttn-uFBqv (accessed March 4, 2008).
Weissberg, Robert. *Polling, Policy, and Public Opinion: The Case Against Heeding the "Voice of the People."* New York: Palgrave Macmillan, 2002.

Western, Jon W. *Selling Intervention and War: The Presidency, the Media, and the American Public.* Baltimore: Johns Hopkins University Press, 2005.

Wildavsky, Aaron. "The Two Presidencies." *Trans-Action* 4, no. 2 (1966): 7–14.

Wittkopf, Eugene R. *Faces of Internationalism: Public Opinion and American Foreign Policy.* Durham: Duke University Press, 1990.

Wittner, Lawrence S. *Toward Nuclear Abolition: A History of the World Nuclear Disarmament Movement, 1971–Present.* Stanford: Stanford University Press, 2003.

Wlezien, Christopher. "On the Salience of Political Issues: The Problem with 'Most Important Problem.'" *Electoral Studies* 24, no. 4 (December 2005): 555–79.

———. "Patterns of Representation: Dynamics of Public Preferences and Policy." *Journal of Politics* 66, no. 1 (2004): 1–24.

Wood, B. Dan, and Jeffrey S. Peake. "The Dynamics of Foreign Policy Agenda Setting." *American Political Science Review* 92, no. 1 (1998): 173–84.

Woodward, Bob. *Bush at War.* New York: Simon and Schuster, 2002.

———. *The Commanders.* New York: Simon and Schuster, 1991.

———. *Plan of Attack.* New York: Simon and Schuster, 2004.

———. *State of Denial.* New York: Simon and Schuster, 2006.

Zaller, John. "The Converse-McGuire Model of Attitude Change and the Gulf War Opinion Rally." *Political Communication* 10, no. 4 (October–December 1993): 369–88.

———. "Elite Leadership of Mass Opinion: New Evidence from the Gulf War." In *Taken by Storm: The Media, Public Opinion, and U.S. Foreign Policy in the Gulf War,* edited by Lance W. Bennett and David L. Paletz, 186–209. Chicago: University of Chicago Press, 1994.

———. *The Nature and Origins of Mass Opinion.* New York: Cambridge University Press, 1992.

———. "Strategic Politicians, Public Opinion, and the Gulf Crisis." In *Taken by Storm: The Media, Public Opinion, and U.S. Foreign Policy in the Gulf War,* edited by Lance W. Bennett and David L. Paletz, 250–76. Chicago: University of Chicago Press, 1994.

Zelikow, Philip. "Foreign Policy Engineering: From Theory to Practice and Back Again." *International Security* 18, no. 4 (Spring 1994): 143–71.

Zhu, Jian-Hua. "Issue Competition and Attention Distraction: A Zero-Sum Theory of Agenda-Setting." *Journalism Quarterly* 69, no. 4 (Winter 1992): 825–36.

Index

acid rain, 203–4
Afghanistan
    embassy bombings, U.S. retaliation after, 72
    Soviet invasion of, 14–16, 76–78
    U.S. war in, 47, 76, 211
agenda setting
    carrying capacity, 42
    Ethiopian famine, 143–44
    Persian Gulf Crisis, 82–84
    problem definition stage, 19, 40–43
Agreed Framework. *See* North Korea
AIDS, 32
al Qaeda, 72
Angola, 60, 72, 78–80
Annan, Kofi, 74
Anti-Ballistic Missile (ABM) Treaty, 62–63
apartheid, 26, 39, 44, 60, 62, 214
Aristide, Jean-Bertrand, 75
arms control
    decision stages, 19
    issue salience, 10, 25–27, 46, 51, 59, 67
    non-crises, 16
    Non-Proliferation Treaty (NPT), 78
    preferences, public, 27
    SALT, 26, 46, 60, 62
    START, 26, 60, 62
attention, public. *See* issue salience
Aziz, Tariq, 135

Baker, James
    congressional authorization for war, 132
    diplomacy, 103–4, 133–35
    economic sanctions, 105, 120
    Operation Desert Storm, 135
    UN ultimatum, 129
Band Aid, 179
Barrett, Mark, 75
beliefs model, 8, 19, 35
Biya, Paul, 38–39
Bolton, John, 151 n. 27, 152
Bonifas, Arthur, 75
Bono, 32
Boomtown Rats, 179
Bosnia, 19, 101, 209, 212
Brady, Nicholas, 84, 103–4
Bread for the World, 166
British Broadcasting Corporation (BBC), 178, 182

Brokaw, Tom, 178
Brooke Amendment to the Foreign Assistance Act, 193–94
bureaucracy, U.S. government
    carrying capacity, 42
    deadlock, Ethiopian famine, 159–60
    emergency food aid in Ethiopian famine, allocation process, 149–51, 165
    issue salience, Ethiopian famine, 172, 174, 176, 181
    standard operating procedures, 50
    decision making, general, 7, 17, 26, 44, 50–51, 218
    problem representation in Ethiopian famine, affect on, 154, 156
Bush, George H. W. *See also* Persian Gulf Crisis
    beliefs about public opinion, 35
    Clean Air Act of 1990, 204
    Haiti, 75
    North Korea Nuclear weapons, 78
    Panama invasion, 70
    Rio Treaty, 1–2, 62–63
Bush, George W.
    ABM Treaty, 60, 62
    Afghanistan, 76
    Iraq War, 47, 53, 209–10, 215
    Kyoto Protocol, 60, 64–66

Cambodia, 71, 211
Camp David Accords, 26
Canada, 203
Cantor, Mickey, 55
carrying capacity. *See* agenda setting
Carter, Jimmy
    Carter Doctrine, 77, 119
    Iran Hostage Crisis, 14–15, 71, 125
    Mariel boatlift, 64–65
    Panama Canal Treaty, 13, 15, 62
    Shaba II, 74
    Soviet Invasion of Afghanistan, 14–16, 76–77
    USAID budget under, 170
Carter-Torrijos Treaty. *See* Panama Canal Treaty
Castro, Fidel, 64
casualties
    air power, 101
    public opinion, affect on during the Persian Gulf Crisis, 98–99, 109, 123–24
    Persian Gulf Crisis: affect on choice for war,

casualties (*continued*)
  108–9, 135–36; affect on decision to end war, 139–40; Iraqi casualties, 110–11, 136; pre-war expectations of, 109, 115–16, 123–24
  public support for war, general, 1, 27, 50–51, 95, 209–12, 229
Catholic Relief Services. *See* Ethiopian famine
Central Intelligence Agency (CIA). *See* Ethiopian famine *and* Persian Gulf Crisis
Chamberlain, Neville, 104
Cheek, James, 195, 201
Cheney, Dick
  Bush's decision to end war, 138
  Bush's handling of Desert Storm, 135–36
  congressional authorization for war, 132
  military options in the Persian Gulf Conflict, 101–2, 106, 110, 115
  problem representation of Persian Gulf Conflict, 87–88
  UN resolution on Iraq, 129
China
  earthquake 2008, 26
  economic threat to the U.S., 46, 56
  global warming, 49, 213
  trade, U.S., 46, 60, 62–63
Clancy, Tom, 56
Clark Amendment, 80
Clean Air Act of 1990, 204
climate change. *See* global warming
Clinton, Bill
  Cuba sanctions, 60, 62–63
  embassy bombings, 72
  Fay, Michael, 55
  Gonzalez, Elian, 68
  Haiti, 75
  Kosovo, 1–2
  Kyoto Protocol, 48–49, 60, 62–63, 213, 229
  Lewinsky, Monica, 72
  North Korea, 78
  Operation Desert Fox, 72
  Operation Desert Strike, 71–72
  Somalia, 53
Clooney, George, 32
CNN, 129, 224
Coats, Stephen, 166
Columbia Pictures, 56
conditional responsiveness, 3, 8–10, 16–24, 28, 81, 204–7
Congress. *See also* Ethiopian famine, Persian Gulf Crisis
  carrying capacity, 42
  food aid policy, 150
  foreign policy making, 7–8, 17

Kyoto Protocol, 49
military force, authorization of, 26–27, 47, 50, 132–33
Connery, Sean, 56
constrained. *See* political context
contested. *See* political context
Copenhagen Accord. *See* global warming
crisis and non-crisis foreign policies, 16–17. *See also* issue salience
Cronkite, Walter, 63, 71
Crow, Sheryl, 32
Crowe, William, Jr., 120, 138
Cuba
  covert action, U.S., 214
  Ethiopia, 151
  Gonzalez, Elian, 67–68
  Grenada, 70
  Mariel boat lift, 64–65
  Missile Crisis, 40–41
  refugees, 41
  sanctions, U.S., 60, 62–63
  Zaire, 74

Damon, Matt, 32
Darfur, 32, 211–12
Darman, Richard, 87, 99, 105–6
Debt of Honor, 56
decision stages. *See also* Ethiopian famine *and* Persian Gulf Crisis
  issue salience, 23–24, 57–80
  operationalization of, 30–31, 224–25
  political context, expectations of, 40–54
  theory, role in, 9, 17–19, 204–5
delegate representation, 216–17
Derg. *See* Ethiopia
diversionary hypothesis, 41 n. 8
Do They Know It's Christmas, 179

Earth Summit Conference, Rio de Janerio. *See* global warming
Egypt, 145, 228 n. 4
electoral cycle, 8
elite cues, 47, 89, 121
embassy bombing, Kenya and Tanzania, 60, 72, 101
Eritrea, 141, 153, 155, 168
Ethiopian famine
  agenda setting, 143–44
  background, 141–43
  Bloch, Julia Chang, xii, 152, 154–55, 160, 162–63, 193, 196
  budget: cuts to, 160–61; Fiscal Year 1986, 195–97; Fiscal Year 1987, 198–201; supplemental debate, 1984, 171–74

INDEX

Bureau of Food for Peace, State Department's, 150 n. 24, 155, 160, 193
Catholic Relief Services (CRS), 143–44, 150, 152, 156, 160–64, 166–71, 180, 187, 198
celebrities, influence of, 142–43, 178–79
Central Intelligence Agency (CIA), 144, 150–51, 163, 170–71
civil war, Ethiopian, 152, 155, 158, 189
complex humanitarian emergencies, 142
Congress, 150–51, 156, 162–63, 166–69, 171–74, 191–92, 196 n. 63
Crocker, Chester, 152, 155–56, 162, 164–65, 186, 193
cross-border operation, 164–66, 170, 184
Danforth, John, 152, 156 n. 45, 171–74
Derg, 141, 151, 161, 163
development projects, 193–95
distribution of food aid, 157, 158 n. 51, 163, 170–71, 191–92, 196, 199
diversion of food aid, 152, 155, 157, 162–63, 171
donor fatigue, 190, 192
economy, 141–42, 151–52, 155–56, 167
emergency food aid, U.S., 149–50
Eritrean People's Liberation Front (EPLF), 153
Ethiopian government cover-up of famine, 155
food aid, 144–46, 188–89, 195–96, 200–201
Government's Tenth Anniversary Celebration, 174–76
Hackett, Kenneth, xii, 152, 156–57, 161
hardliner representation, 151–59, 161–65, 174, 176, 181–82, 187
Heritage Foundation, 152
humanitarian representation, 152, 156–59, 163–67, 169, 171, 174, 176, 181–82, 186–87, 190, 194–95, 198, 213
implementation stage, 187–97
inland transportation of food aid, 155, 163, 191–92, 212
institutionalist representation, 152, 154–56, 158–59, 162–65, 167, 176, 181–82, 190, 193
issue salience, 26, 49, 60, 62, 142, 146–49, 158, 163–64, 168, 174, 178–81, 190, 192, 195, 198, 202, 215
Kasten, Robert, 151 n. 27, 152, 173
Kirkpatrick, Jeanne, 161
Korn, David, xii, 152, 156 n. 45, 157, 168–69, 195 n. 58
Leland, Mickey, 152, 156 n. 45, 166, 186
Lyman, Princeton, 152, 154, 155, 162, 165–66, 181, 194
McPherson, M. Peter, xii, 152, 154, 156, 162–63, 166–67, 169–70, 175–76, 183, 186, 191–93

Mengistu Haile Mariam (Mengistu regime), 141, 151–53, 155–57, 161, 165–67, 174–76, 181–84, 187, 190, 192–93, 201
militarization, of Ethiopia, 141–42
mortality estimates in famine, 142, 195–96
National Security Council, 150–52, 161, 165
New York Times coverage of, 146, 148, 155, 173, 175, 178, 190, 198
Office of Management and Budget (OMB), 150, 156, 169–70
option generation stage, 143–44, 159–76, 181, 188, 197
policy decision stage, 150, 177–88, 190–91, 202, 212
policy review stage, 177, 197–201
political context, constrained, 177–87
political context, guarded, 143–49, 159, 189–90, 192, 202
public preferences for humanitarian aid, 142–45, 154, 157–60, 174, 179–80, 188–90, 195, 197–98
public preferences, latent, 142, 146, 149, 160, 164, 199, 201
problem definition stage, 143–59, 201, 204
problem representation stage, 144–59, 188
problem representation, American public, 157–59
Reagan administration, food aid policy, 49, 143, 173, 181
Rehabilitation and Relief Commission, Ethiopia's, 157
Selassie, Haile, 141, 175
Sheehan, Peggy, 160
Soviet Union, 141, 151, 163, 175, 183, 227–28
State Department, U.S., 144, 150, 154, 156, 170 n. 97, 175, 183, 193–94
Stevens, Ted, 151 n. 27, 152, 173
television, coverage of, 142–43, 146–49, 163–64, 177–80, 182, 190, 201, 207, 213
Tigrayan People's Liberation Front (TPLF), 153
U.S. Agency for International Development (USAID), 144, 150–52, 154–56, 160–63, 166, 168–73, 183, 185, 191, 193–97, 199–200
victims, number of, 188, 195–96
Weiss, Ted, 152, 156 n. 45, 166, 186
Weissman, Steve, xii, 152, 156 n. 45, 157, 169
Wettering, Fred, 151 n. 27, 152
wheat reserve, U.S. enactment of, 184–85
Wolpe, Howard, 152, 156 n. 45, 157, 166–67, 169, 173, 186–87, 191, 198
World Food Programme (WFP), 144, 150, 162, 170 n. 97

ethnic cleansing. *See* genocide
expected utility theory, 44, 113

Fahd, King, 100, 104
Farrow, Mia, 32
Fay, Michael, 55–56
Foley, Thomas, 106, 118
food aid, 149–50. *See also* Ethiopian famine
Ford, Gerald
   Angola, 80
   Mayaguez, 71
   Poplar Tree, 75
foreign aid, 10, 25, 41. *See also* Ethiopian famine
framing
   Ethiopian famine, 157–58, 167, 175
   Persian Gulf Crisis, 90–94, 102, 118, 126, 139, 215
   White House, 4
Frost, David, 138

Gates, Robert, 39
Geldolf, Bob, 179
Geneva Convention, 110
genocide, 1, 32, 51, 211
Gingrich, Newt, 214
Glaspie, April, 83, 122
global warming
   celebrities, 32
   issue-attention cycle, 24–26
   issue salience, 10, 62–63, 203–4, 212–15
   Kyoto Protocol: Clinton, 48–49; Bush, George W., 65–66
   media coverage, 25–26
   preference, 21, 51
   Rio Treaty, 1–2
globalization, 5, 214
going private, 41–42, 144, 159
gold standard, 60, 62–63
Gonzalez, Elian, 60, 67–69
Gore, Al, 25
Goyder, Hugh, 194
Gray, C. Boyden, 132
Grenada, 60, 69–70, 208
guarded. *See* political context
Guns 'N' Roses, 70

Haass, Richard, 87
Haiti, 41, 60, 75
Hay-Bunau-Varilla Treaty. *See* Panama Canal Treaty
Hickenlooper Amendment to the Foreign Assistance Act, 193–94
Hussein, Saddam. *See also* Persian Gulf Crisis
   covert action against, 98
   economic sanctions, 105, 119–21

   extra mile for peace, 133–34
   Hussein-as-Hitler frame, 91–94, 102–4, 122–23
   Israel, threat to, 82
   Kuwait, invasion of, 81–83, 104
   military action against, 97–100, 110
   objectives, 1991 Gulf War, 115–16
   oil, control over, 87–88
   Operation Desert Fox, 74
   Operation Desert Storm, 136–40
   Operation Desert Strike, 74
   overthrow of, 2003, 34, 47, 131 n. 37
   Saudi Arabia, threat to, 85, 88, 100
   UNSCOM, 74
   UN ultimatum, 129

Immigration and Naturalization Service (INS), 68
implementation stage, 9–10, 19, 49–52. *See also* Ethiopian famine; Persian Gulf Crisis
India, 49, 184, 213
insulated. *See* political context
interest groups, 150, 214, 216
International Atomic Energy Agency (IAEA), 78
Iran
   Contra scandal, 52
   Hostage Crisis, 14–16, 50–51, 60, 71, 125
   covert action against, U.S., 214
   Persian Gulf Crisis, 105 n. 76, 115
Iran-Iraq War, 82, 98–99
Iraq. *See also* Persian Gulf Crisis
   ability to withstand economic sanctions, 120
   Operation Desert Fox, 60, 72–73
   Operation Desert Strike, 60, 71–73
   UNSCOM, 60, 74, 77
   2003 War, xi, 16, 47, 25, 51, 53, 70, 76, 208–11, 215
Israel
   Camp David Accords, 26
   Entebbe, raid on, 14
   foreign aid to, 145, 228 n. 4
   Mossad, 171
   Persian Gulf Crisis, 82–83
issue publics, 31, 216
issue salience. *See also* Ethiopian famine *and* Persian Gulf Crisis
   Afghanistan: Soviet invasion of, 14–16, 60, 76–79; U.S. war in, 47, 60, 76–77
   Angola, 60, 74, 78–80
   Anti-Ballistic Missile Treaty, 60, 62–63
   apartheid, 26, 44, 60, 62, 214
   celebrities, affect on, 32, 178–79
   China-U.S. trade, 56, 60, 62–63
   crises and non-crises, 16–17, 23–36, 57–61, 214–15

INDEX

Cuba sanctions, 60, 62–63
embassy bombings, Kenya and Tanzania, 60, 72–73
global trade, 25, 46, 51, 62–64, 214
gold standard, 60, 62–63
Gonzalez, Elian, 60, 67–69
Grenada, 60, 69–70, 73
Haiti, 60, 75, 77
interaction with preferences, 22–23
Iran Hostage Crisis, 14–16, 50–51, 60, 71, 73, 125
Japan-U.S. trade, 56, 60, 62–64, 223
Kosovo, 1–2, 60, 69–71, 73, 209–10, 217–18, 223
Kyoto Protocol: Clinton, 60, 62–63, 213, 215; Bush, George W., 60, 64–67
manipulation of, 213–14
Mariel boatlift, 60, 64–66, 75
Mayaguez, 60, 71, 73
monetary policy, 51
movement of, 23–26
NAFTA, 26, 60, 62–63
North Korea nuclear weapons, 60, 77–79
Operation Desert Fox, 60, 72–73
Operation Desert Strike, 60, 71–73
Panama Canal Treaty, 13, 15, 60, 62
Panama, U.S. Invasion of, 60, 69–70, 73
pattern-breaking crises: option generation, 76–78; policy decision, 72–76; policy review, 78–80
pattern-breaking noncrises: implementation, 66–67; option generation, 64–66; policy review, 67–68
pattern-conforming crises, 69–72
pattern-conforming noncrises, 62–64
patterns of, expected, 57–58
poplar tree, 60, 74–75, 77
potentially attentive public, 28–29, 168
responsiveness, political, x, 21–22, 31–32, 205
Rio Treaty, 1–2, 60, 62–63, 212, 215
SALT Treaty, 26, 46, 60, 62
television coverage, measure of, 9, 21–22, 23, 25, 33, 58–59, 204–6
Shaba II, 60, 74–75, 77
START Treaty, 60, 62
Star Wars, 60, 66–68
UNSCOM, 60, 74, 77
issue-attention cycles, 24, 29, 57
Italy, 38–40

Jackson, Jesse, 183
Jackson, Michael, 179
Jagger, Mick, 179

Japan
Persian Gulf Crisis, 102
trade with U.S., 27–28, 41, 46, 56–57, 60, 62–64, 223
Johnson, Lyndon B., 43 n. 15, 53, 125, 135, 218 n. 30
Johnson, Robert, 109
Jordan, Hamilton, 71
just war, 110

Kennedy, John F., 43 n. 15
Kennedy, Ted, 71
Kenya, 72, 101, 174
Keys, Alicia, 32
Kissinger, Henry, 75
knowledge, American public, 38–39
Knowles, Beyonce, 39
Kosovo, xi, 1–2, 60, 69–71, 101, 208–10, 217–18, 223, 229–30
Kurds, 105
Kuwait. *See* Persian Gulf Crisis

Leahy, Patrick, 118
Lebanon, 53, 209
Lewinsky, Monica, 72
Lincoln, Abraham, 216
Live Aid, 181, 190
Lutheran World Relief, 164, 194
Libya, 151

Manning, Peyton, 39
Mariel boatlift, 60, 64–66, 75
Mayaguez incident, 60, 71
McCain, John, 33
media. *See also* issue salience; Ethiopian famine; Persian Gulf Crisis
  agenda setting, 41
  crises, coverage of, 60, 69–80
  magnifier effect, 179
  non-crisis, coverage of, 25–26, 58–59, 61–68
  patterns of media coverage, 55–61
  peg, use of, 25, 63–64
  political leadership, 5
  public attention, 20, 21 n. 30, 33, 45, 58, 222–25
Mengistu Haile Mariam. *See* Ethiopia
Mercy Corps International, 164
Mitchell, George, 106, 118
Mobutu Sese Seko, 43 n. 15, 74
Mondale, Walter, 182
monetary policy, 25, 51. *See also* gold standard
MTV, 179
Mugabe, Robert, 38
multilateralism, 27, 50, 100, 130–31, 209
Myanmar, 26

National Broadcast Corporation (NBC), 178, 180, 182
National Front for the Liberation of Angola (FNLA). *See* Angola
National Security Council (NSC)
  Ethiopian famine, 150–52, 161, 165
  Persian Gulf Crisis, 84–87, 98–100, 103–5, 109, 232
National Union for the Total Independence of Angola (UNITA). *See* Angola
NATO, 1
New York Times
  Ethiopian famine, coverage of, 146, 148, 155, 173, 175, 178, 190, 198, 223
  Persian Gulf Crisis, coverage of, 92–93
  television coverage, relation to, 223
Nicaragua, 19, 43 n. 15, 173–74, 182
Nikolasen, Niels, 194
9/11, 5, 47, 76, 211
Nixon, Richard M., 53, 62–63
Noriega, Manuel, 37–38, 70
North American Free Trade Agreement (NAFTA), 20, 26, 60, 62–63
North Korea
  nuclear weapons, 60, 77–78
  poplar tree, 60, 74–75
nuclear freeze movement, 214

Obama, Barack
  Copenhagen Accord, 213
  presidential election, 2008, 33
Office of Management and Budget (OMB), 87, 99, 105, 150, 156, 169–70
oil. *See* Persian Gulf Crisis
Olympic Games, 15–16, 26, 77
O'Neill, Tip, 173
Operation Desert Strike. *See* Iraq
Operation Eagle Claw. *See* Iran Hostage Crisis
Operation Just Cause. *See* Panama, U.S. invasion of
Operation Paul Bunyan. *See* Poplar Tree
Operation Uphold Democracy. *See* Haiti refugees
Operation Urgent Fury. *See* Grenada
option generation stage. *See also* Ethiopian Famine *and* Persian Gulf Crisis
  attention to, crisis, 61, 69–80
  attention to, non-crisis, 26, 57, 59, 61–68
  decision stages, role in, 9, 11, 19, 26, 44–47, 50–51, 204
Organization of Eastern Caribbean States (OECS), 70
Organization of the Petroleum Exporting Countries (OPEC), 82, 85, 87

outsourcing, 51
Oxfam, 194

Palestinian Liberation Organization (PLO), 87
Panama
  Canal Treaty, 13, 15, 38, 60, 62
  U.S. invasion of, 37–38, 60, 69–70, 99, 208
Patton, George C., 208
Pebble Beach Golf Course, 56
Pelosi, Nancy, 214
Persian Gulf Crisis
  agenda setting, 82–84
  air power, 99–101, 109–11, 128
  Al Firdos bombing, 136
  Arab problem representation, 84–85
  Bush, George H.W.: beliefs about public opinion, 102–3; decision for war, 81, 122–24; decision for war, end, 138; diplomacy, 103–4, 133–35; economic sanctions, 105; leadership of public opinion in early stages, 90; military options, 100, 101–2, 106–8; Operation Desert Shield, 100, 135–36; problem representation, 85–87, 209; public approval, 105–7, 126–27, 135–36, 138–40; public comments on, 97–98, 104, 106
  causalities: Iraq, 111, 136; U.S., 85, 98–99, 101, 108–10, 115–16, 123–25, 135, 136–40
  Central Intelligence Agency (CIA), 80, 83 n. 2, 98–99
  choice for war, 114–16
  Congress, 91, 96, 104, 106, 115, 118, 120, 123, 126–28, 132–33, 135, 140
  covert action, 95, 98
  delay announcing troop increase, 126–27
  diplomacy, 98, 103–4, 130, 133–35
  economic sanctions, 81, 97–100, 104–8, 110, 114, 117–22, 125, 130
  extra mile for peace, 133–35
  future opinion, 95, 109, 118 n. 10, 119, 122–23, 125
  Hussein-as-Hitler frame, 91–94, 102–4, 116, 139
  implementation stage, 89, 113–14, 119, 125–37, 140
  issue salience, 60, 69–70, 73, 88–90, 96, 108, 117–18, 126, 215
  Kuwait, 81–83
  military options, 97, 99–102, 106–8, 110–11, 122–23
  multinational force, 130–32, 140
  national interest frame, 90–94
  oil, 81–82, 85, 87–88, 93, 97, 99, 102, 105–6, 119–20, 227
  Operation Desert Shield, 96, 104–6; Bush's announcement of, 96, 104, 106

Operation Desert Storm, 135–40
option generation, 81, 89, 94–111, 135
overview of, 81, 206–7
policy decision stage, 81, 89, 95, 107–8, 110–11, 114–25
policy review stage, 81, 89, 116, 137–40
political context: constrained, 82, 94, 108, 111, 113, 118 n. 10, 126, 130, 139–40; contested, 82, 96, 108, 118, 125; insulated, 83, 88–89, 94, 111
political leadership, 88–94, 113–14
political responsiveness, 113, 209
public preferences: on casualties, 124; on congressional authorization for war, 132–33; creating a region of acceptability, 109–10; on diplomacy, 133–35; on early stage of conflict, 96; on economic sanctions, 121–22; on end of war, 138–39; at the implementation stage, 126; on multinational force, 130–31; on Operation Desert Shield, 106, 108; for U.S. intervention, 93; on UN resolution, 130; for war, 32, 116–19, 126–27, 208
problem definition stage, 82–94
problem representation, 84–94
road to Basra attack, 137–38
Saudi Arabia, 81, 83, 85–88, 91–92, 94–95, 98–106, 120–21, 126–27
television coverage of, 60, 88–90, 146
U.S. economy, effect on, 87, 105–6, 120
U.S. ways of starting war, 127–30
UN Resolution, 127–30, 133, 139
weapons of mass destruction, 110
Pitt, Brad, 32
policy decision stage, 9, 11, 16–17, 19, 26, 29, 40, 46–51, 57–58, 61–64, 72–76, 80, 204. *See also* Ethiopian famine *and* Persian Gulf Crisis
policy review stage, 9, 11, 19, 40, 52–54, 57, 67–69, 78–80, 204–6. *See also* Ethiopian famine *and* Persian Gulf Crisis
political context. *See also* Ethiopian famine *and* Persian Gulf Crisis
  constrained, 23, 30, 40, 43, 45, 48–50, 52–54
  contested, 23, 40, 45, 47–49
  guarded, 23, 40, 45, 47, 52, 54
  implementation stage, expectations of, 49–52
  insulated, 23, 40, 45–47
  option generation stage, expectations of, 44–47
  policy decision stage, expectations of, 46–49
  policy review, expectations of, 52–56
  problem definition stage, expectations of, 40–45

political leadership
  option generation, 45
  Persian Gulf Crisis, 81–82, 84, 88–94, 111, 113, 125, 140
  political context, 29–30, 40
  problem representation, 43
  public opinion–foreign policy connection, 3–6
political representation
  normative position, 215–19
  public opinion–foreign policy connection, 3–6, 11
political responsiveness
  conditional, 15–28
  Ethiopian famine, 177–87
  implementation, 50–52
  issue salience, 57–58
  normative position, 215–19
  Persian Gulf Crisis, 81, 101, 111, 125–40
  president's preferences, 33–34
  problem representation, 43
  public opinion–foreign policy connection, 3–7
poverty, global, 25, 32, 63, 145, 154, 179
Powell, Colin
  Bush's early statements on Iraq, 86–87
  casualties, 123
  covert action against Saddam Hussein, 98
  economic sanctions, 105–6
  Hussein-as-Hitler frame, 116
  military options, 98–102, 107, 109, 115–16
  objectives of Operation Desert Storm, 115
  Operation Desert Storm, 136
  policy review, 138
  Powell Doctrine, 210
  Saudi Arabia, defense of, 85
  weapons of mass destruction, 110
preferences, American public. *See also* Ethiopian Famine *and* Persian Gulf Crisis
  arms control, 27
  benchmarks in, 20
  casualties, 1, 27, 41, 50–51, 95, 99, 101, 108–9, 116, 123–25, 135, 139–40, 209–12
  crises, 26–27
  environment, 24, 27, 62
  Fay, Michael, incident, 55
  foreign policy connection, xi, 3–7, 9, 19–21, 26–28, 205
  future preferences, 28–29, 40, 43–49, 52, 54, 95, 118, 119–25
  global warming, 2, 21, 49, 52, 212–13, 215
  humanitarian aid, 24, 27, 51, 142–43, 144–46, 149, 157–59, 160–62, 174, 177, 179–82, 189–90, 192, 197, 207
  interaction with issue salience, 22–23

preferences, American public (*continued*)
  Iran Hostage Crisis, 14–15, 51, 125
  Japan–U.S. trade, 27–28, 46, 56, 63–64
  Mariel boatlift, 64–65
  measures of, 32–33
  military force: Congress authorization of, 26–27, 50; success, 50, 208–9; UN authorization of, 26–27, 50
  multilateralism, 27, 50
  non-crises, 27–28
  objectives of war, 27
  outsourcing, 27, 51
  Panama Canal Treaty, 13, 15
  Soviet invasion of Afghanistan, 14–15
  trade global, 27–28
  unified or divided, 22–23
  war, 46–48, 50, 209
  White House polling of, 20
president, U.S. *See also* Ethiopian Famine *and* Persian Gulf Crisis
  approval of, 8
  foreign policy making, 7–8
  individual v. institutional theories, 34–35
problem definition stage, 9, 11, 19, 40–45, 51, 57, 59, 204. *See also* Ethiopian Famine *and* Persian Gulf Crisis
problem representation stage, 19, 40, 43–44. *See also* problem definition
public attention. *See* issue salience
public opinion. *See* preferences, American public
Putin, Vladimir, 39

Quayle, Dan, 132

rally effect, 26, 29, 43, 48, 99, 103, 106, 108, 122–24, 127, 206
rational choice models. *See* expected utility theory
Reagan, Ronald. *See also* Ethiopian famine
  beliefs about public opinion, 35
  Grenada, 69–70
  Iran Hostage Crisis, 71
  Lebanon bombing, 53
  Star Wars, 66–67
Reid, Harry, 39
Reno, Janet, 68
Ricardo, Lucy, 38–39
Rio Treaty. *See* global warming
Rockefeller Center, 56
Roosevelt, Franklin, 20
Rumsfeld, Donald, 42 n. 14, 76, 210–11
Rwanda, 211

Sassou-Nguesso, Denis, 39
Schaufele, William, 198

Schwarzkopf, Norman
  criticism of Bush's decision to end war, 138
  military strategy, Gulf, 97, 100–101, 137
  pre-war casualty estimate, 123
Scowcroft, Brent
  congressional authorization for war, 132–33
  delay in announcing troop increase, 126
  Desert Shield, 100
  diplomacy, 103–4, 134
  economic sanctions, 97, 105
  military options, 101, 109, 111, 114–15, 128
  Operation Desert Storm, 135
  problem representation, 86–87, 98
  UN resolutions, 130
Selassie, Haile. *See* Ethiopia
September 11. *See* 9/11
sequential decision making. *See* decision stages
Serbia, 1, 217
Shaba II, 60, 74–75
Sheffield, James, 180
Shiites, 105
Shultz, George, 170, 172
Singapore, 55–56
60 Minutes, 178
Snipes, Wesley, 56
Somalia
  Ethiopian famine, 141
  U.S. aid to, 174
  U.S. intervention in, 53, 209, 211–12
South Korea, 78
Soviet Union (USSR)
  Afghanistan Invasion, 14–16, 76–78
  Cuban Missile Crisis, 41
  Ethiopian famine, 70, 141, 151, 163, 175, 183, 227–28
  Grenada, 70
  Persian Gulf Crisis, 97, 103–4
  Strategic Arms Limitation Talks (SALT), 46
  Star Wars, 66–67
  threat to the U.S., 56
  Zaire, 74
Springsteen, Bruce, 179
Star Wars, 60, 66–68, 182
State Department, U.S.
  Ethiopian famine, 144, 150, 154, 156, 170, 175, 183, 193
  Office of Verification Operations (OVO), 42
Stockman, Dave, 169–70
strategic defense initiative. *See* Star Wars
Sudan, 72, 164–65
Sununu, John, 100, 104, 132
Super Bowl, 180
Sweden, 203

Thatcher, Margaret, 86, 129
Tibet, 32
Tigray, 141, 168
Today Show, 172
Torrijos, Omar, 13
trade, international, 5, 20, 25, 27–28, 41, 46, 214. *See also* Japan–U.S. *and* China–U.S. trade
Travolta, John, 32
trustee representation, 217–19
Turner, Tina, 179

U.S. Agency for International Development (USAID). *See* Ethiopia
United Kingdom, 203
United Nations (UN)
    economic sanctions against Iraq, 81, 97, 99, 104–5
    and Haiti, 75
    military force, authorization of, 26, 47, 50, 72, 114–15, 127–30, 132–35, 139–40, 209
United Nations Children's Fund (UNICEF), 180
United Nations Command (UNC), 74–75
United Nations Relief Organization (UNDRO), 144, 150, 164, 166, 188
United Nations Special Commission (UNSCOM), 74
USA for Africa, 179

Vietnam, 14, 51, 53, 94, 103, 106, 109–10, 124–25, 129, 135, 179, 208

Walters, Vernon, 171
War on Terror, 76
Washington Post, 167, 173, 175
Watkins, James, 99
We are the World, 179
Webster, William, 98
White House, 7–8, 20
Whitman, Christine Todd, 66
World Bank, 193
World Trade Organization (WTO), 20, 26, 55, 214
World War II, 47

Zaire, 174. *See also* Shaba II